בס"ד

ראשית חכמה יראת השם

TORAH FROM JERUSALEM
AN ANTHOLOGY OF AGGADOTH
FROM THE JERUSALEM TALMUD

by Yehuda Cahn

VOL. II

Peah, Demai, Kilayim, Shevi'ith, T'rumoth,
Ma'aseroth, Ma'aser Sheni, Bikkurim

DISTRBUTED BY:

Israel Book Shop
501 Prospect Street
Lakewood, NJ 08701

Tel: (732) 901-3009

Fax: (732) 901-4012

Email: isrbkshp@aol.com

ISBN: 0-9707757-3-3 hardcover
0-9707757-4-1 softcover

RABBI MOSHE HEINEMANN
6109 Gist Avenue
Baltimore, MD 21215
Tel. (410) 358-9828
Fax. (410) 358-9838

משה היינעמאן
אב"ד ק"ק אגודת ישראל
באלטימאר
טל. 764-7778 (410)
פקס 764-8878 (410)

בס"ד

הנני בזה להשמיע בשער בת רבים שבח המגיע לכתבים על הספר השני של
ידידי ר' יהודה קאן נ"ו שעבר בעינא פקיחא על האגדות שבתלמוד ירושלמי של
סדר זרעים ותרגם אותם להשפה המדוברת וגם הוסיף עליהם ביאור נחמד ונעים
מדליה.

כמעשהו בראשון על מסכת ברכות,שכבר יצא לו שם טוב בעולם התור––ה, כן
מעשהו בשני ועבדתי בין בתרי ספרו דנן ומצאתי בו דברים מתוקים הראויים
להעלותם על שלחן מלכים.

לכן אמינא לפעולא טובא יישר ויזכה שספרו זה ימצא חן בעיני קוראיו ובזכות
לימוד דברי רבותינו התנאים והאמוראיס, שהם גופי תורה, נזכה לביאת גואל
צדק בב"א.

וע"ז באתי עה"ח לכבוד המחבר ולכבוד לומדי תוה"ק בששי בשבת כסדר
הנמצא כזה איש אשר רוח אלקים בו, יום החמישי דחנוכה,תשעה ועשרים יום
לחדש כסלו שנת חמשת אלפים ושבע מאות ושיש ושתיס לבר––יאת עולס
יעשה בה"ר––– ב––––וך ג––––ליה למשפחת היינעמאן החונה מתא באלטימאר

ACKNOWLEDGMENTS

I would like to thank Rabbi Moshe Heinemann שליט"א, an outstanding *Torah* scholar and leader of rare ability, for taking the time from his busy schedule to read my manuscript and give me a detailed critique which I used to produce the final work.

Rabbi Shaul Abrams, a member of the Kollel at Ner Israel Rabbinical College, also read the manuscript and offered many useful suggestions.

I would also like to acknowledge Mrs. Elaine Mael who assisted me in identifying some of the sources for the bibliography which appears at the end of this work.

Rabbi Doneel Edelson, who offered encouragement in this project, also kindly lent me his copy of *Sefer Mashbiach*, a commentary on parts of the Jerusalem Talmud by Rabbi Moshe Shimon Sivitz.

Finally, I would like to express my gratitude to my wife, Geoula. Besides making sure that I could work on this project without distractions, she used her own vast knowledge of Jewish religious literature to offer several suggestions and insights which I incorporated into the text.

לעילוי נשמות

עליה בת שלמה נזרי ז״ל
פרלה בת שלמה דהן ז״ל
משה בן שלמה בן לולו ז״ל
אליהו בן שלמה בן לולו ז״ל
מחלוף בן שלמה בן לולו ז״ל
אדמונד בן מקסים שחר ז״ל
חוה בת מקסים סנדק ז״ל
אריה בן סנדק ז״ל

INTRODUCTION

The goal of this anthology is to produce a translation which conveys the meaning of the text in easily readable form. Accordingly, it avoids highly technical analyses of linguistic usage or variant manuscript readings except when those have a significant bearing on the basic meaning of the text.

Those with a background in *Talmud* who wish to follow along in the Hebrew should keep in mind that the originators of the Jerusalem *Talmud* spoke a form of Aramaic somewhat different from that used in Babylonia. In particular, they often slurred the guttural letters א, ה, ח, ע. For instance, the word אמר, meaning "he said," is often simply מר, the word אנן, meaning "we," is reduced to נן, and the word כאילו, meaning "as though," becomes כילו. The names of the sages were also often shortened in this fashion. For example, רבי אליעזר became רבי ליעזר and רבי אבא became רבי בא. In addition, the guttural letters were sometimes used interchangeably. By way of illustration, the word היכן, meaning "where" in the Babylonian *Talmud* is איכן in the Jerusalem *Talmud*.

The editors of the Jerusalem *Talmud* also employed many contractions. Thus, the words כי האי, meaning "like this" are contracted to כיי, and the words לית אנא, meaning "should I not?" are contracted to לינא. Although scribes may have employed some contractions and abbreviations partly to ease the time consuming job of copying so much material by hand, these contractions probably reflect the form of Aramaic spoken in the Land of Israel.

As noted in the introduction to Volume I, sometimes the *Talmud* paraphrases a verse from the *Tanach* or even quotes the *Tanach* as saying something which is only derived from a verse but not explicit in it.[1] For the convenience of the reader, when the Hebrew text cites a Biblical reference, it is reproduced in this translation in its full correct form. In addition, to enhance the clarity of the text, names of people and places cited in Biblical verses are translated with their traditional English equivalents (Jacob, Samuel, etc.) while names and places in the *Talmudic* text are transliterated (Yaakov, Shmuel, etc.).

Although later scholars have traditionally studied the Jerusalem *Talmud* less than the Babylonian *Talmud*, the editors of the Babylonian *Talmud* had the highest esteem for their colleagues living in the Land of Israel. For example, the Babylonian *Talmud* portrays the scholars of the Land of Israel as showing great respect for one another and working harmoniously to arrive at the true meaning of the *Torah*.[2] Moreover, the *Midrash* asserts that the sages in the Land of Israel delved into the *Torah* at great length until they had a clear understanding of it.[3] Rabbi Zera valued the learning available in the Land of Israel to such a degree

---

[1] *Tosafoth* on B.T. *Shabbath* 128A, sub verba *"VeNathan HaKessef"* (ונתן הכסף).
[2] B.T. *Sanhedrin* 24A.
[3] *Breishith Rabbah* 70:8.

that before traveling there, he fasted one hundred times to forget what he had learned in Babylonia so that he could study the teachings of the Land of Israel without preconceived ideas.[4]

By contrast, the Babylonian sages viewed their own scholarship as the result of contentious debate.[5] This may explain why the *Halachah* follows the opinion of the Babylonian *Talmud*. Studying *Torah* in a spirit of cooperation is praiseworthy. However, because the Babylonian scholars argued strenuously among themselves, they could be sure that any *Halachic* conclusion they reached had been carefully tested and was correct.[6]

One scholar has suggested that the primacy of the Babylonian *Talmud* reflects the spiritual condition of the Jewish people. Just as, sadly, the Temple has remained destroyed these many years and Jews have been scattered in exile, so the *Talmud* of the Land of Israel has been neglected.[7] Perhaps now that the end of the long exile is

---

[4] B.T. *Baba Metzia* 85A. One might question how Rabbi Zera could do this since the *Mishnah* teaches that "whoever forgets one thing from his learning, Scripture views him as though he forfeits his soul." (*Pirkei Avoth* 3:8). Evidently, Rabbi Zera only prayed to forget what he had learned to the extent that it not interfere with his studies in the Land of Israel. For proof that, in practice, he did not forget his prior learning, see B.T. *Shabbath* 114A-B.

[5] B.T. *Sanhedrin* 24A.

[6] See *Maharal, Nethivoth Olam, Nethiv HaTorah*, chapter 13.

[7] Rabbi Moshe Shimon Sivitz of Pittsburgh, Pennsylvania, *Sefer Mashbiach* (Moshe Shimon ben Yechezkel) (published 1918), Vol. II, Introduction.

approaching, it is especially fitting to study the Jerusalem *Talmud*.

The *Talmud* teaches that since the destruction of the Temple, the situation of the Jewish people has deteriorated so that all that keeps things going is the recital of *Uva LeTzion* (ובא לציון) and the *Kaddish* which follows the study of *Aggadoth*.[8] One reason the study of *Aggadoth* has such power is that it contains material which everyone can understand and appreciate, not only great scholars.[9]

Avoth D'Rabbi Nathan says that whoever has mastered *Halachah* but not *Midrash* has not tasted fear of sin while whoever has mastered *Midrash* but not *Halachah* has not tasted wisdom. One who has mastered *Midrash* but not *Halachah* is like a mighty warrior without weaponry while whoever has mastered *Halachah* but not *Midrash* is like a weak person with weaponry.[10] So it emerges that the study of *Midrashim* and *Aggadoth* as well as *Halachoth* is essential to becoming a good Jew.

The *Zohar* denounces those who would view the *Torah* as mere stories. If that were the case, it would be possible to create similar stories, or perhaps even better ones, today. The reason the *Torah* contains what appear to be simple stories is that its great holiness cannot exist in undiluted form in the physical world nor could the physical

---

[8] B.T. *Sotah* 49A.

[9] *Rashi* on B.T. *Sotah* 49A. *Tur Shulchan Aruch, Orach Chaim* 56 states that the *Aggadoth* were taught in Aramaic so that the masses of people who were unfamiliar with Hebrew could understand them.

[10] *Avoth D'Rabbi Nathan*, chapter 29 (towards the end of the chapter).

world tolerate such holiness. Only by clothing itself in story form can the *Torah* exist in the physical world. Saying that the *Torah* is a mere storybook is as silly as saying that the clothing a person wears is what he or she really looks like.[11]

The same principle applies to the *Aggadoth* of the *Talmud.* What appear on the surface as simple stories actually represent profound spiritual concepts.

---

[11] Zohar III, 152A.

Peah 1:1 (compare B.T. *Shabbath* 133B)

תני רבי ישמעאל: "...זֶה אֵלִי וְאַנְוֵהוּ... ." (שמות טו:ב) וכי
אפשר לו לאדם לנוואות את בוראו? אלא אנווהו לפניו במצות.
אעשה לפניו לולב נאה, סוכה נאה, שופר נאה, ציצית נאין, תפילין
נאין.

אבא שאול אומר: אדמה לו. מה הוא רחום וחנון, אף את
תהא רחום וחנון.

מעשה ברבי ישבב שעמד והחליק את כל נכסיו לעניים.
שלח לו רבן גמליאל, "והלא אמרו, 'חומש מנכסיו למצות?'"
ורבן גמליאל לא קודם לאושא היה?

רבי יוסי ברבי בון בשם רבי לוי: כך היתה הלכה בידם
ושכחוה ועמדו השַׁנָים והסכימו על דעת הראשונים ללמדך שכל דבר
שבית דין נותנין נפשן עליו הוא מתקיים כמה שנאמר למשה מסיני.
ואתייא כיי דאמר רבי מנא: "כִּי לֹא דָבָר רֵק הוּא מִכֶּם..." (דברים
לב:מז) ואם הוא רֵק, מכם הוא. למה? שאין אתם יגיעין בתורה. "...כִּי
הוּא חַיֵּיכֶם... ." (שם שם) אימתי הוא חייכם? כשאתם יגיעין בו.

רבי תנחומא בשם רב הונא: "וּבְצַלְאֵל בֶּן אוּרִי בֶן חוּר לְמַטֵּה
יְהוּדָה עָשָׂה אֵת כָּל אֲשֶׁר צִוָּה ה' אֶת מֹשֶׁה." (שמות לח:כב) "אותו
מֹשֶׁה" אין כתיב כאן, אלא "אֲשֶׁר צִוָּה ה' אֶת מֹשֶׁה." אפילו דברים
שלא שמע מפי רבו הסכימה דעתו כמה שנאמר למשה מסיני.

רבי יוחנן בשם רבי בנ יי: "כַּאֲשֶׁר צִוָּה ה' אֶת מֹשֶׁה עַבְדּוֹ כֵּן
צִוָּה מֹשֶׁה אֶת יְהוֹשֻׁעַ וְכֵן עָשָׂה יְהוֹשֻׁעַ לֹא הֵסִיר דָּבָר מִכֹּל אֲשֶׁר צִוָּה ה'
אֶת מֹשֶׁה." (יהושע יא:טו) "אותו מֹשֶׁה" אין כתיב כאן, אלא "מִכֹּל
אֲשֶׁר צִוָּה ה' אֶת מֹשֶׁה." אפילו דברים שלא שמע מפי משה הסכימה
דעתו כמה שנאמר למשה מסיני. רבי יוחנן בשם רבי בנ יי, רבי חונה
בשם רבי: "תּוֹרַת אֱמֶת הָיְתָה בְּפִיהוּ..." (מלאכי ב:ו) דברים ששמע מפי
רבו. "...וְעַוְלָה לֹא נִמְצָא בִשְׂפָתָיו..." (שם שם) אפילו דברים שלא שמע
מפי רבו.

Torah From Jerusalem

 וּרְבָּנַן אָמְרִי: "כִּי ה' יִהְיֶה בְכִסְלֶךְ וְשָׁמַר רַגְלְךָ מִלָּכֶד." (משלי
ג:כו) אֲפִילוּ דְבָרִים שֶׁאַתָּה כָּסִיל בָּהֶן, "וְשָׁמַר רַגְלְךָ מִלָּכֶד." רבי דוסא
אָמַר: מִן הַהוֹרַיְיה. וּרְבָּנַן אָמְרִי: מִן הָעֲבֵירָה. רבי לוי אָמַר: מִן
הַמַּזִּיקִין.
אָמַר רבי אבא: אִם נִתַּת מְכִיסְךָ צְדָקָה, הַקָּדוֹשׁ בָּרוּךְ הוּא
מְשַׁמֶּרְךָ מִן הַפִּיסִין וּמִן הַזִּימִיּוֹת וּמִן הַגַּלְגָּלוֹת וּמִן הָאַרְנוֹנִיּוֹת.

Rabbi Yishmael taught: "...this is my God and I
will beautify Him... ."[12] Is it then possible for a person to
beautify his Creator? Rather the meaning is, "I will
beautify *Mitzvoth* before Him." I will prepare before Him a
beautiful *Lulav*, a beautiful *Sukkah*, a beautiful *Shofar*,
beautiful *Tzitzioth*, beautiful *Tefillin*.[13]

Abba Shaul says: [The phrase "...this is my God and
I will beautify Him..."[14] means] "I will emulate Him."[15]

---

[12] Exodus 15:2.
[13] However, one should take care not to spend money performing
Mitzvoth in a way which causes others who cannot afford such
expenditures to feel under pressure to do likewise. For example, the
Babylonian *Talmud* tells how people used to bury their dead in
extravagant garments, presumably to fulfill the *Mitzvah* of showing
respect for the dead (כבוד המת). Since many families could not afford
it, Rabban Gamliel put an end to this practice by instructing that he be
buried in simple linen garments. (B.T. *Kethuboth* 8B).
[14] Exodus 15:2.
[15] Abba Saul may mean to render the verse, "I will beautify *myself* by
emulating my Creator." *Rashi*, however, suggests that the term "I will
beautify" (אנוהו) should be interpreted as "I and He" (אני והוא) implying
that one should seek unity with God by emulating Him. See *Rashi* sub
verba *Heveh Domeh Lo* (הוי דומה לו) on B.T. *Shabbath* 133B.

7

Just as He is merciful and gracious, so should you be merciful and gracious.

An incident occurred where Rabbi Yeshavov arose and distributed all his property to the poor [based on this concept of "beautifying" the *Mitzvah* of charity or imitating God by being merciful]. Rabban Gamliel sent him [a message], "Did not the sages say to limit contributions for *Mitzvoth* to one-fifth of one's property?"[16]

[How could Rabban Gamliel have sent such a message?] Did not Rabban Gamliel live at a time before the *Sanhedrin* met in Usha [and made the decree limiting charitable contributions to a fifth of one's wealth]?

Rabbi Yossi bar Bon said in the name of Rabbi Levi: So had the earlier rabbis established the *Halachah*, but it became forgotten. Later ones arose who agreed with the opinion of the first ones. [The *Sanhedrin* in Usha established the exact same rule as existed in earlier times but which had been forgotten in the interim.] This teaches that any issue upon which a court diligently labors becomes correctly established just as it was related to Moses at Sinai.

This accords with that which Rabbi Manna said: "For it [the *Torah*] is not an empty matter for you..."[17] And if it is empty, it is because of you. Why? Because you have not exerted effort in *Torah* study. [Since the *Torah*

---

[16] The *Talmud* mentions this law earlier in the passage. *Rama* on *Shulchan Aruch, Yoreh Deah* 249:1 prohibits donating more than one fifth of one's assets or earnings to charity out of concern that one who does so may himself become a charity case.

[17] Deuteronomy 32:47.

promises success to those who study it, the only reason a person can fail to understand it is lack of effort.[18]] The verse continues, "...for it is your life... ."[19] When is it your life? When you exert effort upon it.

Rabbi Tanchuma said in the name of Rav Huna: "And Bezalel son of Uri, son of Hur, of the tribe of Judah did all which the Lord commanded Moses."[20] It is not written here "which Moses commanded him," but rather "which the Lord commanded Moses." Even things which he did not hear from his master's mouth he deduced on his own just as they were told to Moses at Sinai.

Rabbi Yochanan said in the name of Rabbi Banai: "Just as the Lord commanded Moses, His servant, so Moses commanded Joshua and so did Joshua; he did not omit a thing from all which the Lord commanded Moses."[21] It is not written here "he did not omit a thing from all which Moses commanded him," but rather "from all which the Lord commanded Moses." Even things which he did not hear from Moses's mouth he deduced on his own just as they were told to Moses at Sinai.

---

[18] In addition, the phrase "for you" (מכם) emphasizes that if a deficiency in understanding exists, it derives from *you*, that is, from the people studying it. (*P'nei Moshe* here and *Korban Ha'Eidah* on J.T. *Shabbath* 1:4.)

[19] Deuteronomy 32:47.

[20] Exodus 38:22.

[21] Joshua 11:15.

9

Rabbi Yochanan said in the name of Rabbi Banai and Rav Chuna in the name of Rebbi[22]: "A law of truth was in his mouth..."[23] refers to words which he heard from his master. "...and injustice is not found on his lips..."[24] means even things which he did not hear from his master [were nonetheless correct].

The rabbis say: "For the Lord will be your security [בכסלך] and guard your foot from danger."[25] Even matters concerning which you are a fool [כסיל], God will "...guard your foot from danger." Rabbi Dosa said that "danger" refers to erroneous teaching. The rabbis say it means sin. Rabbi Levi said it refers to demons.

Rabbi Abba said that the above verse means: If you dispense charity from your wallet, then the Holy One, Blessed be He, will guard you from tributes, fines, head taxes and taxes in kind. [The Hebrew term "your security" (בכסלך) is similar to "your wallet" (כיסך)].

The Torah says, "You shall come to the Levite priests and to the judge who shall be in those days and inquire, and they will tell you the words of the law. You shall do according to the words which they tell you from

---

[22] Rabbi Yehudah HaNassi (Judah the Prince), editor of the *Mishnah*, was so widely respected that people simply called him "Rebbi," meaning "master" or "teacher."
[23] Malachi 2:6. The verse refers to the tribe of Levi which was devoted to teaching the Torah.
[24] Ibid.
[25] Proverbs 3:26.

the place which the Lord will choose and be careful to do according to all that they will instruct you. According to the law which they instruct you and the statute which they tell you, you shall do; do not stray from the words which they tell you right or left."[26] *Scripture refers to "the judge who shall be in those days" to emphasize that the Jewish people must rely on the rabbis and teachers of the generation in which they live. It does not matter whether current leaders rise to the level of the those of earlier generations. Moreover, one must obey the rulings of such leaders even if they appear to say that "right is left and left is right," meaning that what they say* **appears** *illogical.*[27]

In the foregoing passage, the Talmud explains that the faith in the rabbinical leadership of the Jewish people which the Torah requires is justified because when one studies Torah with sufficient diligence, he is **bound** *to come to correct conclusions, even correctly figuring out matters which were forgotten over time due to persecution or for other reasons. Accordingly, when dealing with Halachic rulings, one cannot assume that everyone's view is of equal value. Instead, those outstanding rabbis who study with great dedication and self-sacrifice are bound to come to correct conclusions which must be followed.*

---

[26] Deuteronomy 17:9-11.
[27] *Rashi* on Deuteronomy 17:9-11. B.T. *Rosh HaShannah* 25A-B.

Peah 1:1 (continued) (compare B.T. *Baba Bathra* 11A)

מונבז המלך עמד ובזבז כל נכסיו לעניים. שלחו לו קרוביו
ואמרו לו, "אבותיך הוסיפו על שלהן ועל של אבותיהן ואתה ביזבזתה
את שלך ואת של אבותיך."

אמר להו, "כל שכן! אבותי גנזו בארץ ואני גנזתי בשמים
שנאמר, 'אֱמֶת מֵאֶרֶץ תִּצְמָח וְצֶדֶק מִשָּׁמַיִם נִשְׁקָף.' (תהלים פה:יב)
אבותי גנזו אוצרות שאין עושין פירות ואני גנזתי אוצרות שהן עושין
פירות שנאמר, 'אִמְרוּ צַדִּיק כִּי טוֹב כִּי פְרִי מַעַלְלֵיהֶם יֹאכֵלוּ.' (ישעיה
ג:י) אבותי גנזו במקום שהיד שולטת בו ואני גנזתי במקום שאין היד
שולטת בו שנאמר, 'צֶדֶק וּמִשְׁפָּט מְכוֹן כִּסְאֶךָ [חֶסֶד וֶאֱמֶת יְקַדְּמוּ פָנֶיךָ.]'
(תהלים פט:טו) אבותי גנזו ממון ואני גנזתי נפשות שנאמר, '...וְלֹקֵחַ
נְפָשׁוֹת חָכָם.' (משלי יא:ל) אבותי גנזו לאחרים ואני גנזתי לעצמי
שנאמר, '...וּלְךָ תִּהְיֶה צְדָקָה... .' (דברים כד:יג) אבותי גנזו בעולם הזה
ואני גנזתי לעולם הבא שנאמר, '[לֹא יוֹעִיל הוֹן בְּיוֹם עֶבְרָה] וּצְדָקָה
תַּצִּיל מִמָּוֶת.' (משלי יא:ד) ולא מית? אלא שלא ימות לעולם הבא."

King Munbaz arose and distributed all his property
to the poor. His relatives sent him a letter saying, "Your
ancestors added upon their wealth and that of their own
forebears while you disbursed yours and that of your
ancestors!?!"[28]

---

[28] King Munbaz was the son of Queen Helen. Both are mentioned in
the *Mishnah* (*Yoma* 3:10) as making major contributions to the Temple.
Rabbi Shlomo Sirilio writes that King Munbaz was from the line of the
Hasmoneans. *Breishith Rabbah* 46:10, however, states that he and his
brother, both sons of King Ptolemy, circumcised themselves, indicating
that he converted to Judaism. *Otzar HaMidrashim, Esser Galioth* 29
also identifies him as one of ten kings who converted to Judaism.

He answered, "I have accumulated more than they, for my ancestors amassed wealth on Earth whereas I amass it in Heaven, as it says, 'Truth shall sprout forth from the Earth and charity be seen from Heaven.'[29] My ancestors amassed in storehouses which produce no further wealth, whereas I have amassed in storehouses which produce further wealth, as it says, 'Tell the righteous that he is good, for the fruit of their deeds they will eat.'[30] My ancestors amassed in a place which the hand can reach [and, so, may be lost or stolen], whereas I have amassed in a place where the hand cannot reach, as it says, 'Charity and justice are the habitation of Your throne; kindness and truth go before Your countenance.'[31] My ancestors amassed money, whereas I have amassed lives, as it says, '...and a wise one takes lives.'[32] [By providing for the needs of the poor, King Munbaz prolonged or improved their lives. So, in a manner of speaking, he "amassed lives."] My ancestors amassed for others, whereas I have amassed for myself, as it says, '...and for you it shall be charity... .'[33] [When one dies, others inherit his or her wealth. By contrast, the merit

---

[29] Psalms 85:12. The word צדק is translated as "charity" in this verse and those which follow consistent with the point King Munbaz is making. The literal meaning of צדק, however, is "justice." The term "charity" in English connotes doing an undeserved favor for someone, but because the *Torah* commands Jews to help the poor, such help is not a favor but something to which the poor are rightfully entitled.
[30] Isaiah 3:10.
[31] Psalms 89:15.
[32] Proverbs 11:30.
[33] Deuteronomy 24:13.

of giving charity belongs to the donor forever. The expression "for you" in the verse highlights this point.] My ancestors amassed in this world, whereas I have amassed in the world to come, as it says, 'Wealth will not help on the day of wrath, but charity saves from death.'[34] Will one who gives charity never die? Rather, the verse means that he will not die in the world to come."

The Babylonian Talmud tells how astrologers predicted that a snake would bite the daughter of Rabbi Akiva on her wedding day and kill her. In those times it was customary for people to store small items between the cracks in the stone walls of the houses they inhabited. As she undid her hair after her wedding, Rabbi Akiva's daughter stuck her hairpin into a crack in the wall of her room. In the morning, she discovered that she had thus killed a poisonous snake which had been hiding there.

When Rabbi Akiva discovered what had happened, he asked his daughter whether she had done anything unusual that day. She replied that a poor person had come begging at the entrance to the wedding hall, but none of the guests paid any attention because they were preoccupied with the banquet, so she herself got up and gave her meal to the beggar. Citing the verse, "...charity saves from death,"[35] Rabbi Akiva declared that the Mitzvah of Tzedakah had saved his daughter's life. He added that not

---

[34] Proverbs 11:4. (Proverbs 10:2 contains similar wording.)
[35] Proverbs 11:4. (Proverbs 10:2 contains similar wording.)

only does Tzedakah save one from an unusual death, but even from death itself.[36]

The Talmud cites a similar story about a man whom Shmuel observed going out to chop wood. Although an astrologer predicted his death, an act of Tzedakah saved him. Shmuel then proclaimed that Tzedakah saves one both from an unusual death and even from death itself.[37]

The above incidents appear to contradict the passage of the Jerusalem Talmud just translated which points out that all people eventually die so that the expression "...charity saves from death"[38] must refer to death in the world to come rather than to physical death. What do Rabbi Akiva and his colleagues say about the fact that people do eventually die? How can charity save one even from death itself?

The expression "...charity saves from death" occurs twice in the book of Proverbs.[39] This repetition serves as the basis for the teaching that Tzedakah saves a person from two deaths: an unusual death and death itself.[40] True everyone dies, but death can be a gruesome ordeal or relatively painless.[41] Accordingly, one benefit Tzedakah

---

[36] B.T. *Shabbath* 156B.
[37] Ibid.
[38] Proverbs 11:4. (Proverbs 10:2 contains similar wording.)
[39] Ibid.
[40] B.T. *Baba Bathra* 10A.
[41] The *Talmud* deems a choking death to be the most grisly in contradistinction to the ideal death which is "a kiss resembling the drawing of a hair from milk." (B.T. *Brachoth* 8A.)

provides its donors is protection from an unusual, gruesome death when the time to die arrives.

There is, however, also the issue of a person living out the normal term of a human lifespan. The Psalms state that "The days of our years total seventy years and if with strength, eighty years....."[42] This implies that one who dies prior to the age of seventy has not completed the standard human lifespan.[43] Thus, although the natural forces of the universe (מזל) dictated that Rabbi Akiva's daughter die at a younger age than the standard human lifespan, Tzedakah prevented that from occurring. Tzedakah saved her from "death itself," meaning a premature death.[44]

Throughout the long period during which Jews have lived outside the Land of Israel, the Gentiles among whom they have dwelled have often restricted their activities. In many instances, Jews could only live in certain places and could not own land. In some places, Jews could not engage in certain crafts controlled by guilds which did not admit them. Ironically, these very restrictions often worked to the

---

[42] Psalms 90:10.

[43] B.T. *Mo'ed Katan* 28A and see below pp. 381-382 and 385.

[44] This explanation of Rabbi Akiva's position resembles that of the *Maharsha* on B.T. *Shabbath* 156B. Alternatively, perhaps Rabbi Akiva indeed means the same thing as what our passage says. Rabbi Yochanan states in the Babylonian *Talmud* that *Tzedakah* saves one from an unusual death as well as from the judgment of *Gehinnom*. (B.T. *Baba Bathra* 10A). Rabbi Akiva may mean that charity saved his daughter from the gruesome death by snakebite and also saves from "death itself," meaning the punishment of *Gehinnom*, the equivalent of death in the world to come.

economic advantage of the Jews because they forced them to engage in more lucrative business activities. For example, many Gentiles shunned foreign trade because they had difficulty making reliable contacts in other countries. Jews, on the other hand, succeeded well in international business since they could deal with Jews in other countries who spoke the same language, usually Yiddish, and whom they could trust. Although the inclination to be merchants and businesspeople derived from gentile oppression, it became so ingrained among Jews that both groups came to think of Jews as possessing a "commercial instinct."[45]

The Torah teaches that nothing happens by coincidence. Whatever takes place in the world, is directed by God. As Rabbi Akiva used to say, "Whatever the Merciful One does is for the best."[46] Perhaps the reason Hashem directed the course of history so that Jews came to engage so heavily in business pursuits was to drive home the message of King Munbaz. The most fundamental business concept is to "buy low and sell high," since,

---

[45] A classic example of this attitude is found in a lengthy essay entitled, "Concerning The Jews," written by Samuel L. Clemens popularly known by the pen name, "Mark Twain" (1835-1910). Mr. Clemens claimed that the main reason for persistent persecution and bias against Jews was envy of their success in business coupled with the inability to compete against them effectively. He wrote, "...the Jew is a money-getter; and in getting his money he is a very serious obstruction to less capable neighbors who are on the same quest."

[46] B.T. *Brachoth* 60B.

obviously, no business can succeed without a profit margin. King Munbaz pointed out that this concept applies to Tzedakah too. Although his ancestors accumulated large treasures, their holdings were insecure and could produce little, if any, reliable profit. By contrast, King Munbaz chose to "invest" in Tzedakah, a secure "business venture" guaranteed to yield a high profit margin.

Peah 1:1 (continued) (Compare B.T. *Sukkah* 49B)

צדקה וגמילת חסדים שקולות כנגד כל מצותיה של תורה
שהצדקה נוהגת בחיים וגמילת חסדים נוהגת בחיים ובמתים. הצדקה
נוהגת לעניים וגמילות חסדים נוהגת לעניים ולעשירים. הצדקה
נוהגת בממונו של אדם וגמילות חסדים נוהגת בין בממונו בין בגופו.
רבי יוחנן בר מריא בשם רבי יוחנן: אין אנו יודעין איזה מהן
חביב, או צדקה או גמילות חסדים. כשהוא אומר, "וְחֶסֶד ה' מֵעוֹלָם
וְעַד עוֹלָם עַל יְרֵאָיו וְצִדְקָתוֹ לִבְנֵי בָנִים." (תהלים קג:יז) הדא אמרה
שגמילות חסדים חביבה יותר מן הצדקה.

Charity and acts of kindness are valued as the equivalent of all the commandments of the *Torah* [and acts of kindness are greater than charity],[47] for charity applies to the living while acts of kindness apply to both the living and the dead. [Although the dead obviously have no use for money, one can show kindness towards them by burying them, attending their funerals or eulogizing them.] Charity applies to the poor, while acts of kindness apply both to the poor and to the rich. Charity may be done with a person's money while acts of kindness may be done with either one's money or one's person.

Rabbi Yochanan bar Maryah said in the name of Rabbi Yochanan: We do not know which of them is more beloved, charity or acts of kindness. When Scripture says,

[47] Rabbi David Oppenheim of Nikholsburg (Moravia) suggests the addition of this phrase to the text. A similar text in B.T. *Sukkah* 49B also reads this way.

"The kindness of the Lord is from eternity unto eternity upon those who fear Him and His charity to the children of their children,"[48] it is saying that acts of kindness are more beloved than charity. [God rewards people measure for measure. Accordingly, when they act kindly, He rewards them with kindness and when they give charity, He acts charitably towards them. Because the verse declares that God's kindness is eternal whereas His charity only extends to grandchildren, one may conclude that acts of kindness are greater.]

The Talmud points out that the Mitzvah of kindness has a broader application than charity does. The Torah does not teach that Mitzvoth which apply more frequently are therefore more important, so why does the Talmud say that acts of kindness are greater than charity?

The reward for Mitzvoth is commensurate with the amount of effort one puts into their performance.[49] A person readily sympathizes with the plight of a beggar who needs money, but it is more difficult to appreciate the importance of honoring the dead by attending a funeral since it may appear that the beneficiary of such kindness cannot enjoy it. In addition, the deceased cannot repay such kindness. Similarly, people tend to feel sorry for those who are poverty-stricken, but not for those who are well

---

48 Psalms 103:17. The term בנים in this verse means "children," not "sons." Compare B.T. *Baba Bathra* 110B.
49 *Pirkei Avoth* 5:22.

off. For this reason, it may be more of a challenge to behave kindly towards the rich. Finally, it is sometimes a simple matter to give some money to help out a poor person, whereas an act of kindness such as visiting the sick or rejoicing with a bride and groom requires much more active personal involvement. The above passage of the Jerusalem Talmud is not suggesting that acts of kindness are greater than charity because they occur more frequently. Rather, the greater challenges a person faces when performing acts of kindness than when donating to charity make the rewards much greater.

Peah 1:1 (J.T. *Sotah* 9:15 and compare B.T. *Menachoth* 99B)

שאלו את רבי יהושע: מהו שילמד אדם את בנו יוונית?
אמר להם: ילמדנו בשעה שאינו לא יום ולא לילה דכתיב, "...וְהָגִיתָ בּוֹ
יוֹמָם וָלַיְלָה... ." (יהושע א:ח) והתני רבי ישמעאל: "...וּבָחַרְתָּ בַּחַיִּים..."
(דברים ל:יט), זו אומנות. מעתה אסור ללמד את בנו אומנות בגין
דכתיב, "...וְהָגִיתָ בּוֹ יוֹמָם וָלַיְלָה... ." (יהושע א:ח).
רבי [בא] בריה דרבי חייא בר ווא בשם רבי יוחנן: מפני
הַמָּסוֹרוּת.
רבי אבהו בשם רבי יוחנן: מותר לאדם ללמד את בתו יוונית
מפני שהוא תכשיט לה. שמע שמעון. אמר, "בגין דו בעי מלפה בנתי
הוא תליה ליה ברבי יוחנן."
"יבוא עלי אם שמעתיה מרבי יוחנן."

They asked Rabbi Yehoshua: What is the rule with respect to a person teaching his son Greek? He answered them: Let him teach him at a time when it is neither day nor night, as it is written, "...and you shall meditate upon it [the *Torah*] day and night... ."[50]

But did not Rabbi Yishmael teach: "...and you shall choose life..."[51] refers to a trade [whereby one may sustain one's life[52]], yet now [according to Rabbi Yehoshua] it is

---

[50] Joshua 1:8.
[51] Deuteronomy 30:19.
[52] *Etz Yosef.*

forbidden to teach one's son a trade because it is written, "...and you shall meditate upon it day and night."[53]

Rabbi Ba,[54] the son of Rabbi Chiya bar Vava, said in the name of Rabbi Yochanan: [The reason one is forbidden to study Greek has nothing to do with the above verse, but is] because of treason. [Jews who studied Greek language and its attendant literary and philosophical traditions tended to turn against their own people.[55]]

Rabbi Abahu in the name of Rabbi Yochanan says: It is permissible for a person to teach his or her daughter Greek because it is an adornment for her.

Shimon bar Vava[56] heard this remark and said, "Because he wants to teach his daughters Greek, he claims

---

[53] Joshua 1:8.

[54] Although the Romm Vilna text reads simply "Rebbi," evidently referring to Rabbi Yehuda HaNassi, its editors point out that the Venice edition reads "Rabbi Ba." In addition, the version of this text in J.T. *Sotah* 9:15 has "Rabbi Ba, son of Rabbi Chiya bar Ba." To this day, it is customary to name a son after one's father, so that reading of the text makes the most sense. "Ba," is an abbreviation or nickname for "Abba." Rabbi Chiya bar Abba was an *Amora* who lived in the third century in the Land of Israel and is widely quoted throughout both the Jerusalem and Babylonian *Talmud.*

[55] *P'nei Moshe* on J.T. *Sotah* 9:15. There is some difference of opinion among the sages as to whether it is the language or the philosophy which is forbidden. Familiarity with a foreign philosophical system would have tended to lure Jews away from their own culture, making them more likely to commit treason. On the other hand, knowledge of the Greek language made it easier for Jews to betray their fellows without detection. See *Etz Yosef* on this text and see B.T. *Sotah* 49B.

[56] Although the Romm Vilna text reads simply "Shimon," the editors

to rely upon Rabbi Yochanan [who never would have said such a thing]."

Rabbi Abahu then said, "May a curse come upon me if I did not hear it from Rabbi Yochanan."[57]

The Mishnah itself forbids a person to teach his son Greek philosophy.[58] *The Babylonian Talmud explains that the reason for the prohibition has to do with a war which once broke out between two Hasmonean kings. Hyrcanus's forces took control of the Temple while Aristobolus's army laid siege from without. Each day, Hyrcanus's soldiers lowered a basketful of money to the enemy who then supplied the lambs necessary for the sacrificial service. A certain old man used Greek philosophy to convince Aristobolus's soldiers that as long as the sacrificial service continued, they would never prevail. The very next day, instead of sending lambs, the soldiers placed a pig in the basket, thereby disrupting the Temple service. This led the rabbis to say, "Cursed be the man who teaches his son Greek philosophy."*[59]

At first glance, the preceding story seems strange. If the merit of the Temple service prevented the downfall of the army inside the Temple, then any believing Jew might

---

point out that the Venice edition reads "Shimon bar Vava."

[57] This reading is based on the cross-reference of *P'nei Moshe* to the text in J.T. *Sotah* 9:15 and on the commentary of *Korban HaEidah* ad. loc.

[58] *Sotah* 9:14.

[59] B.T. *Sotah* 49B.

have suggested interrupting it. Indeed, if the study of Greek philosophy tends to harm one's faith, it would seem that precisely those Jews who were never exposed to it would be more likely to come up with this idea because their belief in the merit of the Temple service would be stronger.

*Contemporary Jews participate fully in non-Jewish society, immersing themselves in all types of thinking which may be contrary to the outlook of Judaism. While it would be futile to suggest that Jews isolate themselves from all outside influences, it is important to understand what such influences can lead to if one is not careful. Surely there were believing Jews who realized how interruption of the Temple service would affect the outcome of the war, but it never occurred to anyone to **do** such a terrible thing until an individual whose thinking was tainted with a foreign philosophy suggested it. Many of the ideas of Greek philosophy are compatible with the Torah. However, in subtle ways, such a non-Jewish philosophy can undermine one's value system, leading a person to do things he or she would never have considered doing otherwise.*

The Babylonian Talmud raises a question. The members of the family of Rabban Shimon ben Gamliel, the head of the Sanhedrin, studied Greek philosophy. How could they do so if the Mishnah forbids it? The Talmud answers that as leaders of the Jewish people, they had to study Greek philosophy to be able to deal with the gentile government.[60]

One might wonder why this was permitted. If the danger of foreign influence is so great, then the combination of dealing with Gentiles and studying their philosophy should be even worse. The answer is as follows. The Mishnah discusses a dispute between Rabbi Yehudah and the other sages regarding when to perform the Mitzvah of searching for Chametz at Passover. Rabbi Yehudah says one should check on the evening of the fourteenth day of Nissan (the day before Passover), but if one forgot, he or she can perform the inspection early the next morning or later on when the time arrives for the Chametz to be destroyed. After that, one may no longer perform the Mitzvah of searching for Chametz. The other rabbis, however, say that if one failed to check for Chametz on the night of the fourteenth, he or she may do so any time on the fourteenth, or, failing that, on the holiday itself, or, failing that, even during the intermediate days of the holiday.[61]

The Talmud raises a question about the view of the sages. Throughout the rest of the year people eat Chametz every day. Why are the sages not worried that if a person inspects for Chametz on Passover itself, he may forget that its consumption is temporarily forbidden and eat whatever

---

[60] Ibid.

[61] *Pesachim* 1:3 according to the commentary of *Tosafoth* sub verba "*V'eem Lo*" (ואם לא).

Chametz he finds? The Talmud answers, "If he himself is searching around to burn it, will he then eat it?"[62] *Since the entire purpose of the search is to destroy the Chametz, the person doing the checking will not make this type of mistake.*

As leaders of the Jewish nation, the family of Rabban Shimon ben Gamliel studied Greek philosophy for the express purpose of being able to deal with the gentile government for the benefit of the people. Consequently, there was no need to worry that they might turn around and become traitors. The Rambam and other Jewish leaders and scholars of the Middle Ages delved into Greek philosophy for the same purpose of dealing with non-Jews as well as convincing those Jews who might be lured away from Torah observance by such philosophy that they should remain loyal to the Torah. Because they studied Greek philosophy for the specific purpose of defending Judaism, they were clearly not going to be subverted by it.[63]

In addition, the Mishnah teaches that, "No sin will come through anyone who causes merit for the public."[64] *Since Rabban Shimon ben Gamliel and other Jewish leaders studied Greek philosophy for the express purpose of helping the community, they were protected from the harmful influence of the material they were studying.*

---

[62] B.T. *Pesachim* 11A.

[63] Rabbi Moshe Feinstein rules that such study is permitted today as well if it is for the purposes outlined here. (*Iggroth Moshe, Yoreh Deah* II, Responsa 111).

[64] *Pirkei Avoth* 5:18.

Along these lines, there is an apparently inconsistent pair of verses in the Book of Proverbs: "Do not answer a fool according to his folly lest you become equal to him yourself. Answer a fool according to his folly lest he be wise in his own eyes."[65] One interpretation of these verses is that if a person seeks out an argument with an adherent of a non-Jewish philosophy merely because he finds the topic interesting, he runs the risk of becoming equal to that person and adopting that philosophy. However, if one becomes involved with foreign systems of thought because he must respond to a challenge to the Torah, then the merit of trying to help the Jewish people will protect him from its negative influence.

---

[65] Proverbs 26:4-5.

Peah 1:1 (Compare B.T. *Kiddushin* 31A-B)

רבי אבוה בשם רבי יוחנן: שאלו את רבי אליעזר, "עד היכן כיבוד אב ואם?"

אמר להם, "ולי אתם שואלין? לכו ושאלו את דמה בן נתינה!"

דמה בן נתינה ראש פַּטְרְבּוּלִי היה. פעם אחת היתה אמו מסטרתו בפני כל בולי שלו ונפל קורדקן שלה מידה והושיט לה שלא תצטער.

אמר רבי חזקיה: גוי אשקלוני היה וראש פַּטְרְבּוּלִי היה, ואבן שישב אביו עליו לא ישב עליו מימיו. וכיון שמת אביו, עשה אותה יראה שלו.

פעם אחת אבדה יָשְׁפֵּה של בנימין. אמרו, "מאן דאית ליה טבא דכוותה?"

אמרו, "אית ליה לדמה בן נתינה."

אזלון לגביה ופסקו עמיה במאה דינר. סליק ובעי מייתו להו ואשכח אבוה דמיך. אית דאמרין מפתח דתיבותא הוה יתיב גו אצבעתיה דאבוי. ואית דאמרין ריגלוייה דאבוה הוות פשיטא על תיבותא. נחת לגבון. אמר לון, "לא יכילית מייתותיה לכון."

אמרי, "דילמא דו בעי פריטן טובא. אסקוניה למאתיים. אסקוניה לאלף. כיון דאיתער אבוה מן שינתיה, סליק ואייתותיה לון. בעון מיתן ליה בסיפקולא אחרייא, ולא קביל עלוי. אמר, "מה? אנא מזבין לכון איקרא דאבהתי בפריטין? איני נהנה מכבוד אבותי כלום!"

מה פרע ליה הקדוש ברוך הוא שכר? אמר רבי יוסי בי רבי בון: בו בלילה ילדה פרתו פרה אדומה ושקלו לו כל ישראל משקלה זהב ונטלוה.

אמר רבי שבתי: כתיב, "...וּמִשְׁפָּט וְרֹב צְדָקָה לֹא יְעַנֶּה." (איוב לז:כג) אין הקדוש ברוך הוא משהא מתן שכר של עושה מצות בגוי.

Rabbi Abahu in the name of Rabbi Yochanan said: They asked Rabbi Eliezer, "How far does the obligation of honoring a father and mother extend?"

He answered them, "Do you ask me? Go ask Dama ben Nathina!"

Dama ben Nathina was head of the town councilors.[66] One time his mother slapped his face in front of his entire staff. When her glove dropped from her hand, he picked it up and passed it to her so that she would not be troubled [bending over for it].

Rabbi Chizkiah said: He was a Gentile from Ashkelon and head of the town councilors. The stone upon which his father used to sit, he never sat upon all his life. Once his father died, he made it into an idol.

One time the gem of Benjamin was lost [from the High Priest's breastplate].[67] Those in charge of the Temple said, "Is there anyone who possesses one as fine as it was?"

---

[66] Paterbulli (פטרבולי) is a Latin or Greek word which appears to derive from "pater" which means "father," or, as used here, "leader," and "bulli" which the *Talmud* says means "tycoon" (B.T. *Gittin* 37A) and, in the present context implies "aristocrat." The Latin word "bulla" means "seal." The aristocrats of the town council probably came to be called by this name because they placed a seal upon the decrees they issued. It is also possible that the town councilors wore distinctive seals on their tunics. Some versions of the text read "Paterculli" which may mean "leader of underlings" since the word "cul" in Latin means "bottom." See *P'nei Moshe*, however, for a different interpretation.

[67] The High Priest's breastplate contained twelve gemstones, one for each tribe. (Exodus 28:21) The exact identity of *Yashfeh* (ישפה), the gem which represented Benjamin, is not known.

Others said, "Dama ben Nathina has one."

Those in charge of the Temple went to him and fixed a price of one hundred *dinarii*. He arose, seeking to bring it for them and found his father sleeping. Some say that the key to his treasure box was resting in his father's fingers while others say that his father's feet were stretched out on the box. He descended to those in charge of the Temple and said to them, "I cannot bring it for you."

They said, "Perhaps he wants more money." They went up to two hundred *dinarii*. They went up to a thousand. [However, Dama ben Nathina still refused.]

After his father awakened from his sleep, he arose and brought the gem to those in charge of the Temple. They wanted to pay him according to their last offer, but he would not accept it. He told them, "What? Should I sell you the honor of my father for money? I will not benefit from the honor of my parents whatsoever!"

How did the Holy One, Blessed be He, pay him a reward? Rabbi Yossi, the son of Rabbi Bon, said: That very night his cow gave birth to a red heifer and all Israel measured out its weight in gold and they purchased it.[68]

Rabbi Shabbethai said: It is written, "...and judgment and great justice He does not delay."[69] The Holy

---

[68] For purposes of ritual purification, the *Torah* requires the sacrifice of a red heifer, the ashes of which are mixed with spring water for use in the purification ceremony. However, a completely red heifer which meets the *Torah's* specifications is exceedingly rare so the Jews were prepared to pay its weight in gold.

[69] Job 37:23.

One, Blessed be He, does not delay the rendering of reward for those among the nations who do *Mitzvoth*.

The Ten Commandments say, "Honor your father and mother so that your days may be lengthened upon the land which the Lord your God gives you."[70] *Rabbi Yaakov Culi asks: If, ordinarily, the reward for honoring one's parents is long life, why did God instead reward Dama ben Nathina with a red heifer so that he could recoup his money?*

Ideally people should perform Mitzvoth because they wish to obey God. This is true even when the Mitzvoth appear to have a logical basis which all people recognize. Although Dama ben Nathina excelled at fulfilling the Mitzvah of honoring his parents, he did so because of his personal belief that such behavior was good. Anyone who performs a Mitzvah deserves a reward, regardless of his or her intentions, but God wished to point out to this Gentile that the true motivation for observing the commandments should be to serve Him. Whether they appear to make logical sense or not is of no importance.

The rules governing the red heifer sacrifice defy human logic. For example, when the ashes of the red heifer are mixed with spring water and sprinkled upon a person who is ritually impure, he or she becomes purified, while the one who did the sprinkling becomes impure.[71] *Jews*

---

[70] Exodus 20:12.
[71] Numbers 19:19.

32

obey these rules despite the fact that they make no logical sense because they trust God's Divine wisdom. God rewarded Dama ben Nathina with a red heifer to hint at the idea that people should obey even those commandments which are understandable to human intelligence, such as honoring one's parents, because God ordained them and not merely because they make sense.[72]

In addition, the Torah's promise of long life does not necessarily refer to life in this world, but to eternal life in the hereafter.[73] To merit that reward, perhaps one must perform the Mitzvoth as decrees of God and not merely because they make sense. Since Dama ben Nathina honored his parents only because it seemed sensible to him to do so, God rewarded him in this world rather than in the next.

---

[72] *Me'Am Loez* on Exodus 20:12.
[73] B.T. *Kiddushin* 39B.

Peah 1:1 (Compare B.T. *Kiddushin* 31A-B)

אמו של רבי טרפון ירדה לטייל לתוך חצירה בשבת והלך
רבי טרפון והניח שתי ידיו תחת פרסותיה והיתה מהלכת עליהן עד
שהגיעה למיטתה. פעם אחת, חלה ונכנסו חכמים לבקרו. אמרה להן,
"התפללו על טרפון בני שהוא נוהג בי כבוד יותר מדאי."
אמרו לה, "מה עביד ליך?"
ותניית להון עובדא.
אמרו לה, "אפילו עושה כן אלף אלפים עדיין לחצי כבוד
שאמרה התורה לא הגיע."
אמו של רבי ישמעאל באה וקיבלת עלוי לרבותינו. אמרה
להן, "גיערו בישמעאל בני שאינו נוהג בי בכבוד."
באותה שעה נתכרכמו פניהם של רבותינו. אמרו, "איפשר
רבי ישמעאל לא נהג בכבוד אבותיו?" אמרו לה, "מה עביד ליך?"
אמרה, "כד דו נפק מבית וועדה, אנא בעי משנז ריגלוי
ומישתי מיהן ולא שביק לי."
אמרו לו, "הואיל והוא רצונה, הוא כבודה."
אמר רבי מנא יאות אילין טחונייא אמרין, "כל בר נש ובר נש
זכותיה גו קופתיה." אימיה דרבי טרפון אמרה לון אכין ואגיבונה
אכין. אימיה דרבי ישמעאל אמרה לון אכין ואגיבוניה אכין.
רבי זעירא הוה מצטער ואמר, "הלואי היה לי אבא ואימא
דאיקרינון דנירת גן עדן." כד שמע אילין תרתין אולפניא, אמר,
"בריך רחמנא דלית לי לא אבא ואימא! לא כרבי טרפון הוות יכילנא
למעבד ולא כרבי ישמעאל הוינא מקבלה עלוי."

The mother of Rabbi Tarfon went down to stroll in
her courtyard on the Sabbath. [While strolling, her sandal

broke and she could not repair it on the Sabbath.[74]] Rabbi Tarfon went and placed his two hands under her soles and she was walking upon them until she reached her couch. One time, he became ill and the sages came to visit him. His mother told them, "Pray for Tarfon, my son, for he behaves towards me with extreme respect."

They asked her, "What did he do for you?"

She repeated the foregoing incident to them.

They told her, "Even if he would do so thousands upon thousands of times, he still would not reach half the honor prescribed by the *Torah*."

The mother of Rabbi Yishmael came and complained about him to the rabbis. "Scold Rabbi Yishmael, my son," she told them, "for he does not behave with respect towards me."

At that moment, the faces of the rabbis paled. They said to themselves, "Is it possible that Rabbi Yishmael did not behave respectfully towards his parents?" They then asked her, "What does he do to you?"

"When he departs from the study hall, I seek to wash his feet and drink from the water, but he does not permit me."

The sages told Rabbi Yishmael, "Since this is her desire, this is her honor."

---

[74] *P'nei Moshe*, citing B.T. *Kiddushin* 31B. This language does not actually appear in the text there, but in *Tosafoth* sub verba *Rabbi Tarfon Havya* (ר' טרפון הויא).

Rabbi Manna said: How right are those millers who say, "Each and every person's rightful portion is in his hopper." [When people bring hoppers of wheat for grinding, the amount and quality of the finished product varies according to the owner's merit and luck.[75]] The mother of Rabbi Tarfon told the sages thus and they answered her thus, while the mother of Rabbi Yishmael told them thus and they answered her thus. [The mother of Rabbi Tarfon praised her son's extreme willingness to honor her, yet the rabbis declared that he did not even approach fulfilling his true obligation. By contrast, when Rabbi Yishmael's mother complained, the rabbis instructed him to permit her to degrade herself, insisting that such constituted honor.]

Rabbi Z'eira said regretfully, "If only I had a father and mother whom I might honor so as to inherit Paradise!" When he heard these two anecdotes, he said, "Blessed is the Merciful One that I have neither father nor mother! I could not have done as Rabbi Tarfon and I could not have accepted upon myself what Rabbi Yishmael did."

Based upon the verse, "Do not make your souls repulsive... ,"[76] Jewish law forbids a person to eat or drink substances which are disgusting even if they are Kosher. For example, one should not eat or drink with

---

75 *P'nei Moshe.*
76 Leviticus 11:43 and 20:25.

dirty hands or from utensils which are dirty.[77] *Hence, it is forbidden to drink water that was used to wash someone's feet.*

The Torah says, "[Each] man his mother and father you shall fear and my Sabbaths you shall observe, I am the Lord your God."[78] *By including a reference to Sabbath observance in the same verse which obligates each person to fear his or her parents, the Torah teaches that if a parent orders a child to violate the Sabbath, he or she must disobey. Thus, one may not obey a parent to violate any commandment of the Torah.*[79] *Indeed, Jewish law provides that if a parent orders a child to violate even a rabbinical ordinance, he or she must refuse.*[80]

In Rabbi Yishmael's case, his mother sought to disobey the Torah's prohibition against consuming disgusting substances. Although she did not command him to transgress anything himself, the Torah also forbids strengthening the hands of wrongdoers.[81] *For example, one should not purchase goods from known thieves as this*

---

[77] *Shulchan Aruch, Yoreh Deah* 116:6 based on B.T. *Makkoth* 16B. Whether this is a Torah prohibition or only a rabbinical one is a matter of dispute. See *Torah Temimah* on Leviticus 11:43 and *Encyclopedia Talmudith*, Vol. 3, pp. 338-339.

[78] Leviticus 19:3.

[79] The conclusion, "...I am the Lord your God" emphasizes that both the individual and his or her parents must honor God. *Rashi* ad. loc. based on B.T. *Kiddushin* 5B-6A and 32A.

[80] *Shulchan Aruch, Yoreh Deah*, 240:15.

[81] Mishnah, *Gittin* 5:9.

encourages them in their dishonest enterprises.[82] *Moreover, the Talmud questions whether one is permitted to give a child a Kosher grasshopper as a pet because, if the grasshopper dies, perhaps the child will eat it and violate the prohibition against eating something disgusting.*[83] *If so, how could the rabbis suggest that Rabbi Yishmael honor his mother's request that she wash his feet and drink the water?*

The answer may be that the prohibition against consuming something disgusting does not apply when it is done for purposes of medical treatment even in circumstances where no danger to life exists.[84] *Rabbi Yishmael's mother was obviously not in her right mind to want to drink water which had been used to wash his feet. However, agitating someone who is mentally unstable may cause negative health consequences. Perhaps the sages thought that if Rabbi Yishmael persisted in refusing her demands, his mother would grow ill. Thus, when they said, "Since it is her desire, it is her honor," they meant that her desire to do so was so great that if her son failed to comply, she could become sick. Accordingly, it was permitted.*

In the alternative, perhaps Rabbi Manna's statement at the end of the passage was a criticism of the viewpoint of the other rabbis. A person's ability to fulfill the Mitzvah of honoring his or her parents depends largely

---

[82] *Shulchan Aruch, Choshen Mishpat* 356:1.

[83] B.T. *Shabbath* 90B.

[84] See, for example, *Aruch HaShulchan, Yoreh Deah* 81:10.

upon that individual's circumstances. Thus, if Dama ben Nathina had not found his father sleeping upon his treasure box, he would not have had the opportunity to honor him. Similarly, had his mother not slapped him in front of the town council, he would not have had the chance to honor her as he did. Had similar opportunities arisen for Rabbi Tarfon, perhaps he would have done the same. Thus, Rabbi Manna held that the statement that Rabbi Tarfon had not achieved anywhere near complete fulfillment of the commandment to honor parents was not really a fair criticism. By the same token, Rabbi Yishmael behaved properly by refusing to permit his mother to wash his feet and drink the water. Accordingly, Rabbi Manna objected to the responses the rabbis gave in these two situations.

Peah 1:1 continued (B.T. *Kiddushin* 31A-B)

יש שהוא מאכיל את אביו פטומות ויורש גיהנם ויש שהוא
כודנו ברחיים ויורש גן עדן.

כיצד מאכיל את אביו פטומות ויורש גיהנם? חד בר נש הוה
מייכיל את אביו תרנגולים פטומים. חד זמן אמר ליה אביו, "ברי,
אילין מנן ליך?" אמר ליה, "סבא, סבא, אכול ואדיש דכלבין אכלין
ואדשין!" ונמצא מאכיל את אביו פטומין ויורש גיהנם.

כיצד כודנו ברחיים ויורש גן עדן? חד בר נש איטחין
בריחיים. אתית מצוותא לטיחנייא. אמר ליה, "אבא, עול טחון תחתי.
אין מטת מבזייא, טב לי אנא ולא את. אין מטת מילקי, טב לי אנא
ולא את." נמצא כודנו בריחייא ויורש גן עדן.

There is one who feeds his father delicacies yet inherits *Gehinnom* while there is one who binds him to a mill yet inherits Paradise.

How does it come about that one feeds his father delicacies yet inherits *Gehinnom*? One person used to feed his father fattened roosters. One time, his father said to him, "My son, from where do you get these?" He answered, "Old man, old man, eat and shut up, for dogs eat and shut up!" So it comes about that one feeds his father delicacies yet inherits *Gehinnom*.

How does it come about that one binds him to a mill yet inherits Paradise? One person was grinding at a mill when a conscription order for millers arrived. [At certain times, the king required each household to supply a person to work in his mills. Those who directed the work were often very harsh.[85]] He said, "Father, go in and mill in my stead [whereas I will go serve the king]. If taskmasters who degrade come, better I should suffer and not you. If taskmasters who whip come, better I should suffer and not you." So it comes about that one binds him to a mill yet inherits Paradise.

The value of Torah study and Mitzvah performance is commensurate with the sincere devotion of the person who does them. For instance, while not everyone has the ability to become an expert Torah scholar, "it is the same whether one does much or does little provided that he directs his heart to Heaven."[86] Moreover, "The Holy One, Blessed be He, desires the heart."[87] The sincere devotion one puts into his or her Torah study is more important than the quantity learned.

Along similar lines, Rabbi Yitzchak taught that one who gives a coin to a beggar merits six blessings while one who soothes and encourages him merits eleven blessings.[88]

---

[85] *P'nei Moshe. Rashi* sub verba *"Umevio"* (ומביאו) on B.T. *Kiddushin* 31B and *Tosafoth* sub verba *"V'Tordo"* (וטורדו) on B.T. *Kiddushin* 31A state that the king's men were specifically coming to draft the father.

[86] B.T. *Brachoth* 5B.

[87] B.T. *Sanhedrin* 106B. A similar expression is found in *Zohar, Parshath T'rumah* 162B.

[88] B.T. *Baba Bathra* 9B. *Tosafoth* points out that the eleven blessings are additional to the six blessings bestowed for the contribution itself.

The kind thoughts and words that accompany the charitable contribution are more important than the contribution itself. Likewise, the merit of honoring parents depends not so much on what one does as on how he or she does it.

The passage under consideration takes matters a step further. Here, the Talmud points out that when a person says or does something contradictory to a Mitzvah, he thereby converts the Mitzvah into a grievous sin. Hence, the Talmud does not say that the son who fed his father fattened roosters but insulted him gained less merit from his actions, but rather that he will be punished in Gehinnom. The son did not merely lack the best of motives. Rather, he converted the Mitzvah into a sin.

Along these lines, the Talmud teaches that if one steals wheat, performs all required rituals such as removing the tithe and Challah donations, processes it into bread and utters a blessing over it, "this is not one who blesses but one who blasphemes."[89] *By reciting a blessing, one shows his belief that Hashem supplies all his needs. One who steals, however, shows that he does not trust God to provide for him. Hence, the act of stealing contradicts the act of making a blessing so that one who utters a blessing over stolen food does not perform a Mitzvah. To the contrary, such action constitutes a sin.*

---

[89] B.T. *Baba Kama* 94A. See also B.T. *Sukkah* 30A that a *Mitzvah* performed by means of a sin does not count as a *Mitzvah*.

The Talmud states that one who studies Torah with impure motives, such as a desire to be respected, should nonetheless continue to study because as a result of learning with impure motives, he will eventually come to learn with pure motives.[90] *However, if one studies the Torah for the purpose of ridiculing others by trying to contradict and disparage their learning, it would have been better for him if he had never been created.*[91] *The purpose of Torah study is to understand and fulfill God's will. If one studies it in order to refute it, God forbid, he thereby acts contrary to its purpose and does not perform the Mitzvah of Torah study. One who studies merely for the sake of being able to contradict the learning of others falls into this category.*

Likewise, whenever one converts a Mitzvah to a purpose directly contrary to that Mitzvah, it becomes transformed into a sin. In the passage of the Talmud translated here, the son used the outer trappings of the Mitzvah, a gift to his father, as a means to disgrace him, saying, in so many words, "Look at how you have to depend on me like a dog!" In this way, he converted what should have been a Mitzvah into a sin.

---

[90] B.T. *Pesachim* 50B.

[91] B.T. *Brachoth* 17A according to *Tosafoth* sub verba "*HaOseh Shelo*" (העושה שלא).

Peah 1:1

רבי אחא בשם רבי אבא בר כהנה: כתיב, "אֹרַח חַיִּים פֶּן
תְּפַלֵּס נָעוּ מַעְגְּלֹתֶיהָ לֹא תֵדָע." (משלי ה:ו) טילטל הקדוש ברוך הוא
מתן שכרן של עושי מצות כדי שיהיו עושין אותן באמונה.

רבי אחא בשם רבי יצחק: כתיב, "מִכָּל מִשְׁמָר נְצֹר לִבֶּךָ כִּי
מִמֶּנּוּ תוֹצְאוֹת חַיִּים." (משלי ד:כג) מכל מה שנאמר לך בתורה השמר
שאין אתה יודע מאיזה מהן יוצא לך חיים.

אמר רבי אבא בר כהנה: השוה הכתוב מצוה קלה שבקלות
למצוה חמורה שבחמורות. מצוה קלה שבקלות זה שלוח הקן ומצוה
חמורה שבחמורות זה כיבוד אב ואם ובשתיהן כתיב, "...וְהַאֲרַכְתָּ יָמִים."
(דברים כב:ז)

אמר רבי אבון: ומה אם דבר שהוא פריעת חוב כתיב בו,
"...לְמַעַן יַאֲרִיכֻן יָמֶיךָ וּלְמַעַן יִיטַב לָךְ..." (דברים ה:טז), דבר שיש בו
חסרון כיס וסיכון נפשות לא כל שכן?

אמר רבי לוי והוא דרבה מינה: גדול הוא דבר שהוא פריעת
חוב מדבר שאינו בפריעת חוב.

רבי שמעון בר יוחאי אומר: כשם שמתן שכרן שוה, כן
פורענותן שוה. מה טעם. "עַיִן תִּלְעַג לְאָב וְתָבֻז לִיקֲהַת אֵם [יִקְּרוּהָ
עֹרְבֵי נַחַל וְיֹאכְלוּהָ בְנֵי נָשֶׁר.]" (משלי ל:יז) עין שהלעיגה על כיבוד
אב ואם ובזית על "...לֹא תִקַּח הָאֵם עַל הַבָּנִים." (דברים כב:ו) יקרוה
עורבי נחל. יבא עורב שהוא אכזרי ויקרנה ואל יהנה ממנה ויבא נשר
שהוא רחמן ויאכלנה ויהנה ממנה.

Rabbi Acha in the name of Rabbi Abba bar Kahana said: It is written, "Lest you assess the path of life, [God] moved its ways; you do not know [them]."[92] The Holy

---

[92] Proverbs 5:6. This translation accords with the interpretation that

One, Blessed be He, transferred the granting of reward for those who perform *Mitzvoth* so that they should perform them with faith. [*Hashem* transferred the reward for *Mitzvah* performance to the hereafter so that people cannot know the relative importance of one *Mitzvah* compared to another. They cannot "assess the path of life." Thus, God forestalled the problem of people ignoring "minor" commandments in order to focus their energy on "important" ones.[93]]

Rabbi Acha in the name of Rabbi Yitzchak said: It is written, "From every admonition [of the *Torah*] guard your heart, for from it are emanations of life."[94] From everything which is stated to you in the *Torah* take heed, for you do not know from which of them life will emanate for you.

Rabbi Abba bar Kahana said: Scripture equated the very easiest *Mitzvah* with the most stringent *Mitzvah*. The

---

follows here, but see *Rashi* ad. loc. for an alternative reading.

[93] *P'nei Moshe*; *Rashi* on Proverbs 5:6. This passage appears at odds with B.T. *Mo'ed Katan* 9A-B according to the commentary of *Rabbeinu Nissim* as cited there by *HaKothev*. He says that if others are available to perform a less important *Mitzvah*, one should let them do it and go on to perform the more important *Mitzvah*. Only if no one else is available, should one perform whichever *Mitzvah* happens along first. *Rashi*, however, understands that passage as referring to whether *Torah* study should take priority over *Mitzvah* performance, stating that if others are available to handle the *Mitzvah*, one should not interrupt his studies to do so. Thus, according to *Rashi*, that passage does not contradict this section of the Jerusalem *Talmud*.

[94] Proverbs 4:23 according to *Rashi* ad. loc.

very easiest *Mitzvah* is sending away the mother bird before seizing her eggs or goslings, whereas the most stringent *Mitzvah* is honoring a father and mother, yet for both of them it is written, "you shall lengthen days."[95] [One can scare a mother bird away from her nest with a trifling effort, whereas the previous passages show the demanding nature of the commandment to honor one's parents.]

Rabbi Abon said: If regarding something which constitutes repayment of a debt it is written, "...so that your days may be long and so that it will be good for you...,"[96] then regarding something which entails financial loss or hazard to life shall it not be even more so? [Honoring one's parents may be viewed as merely repaying a debt of gratitude. If one may anticipate great reward for a *Mitzvah* which ordinary human logic and emotion dictate, certainly one may do so concerning *Mitzvoth* the purpose of which is not readily apparent. Rabbi Abon disagrees with the rabbis who maintain that the commandment to respect one's parents is among the most difficult to fulfill. He points out that although this *Mitzvah* may demand sacrifices at times, from a psychological perspective it is easier to perform than other *Mitzvoth* because a person feels he or she owes respect to a parent.]

---

95 Deuteronomy 22:7. A similar phrase is found in Deuteronomy 5:16.
96 This is how the verse actually reads in Deuteronomy 5:16. The Romm Vilna text of the Jerusalem *Talmud* has the phrases in the opposite order.

Rabbi Levi and one who is greater than him[97] said: Greater is something which is repayment of a debt than that which is not repayment of a debt. [Because the requirement to honor one's parents is not only a *Mitzvah*, but also compelled by human logic, a person feels more worry and anxiety about fulfilling it. Hence, contrary to the position of Rabbi Abon, even from a psychological standpoint, fulfilling this *Mitzvah* is more difficult than fulfilling other *Mitzvoth*.[98]]

Rabbi Shimon bar Yochai said: Just as their reward is equal, so their punishment is equal. What is the Scriptural basis for this? "An eye which mocks a father and despises gathering of a mother, ravens of the valley shall gouge it and eaglets shall consume it."[99] [The plain meaning of the verse is that "gathering of a mother" refers to the wrinkles that gather upon an elderly person's face.[100] The *Talmud*, however, understands "gathering of a mother" as alluding to the commandment to shoo away the mother bird before seizing her eggs or offspring.] An eye which mocked at the *Mitzvah* of honoring father and mother and despised the *Mitzvah* of "When it shall happen before you a bird's nest upon the way in any tree or upon the ground

---

[97] The Romm Vilna text reads this way and does not identify which rabbi joined Rabbi Levi in making this pronouncement. According to the text of Rabbi Shlomo Sirilio, however, the passage should read, "Rabbi Levi said that which Rabbi Muna said, for Rabbi Muna said... ."

[98] *P'nei Moshe.*

[99] Proverbs 30:17.

[100] *Rashi* ad. loc.

[with] goslings or eggs and the mother crouches upon the goslings or upon the eggs, you shall not take the mother with the offspring. You shall surely send away the mother and the offspring you shall take for yourself so that it will be good for you and you may lengthen your days,"[101] ravens of the valley shall gouge it. A raven which is cruel shall come and gouge it, but will not benefit from it. An eagle will come which is merciful and eat it and benefit from it. [A person who views his or her parents with disrespect is punished measure for measure. Such an individual did not wish to benefit his parents, so he is punished by the raven which cruelly refuses to provide for its offspring and derives minimal benefit from the food it scavenges.[102] Alternatively, a person may try to avoid the obligation of honoring parents by refusing to take notice of their needs. He or she may likewise avoid sending away the mother bird by refusing to take notice of it. A person who avoids *Mitzvoth* by closing his or her eyes to them deserves a punishment involving the eyes.[103]]

The overall message of this section of the Talmud parallels the statement of Rabbi Yehudah HaNasi that one should be just as careful with a seemingly trivial Mitzvah

---

[101] Deuteronomy 22:6-7.
[102] *P'nei Moshe.*
[103] *Etz Yosef.*

as with one which appears important because one does not know what reward they will ultimately bring.[104]

People can understand why fulfillment of the commandment to honor parents should warrant a reward of long life. A person's parents bring him or her into life, so, measure for measure, honoring them causes long life. However, the connection between performance of the Mitzvah of sending away the mother bird and meriting long life is not readily apparent. Hence, the Talmud makes the point that such matters may not follow a logic which human beings can understand. Accordingly, a person should take care to perform all commandments diligently.[105]

The Maharal explains that the reward for performing Mitzvoth has two aspects. On the one hand, God rewards the person according to the effort he exerts and the thoughtfulness he applies when performing them. Hence, the more difficult the Mitzvah is, the more reward it entails. On the other hand, the Mitzvoth have a certain

---

[104] *Pirkei Avoth* 2:1. This is not to suggest that for *Halachic* purposes there may not be situations where performance of one *Mitzvah* takes precedence over another. (See *Maharsha* on B.T. *Mo'ed Katan* 9A-B.) That fact, however, should not lead one to conclude that the reward for one is necessarily greater than the reward for the other or that one should take performance of the "less serious" *Mitzvah* lightly.

[105] Rabbi Chaim Vital in *Sefer HaGilgulim, Hakdamah* 16, says that a person's soul must go through repeated reincarnations until it has fulfilled certain commandments. Since no one knows which commandment he was sent here to perform, one must be meticulous in doing all of them.

function and value in and of themselves which is not known. For this reason, one must be careful to perform as many as possible.[106]

The Talmud's reference to losing one's sight for failing to observe these commandments is, of course, figurative. Classical Jewish literature often analogizes spiritual insight to physical sight. Thus, for example, when Rav Shesheth, who was blind, went out to greet a royal procession, a certain Sadducee mocked him, questioning what benefit a blind person could have from attending a royal procession. Rav Shesheth responded, "Come and see that I know more than you." He then proceeded to correctly predict the approach of the king's entourage based upon his interpretation of Scripture.[107] *Hence, although he was blind, Rav Shesheth possessed a kind of intellectual or spiritual "sight."*[108] *Similarly, the Tanach refers to prophetic experiences as "visions" although the prophets did not physically see anything during them.*[109]

Although the Talmud contrasts the commandments of honoring one's parents and sending away the mother bird in terms of the relative ease of their fulfillment, it also points out how both commandments have something in common: one who fails to perform them is exceedingly stingy and self-centered. After all, if one cannot show

---

[106] *Tifereth Yisrael*, chapter 61.
[107] B.T. *Brachoth* 58A.
[108] *Ben Yehoyada* ad. loc.
[109] *Moreh Nevuchim* II:41.

kindness towards one's parents for whom one should have natural feelings of affection and from whom one has received so much, to whom can he or she show kindness? Similarly, when a person finds a nest with eggs or goslings in it, he has found a windfall, something into which he has invested neither time nor money. It is such a simple matter to shoo away the mother bird that only a very greedy person would be so anxious to grab the prize that he or she would fail to do so.

The character traits of greed, stinginess and selfishness which motivate people who do not wish to spend time or money honoring parents or shooing away a mother bird reflect lack of faith in God, for if God commands a person to do something, He has the power to see to it that those who obey Him will not lose out. Thus, one who refuses to honor parents or send away the mother bird destroys his spiritual sensitivity because he acknowledges only the physical world. He destroys his spiritual "sight."

The Talmud often refers to a stingy, greedy person as one who has "an evil eye," again emphasizing how these characteristics demonstrate lack of spiritual vision.[110] *Rabbi Yehoshua said, "An evil eye, evil impulse and hatred of humanity remove a person from the world."*[111] *Similarly, Rava said that, "Ninety nine die*

---

[110] This is similar to the English expression that such a person has a "jaundiced view" of the world.

[111] *Pirkei Avoth* 2:11.

from an evil eye and one from natural causes."[112]
*Stinginess and greed cause death because a person with
these traits is reluctant to perform the many Mitzvoth which
entail sacrificing one's resources or showing generosity
towards others and it is the performance of Mitzvoth that
gives life.*

*The long life which the Torah promises as a reward
for observing these Mitzvoth does not necessarily mean
long life in this world, but life in the hereafter.*[113] *When a
person is stingy or greedy, he thereby shows that he values
only the material world. Only one who has a recognition
that this world is but a means through which to reach the
next can overcome the natural temptation to stinginess and
greed. Measure for measure, such recognition merits
reward in the world to come.*

---

[112] B.T. *Baba Metzia* 107B.
[113] B.T. *Kiddushin* 39B.

Peah 1:1 (Compare B.T. *Kethuboth* 17A)

וגמילות חסדים: דכתיב, "רֹדֵף צְדָקָה וָחָסֶד יִמְצָא חַיִּים
צְדָקָה וְכָבוֹד." (משלי כא:כא) כבוד בעולם הזה וחיים לעולם הבא.
רבי שמואל בר רב יצחק הוה נסיב שיבשתיה והוה מהדס
קומי כליא. והוה רבי זעירא חמי ליה ומיטמר מן קומוי. אמר, "חמי
להדין סבא איך הוא מבהית לן." וכיון דדמך, הוה תלת שעין קלין
וברקין בעלמא. נפקת ברת קלא ואמרה, "דדמוך רבי שמואל בר רב
יצחק, גמיל חסידים נפקון למגמל ליה חסד." נחתת אישתא מן שמיא
ואיתעבידת כעין שבשא דנור בין ערסיה לציבורא. והוון בריתי
אמרין, "היא דהדין סבא דקמת ליה שבשתיה."

[The first *Mishnah* of this Tractate declares that,
**"These are things the proceeds of which a person
consumes in this world while the principal remains for
the world to come: honoring father and mother,
bestowing kindness, creating peace between a person
and his or her comrade, and study of *Torah* which is
more valuable than all of them."** The *Talmud* now
adduces Scriptural proof that bestowing kindness merits
this reward.]

It is written, "One who pursues charity and kindness
will find life, charity and honor."[114] The verse means that
one who is kind will receive honor in this world and life in
the world to come.

Rabbi Shmuel bar Rabbi Yitzchak used to take up a
myrtle branch and dance before the bride [it being an act of

---

[114] Proverbs 21:21.

kindness to cause the bride and groom to rejoice.] Rabbi Z'eira used to observe him do so and would hide from his presence, saying, "Do you see how this old man shames us?" When Rabbi Shmuel bar Rabbi Yitzchak died, there were three hours of thunder and lightning throughout the world. A Heavenly voice emerged and said, "Since Rabbi Shmuel bar Rabbi Yitzchak has died, let those who bestow kindness go forth and bestow kindness to him." Fire descended from the Heavens and formed a kind of flaming branch between his coffin and the public. The people said, "Observe how his branches stand by this old man."

The Talmud rules that one must set aside Torah study for the sake of accompanying a funeral or causing a bride and groom to rejoice.[115] However, there is a difference between interrupting one's study to greet a bride and groom on the one hand, and behaving in an undignified way on the other. Rabbi Z'eira feared that when the general public viewed an elderly Torah scholar dancing and carrying on before a bride, they would come to view Torah scholars with disrespect.

Rabbi Z'eira seems to have a valid point. Torah scholars are required to maintain their dignity before the public. For instance, when the townsfolk used to pitch in to build or maintain parts of a town, a Torah scholar was forbidden to join them because doing so might cause

---

[115] B.T. *Kethuboth* 17A. See *Shulchan Aruch, Yoreh Deah* 361:1 for details of the practical *Halachah* in this regard.

disrespect.[116] *Moreover, Rabbi Yochanan used to say that a scholar who had a grease stain on his garments deserved death for bringing Torah study into contempt.*[117] *If so, why does the Talmud reject Rabbi Z'eira's criticism of Rabbi Shmuel bar Rabbi Yitzchak?*

The answer appears to be that there is a distinction between disgracing oneself over an optional activity and doing so for the sake of a Mitzvah. The Tanach tells how King David danced energetically during the procession which accompanied the Ark of the Covenant to Jerusalem. "...Michal, daughter of Saul, went out towards David and said [sarcastically], 'How honorable is this day when a king of Israel is exposed today to the eyes of maidservants and manservants as one of the good-for-nothings might be exposed!' And David said to Michal, '...I would abase myself more than this and I would be degraded in my eyes and with the maidservants of whom you spoke, [for] with such I would gain honor.'"[118] *The Talmud comments that one of the great merits of King David was that while other kings delighted in worldly honor, holding elaborate banquets, he dealt with making Halachic rulings even when doing so required him to dirty his hands.*[119]

---

[116] *Shulchan Aruch, Yoreh Deah* 243:1.
[117] B.T. *Shabbath* 114A. See also B.T. *Brachoth* 43B which enumerates other things a scholar must take care to avoid such as wearing overly ragged shoes or arriving late at the house of study.
[118] II Samuel 6:20-22 according to *Metzudoth David.*
[119] B.T. *Brachoth* 4A.

The purpose of creating an atmosphere of reverence towards Torah scholars is not for the sake of the scholars, but so that people will respect the Torah which they represent. Accordingly, it makes sense that they should set aside their personal honor for the sake of carrying out Mitzvoth. Indeed, the very willingness of a highly respected person to engage in behavior that otherwise might be considered beneath his or her dignity for the sake of a Mitzvah brings honor to the Torah because onlookers will gain a greater appreciation of the importance of Mitzvoth.

Peah 1:1 (Compare B.T. *Kiddushin* 40A)

וַהֲבָאַת שָׁלוֹ-ם בֵּין אדם לחבירו: כתיב, "סוּר מֵרָע וַעֲשֵׂה טוֹב
בַּקֵּשׁ שָׁלוֹ-ם וְרָדְפֵהוּ." (תהלים לד:טו) בקשיהו במקומך ורדפהו
במקום אחר.
אמר רבי טביומי: נאמר כאן "רדיפה" ונאמר להלן "רדיפה."
מה רדיפה שנאמר להלן כבוד בעולם הזה וחיים לעולם הבא, אף הכא
כן.

[What Scriptural basis is there for the *Mishnah's* promise of reward both in this world and the next for] creating peace between a person and his or her comrade? It is written, "Turn from evil and do good; seek peace and pursue it."[120] Seek it in your place and pursue it in another place. [One should not only strive for harmonious relations with his or her immediate acquaintances, but pursue creating such harmony among other people as well.]

Rabbi Tavyomi said: It is said here "pursuit" and it is said elsewhere "pursuit" [in the verse, "One who pursues charity and kindness will find life, charity and honor."[121]] Just as the "pursuit" mentioned elsewhere merits honor in this world and life in the world to come, so it is here.

When people quarrel, they often develop bitter feelings towards one another. Hence, they may rebuff the initial efforts of one who wishes to create peace between

---

120 Psalms 34:15.
121 Proverbs 21:21.

*them. They may also resent those who try to reconcile them, viewing such people as "outside meddlers." For this reason, the Tanach proclaims that one must **pursue** peace, making repeated efforts, if necessary, and not growing discouraged.* [122]

---

[122] Rabbi Yaakov Ibn Chaviv, *HaKothev*.

Peah 1:1 (Compare *Breishith Rabbah* 35:3)

רבי ברכיה ורבי חייא דכפר דחומין. חד אמר: אפילו כל
העולם כולו אינו שוה לדבר אחד של תורה. וחד אמר: אפילו כל
מצותיה של תורה אינן שוות לדבר אחד מן התורה.

רבי תנחומא ורבי יוסי בן זימרא: חד אמר כהדא וחד אמר
כהדא.

רבי אבא אבוי דרבי אבא בר מרי בשם רבי אחא: כתוב אחד
אומר, "[כִּי טוֹבָה חָכְמָה מִפְּנִינִים] וְכָל חֲפָצִים לֹא יִשְׁווּ בָהּ." (משלי
ח:יא) וכתוב אחד אומר, "[יְקָרָה הִיא מִפְּנִיִים [מִפְּנִינִים קרי]] וְכָל
חֲפָצֶיךָ לֹא יִשְׁווּ בָהּ." (משלי ג:טו) "חֲפָצִים," אלו אבנים טובות
ומרגליות. "חֲפָצֶיךָ," אלו דברי תורה דכתיב, "[כִּי אִם בְּזֹאת יִתְהַלֵּל
הַמִּתְהַלֵּל הַשְׂכֵּל וְיָדֹעַ אוֹתִי כִּי אֲנִי ה' עֹשֶׂה חֶסֶד מִשְׁפָּט וּצְדָקָה בָּאָרֶץ]
כִּי בְאֵלֶּה חָפַצְתִּי נְאֻם ה'." (ירמיה ט:כג)

Rabbi Berachya and Rabbi Chiya of the village of
Chumin each expressed a different view concerning *Torah*
study. One said: Even all the world in its entirety is not
worth a single word of *Torah*. The other said: Even all the
Mitzvoth of the *Torah* are not worth a single word of *Torah*.

Rabbi Tanchuma and Rabbi Yossi ben Zimra
expressed the foregoing views, one like this one and one
like that one.[123]

---

[123] The ancient redactors of the *Talmud* were highly conscientious
about maintaining a precise record of tradition. As they put it,
"Whoever recites something in the name of the one who said it brings
redemption to the world." (B.T. *Chullin* 104B and see *Pirkei Avoth*
6:6). For this reason they felt it important to let the reader know that
other sages held views similar to those just expressed by Rabbi

Rabbi Abba, the father of Rabbi Abba bar Mari, in the name of Rabbi Acha said: One verse says, "For wisdom is better than jewels and all desirable things are not equal to it,"[124] while another verse says, "It is more dear than jewels and all your desirable things are not equal to it."[125] [Why does one verse refer to "*all* desirable things" generally while the other speaks of "*your* desirable things" specifically?] "Desirable things" alludes to jewels and pearls while "your desirable things" alludes to words of *Torah* as it is written, "Rather in this shall one who takes pride, pride himself: comprehend and know Me for I am the Lord who does kindness, judgment and charity in the Earth for in these I desire,' says God."[126]

[The *Talmud* uses the expression "words of *Torah*" to refer to the *Mitzvoth* which derive from the *Torah*.[127]]

This passage is one of several in the Talmud which state that Torah study takes priority over Mitzvah

---

Berachya and Rabbi Chiya of Chumin.

[124] Proverbs 8:11.

[125] Proverbs 3:15.

[126] Jeremiah 9:23.

[127] This is apparent because God says in the verse that He desires "kindness, judgment and charity," which are *Mitzvoth*. (*P'nei Moshe* and *Mareh HaPanim*). In addition, the phrase "דברי תורה," usually translated as "*words* of *Torah*" could also be rendered "*things* of *Torah*," a "thing of *Torah*" being a commandment. (Rabbi Moshe Heinemann שליט"א). Thus, the study of *Torah* exceeds in greatness both any worldly delights as well as the performance of *Mitzvoth* as Rabbi Berachya and Rabbi Chiya asserted above.

---

performance. The Babylonian Talmud rules that this is indeed the case when others can perform the Mitzvah. However, if an opportunity to do a Mitzvah arises which only a Torah scholar can do, he should set aside his studies to perform the Mitzvah unless the Mitzvah itself involves Torah study.[128] *Thus, for example, reciting Shema is actually a form of Torah study. Accordingly, an outstanding scholar who never stops learning for even a moment need not interrupt to say Shema since he is in any event engaged in Torah study.*[129]

In addition to the foregoing Halachic principles, this passage presents an interesting philosophical issue. For one thing, Rabban Shimon ben Gamliel said that, "Homiletics are not the main thing, but rather action,"[130] *which seems to imply that Mitzvah performance is more important than Torah study.*[131] *Moreover, Rabbi Chanina ben Dosa said, "Anyone whose deeds exceed his wisdom, his wisdom will last, while anyone whose wisdom exceeds his deeds, his wisdom will not last."*[132] *Thus, there exists a*

---

[128] B.T. *Mo'ed Katan* 9B.

[129] *Tosafoth* sub verba "*Kan B'Mitzvah*" (כאן במצוה) on B.T. *Mo'ed Katan* 9B citing J.T. *Shabbath* 1:2.

[130] *Pirkei Avoth* 1:17.

[131] It is possible that Rabban Shimon ben Gamliel means that homiletics (מדרש) which rabbis employ to inspire people to observe the commandments are secondary to actual *Mitzvah* performance. He may agree that other forms of *Torah* study are superior to *Mitzvah* performance. However, this is not how most commentators explain his statement.

[132] *Pirkei Avoth* 3:12 and see also 3:22 where Rabbi Elazar ben

body of rabbinic opinion that Mitzvah performance is more important than Torah study.

Rabbi Akiva and Rabbi Tarfon debated this very issue before the sages in Lod. Rabbi Akiva claimed that study is more important while Rabbi Tarfon claimed that deeds are more important. Those present concluded, "Great is study for study brings to action,"[133] resolving the question by pointing out that Torah study and Mitzvah performance complement one another.

*Rabbi Shneur Zalman of Liadi taught that Mitzvah performance **surrounds** the soul with Divine light, a spiritual emanation of God, while Torah study permits a person's limited intellect to commune with the infinite wisdom of God so that the soul actually **absorbs** the Divine light. Thus, Torah study is "food" for the soul while Mitzvah performance creates "garments" for the soul.[134] Each has its own importance. By studying Torah, a person elevates his or her mind to a sublime level of spirituality. By performing Mitzvoth, he or she puts God's will into effect in the physical world. Both forms of service create a nexus between the corporeal and spiritual realms. One cannot perform Mitzvoth without studying Torah to know how to perform them. On the other hand, pure study does not complete the job of connecting the physical and spiritual realms. It is actual Mitzvah performance which*

Azariah expands on this theme.

[133] B.T. *Kiddushin* 40B.

[134] *Likutei Amarim Tanya*, Part I, Chapter 5.

accomplishes that.[135] *Thus, from a philosophical perspective, these two forms of Divine service complement one another and it cannot be said in any absolute sense that one is greater than the other.*

Rabbi Yitzchak Isaac Chaver expresses a similar view. He points out that Torah study is both a preparation for Mitzvah performance as well as a Mitzvah in and of itself. For this reason, Torah study is greater than the performance of any particular Mitzvah. Moreover, with most Mitzvoth, if one did not complete performance of the Mitzvah it counts for nothing whereas each word of Torah study counts as a Mitzvah even if one did not fully master the topic of study.[136] *He further notes that, according to the Kabbalah, each Mitzvah affects certain spiritual realms. By contrast, Torah study does not merely affect a particular aspect of the spiritual universe. Rather, all the upper worlds depend upon and are sustained by Torah study. Moreover, performance of most Mitzvoth is limited by time and space. For example, many Mitzvoth can be performed only in the Land of Israel. Others, such as*

---

[135] *Likutei Amarim Tanya*, Part I, Chapter 37.

[136] Rav Ashi taught that if one seeks to do a *Mitzvah* but circumstances prevent him from completing it, it counts as though he did it. (B.T. *Brachoth* 6A). Rabbi Yitzchak Isaac Chaver apparently distinguishes between a situation where it is *as though* one performed the *Mitzvah* (a lower level) and one where a person *actually* completed performance of the *Mitzvah* (a higher level). When one learns *Torah*, he *actually* fulfills the *Mitzvah* of *Torah* study even if his limited ability prevents him from comprehending the material fully.

holiday and Sabbath observance, are limited to certain times. Torah study, however, is a Mitzvah which does not have these limitations. This reflects the higher spiritual nature of Torah study for that which is spiritual is not bound by time and space.

Despite the many ways in which Torah study excels over Mitzvah performance, Rabbi Chaver notes that Torah study and Mitzvah observance are interdependent. The physical world derives its life force from the lofty spiritual worlds through which God channels His Divinity. However, the purpose of Creation is not those spiritual worlds, but the physical one which people inhabit. Likewise, Torah study is the life force of the Mitzvoth, but was only created so that Mitzvoth could exist. [137]

The Talmudic story of how Moses ascended to Heaven at the time of the Giving of the Torah also supports this thesis. The angels objected against God bestowing something as holy as the Torah to mere mortals. To this, Moses responded that the Mitzvoth contained in the Torah do not apply to angels. For example, the angels were never enslaved in Egypt, so all the Mitzvoth related to that episode of Jewish history cannot apply to them. Similarly, angels do not work, so resting on the Sabbath is meaningless for them. Again, angels do not conduct business, so they cannot fulfill the many Torah laws concerning business activity. In this manner, Moses

---

[137] *Siach Yitzchak*, Part I, Sermon on the Topic of the Two *Nunin* of "*VaYehi Binso'a Ha'Aron.*"

convinced the angels that the proper place for the Torah is on Earth and not in Heaven. [138] *As lofty as the Torah is, its true purpose is its fulfillment in this physical world through Mitzvah performance.*

This concept is further reflected in the dictum of Rabbi Elazar ben Azariah: "Anyone whose wisdom exceeds his deeds, to what is he compared? To a tree whose branches are many but whose roots are few. The wind comes, uproots it and turns it on its face... But one whose deeds exceed his wisdom, to what may he be compared? To a tree whose branches are few but whose roots are many. Even if all the winds of the world come and blow upon it, they cannot move it from its place." [139] *While Rabbi Elazar ben Azariah appears to emphasize the importance of Mitzvah performance, he also compares Torah study and Mitzvah performance to parts of a tree. Just as the branches and roots of a tree represent an integrated unit, both elements essential to the existence of the tree, so Torah study and Mitzvah observance are both essential and interdependent elements of a person's service to God.*

---

[138] B.T. *Shabbath* 88B-89A.
[139] *Pirkei Avoth* 3:22.

Peah 1:1

ארטבון שלח לרבי הקדוש חד מרגלי טבא אטימיטון. אמר
ליה, "שלח לי מילה דטבא דכוותה." שלח ליה חד מזוזה.
אמר ליה, "מה? אנא שלחי לך מילה דלית לה טימי ואת
שלחת לי מילה דטבא חד פולר?!?"
אמר ליה, "חפציך וחפצי לא ישווה בה. ולא עוד, אלא דאת
שלחית לי מילה דאנא מנטיר לה ואנא שלחית לך מילה דאת דמך לך
והיא מנטרא לך דכתיב, 'בְּהִתְהַלֶּכְךָ תַּנְחֶה אֹתָךְ בְּשָׁכְבְּךָ תִּשְׁמֹר עָלֶיךָ
וַהֲקִיצוֹתָ הִיא תְשִׂיחֶךָ.'" (משלי ו:כב)

Artebon[140] sent a priceless jewel to the holy Rebbi,
saying, "Send me something of similar value." He sent him
a *Mezuzah*.

"What!" exclaimed Artebon. "I sent you something
priceless and you send me something worth one *Folleron* [a
small coin]!?!"

He answered, "Your property and my property do
not equal its value. Not only that, but you sent me
something which I must guard while I sent you something
where you can sleep and it will guard you, as it is written,

---

[140] Artebon's identity is unclear. *P'nei Moshe* claims he was an
extremely wealthy Jew. However, Rabbi Yisrael Eisenstein in *Amudei
Yerushalayim* suggests that he may have been a non-Jew who rejected
idolatry. *Etz Yosef* cites *Sefer Yuchasin* that he was a Persian king.
Rashi on B.T. *Yoma* 11A sub verba "*B'Artebin*" (באַרטבין) says that a
similar term used there may be a proper name or may indicate the
person's profession, presumably a tribune. (The word resembles
"tribune" if the א is dropped and the letters are transposed.)

'In your walking it will guide you, in your lying down it will watch over you and when you awaken it will advocate for you.'"[141]

This story is reminiscent of a widely known tale about Onkelos, a nephew of the Roman emperor Hadrian, who converted to Judaism. Upset and embarrassed that his nephew had joined the "lowly" Jewish people, Hadrian sent a group of soldiers to return him to Rome by force. Through his great eloquence, however, Onkelos persuaded them to remain with him and also convert to Judaism. A second party of soldiers fared no better. Finally, the emperor sent a third contingent of soldiers, this time instructing them not to engage in any type of conversation with Onkelos. As the soldiers led Onkelos out the door, he touched the Mezuzah and smiled.

"Why do you smile?" demanded one of the soldiers.

"The way of the world," explained Onkelos, "is that the king sits inside his palace while his servants stand outside guarding him. God, however, allows his servants to sit inside while He protects them."

Hearing this, these soldiers also converted to Judaism.[142]

At first glance, this story seems strange. What exactly persuaded these Gentiles to convert to Judaism? Similarly, in the passage translated above, why did Rabbi

---

[141] Proverbs 6:22.
[142] B.T. *Avodah Zarah* 11A and *Tanchuma, Mishpatim* 5.

Yehudah HaNassi think that Artebon would find the idea of God protecting the Jewish people so impressive?

Ancient Greek and Roman mythology depicted the pagan gods as glorified humans. They ate and drank as humans do. They schemed against one another as humans do. They felt all the same emotions of love, jealousy, greed and pride that humans do. They were even supposed to be capable of mating with humans to produce demigods.

The purpose of worshiping such gods was to curry favor with them or to avoid their wrath, just as one might try to appease a powerful human being. Many pagans did recognize an ultimate "God" who created the universe. Aristotle referred to Him as the "First Cause."[143] However, while the pagans believed that the Supreme God created the world, they also held that He cared little about it, leaving all terrestrial matters in the hands of subordinate "gods" who must be appeased "or else."

*The idea of a Supreme God who does **not** behave as humans do, who not only cares about what happens in the world but expects people to do justice and love mercy as He does and, on top of all that, cares for and protects those who obey Him, was a radical idea to ancient heathens. So impressed were they by this novel concept that they converted to Judaism.*

---

[143] *Moreh Nevuchim*, **Part II, Chapters 20-21.**

Peah 1:1

רבי מנא שמע כולהון מן הדין קריא: ["כִּי לֹא דָבָר רֵק הוּא
מִכֶּם כִּי הוּא חַיֵּיכֶם וּבַדָּבָר הַזֶּה תַּאֲרִיכוּ יָמִים עַל הָאֲדָמָה אֲשֶׁר אַתֶּם
עֹבְרִים אֶת הַיַּרְדֵּן שָׁמָּה לְרִשְׁתָּהּ." (דברים לב:מז)] "כִּי לֹא דָבָר רֵק הוּא
מִכֶּם..." זה תלמוד תורה. "...כִּי הוּא חַיֵּיכֶם..." זה כיבוד אב ואם.
"...וּבַדָּבָר הַזֶּה תַּאֲרִיכוּ יָמִים..." זו גמילת חסדים. "...עַל הָאֲדָמָה..." זה
הבאת שלו-ם בין אדם לחבירו.

[The first *Mishnah* of this Tractate declares that
**"These are things the proceeds of which a person
consumes in this world while the principal remains for
the world to come: honoring father and mother,
bestowing kindness, creating peace between a person
and his or her comrade, and study of *Torah* which is
more valuable than all of them."**]

Rabbi Manna derived all of them from this verse:
"For it is not an empty matter for you, for it is your life and
with this thing you shall lengthen your days upon the land
which you are passing over the Jordan, there to inherit
it."[144] "For it is not an empty matter for you..." refers to
Torah study [which you can master and make meaningful if
you apply sufficient effort]; "...for it is your life..." refers to
honoring father and mother [concerning which the Torah
promises long life[145]]; "...and with this thing you shall
lengthen your days..." refers to bestowing kindness, [as the

---

[144] Deuteronomy 32:47.
[145] Exodus 20:12.

Tanach says, "One who pursues charity and kindness will find life... ."[146]; "...upon the land..." refers to creating peace between a person and his or her comrade. [The end of the verse says, "...which you are passing over the Jordan, there to inherit it." When the Jews arrived in the Land of Israel, each tribe received a share by drawing lots.[147] Since Divine Providence determined just which portion of land went to whom, everyone was satisfied and no one quarreled. Thus, the reference to "the land" alludes to creating peace among people.]

The verse Rabbi Manna cites as a source for the Mishnah employs the repetitive phrase "...for it is your life and with this thing you shall lengthen your days...," thereby suggesting that there are two rewards: one in this world and one in the next.[148]

In the preceding passages, the sages discussed at length how performance of each of the four Mitzvoth mentioned in the Mishnah yield proceeds in this world while the principal reward remains for the hereafter. Why, then, did Rabbi Manna think it important to derive them all from this particular verse?

Rabbi Yitzchak Albo points out that the verse Rabbi Manna uses comes towards the very end of the Torah when Moses was taking leave of the Jewish people and charging

---

146 Proverbs 21:21. *Etz Yosef.*
147 B.T. *Baba Bathra* 122A.
148 *Etz Yosef.*

them to remain loyal to its teachings. According to Jewish law, when one writes a document, one should repeat the general topic of the document at the end before the witnesses sign it.[149] *In the same manner, Moses sought to sum up the substance of the Torah towards the end.*[150] *Thus, Rabbi Manna sought to demonstrate that these four Mitzvoth represent the essence of the Torah, that by which the totality of the Torah may be summed up.*

[149] *Shulchan Aruch, Choshen Mishpat* 44:1.
[150] *Sefer Halkarim,* Dissertation IV, Chapter 40.

Peah 1:1

וכנגדן ארבעה דברים שהן נפרעין מן האדם בעולם הזה
והקרן קיימת לו לעולם הבא. ואלו הן: עבודה זרה, גילוי עריות,
שפיכות דמים ולשון הרע כנגד כולן.

עבודה זרה מניין? "[כִּי דְבַר ה' בָּזָה וְאֶת מִצְוָתוֹ הֵפַר] הִכָּרֵת
תִּכָּרֵת הַנֶּפֶשׁ הַהִוא עֲוֹנָה בָהּ." (במדבר טו:לא) מה תלמוד לומר "עֲוֹנָה
בָהּ?" מלמד שהנפש נכרתת ועונה בה. וכתיב "[וַיָּשָׁב מֹשֶׁה אֶל ה'
וַיֹּאמַר] אָנָּא חָטָא הָעָם הַזֶּה חֲטָאָה גְדֹלָה וַיַּעֲשׂוּ לָהֶם אֱלֹהֵי זָהָב." (שמות
לב:לא)

גלוי עריות מניין? "...וְאֵיךְ אֶעֱשֶׂה הָרָעָה הַגְּדֹלָה הַזֹּאת
וְחָטָאתִי לֵא-לֹהִים." (בראשית לט:ט)

שפיכות דמים מניין? "וַיֹּאמֶר קַיִן אֶל ה' גָּדוֹל עֲוֹנִי מִנְּשֹׂא."
(בראשית ד:יג)

כשהוא בא אצל לשון הרע, מהו אומר? לא "גדול" ולא
"גדולה" ולא "הגדיל," אלא, "גדולות." "יַכְרֵת ה' כָּל שִׂפְתֵי חֲלָקוֹת
לָשׁוֹן מְדַבֶּרֶת גְּדֹלוֹת." (תהלים יב:ד)

And corresponding to them are four things for
which retribution is exacted from a person in this world
while the principal remains for the world to come. They
are: idol worship, sexual immorality, bloodshed and evil
gossip (לשון הרע) which is worse than all the others.

From where is there proof that this is so with
respect to idolatry? "Because the word of the Lord he
despised and His commandment he violated, surely that
soul shall be cut off, its sin shall be upon it."[151] Why does

---

[151] Numbers 15:31.

72

Scripture say "its sin shall be upon it?" Because the soul is cut off yet its sin remains upon it. [The reference to "His commandment" without specifying which one implies idolatry because that sin is tantamount to violation of all the laws of the *Torah*.[152] His or her sin remains upon the soul of the idolater who will suffer further punishment in the hereafter.] And it is written, "Moses returned to the Lord and said, 'Please, this people has sinned a great sin and they made for themselves gods of gold.'"[153] [The term "great sin" implies that idolatry is far more grievous than "ordinary" sins and that retribution occurs both in this world and the next.[154]]

From where is there proof that this is so with respect to sexual immorality? [When Joseph served as a slave in Egypt and Potiphar's wife attempted to seduce him, he refused, saying,] "...and how can I do this great evil and sin unto God."[155] [The term "great evil" suggests that sexual immorality is far worse than other sins.]

From where is there proof that this is so with respect to bloodshed? "And Cain said to the Lord, 'My sin

---

[152] *Etz Yosef.*

[153] Exodus 32:31.

[154] The first verse the *Talmud* cited as proof of the severe nature of idolatry only alludes to that sin by implication. According to its context, the verse actually refers to blasphemy, not idol worship. Because that verse is not precisely on point, the *Talmud* presents an additional one.

[155] Genesis 39:9.

is too great to bear.'"[156]   [Once again, the expression "great" alludes to unusual severity.]

When Scripture comes to evil gossip, what does it say? Not "great sin" or "great evil" or "too great," but "great things." "May the Lord eradicate all lips of deception, a tongue which speaks exaggerations [literally, "great things" (גדולות)]."[157] [The plural form indicates that sins of speech are even worse than those previously mentioned.]

The Talmud's proof that evil gossip is worse than any of the other three cardinal sins is based upon a verse which does not appear to talk about evil gossip at all, but deception. How are the two connected?

Deceit does not necessarily entail outright lying. As the verse states, it can mean "exaggerating" the truth. The Talmud relates how a lender once took a borrower to court and demanded payment. The borrower claimed that he had already given the lender the money. Rava, who was the judge, told the borrower that he would have to swear that he had already paid. The borrower surreptitiously placed money inside a hollow walking stick. When he arrived in court to take the oath, he asked the lender to hold his walking stick while he held the Torah scroll and swore that he had given the lender his money. Upon hearing the oath, the lender grew so incensed that he broke

---

[156] Genesis 4:13.
[157] Psalms 12:4.

the stick. The money fell out and everyone discovered the deception.[158]

Evil gossip (לשון הרע) does not entail lying. The Torah tells how Miriam gossiped to her brother Aaron about Moses. She and Aaron were both prophets who had also scaled lofty spiritual heights, yet they continued their normal family life. Accordingly, Miriam questioned why Moses found it necessary to separate from his wife. Not only was Miriam's statement true, but she also intended it in a positive way. She thought that someone should admonish Moses not to abandon his wife if such was not necessary to carry out his prophetic mission. Miriam did not realize that Moses's much higher level of prophecy required him to separate from his spouse. The Torah describes how Miriam was punished for what she said even though her statements were true and her intentions proper because she should not have suspected Moses of doing anything amiss.[159]

Accordingly, evil gossip and deception have a common element: subtlety. Just as one who deceives may do so by very refined means, even using statements which are technically true, so it is with evil gossip. For this reason, a verse which talks about deception may also be taken to allude to evil gossip.

---

[158] B.T. *Nedarim* 25A.

[159] Numbers 12. As the reader will see in the passages which follow, the *Talmud* discusses how Joseph spoke apparently evil gossip about his brothers. The fact that Joseph was a highly righteous person again shows how difficult it is to detect evil gossip and avoid it.

A question remains, however: Why is evil gossip singled out as the most egregious sin a person can commit, worse than any other? The Talmud teaches that the more serious a sin is, the more serious is its punishment. Thus, if one fails to perform a positive commandment and repents, his or her repentance is immediately accepted. By contrast, one who violates a negative precept for which a Jewish court might impose the punishment of lashes may repent, but his or her repentance is not fully accepted until Yom Kippur. One who transgresses a commandment for which a court might impose the death penalty may repent and observe Yom Kippur, but such repentance is not fully accepted until after the sinner has suffered hardships during his or her lifetime. The Talmud identifies desecration of God's Name as the worst possible sin and declares that it cannot be atoned until the sinner dies.[160] Evil gossip is not mentioned in this scheme and since a Jewish court imposes no penalty on someone who speaks it, how can it be the most serious transgression of all?

A simple answer would be to say that the rabbis only spoke metaphorically here. As noted above, it is very easy for someone to make the mistake of speaking evil gossip without realizing that he or she is doing something wrong because the subject matter is true and because the speaker may have positive motives. By contrast, the wrongfulness of idolatry, murder and sexual immorality are readily apparent to even the simplest Jew. Accordingly, the

---

[160] B.T. *Yoma* 86A.

rabbis thought it necessary to emphasize the serious nature of evil gossip by comparing it to these grievous sins even though in reality it is not as grave.[161]

*However, the Talmud states that the first Temple was destroyed because people engaged in the three sins of idolatry, murder and sexual immorality, whereas the second Temple was destroyed due to evil gossip. This shows that evil gossip is **literally** as bad as those three terrible sins.*[162]

Evil gossip indeed represents the very root of all evil because, as noted earlier, it is related to sly deception. The very first sin, that of Adam and Chavah, resulted from deception and self-delusion. God forbade Adam to eat from the fruit of the Tree of Knowledge, but when the snake questioned Chavah about it, she told him that she and

---

[161] Rabbi Tzvi Hirsch Chajes in *Mavoh HaAggadoth* ("Introduction to the *Aggadoth*"). Rabbi Chajes points out that the rabbis of the *Talmud* frequently exaggerated the severity of various sins to cause their listeners to avoid them. One may not commit the sins of murder, idolatry or sexual immorality even if he or she will die as a result. Since the same is not the case with evil gossip, it is clearly not as serious as they are. The rabbis only make this comparison as a way of stressing the degree to which people must avoid evil gossip.

[162] The *Chafetz Chaim* in *Shmirath HaLashon*, Part I, Chapter 4 bases this on *Rashi* sub verba "*VeHaynu*" (והיינו) in B.T. *Gittin* 57B. In addition, B.T. *Yoma* 9B states that the Second Temple was destroyed due to unwarranted hatred (שנאת חנם), proving that such hatred is equivalent to the three major sins. The *Talmud* then goes on to imply that unwarranted hatred is identical to evil gossip, probably because it causes it.

Adam were also forbidden to touch it.[163] *This very minor and seemingly innocent deviation from the truth gave the snake the opportunity to deceive Chavah. He pushed her against the tree and, when nothing happened, argued that just as touching the tree was harmless so eating its fruits would prove harmless.*[164]

The evil inclination always starts to incite a person to sin in subtle ways which gradually lead to more and more.[165] *Thus, in reality, it can be said that evil gossip is the worst of all sins. Because its nature is so subtle and its evil so difficult to detect, it is, indeed, the most serious sin, a paradigm and source for all others. Indeed, part of the snake's incitement of Chavah included the malicious accusation that God forbade Adam and Chavah to eat from the Tree of Knowledge not for their own benefit but merely to prevent them from becoming like Him.*[166] *Consequently, the first sin was* **not** *the eating of the forbidden fruit, but listening to evil gossip!*

In light of the above, it is not surprising that as soon as Hashem confronted Adam with his sin, Adam's response was to speak evil gossip, immediately blaming Chavah for what happened. Chavah, in turn blamed the serpent.[167] *This is another fundamental aspect of evil gossip: people who gossip about others often do so as a*

---

163 Genesis 3:3.
164 *Rashi* on Genesis 3:3-4.
165 See B.T. *Sukkah* 52A and *Shabbath* 105B.
166 Genesis 3:5.
167 Genesis 3:12-13.

way of making themselves feel superior. By pointing out defects in others, they can divert attention from their own faults. This is also the root of all evil because one who deflects blame onto others and ignores his or her own failings will never repent. True the snake led them astray, but had Adam and Chavah admitted their wrongdoing and expressed regret, God may not have punished them.

This idea may help explain the parallel between Torah study and evil gossip. Honoring one's parents, performing acts of kindness and creating peace between a person and his or her comrade are good deeds which everyone can readily appreciate. Even non-Jews recognize the importance of these Mitzvoth as illustrated by the fact that the Talmud identifies Nathina ben Dama, an idolater, as the ideal of a person who truly fulfilled the Mitzvah of respecting one's parents.[168] *Even so, there are Halachoth which define how to perform these Mitzvoth. There is a "Torah way" of doing them. Hence, Torah study reveals the subtleties of these Mitzvoth and is a counterpoint to evil gossip which is a paradigm for all other sins because of its subtlety.*

The Talmud taught in earlier passages that studying Torah is not only greater than other Mitzvoth in some respects, but also that one cannot perform other Mitzvoth properly without learning Torah and, thus, knowing how to do them. Just as "Great is study for study brings to

---

[168] See above and B.T. *Kiddushin* 31A.

action,"[169] *so evil gossip can lead to the three major sins discussed here. Thus, the Talmud declares in an upcoming passage that a person does not speak evil gossip unless he or she denies God, alluding to idolatry.*[170] *Moreover, evil gossip "murders" three people: the one who says it, the one who listens to it and the one about whom it is said.*[171] *In addition, when the Jews sent spies to the Land of Israel prior to entering it, the spies came back and reported that it was too difficult to conquer or inhabit. As a result of this evil gossip about the Holy Land, God ordered that all that generation had to wander in the desert until it died out. Only their children could enter the Land.*[172] *Thus, evil gossip is related to bloodshed. Finally, David married the daughter of King Saul. Later, King Saul falsely believed that David had rebelled against his rule. The Midrash tells how Doeg gossiped about David to King Saul, arguing that because David rebelled against the kingdom, his life was forfeit. King Saul reasoned that if David was regarded as dead, his wife was permitted to marry another man and he indeed married her off to someone else. Hence, evil gossip caused sexual immorality.*[173]

---

[169] B.T. *Kiddushin* 40B.
[170] See below pp. 85-87.
[171] See below p. 103.
[172] Numbers 13 and 14. The *Mishnah* in *Arachin* 3:5 says "the final judgment against our ancestors was not sealed except because of evil gossip."
[173] *Etz Yosef. Breishith Rabbah* 32:1.

Peah 1:1 (Compare *Breishith Rabbah* 84:7)

כתיב, "וַיָּבֵא יוֹסֵף אֶת דִּבָּתָם רָעָה אֶל אֲבִיהֶם." (בראשית לז:ב)
מה אמר? רבי מאיר אמר: חשודים הן על אבר מן החי. רבי יהודה
אומר: מזלזלין הן בבני השפחות ונוהגין בהן כעבדים. ורבי שמעון
אומר: נותנין הן עיניהן בבנות הארץ.

אמר רבי יודה בן פזי: "פֶּלֶס וּמֹאזְנֵי מִשְׁפָּט לַה' מַעֲשֵׂהוּ כָּל
אַבְנֵי כִיס." (משלי טז:יא) מה אמר? חשודין הן על אבר מן החי. אמר
הקדוש ברוך הוא, "כך אני מוכיח עליהן שהן שוחטין ואזלין. 'וַיִּקְחוּ
אֶת כְּתֹנֶת יוֹסֵף] וַיִּשְׁחֲטוּ שְׂעִיר עִזִּים וַיִּטְבְּלוּ אֶת הַכֻּתֹּנֶת בַּדָּם.'
(בראשית לז:לא) מה אמר? מזלזלין הן בבני השפחות ונוהגים בהן
כעבדים. "...לְעֶבֶד נִמְכַּר יוֹסֵף." (תהלים קה:יז) מה אמר? נותנים
עיניהם בבנות הארץ. הא דובא מתגרי לך! "וַתִּשָּׂא אֵשֶׁת אֲדֹנָיו אֶת
עֵינֶיהָ אֶל יוֹסֵף וַתֹּאמֶר שִׁכְבָה עִמִּי." (בראשית לט:ז)

It is written, "...and Joseph brought their evil report to their father."[174]   What did he say concerning his brothers? Rabbi Meir said: They are suspected of violating the prohibition against eating the limb of a living animal. Rabbi Yehudah said: They show disrespect towards the children of the maidservants and treat them as slaves. Rabbi Simeon said: They set their eyes upon the women of the land.

Rabbi Yehudah ben Pazi said: "A balance and scales of justice has the Lord; His deeds are all weights of a pouch."[175] [Just as merchants used to carry weights of

---

[174] Genesis 37:2.
[175] Proverbs 16:11.

varying sizes in a pouch to set upon a balance scale, so God weighs the deeds of each person and rewards or punishes measure for measure.] What did Joseph say? They are suspected of violating the prohibition against eating the limb of a living animal. The Holy One, Blessed be He said, "So shall I prove that they constantly abide by the laws of ritual slaughter. [After his brothers sold Joseph into slavery, the *Torah* says,] 'They took the robe of Joseph and slaughtered a young goat and dipped the robe in the blood.'"[176] What did Joseph say? They show disrespect towards the children of the maidservants and treat them as slaves. Accordingly, "...Joseph was sold as a slave."[177] What did Joseph say? They set their eyes upon the women of the land. [God said:] I will incite against you the female bear. "...the wife of his master set her eyes on Joseph and she said, 'Lie with me.'"[178]

The Talmud states that the forebears of the Jewish people observed all the Mitzvoth of the Torah.[179] If so, how could they commit such grievous sins and how could Joseph have made the mistake of speaking evil gossip? On the other hand, since the observance of the Mitzvoth by the ancestors of the Jewish people was purely voluntary, how

---

[176] Genesis 37:31.
[177] Psalms 105:17.
[178] Genesis 39:7.
[179] *Kiddushin* 4:14; B.T. *Yoma* 28B; *Ramban* on Genesis 26:5.

could God punish Joseph for speaking evil gossip, a Mitzvah he was not obliged to keep?

Rabbi Eliyahu Mizrachi explains that Joseph's brothers did not really commit the offenses he reported to Jacob. They merely engaged in activities which could be interpreted in a negative way. For example, they referred to their brothers as "sons of maidservants" alluding to the original status of Bilhah and Zilpah who were maidservants before they married Jacob. Joseph interpreted this remark in a derogatory manner although the brothers did not intend it that way. Similarly, the brothers engaged in trading activities with the local women. Such business activity is permitted, but Joseph again read something negative into the situation. It thus emerges that God punished Joseph because he failed to give his brothers the benefit of a doubt, a common cause of evil gossip.[180]

The Talmud relates how the Romans murdered the great sage, Rabbi Chanina ben Tradyon. The rabbis explain that he deserved this because he taught how to pronounce the Tetragrammaton publicly. Rabbi Chanina ben Tradyon did not violate any Halachah because one may pronounce the Tetragrammaton for purposes of teaching it to others, but he should not have done so publicly because unworthy people might thereby learn how

---

[180] Rabbi Eliyahu Mizrachi on *Rashi* on Genesis 37:2.

to pronounce it.[181] *God punished him for this indiscretion because He is highly exacting with the righteous.*[182]

  This explains how God could hold Joseph accountable for speaking evil gossip even though Joseph had no duty to observe the commandments and even though he only reported to Jacob what he thought was improper behavior of his brothers. The closer one draws to God, the more He expects of a person.[183] *Observance of the strict letter of the law may be sufficient for some, but God expects more from those who have the ability and insight to do more.*

---

[181] B.T. *Avodah Zarah* 17B-18A.

[182] *Rashi* sub verba "*LeHithlamed*" (להתלמד) on B.T. *Avodah Zarah* 18A.

[183] B.T. *Ta'anith* 8A.

Peah 1:1

רבי יוסי בשם רבי יוחנן: זה שהוא אומר לשון הרע אינו אומר
עד שהוא כופר בעיקר. ומה טעמא? "אֲשֶׁר אָמְרוּ לִלְשֹׁנֵנוּ נַגְבִּיר
שְׂפָתֵינוּ אִתָּנוּ מִי אָדוֹן לָנוּ." (תהלים יב:ה)
כל העבידות אדם חוטא בארץ ואלו חוטאין בשמים ובארץ.
מה טעמא? "שַׁתּוּ בַשָּׁמַיִם פִּיהֶם וּלְשׁוֹנָם תִּהֲלַךְ בָּאָרֶץ." (תהלים עג:ט)
אמר רבי יצחק: "[פִּיךָ שָׁלַחְתָּ בְרָעָה וּלְשׁוֹנְךָ תַּצְמִיד מִרְמָה.
תֵּשֵׁב בְּאָחִיךָ תְדַבֵּר בְּבֶן אִמְּךָ תִּתֶּן דֹּפִי] ...בִּינוּ נָא זֹאת שֹׁכְחֵי אֱ-לוֹהַּ
פֶּן אֶטְרֹף וְאֵין מַצִּיל." (תהלים נ:יט-כב)
אמר רבי יהושע בן לוי: "תֵּשֵׁב בְּאָחִיךָ תְדַבֵּר בְּבֶן אִמְּךָ תִּתֶּן
דֹּפִי." (תהלים נ:כ) מה כתיב תמן? "וְלָרָשָׁע אָמַר אֱ-לֹהִים מַה לְּךָ
לְסַפֵּר חֻקָּי וַתִּשָּׂא בְרִיתִי עֲלֵי פִיךָ." (תהלים נ:טז)

Rabbi Yossi said in the name of Rabbi Yochanan:
One who speaks evil gossip does not do so without first
denying the most fundamental principle of the Jewish
religion. What is the Scriptural basis for this? "Those who
said, 'With our tongues we shall overcome. Our lips are
with us. Who is master over us?'"[184] [The last phrase
implies a denial of God's existence.]

    With all other sins, a person sins upon the Earth, but
those who speak evil gossip sin in Heaven and upon the
Earth. What is the Scriptural basis for this? "They set their
mouths against Heaven and their tongues travel upon the
Earth."[185]

---

[184] Psalms 12:5 according to *Rashi's* commentary ad. loc.
[185] Psalms 73:9.

Rabbi Yitzchak adduced proof that one who speaks evil gossip denies God from the following: "You send forth your mouth with evil and your tongue you attach to deceit. [When] you sit [among others] you speak of your brother, against the son of your mother you issue calumny... Understand this now, those who forget God, lest I punish and there be none to help."[186]

Rabbi Yehoshua ben Levi said: "[When] you sit [among others] you speak of your brother, against the son of your mother you issue calumny."[187] What is written there? "To the wicked one God said, 'Why should you discuss My laws and raise my covenant upon your mouth?'"[188] [The chapter of the Psalms which contains these verses also speaks of such sins as theft and adultery.[189] Accordingly, one might think that the threat against "those who forget God" applies to them as well. Rabbi Yehoshua ben Levi points out that an earlier verse, "Why should you discuss My laws and raise my covenant upon your lips?" refers to sins of speech so those are the primary focus of this verse as well.[190]]

How is it that one who speaks evil gossip denies God? When a person speaks evil gossip, pointing out faults in others, he or she is actually judging that person.

---

[186] Psalms 50:19-22 according to *Metzudoth* ad. loc.
[187] Psalms 50:20.
[188] Psalms 50:16.
[189] Psalms 50:18.
[190] *P'nei Moshe.*

However, it is impossible for one human being to judge another fairly. Only God can know a person's innermost thoughts and motivations. Only He can fully understand all the circumstances that cause a person to act. This means that one who speaks negatively about another person usurps God's authority. In this sense, he or she denies God.

Peah 1:1 (Compare *VaYikra Rabbah* 26:2; B.T. *Yevamoth* 65B)

אזהרה ללשון הרע מנין? "[כִּי תֵצֵא מַחֲנֶה עַל אֹיְבֶיךָ]
וְנִשְׁמַרְתָּ מִכֹּל דָּבָר רָע." (דברים כג:י)

אמר רבי: לא תני רבי ישמעאל: "לֹא תֵלֵךְ רָכִיל בְּעַמֶּיךָ...."
(ויקרא יט:טז) זו רכילת לשון הרע.

תני רבי נחמיה: שלא תהא כרוכל הזה מטעין דבריו של זה
לזה ושל זה לזה.

אמר רבי חנינא: בא וראה כמה קשה הוא אבק לשון הרע
שדברו הכתובים לשון בדאי בשביל להטיל שלו-ם בין אברהם לשרה.
"וַתִּצְחַק שָׂרָה בְּקִרְבָּהּ לֵאמֹר אַחֲרֵי בְלֹתִי הָיְתָה לִּי עֶדְנָה וַאדֹנִי זָקֵן."
(בראשית יח:יב) ולאברהם אינו אומר כן, אלא, "[וַיֹּאמֶר ה' אֶל
אַבְרָהָם] לָמָּה זֶּה צָחֲקָה שָׂרָה לֵאמֹר הַאַף אֻמְנָם אֵלֵד וַאֲנִי זָקַנְתִּי"
(בראשית יח:יג) "וַאדֹנִי זָקֵן" אין כתיב כאן, אלא, "וַאֲנִי זָקַנְתִּי."

אמר רבן שמעון בן גמליאל: בא וראה כמה קשה הוא אבק
לשון הרע שדברו הכתובים דברי בדאי כדי להטיל שלו-ם בין יוסף
לאחיו. הדא הוא דכתיב, "[וַיִּרְאוּ אֲחֵי יוֹסֵף כִּי מֵת אֲבִיהֶם וַיֹּאמְרוּ לוּ
יִשְׂטְמֵנוּ יוֹסֵף וְהָשֵׁב יָשִׁיב לָנוּ אֵת כָּל הָרָעָה אֲשֶׁר גָּמַלְנוּ אֹתוֹ.] וַיְצַוּוּ אֶל
יוֹסֵף לֵאמֹר אָבִיךָ צִוָּה לִפְנֵי מוֹתוֹ לֵאמֹר. כֹּה תֹאמְרוּ לְיוֹסֵף אָנָּא שָׂא
נָא פֶּשַׁע אַחֶיךָ וְחַטָּאתָם כִּי רָעָה גְמָלוּךָ וְעַתָּה שָׂא נָא לְפֶשַׁע עַבְדֵי
אֱ-לֹהֵי אָבִיךָ..." (בראשית נ:טו-יז) ולא אשכחן דפקד כלום.

רבי שמואל בר נחמן בשם רבי יונתן: מותר לומר לשון הרע
על בעלי המחלוקת. ומה טעם? "[לְכִי וּבֹאִי אֶל הַמֶּלֶךְ דָּוִד וְאָמַרְתְּ
אֵלָיו הֲלֹא אַתָּה אֲדֹנִי הַמֶּלֶךְ נִשְׁבַּעְתָּ לַאֲמָתְךָ לֵאמֹר כִּי שְׁלֹמֹה בְנֵךְ
יִמְלֹךְ אַחֲרַי וְהוּא יֵשֵׁב עַל כִּסְאִי וּמַדּוּעַ מָלַךְ אֲדֹנִיָּהוּ. הִנֵּה עוֹדֵךְ מְדַבֶּרֶת
שָׁם עִם הַמֶּלֶךְ] וַאֲנִי אָבוֹא אַחֲרַיִךְ וּמִלֵּאתִי אֶת דְּבָרָיִךְ." (מלכים א
א:יג-יד)

רבי זעירא בעי קומי רבי יוסא: מפני מה נהרג אדוניה בן

חגית? מפני שתבע את אבישג השונמית?

אמר ליה: עילא היו מבקשין להתיר דמן של בעלי המחלוקת.

בעון קומי רבי יוחנן: איזהו לשון הרע? האומרו והיודעו. חנותה דכיתנא הווה לון צמית. והוה תמן חד מתקרייא בר חובץ ולא סליק. אמרי, "מה אנן אכלין יומא דין?" אמר חד, "חובצה." אמר, "ייתי חובץ."

אמר רבי יוחנן: זה לשון הרע בהצנע.

בולוותים דציפורין הוה להון צומות והוה תמן חד מתקרייא יוחנן ולא סליק. אמר חד לחבריה, "לית אנן סלקין מבקרא לרבי יוחנן יומא דין?" אמרין, "ייתי יוחנן!"

אמר רבי שמעון בן לקיש: זה לשון הרע בצנעה.

From where does one see an admonition against evil gossip? "When you go forth to encamp against your enemy, you shall guard yourself against every evil thing."[191] [In the ensuing verses, the Torah details how members of a Jewish army should maintain high standards of behavior. For example, one who becomes ritually impure must leave the camp. Since the Torah explicitly defines the type of behavior it expects, the reference to guarding against "every evil thing" is superfluous. Accordingly, the Talmud interprets that phrase as an allusion to evil gossip because, as explained above, that is the quintessential evil.]

---

[191] Deuteronomy 23:10.

Rebbi[192] said: Did not Rabbi Yishmael teach: "Do not go as a spy among your people..."[193] This refers to spying out evil gossip. [One need not rely on the implication of the phrase "every evil thing" in the above-cited verse to show that evil gossip is prohibited by the *Torah* because this verse is directly on point.]

Rabbi Nechemiah taught: "Do not go as a peddler among your people..."[194] Do not be like a peddler who carries the words of this one to that one and that one to this one.

Rabbi Chanina said: Come and see how serious the taint of evil gossip is for Scripture employed inexact language to foster peace between Abraham and Sarah. At first the *Torah* reports that "Sarah laughed to herself, saying, 'After I have become worn out, shall I have rejuvenation and my husband is old?'"[195] But to Abraham it does not say so. Rather, "The Lord said to Abraham, 'Why did Sarah laugh saying, "Shall I indeed give birth and I have grown old?"'"[196] "My husband is old" is not written

---

[192] The text may refer to Rabbi Yehudah HaNassi (see footnote 22 above). Alternatively, Rabbi Moshe Shimon Sivitz understands the phrase אמר רבי לא to mean, "Rabbi Law said." As noted above in the introduction, the Jerusalem *Talmud* often abbreviates names, so "Rabbi Law" (רבי לא) could refer to Rabbi Illah (רבי אילא), a well known *Amora*.

[193] Leviticus 19:16 according to *Rashi* who says that the letter כ in the word רכיל interchanges with ג so that the word denotes "spying."

[194] Leviticus 19:16 reading the word רכיל as "peddler."

[195] Genesis 18:12.

[196] Genesis 18:13.

here, but rather "I have grown old." [Sarah did not intend anything disparaging when she made the truthful observation that both she and Abraham were too old to have children. She also did not speak evil gossip since she was merely thinking to herself. Even so, God altered her words rather than repeat them verbatim so as to avoid even the mere taint of evil gossip.]

Rabban Shimon ben Gamliel said: Come and see how serious the taint of evil gossip is for Scripture employed inexact language to foster peace between Joseph and his brothers. Thus it is written, "The brothers of Joseph saw that their father had died and they said, 'Perhaps Joseph will bear a grudge against us and repay us the evil which we dispensed to him.' They commanded Joseph, saying, 'Your father ordered before his death saying, "So shall you say to Joseph, 'Please pardon now the offense of your brothers and their sin for they dispensed evil to you and now please pardon the offense of the servants of the God of your father... .'""197 However, we do not find that Jacob commanded anything of the sort. [Jacob was apparently satisfied that Joseph was a person of sufficiently high caliber that he would not seek revenge from his brothers for having sold him into slavery. Accordingly, he did not see a need to admonish Joseph in this regard. The brothers, however, feared that someone might have a discussion with Joseph tainted with evil

---

197 Genesis 50:15-17.

gossip that would remind him of the past and kindle a desire for revenge.[198]]

Rabbi Shmuel bar Nachman in the name of Rabbi Yonathan said: It is permitted to speak evil gossip about those who foment conflict. What is the Scriptural source for this? [When King David's son, Adonijah, tried to incite a revolution to usurp the throne, the prophet Nathan told Bathsheba,] "Go and appear before King David, and say to him, 'Did you not my lord, the king, swear to your maidservant saying that "Solomon your son shall reign after me and he shall sit upon my throne?" Then why has Adonijah claimed rulership?' Behold, while you are still talking with the king, I will come after you and complete your words."[199] [*Gilyon HaShas* points out that this type of gossip is only permitted to resolve a conflict, but not if it will inflame it. In this case, Bathsheba rightly pointed out that if King David did not declare his choice for a successor, a dispute would arise after his death between Solomon's supporters and those of Adonijah.[200]]

Rabbi Z'eira raised a question before Rabbi Yossa: Why was Adonijah ben Chagith killed? Was it only because he sought to marry Abishag the Shunamite? [Abishag was one of King David's female servants.[201] Although the king never had intimate relations with

---

198 *P'nei Moshe.*
199 I Kings 1:13-14.
200 I Kings 1:20-21.
201 I Kings 1:3-4.

92

Abishag, it would have been unseemly for Adonijah to actually marry Abishag since she had served the king. The *Tanach* tells how Adonijah asked Bathsheba to request permission from King Solomon to marry Abishag. Not only did King Solomon refuse, but he ordered Adonijah to be executed that very day.[202] Rabbi Z'eira questions why Adonijah's request warranted such an extreme response.[203]]

Rabbi Yossa answered: They sought an excuse to permit spilling the blood of those who foment conflict. [Adonijah had tried to usurp the throne even during King David's lifetime. King David had settled the conflicting claims to succession by ordering the installation of Solomon as king.[204] When Adonijah later asked to marry Abishag, King Solomon realized that Adonijah was still maneuvering to take over the throne since marrying a servant of the late king would revive Adonijah's claim.[205] As a rebel against the rightful king, Adonijah's life was forfeit.]

They asked in the presence of Rabbi Yochanan: What counts as evil gossip? Even when one says it by implication. A group of flax store owners were subject to conscription [to serve the king]. There was one there called Bar Chovetz who did not go with the others. They said to

---

202 I Kings 2:13-25.
203 *P'nei Moshe*.
204 I Kings 1:32-34.
205 See *Rashi* on I Kings 2:22.

one another, "What will we eat today?" One of them spoke up, "Mash." [The word for "mash" is *Chuvtzah* (חובצה) which sounds similar to Chovetz (חובץ). Thus, the speaker indirectly reminded the king's taskmasters that Bar Chovetz was missing.] The taskmasters said, "Bring Bar Chovetz!"

Rabbi Yochanan said: This is a sneaky form of evil gossip.

Certain groups of distinguished men in Sepphoris were subject to conscription, but there was one there called Yochanan who did not go with the others. One remarked to his comrade, "Aren't we going up to visit Rabbi Yochanan today?" The taskmasters said, "Bring Yochanan!" [The comment reminded them of his absence.]

Rabbi Shimon ben Lakish said: This is a sneaky form of evil gossip.[206]

The literal translation of the expression "taint of evil gossip" is "dust of evil gossip" (אבק לשון הרע). Sefer Chareidim explains that every sin has a "dust" aspect.[207] The term denotes something secondary to the principal prohibition, similar to the dust which rises when something is ground in a mortar.[208]

---

[206] Some versions of the text read "This is a 'righteous' form of evil gossip," because the speaker made himself sound very pious by referring to the *Mitzvah* of visiting a *Torah* scholar. (*P'nei Moshe*).

[207] *Sefer Chareidim*, chapter 66. Although *Tosefta Avodah Zarah* 1:3 lists only four sins which have "dust," that is apparently not an exhaustive list.

[208] Rashi on B.T. *Sukkah* 40B sub verba *"D'Rabbi Yossi"* (דרבי יוסי).

The Talmud teaches that no one escapes the sin of saying something tainted with evil gossip daily.[209] *This is because a seemingly innocent remark might still imply something negative about another person. In addition, even saying something nice about someone else can lead to evil gossip because it may remind a listener of something else negative.*[210]

The Sefer Chareidim comments that because the taint of evil gossip is so prevalent, we say "My God, guard my tongue from evil..." (א–להי נצור לשוני מרע) *after every Amidah prayer.*[211] *The special incense service in the Temple on Yom Kippur atoned for the sin of speaking evil gossip. The Maharal explains that because everyone stumbles in the sin of speaking words tainted with evil gossip every day, it would be inappropriate to try to atone for that sin throughout the year when people are still sinning. However, on Yom Kippur, when Jews are like angels, they are careful not to say things in any way related to evil gossip. This also explains why the incense offering on Yom Kippur had to be ground more finely than the incense used in the Temple throughout the year. The*

[209] B.T. *Baba Bathra* 164B-165A.

[210] B.T. *Arachin* 16A. According to *Arvei Nachal*, the very fact that one speaks positively about another suggests a deficiency in that person because if the subject of discussion were of good character such comments would be unnecessary. (*Arvei Nachal, Parshath Noach* as cited in *Be'urei HaChassiduth Le'Shas*, Rabbi Yisrael Yitzchak Chassidah (Mossad HaRav Kook, Jerusalem, 1975) p. 674).

[211] *Sefer Chareidim*, chapter 67.

"dust" of evil gossip is very rarefied and difficult to detect so only incense which is finely ground can atone for it. In fact, the tongue itself, the organ which generates gossip, alludes to this because it is the only organ of the body which is sometimes concealed and sometimes exposed just as evil gossip is sometimes obvious and at other times difficult to detect.[212]

---

[212] *Nethivoth Olam, Nethiv HaLashon*, chapter 11.

Peah 1:1

אמר רבי אבא בר כהנא: דורו של דוד כולם צדיקים היו ועל
ידי שהיה להן דילטורים, היו יוצאים במלחמה והיו נופלים. הוא שֶׁדִּבֵּר
דוד, "נַפְשִׁי בְּתוֹךְ לְבָאִם אֶשְׁכְּבָה לֹהֲטִים בְּנֵי אָדָם שִׁנֵּיהֶם חֲנִית וְחִצִּים
וּלְשׁוֹנָם חֶרֶב חַדָּה." (תהלים נז:ה) "נַפְשִׁי בְּתוֹךְ לְבָאִם," זה אבנר
ועמשא שהיו לבאים בתורה. "אֶשְׁכְּבָה לֹהֲטִים," זה דואג ואחיתופל
שהיו לוהטים אחר לשון הרע. "בְּנֵי אָדָם שִׁנֵּיהֶם חֲנִית וְחִצִּים," אלו
בעלי קעילה דכתיב, "הֲיַסְגִּרֻנִי בַעֲלֵי קְעִילָה בְיָדוֹ הֲיֵרֵד שָׁאוּל [כַּאֲשֶׁר
שָׁמַע עַבְדֶּךָ ה' אֱ-לֹהֵי יִשְׂרָאֵל הַגֶּד נָא לְעַבְדֶּךָ... וַיֹּאמֶר ה' יָסְגִּירוּ.]"
(שמואל א כג:יא-יב) "וּלְשׁוֹנָם חֶרֶב חַדָּה," אלו הזיפים דכתיב, "בְּבוֹא
הַזִּיפִים וַיֹּאמְרוּ לְשָׁאוּל הֲלֹא דָוִד מִסְתַּתֵּר עִמָּנוּ." (תהלים נד:ב)
באותה שעה אמר דוד לפני הקדוש ברוך הוא, "רבון
העולמים, מה שכינתך לירד בארץ? סליק שכינתך מביניהון!" הדא
הוא דכתיב, "רוּמָה עַל הַשָּׁמַיִם אֱ-לֹהִים עַל כָּל הָאָרֶץ כְּבוֹדֶךָ." (תהלים
נז:ו,יב)
אבל דורו של אחאב עובדי עבודה זרה היו ועל ידי שלא היה
להן דילטורין, היו יורדים למלחמה ונוצחין. הוא שעבדיהו אמר
לאליהו, "הֲלֹא הֻגַּד לַאדֹנִי אֵת אֲשֶׁר עָשִׂיתִי בַּהֲרֹג אִיזֶבֶל אֵת נְבִיאֵי ה'
וָאַחְבִּא מִנְּבִיאֵי ה' מֵאָה אִישׁ חֲמִשִּׁים חֲמִשִּׁים אִישׁ בַּמְּעָרָה וָאֲכַלְכְּלֵם
לֶחֶם וָמָיִם." (מלכים א יח:יג) אם לחם, למה מים? אם מים, למה לחם?
אלא מלמד שהיו המים קשים לו להביא מן הלחם. ואליהו מכריז
בהר הכרמל, "...אֲנִי נוֹתַרְתִּי נָבִיא לַה' לְבַדִּי..." (מלכים א יח:כב) וכל
עמא ידעין ולא מפרסמין למלכא.

Rabbi Abba bar Kahana said: The generation of
King David was entirely righteous but due to slander they

would drop in battle.[213] This is what David meant when he said, "My soul lies among young lions, fiery men whose teeth are a spear and arrows, and their tongue a sharp sword."[214] "My soul lies among young lions..." refers to Abner and Amasa who were young lions in *Torah*; "...fiery men..." refers to Doeg and Ahitophel who were chasing passionately after evil gossip. [During the time when King Saul falsely accused David of treason, Doeg told the king that David had received help from the priests of Nob. As a result of this evil gossip, King Saul ordered the massacre of all the inhabitants of Nob.[215] Ahitophel was one of David's chief advisers who betrayed him and joined Absalom's revolt.[216] However, it is unclear how he was involved with evil gossip.[217]]; "...men whose teeth are a spear and arrows..." refers to the nobles of Keilah as it is written, "Will the nobles of Keilah turn me over into his

---

[213] As the following text will show, it was actually King Saul's men who fell in battle, not King David's, but since the gossip was spoken about David, the *Talmud* refers to him. (*P'nei Moshe*).

[214] Psalms 57:5.

[215] I Samuel 22:9-10.

[216] II Samuel 15:12.

[217] King David ordered his general, Joab, to station Uriah the Hittite in combat in such a position that he would be killed by the Amonite enemy. (II Samuel 11:14-15). The *Malbim* states that Ahitophel, who was Uriah's grandfather, despised King David because of this. (*Malbim* on II Samuel 11:6). Possibly, Ahitophel heard about the king's secret orders as a result of evil gossip. Alternatively, although King David was legally correct to order Uriah's execution in this fashion because Uriah had rebelled against him (B.T. *Shabbath* 56A), there may have been rumors that the king had acted improperly.

hand? Will Saul descend as your servant has heard? Lord God of Israel, please tell your servant...and the Lord said, 'they will hand [you] over.'"[218]; "...a sharp sword" refers to the Ziphites as it is written, "When the Ziphites came and said to Saul, 'Is not David hiding with us?'"[219]

At that time, David said before the Holy One, Blessed be He, "Master of the Universe, why does Your Divine Presence descend to the world? Remove Your Divine Presence from among them!" Thus it is written, "God is exalted above the heavens; above the Earth is Your glory."[220] [Because David just finished declaring how evil people were betraying him in the verse "My soul lies among young lions, burning men whose teeth are a spear and arrows, and their tongue a sharp sword,"[221] it seems out of place for the very next verse to suddenly shift to an assertion of God's greatness. Accordingly, it must be a request that God exalt His Divine Presence by removing it from the Earth.]

By contrast, although the generation of Ahab were idolaters, by virtue of the fact that they did not have slander among them, they went to war and won! This was what Obadiah meant when he said to Elijah, "Was it not told to my lord that which I did when Isabel killed the prophets of the Lord and Ahab [killed] the prophets of the Lord. [I hid]

---

[218] I Samuel 23:11-12.
[219] Psalms 54:2 and see I Samuel 23:19.
[220] Psalms 57:6 and 12.
[221] Psalms 57:5.

one hundred men, fifty each to a cave, and I supplied them with bread and water."[222]   If he mentions bread, why mention water and if water, why bread? [Since bread was the basic staple during that era, mention of it implied that other necessary elements of the meal such as water were also provided. Additionally, the expression "I supplied them" (אכלכלם) connotes feeding them, so had Obadiah used just that word and water, he could have omitted mentioning bread.[223]] Rather it is to show that the water was more difficult to provide than bread.   [Elijah had decreed that no rain fall for three years so there was a severe drought at the time.[224]   Because of the great difficulty in providing for the prophets he saved, Obadiah had to seek supplies from other people. In this way his rescue activities became known. Even so, no one reported him to the king and queen which shows how that generation avoided the type of evil gossip that plagued David.[225]]

Furthermore, Elijah announced at Mount Carmel, "...I remain a prophet to the Lord by myself... ."[226] [Since Elijah knew that Obadiah had hidden other prophets, his identification of himself as the only remaining prophet must mean that he was the only one who remained in the

---

222 I Kings 18:13.
223 *P'nei Moshe.*
224 I Kings 17:1.
225 *P'nei Moshe* and *Etz Yosef.*
226 I Kings 18:22.

open.[227]] All the people knew yet no one informed the king.

The Talmud reiterates not only the severe nature of the sin of evil gossip, but also that it is the paradigm of evil. Thus, although the people of King David's generation were righteous, they were severely punished for speaking evil gossip while the idolaters of King Ahab's generation merited Divine protection because they refrained from such speech.

This is best understood by the explanation offered above that evil gossip entails the fundamental defect of self-deception.[228] An idolater who avoids such self-deception may eventually see the error of his or her ways and repent. Accordingly, such a person merits Divine protection. By contrast, although a person appears meticulous in Mitzvah observance, the subtle self-deception manifested by evil gossip is bound to lead him or her astray from the Torah.

---

227 *Me'Am Loez* on I Kings 18:22.
228 See above pp. 74-79.

Peah 1:1 (B.T. *Arachin* 15B and *VaYikra Rabbah* 26:2)

ולמה הוא קורא אותו שלישי?‎ שהוא הורג שלשה:‎ האומרו
והמקבלו וזה שנאמר עליו.‎ ובימי שאול נהרגו ארבעה:‎ דואג שאמרו,‎
שאול שקיבלו,‎ אחימלך ואבנר.‎

אבנר למה נהרג?‎ רבי יהושע בן לוי ורבי שמעון בן לקיש
ורבנן.‎ רבי יהושע בן לוי אמר:‎ על שעשה דמן של נערים שחוק
שנאמר,‎ "וַיֹּאמֶר אַבְנֵר אֶל יוֹאָב יָקוּמוּ נָא הַנְּעָרִים וִישַׂחֲקוּ לְפָנֵינוּ וַיֹּאמֶר
יוֹאָב יָקֻמוּ.‎"‎ (שמואל ב ב:יד)‎

ורבי שמעון בן לקיש אמר:‎ על שהקדים שמו לשמו של דוד.‎
הדא הוא דכתיב,‎ "וַיִּשְׁלַח אַבְנֵר מַלְאָכִים אֶל דָּוִד תַּחְתָּו [תַּחְתָּיו קרי]‎
לֵאמֹר לְמִי אָרֶץ...‎ .‎"‎ (שמואל ב ג:יב)‎ כתב,‎ "מִן אבנר לדוד...‎ .‎"‎

ורבנן אמרו:‎ על שלא הניח לשאול להתפייס מן דוד.‎ הדא
הוא דכתיב,‎ "וְאָבִי רְאֵה גַם רְאֵה אֶת כְּנַף מְעִילְךָ בְּיָדִי [כִּי בְּכָרְתִי אֶת
כְּנַף מְעִילְךָ וְלֹא הֲרַגְתִּיךָ דַּע וּרְאֵה כִּי אֵין בְּיָדִי רָעָה וָפֶשַׁע וְלֹא חָטָאתִי
לָךְ וְאַתָּה צֹדֶה אֶת נַפְשִׁי לְקַחְתָּהּ.]‎"‎ (שמואל א כד:יב)‎

אמר ליה,‎ "מה את בעי מן הדין גלגולי?‎ בסירה הוערת!"‎
וכיון שבאו למעגל,‎ אמר ליה,‎ "...הֲלוֹא תַעֲנֶה אַבְנֵר...‎ .‎"‎
(שמואל א כו:יד)‎ "גבי כנף אמרת,‎ 'בסירה הוערת.'‎ חנית וצפחת
בסירה הוערו?"‎

ויש אומרים:‎ על ידי שהיתה ספיקה בידו למחות בנוב עיר
הכהנים ולא מיחה.‎

"חֲצֵי גִבּוֹר שְׁנוּנִים עִם גַּחֲלֵי רְתָמִים.‎"‎ (תהלים קכ:ד)‎ כל כלי
זיין מכין במקומן,‎ וזה מכה מרחוק.‎ כל הגחלים:‎ כבו מבחוץ,‎ כבו
מבפנים,‎ ואלו אף על פי שכבו מבחוץ,‎ לא כבו מבפנים.‎ מעשה באחד
שהניח גחלים בוערות בחג ובא ומצאן בוערות בפסח.‎

אמר רב שמואל בר נחמן:‎ אומרים לנחש,‎ "מפני מה את
מהלך ולשונך שותת?"‎

אמר לון,‎ "דו גרם לי."‎

102

"מה הנייה לך שאתה נושך? אריה טורף ואוכל, זאב טורף
ואוכל. את, מה הנייה לך?"

אמר להן, "'אם יִשֹּךְ הַנָּחָשׁ בְּלוֹא לָחַשׁ...' (קהלת י:יא)
אילולי איתאמר לי מן השמים, 'נכית,' לא הוינא נכית."

"מפני מה את נושך אבר אחד וכל האיברים מרגישים?"

אמר להם, "ולי אתם שואלין? אמרו לבעל הלשון שהוא
אומר כאן והורג ברומי, אומר ברומי והורג בסוריא."

"ומפני מה אתה מצוי בין הגדירות?"

אמר להו, "אני פרצתי גדרו של עולם."

Why do they call evil gossip "the third
language?"[229] Because it kills three: the one who says it,
the one who accepts it, and the one about whom it is
spoken. In the days of Saul, four were killed: Doeg who
said it, Saul who accepted it, Ahimelech [the chief priest of
Nob about whom it was said], and Abner. [King Saul
ordered the massacre of the priests of Nob because Doeg
told him that they helped David. As a result of listening to
that evil gossip, King Saul was eventually killed in battle.
His repentance before his death assured him a share in the
world to come.][230]

.   Why was Abner killed? [The *Talmud* now offers
several opinions about this question, including how
Abner's death might have been related to evil gossip.]

---

[229] This was the expression by which Rabbi Yochanan called it in
B.T. *Arachin* 15B. (*P'nei Moshe*)
[230] See B.T. *Brachoth* 12B.

103

Rabbi Yehoshua ben Levi, Rabbi Shimon ben Lakish and the sages each held a different view.

Rabbi Yehoshua ben Levi said: Because he made sport of the blood of the soldiers, as it is said, "Abner said to Joab, 'Let the soldiers rise now and play before us, and Joab said, 'Let them rise.'"[231] [Abner commanded an army on behalf of King Saul's son, Ish-bosheth, while Joab commanded an army loyal to King David. Relations between the two groups were peaceful until Abner suggested that they engage in war games which led to a full scale conflict between the two sides.[232]]

Rabbi Shimon ben Lakish said: Because he mentioned his name before the name of King David. Thus it is written, "Abner sent messengers to David in his stead, saying, '[In the Name of the One] whose is the Earth... .'"[233] He wrote a letter which read, "From Abner to David... ." [Since David was rightful king, having been anointed by the prophet Samuel, it was disrespectful for Abner not to mention David's name before his own and this led to Abner's downfall.]

The sages said: Because he did not permit Saul to be appeased by David. [When King Saul and his army pursued David, the king entered a cave to relieve himself, not realizing that David and his men were hiding within. David approached King Saul and, without being detected,

---

231 II Samuel 2:14.
232 II Samuel 2:12-17.
233 II Samuel 3:12.

cut off a piece of the king's clothing. After King Saul left
the cave, David revealed himself and said,] "Observe, my
Sovereign, and take note: the corner of your garment is in
my hand for I cut off the corner of your garment and did not
slay you. Know and observe that there is no evil nor
offense in my hand and I have not sinned against you, yet
you hunt down my soul to seize it."[234]

[Seeing this, King Saul was prepared to reconcile
with David,[235] but Abner said to him], "What do you want
with this chicanery? You were stuck on a thornbush!"
[David found a piece of your garment which was
accidentally torn away when it became entangled on a
thornbush. His claim to have cut it off in the cave is a
sham.]

[After this event, the *Tanach* tells how the Ziphites
denounced David whereupon King Saul pursued him with
an army of three thousand men.[236] David and Abishai
secretly penetrated King Saul's camp while he and his
soldiers slept. There they seized the king's spear and water
flask.[237] David again argued that the fact that he had the
opportunity to kill King Saul but refrained proved his
peaceful intentions.] Once they reached the encampment,
David said to him, "How do you answer, Abner?"[238] by

---

[234] I Samuel 24:12.
[235] I Samuel 24:17-23.
[236] I Samuel 26:1-2.
[237] I Samuel 26:12.
[238] I Samuel 26:14. Although the straightforward meaning of the
verse has nothing to do with this, the expression "answer" implies that

which he meant, "Respecting the corner of the garment you said, 'You were stuck on a thornbush!' Do a spear and water flask become stuck in a thornbush?"

There are those who say that Abner was killed because he had ample opportunity to object to the destruction of Nob, the city of priests, but did not object.

"The arrows of a hero are sharp like coals of broom."[239] [Broom (רתם) is a species of shrubbery.] All other weapons strike where they are while arrows strike from a distance. [Likewise, evil gossip which is spoken in one location injures its subject who is distant.] When all other coals are extinguished on the outside, they are also extinguished on the inside. Although broom coals are extinguished on the outside, they are not extinguished on the inside. An incident took place where someone left broom coals burning at *Sukkoth* and came and found them burning at Passover. [Likewise, evil gossip may appear to be forgotten or ignored, but tends to resurface later.]

Rabbi Shmuel bar Nachman said: They asked the snake, "Why does your tongue flicker as you travel?"

It answered, "It caused me to be cursed."

"What benefit do you have from biting? A lion tears its prey and eats it. A wolf tears its prey and eats it. As for you, what benefit do you have [from attacking a human whom you cannot eat]?"

Abner had said something before. (*Maharzu* on *VaYikra Rabbah* 26:2)
[239] Psalms 120:4.

It said to them, "Does a snake bite without a whisper?..."[240] Were it not said to me from Heaven to bite, I would not bite. [The word "whisper" alludes to Divine instruction. Moreover, the end of the verse says, "and the gossip has no advantage," implying that "whispering" evil gossip causes retribution.]

"Why do you bite one limb, yet all the limbs feel it?"

"You ask me?" replied the snake. "Ask the gossip who says something here and kills in Rome, says something in Rome and kills in Syria!"

"Why are you found among stone fences?"

"I breached the fence of the world."

King Saul had a grandson named Mipibosheth. When King David's son, Absalom, deposed King David, the king fled to the desert. Ziba, one of the slaves of Mipibosheth, brought provisions to King David. When the king asked where Mipibosheth was, Ziba lied and said, "Behold he dwells in Jerusalem for he said, 'Today the House of Israel will restore to me the kingdom of my father.'"[241] In reality, Mipibosheth was completely loyal to King David.

The Babylonian Talmud reports a dispute between Rav and Shmuel as to whether King David believed Ziba's evil gossip. Rav maintains that King David accepted

---

240 Ecclesiastes 10:11.
241 II Samuel 16:3.

Ziba's statement and consequently awarded him half of Mipibosheth's property.[242] *Shmuel, however, contends that King David did not give credence to the evil gossip. Rather, when the king was restored to the throne, Mipibosheth greeted him in bare feet, wearing dirty clothing and with his mustache and beard overgrown.*[243] *Although Mipibosheth did so because he was mourning over King David's troubles, the king interpreted it as a sign that Mipibosheth was upset about his return to power. It was only as a result of this erroneous "confirmation" of Mipibosheth's treason that King David believed Ziba's evil gossip.*[244]

According to Rav who holds that King David immediately accepted Ziba's evil gossip, the following question arises: If King David suffered so much from evil gossip as shown by the passage of the Talmud under consideration, how could he himself commit such an error?[245]

---

[242] II Samuel 19:30.

[243] II Samuel 19:25.

[244] B.T. *Shabbath* 56A-B.

[245] The Babylonian *Talmud* asks a similar question regarding Joseph. After revealing himself to his brothers, the *Torah* says, "To each man he gave changes of clothing and to Benjamin he gave three hundred [pieces of] silver and five changes of clothing." (Genesis 45:22) Joseph himself was a victim of the jealousy aroused when his father singled him out for the gift of the multi-colored coat. How, then, could he himself repeat the error of showing favoritism to one brother? (B.T. *Megillah* 16A-B).

Perhaps this shows how pervasive the problem of evil gossip is. As Rav Amram said in the name of Rav, "There are three sins from which a person is not saved every day: sinful thought, anticipating results from prayer[246] and evil gossip." Continues the Talmud, "Do you really think evil gossip is meant literally? Rather, the taint of evil gossip." Rav Yehudah said in the name of Rav: "Most people engage in [some form of] theft, a few engage in sexual immorality and all in evil gossip." The Talmud again explains that Rav means "the taint of evil gossip."[247] Thus, Rav consistently held that almost no one can completely avoid some type of involvement with evil gossip. This position led him to conclude that even King David, himself a victim of evil gossip, nonetheless listened to it from Ziba and acted upon it.

According to Shmuel, however, who says that King David did not give credence to Ziba's evil gossip until he observed what he believed to be confirmation of it, perhaps the conflict between King Saul and King David reflects a deep-seated difference in the overall outlooks and attitudes of these two great men.

God stripped King Saul of the right to establish a royal dynasty because the king could not escape viewing

---

[246] Although one should pray to God for his or her needs with devotion and sincerity, one should not look for results in subsequent events either because he or she may not be worthy of a positive answer or because God, in His infinite wisdom, may not consider the request as being in the person's best interests.

[247] B.T. *Baba Bathra* 164B-165A.

matters from his own limited perspective. For instance, the Tanach reports that although Samuel instructed Saul to await his arrival before offering a sacrifice, Saul, following his own logic, disobeyed.[248] *Similarly, God commanded King Saul to destroy every trace of the Amalekite nation. Instead, the king saved the cattle and sheep, reasoning that they could be used for sacrifices. In explaining why God no longer wished to continue King Saul's dynasty, Samuel said, "Does the Lord have a desire for sacrifices and offerings as for listening to the voice of the Lord? Behold, listening is better than offering; better obedience than the fat of rams."*[249]

Unwillingness to strictly obey God's words usurps God's authority to determine what is right, just as speaking evil gossip usurps God's authority to judge other people. A Jewish king must be totally subservient to God. He cannot permit his own logic to interfere with obeying God's words no matter how well-intentioned or apparently reasonable such logic may be. This trait was so ingrained in King Saul that God could not reinstate him even after he begged forgiveness.[250]

King David had a completely opposite attitude. The Tanach tells how he danced in the streets when the Holy Ark came to Jerusalem even though some people, including

---

[248] I Samuel 13:11-13.

[249] I Samuel 15:22. See B.T. *Yoma* 22B for a full discussion of the logic King Saul used when he disobeyed God.

[250] God eventually forgave him, (see B.T. *Brachoth* 12B), but did not restore his right to establish a dynasty.

his wife, Michal, King Saul's daughter, thought it undignified.[251] *When Michal expressed disdain for King David's behavior, part of his response included the very telling phrase, "Before the Lord who chose me instead of your father and instead of his entire house to appoint me leader over the people of the Lord, over Israel, and I have rejoiced before the Lord."*[252] *Certainly Michal had a point. A king must maintain the dignity of his office. Otherwise, no one will respect his commands. King David, however, used complete objectivity in serving God. He was able to distinguish between his own personal desire for honor and the honor required by his position. This permitted him to understand that dancing before the Ark did not conflict with the dignity of his office. It was this willingness to ignore his own reasoning when serving God which made King David fit to rule in contrast to King Saul who permitted his own notions of right and wrong to have an impact upon the way he obeyed God.*[253]

As the passage under review notes, David had two opportunities to murder King Saul, but refrained, even though he had ample justification for doing so. Samuel had

---

[251] II Samuel 6:14-16.
[252] II Samuel 6:21.
[253] The *Talmud* further stresses this aspect of King David's personality when it says that whereas other kings made sumptuous banquets in their honor, King David often dirtied his hands to make *Halachic* rulings. In contrast to other kings who slept late, King David rose well before midnight to sing God's praises and study the *Torah*. (B.T. *Brachoth* 4B-5A.)

already declared that King Saul would not establish a dynasty of kings.[254] *David also knew that Saul had committed a great sin by killing out the inhabitants of Nob.*[255] *According to Jewish law, one may kill a person who is pursuing another with the intent to murder him.*[256] *David could easily have reasoned that King Saul fell into that category because the king repeatedly pursued him with such intent. In fact, David's men repeatedly urged him to kill King Saul.*[257] *David, however, maintained complete objectivity in his obedience to God's will and refused to do so.*[258]

A Jewish king must judge the people and serve them in absolute harmony with the dictates of the Torah and not according to his personal subjective view. King David represented this ideal and thus, according to Shmuel, could not speak or believe evil gossip. Only when confronted with apparently objective evidence of Mipibosheth's disloyalty did he act.

This perhaps explains why Jewish tradition teaches that King David destroyed his evil inclination (יצר הרע).[259]

---

[254] I Samuel 15:26-28.
[255] I Samuel 22:21.
[256] *Shulchan Aruch, Choshen Mishpat* 425:1.
[257] I Samuel 24:5 and I Samuel 26:8.
[258] B.T. *Brachoth* 62B says that David entertained but rejected the possibility that King Saul was a "pursuer" (רודף). (See commentary of *Kavod HaBayith* in *Chiddushei Gaonim* ad. loc.) See also *Degel Machneh Ephraim, Parshath MiKetz*, sub verba "*VeHinei*" (והנה).
[259] *Sefer HaBahir* I:196.

Evil gossip is the essence and root of all evil because it represents the type of subtle deviation from the truth to which King Saul fell prey. By contrast, King David avoided this pitfall and conquered his evil inclination.

Peah 1:1 (Compare B.T. *Kiddushin* 40A)

הזכות יש לה קרן ויש לה פירות. עבירה יש לה קרן ואין לה
פירות. הזכות יש לה קרן ויש לה פירות שנאמר, "אָמְרוּ צַדִּיק כִּי טוֹב
כִּי פְרִי מַעַלְלֵיהֶם יֹאכֵלוּ." (ישעיה ג:י) עבירה יש לה קרן ואין לה
פירות שנאמר, "אוֹי לְרָשָׁע רָע כִּי גְמוּל יָדָיו יֵעָשֶׂה לּוֹ." (ישעיה ג:יא)
מה אני מקיים, "יֹאכְלוּ מִפְּרִי דַרְכָּם..."? (משלי א:לא)   אלא, כל עבירה
שעשת פרי יש לה פרי ושלא עשת פרי אין לה פרי.
מחשבה טובה המקום מצרפה למעשה. מחשבה רעה אין
המקום מצרפה למעשה. מחשבה טובה המקום מצרפה למעשה דכתיב,
"אָז נִדְבְּרוּ יִרְאֵי ה' אִישׁ אֶל רֵעֵהוּ וַיַּקְשֵׁב ה' וַיִּשְׁמָע וַיִּכָּתֵב סֵפֶר זִכָּרוֹן
לְפָנָיו לְיִרְאֵי ה' וּלְחֹשְׁבֵי שְׁמוֹ." (מלאכי ג:טז) מחשבה רעה אין הקדוש
ברוך הוא מצרפה למעשה שנאמר, "אָוֶן אִם רָאִיתִי בְלִבִּי לֹא יִשְׁמַע
אֲ-דֹנָי." (תהלים סו:יח)

Merit has principal and has proceeds [meaning reward both in the next world and in this world]. Sin has principal but no proceeds. Merit has principal and has proceeds as it says, "Praise a righteous person that he is good, for the fruits of their deeds they consume."[260] Sin has principal but no proceeds as it says, "Woe unto the wicked one [who does] evil for the work of his hands shall be done to him."[261] How, then, do I interpret the verse, "They will consume the fruit of their way... ."?[262] Rather, any sin which generates proceeds has proceeds while any

---

[260] Isaiah 3:10.
[261] Isaiah 3:11.
[262] Proverbs 1:31.

which does not generate proceeds has no proceeds. [The four sins mentioned earlier fall into the category of yielding proceeds. Evil gossip tends to spread from mouth to mouth amplifying its original effect. Likewise, when one commits murder, he or she causes damage not only momentarily but also for whatever period of time the victim might have lived. Moreover, murder precludes the victim from having children or engaging in other activities which might have had long-term effects in the world. Engaging in sexual immorality may produce a line of illegitimate descendants who cannot marry other Jews. Idolatry, too, may have long-term effects because one may commit other sins yet recognize the basic truth of the *Torah* and repent. Idolatry, however, represents such an extreme denial of God and the *Torah* that it is much more difficult for a person to repent. Consequently, it "generates proceeds."[263]]

God connects a good thought to a good deed, but God does not connect an evil thought to an evil deed. [If one planned to do a good deed but circumstances prevented its actual execution, he or she still receives a reward. By contrast, God does not count the evil intention of the sinner against him unless a deed actually resulted.[264]] God connects a good thought to a good deed as it is written, "Then spoke those who feared the Lord, a man to his

---

263 This explanation is similar to *P'nei Moshe*. *Etz Yosef*, however, maintains that when one does a *Mitzvah*, he or she earns reward not only for the *Mitzvah itself* (the principal), but for all the preparation that went into it (the proceeds).
264 B.T. *Kiddushin* 40A.

comrade and the Lord heard and listened, and a book of remembrance was written before Him for those who fear the Lord and those who revere His name."[265] [Not only the deeds of the righteous merit recognition, but even their fear and reverence.] The Holy One, Blessed be He, does not connect an evil thought to an evil deed as it is said, "If I saw iniquity in my heart, the Lord shall not harken."[266]

Rabbi Shneur Zalman of Liadi asks: If the Talmud means to say that when someone plans to do a good deed but circumstances prevent its actual execution, he or she still receives a reward, why not say so outright? Why use the expression, "God connects a good thought to a good deed?" He explains that the degree of spiritual benefit which a good deed produces is commensurate with the thoughts and intentions which accompany it. Thus, a Mitzvah performed with a greater degree of love and fear of Hashem reaches a higher spiritual level than one performed with less love and fear of Hashem. Certain lofty levels of love and fear for Hashem are hidden deep within the recesses of a person's mind and heart so that they are difficult to achieve or maintain and are usually not present when one performs the commandments or studies Torah. God Himself, however, attaches those lofty intentions to the

---

[265] Malachi 3:16.
[266] Psalms 66:18.

Mitzvoth a person performs so that the latter can rise to great spiritual heights.[267]

Rabbi Menachem Azariah of Fano offers an alternative view. Sometimes a person has a great desire to perform a Mitzvah but is not able to do so for various reasons beyond his or her control. Another person may actually perform that same Mitzvah, but do so with less than perfect intentions. Hashem combines the intention of the one person with the deed of his or her comrade so that both are rewarded.[268]

---

[267] *Likutei Amarim Tanya*, chapter 16. See also *Maor VeShemesh*, *Rimzei Rosh HaShannah*, sub verba *"Oh"* (אױ).

[268] *Maamar HaNefesh*, Part II, chapter 8. As the *Talmud* says, "All Israel are responsible for one another." (B.T. *Shavuoth* 39A). Rabbi Elimelech of Lizensk offers a similar explanation but says that the person with the positive thoughts receives all the reward for the *Mitzvah*. (*Noam Elimelech, Parshath Metzora*).

Peah 1:1 (Compare B.T. *Kiddushin* 40A)

הדא דתימא בישראל, אבל בגוים חילופא. מחשבה טובה אין
הקדוש ברוך הוא מצפרה למעשה. מחשבה רעה הקדוש ברוך הוא
מצרפה למעשה.

מחשבה טובה אין הקדוש ברוך הוא מצרפה למעשה דכתיב,
"[אֱדַיִן מַלְכָּא כְּדִי מִלְּתָא שְׁמַע שַׂגִּיא בְּאֵשׁ עֲלוֹהִי וְעַל דָּנִיֵּאל שָׂם בָּל
לְשֵׁיזָבוּתֵהּ] וְעַד מֶעָלֵי שִׁמְשָׁא הֲוָה מִשְׁתַּדַּר לְהַצָּלוּתֵהּ." (דניאל ו:טו)
ולא כתיב, "ושזביה."

מחשבה רעה הקדוש ברוך הוא מצרפה למעשה דכתיב,
"[וְחַתּוּ גִבּוֹרֶיךָ תֵּימָן לְמַעַן יִכָּרֶת אִישׁ מֵהַר עֵשָׂו] מִקָּטֶל. מֵחֲמַס אָחִיךָ
יַעֲקֹב [תְּכַסְּךָ בוּשָׁה וְנִכְרַתָּ לְעוֹלָם]." (עובדיה א:ט-י) וכי הורגו? אלא
מלמד שחשב עליו להורגו והעלה עליו הכתוב כאלו הרגו.

This is what is said respecting Israel, but with other
nations it is the opposite. The Holy One, Blessed be He,
does not connect a good thought to a good deed whereas
the Holy One, Blessed be He, does connect an evil thought
to an evil deed.

Scriptural proof that the Holy One, Blessed be He,
does not connect a good thought to a good deed is as
follows. [King Darius's ministers were jealous of Daniel's
high position in the Persian/Medean government. Plotting
his downfall, they had the king issue a decree prohibiting
anyone from making a request from any entity other than
the king for a period of thirty days. Daniel violated the
decree by praying to God.[269] When the schemers

---

[269] Daniel 6:4-14.

denounced Daniel to the king,] it is written, "Then the king, when he heard this thing, was sorely grieved and made a denial concerning Daniel to help him and until sunset tried to save him."[270] [The king told his ministers that he refused to believe their accusation. At sunset, however, Daniel recited the afternoon prayer, thus proving the charges against him.[271]] It is not written "and he helped him." [Scripture tells how King Darius *tried* to save Daniel, but does not view it as though he really helped him. This shows that when a heathen tries to do good, his efforts do not count unless good is actually accomplished.]

Scriptural proof that the Holy One, Blessed be He, does connect an evil thought to an evil deed is as follows. [Obadiah prophesied that many nations would join forces to attack Edom, the nation which descended from Esau.] "Your heroes will be crushed, [inhabitants of the] South, so that [all] men from the mountain of Esau will be annihilated by a massacre. Because of violence [against] your brother Jacob, shame will cover you and you will be annihilated forever."[272] Did Esau actually kill Jacob? Rather this teaches that because he planned to kill him, Scripture regarded it as though he killed him.

---

[270] Daniel 6:15.
[271] *Rashi* ad. loc.
[272] Obadiah 1:9-10.

The Talmud teaches that one should "judge all people favorably."[273] The Rambam explains that when one observes individuals with no clear reputation for being righteous or for being wicked, he or she should try to view their actions in a favorable light. However, if a person is known to be righteous it is forbidden to think that he did something wrong if it is possible to interpret his actions favorably. Conversely, if a person is notorious for wrongdoing, but does something which appears proper, one may suspect wrongdoing.[274] This rule applies to both Jews and non-Jews.[275] Accordingly, the passage of the Talmud under consideration cannot mean that God does not count the good thoughts of righteous non-Jews in their favor, yet counts their bad intentions against them. Instead, this rule applies only to wicked Gentiles.[276]

---

[273] *Pirkei Avoth* 1:6.

[274] *Perush HaMishnayoth* on *Pirkei Avoth* 1:6.

[275] *Tosafoth* sub verba "*V'Ain*" (ואין) on B.T. *Yevamoth* 61A quotes *Rabbeinu Tam* as saying that the expression האדם refers to all humankind and that is the expression the *Mishnah* in *Pirkei Avoth* uses.

[276] Further support for this position comes from the following: The *Torah* says, "I will bless those who bless you and those who curse you I will curse." (Genesis 12:3) It would seem more consistent to say "I will bless those who bless you and curse those who curse you." Why does the *Torah* switch around the wording? Rabbi Levi Yitzchak of Berditchev explains that because God connects a good thought to a good deed, He promised to bless those who bless Abraham even when they merely think to do so but have not yet uttered a blessing. Conversely, because God does not connect an evil thought to an evil deed, God will not curse those who curse Abraham until they actually utter the curse. (*Kedushath Levi* ad. loc.) Since there were no Jews at

Indeed, the attitude of King Darius resembles that of Nazi war criminals following the Holocaust. First the king agreed with his ministers to issue an absurd decree forbidding the entreaty of any entity other than himself. The laws of the Medean/Persian empire forbade revocation of a decree, so when the ministers denounced Daniel to the king for the "treasonous" act of praying, the king could not nullify the decree.[277] In other words, King Darius, though sorry for the situation, was "just obeying the law" when he had Daniel thrown into the pit of lions just as many Nazi mass murderers claimed that they were only carrying out orders of their superiors and should not be blamed for what they did. It would obviously be unjust for God to view King Darius's spurious "good intentions" as though they were accomplished.

On the other hand, God views a wicked non-Jew whose evil plans are thwarted as though he had accomplished his evil designs. Thus, Esau sought to kill Jacob. He only held back because he did not wish to do so while his father Isaac lived and because Jacob fled to Aram.[278] With other people who plan evil but whose plans fall apart, it may be that they would never have carried them through to fruition. With evil people such as Esau,

---

the time God said this to Abraham, it must apply to righteous non-Jews.

[277] Daniel 6:9.

[278] Genesis 27:41-43.

however, one may assume that he would not have repented but would have carried out his evil intentions.[279]

---

[279] See *Etz Yosef.*

Peah 1:1 (Compare B.T. *Kiddushin* 40B)

תני רבי שמעון בר יוחאי: הרי שהיה אדם צדיק גמור כל
ימיו ובאחרונה מרד, איבד זה כל מה שעשה כל ימיו. מה טעם?
"בְּשׁוּב צַדִּיק מִצִּדְקָתוֹ וְעָשָׂה עָוֶל וּמֵת בָּהֶם." (יחזקאל לג:יח) רבי
שמעון בן לקיש אמר: בתוהא על הראשונות.

הרי שהיה אדם רשע גמור כל ימיו ובסוף עשה תשובה,
הקדוש ברוך הוא מקבלו. מה טעם? "וּבְשׁוּב רָשָׁע מֵרִשְׁעָתוֹ וְעָשָׂה
מִשְׁפָּט וּצְדָקָה עֲלֵיהֶם הוּא יִחְיֶה." (יחזקאל לג:יט) אמר רבי יוחנן: ולא
עוד, אלא כל העבירות שעשה הן נחשבין לו כזכיות. מה טעם? "מֹר
וַאֲהָלוֹת קְצִיעוֹת כָּל בִּגְדֹתֶיךָ... ." (תהלים מה:ט) כל בגידות שבגדת בי
הרי הן כמור ואהלות וקציעות.

Rabbi Shimon bar Yochai taught: If a person was
completely righteous all his days but at the end rebelled, he
loses all that he did throughout his life. What is the
Scriptural basis for this? "When a righteous one turns from
his uprightness and commits perversity, he shall die from
it."[280] Rabbi Shimon ben Lakish said: This applies when
he regrets his former deeds. [If a righteous persons does
something wrong, he obviously has abandoned his
uprightness, so the expression "turns from his uprightness"
is unnecessary. This extra phrase implies that he went
further and regretted his earlier good deeds, so he is not
only punished for his present wrongdoing, but loses the
merit of what he did before.[281] This conclusion is further

---

[280] Ezekiel 33:18.
[281] *P'nei Moshe.*

supported by the fact that the verse states that the righteous person "shall die from it." One would think that the great merit he accumulated throughout his life might protect a righteous person from the results of a present sin. Accordingly, it must be that he has lost that merit because he regrets his former good deeds.]

Rabbi Shimon bar Yochai continued: If a person was a complete villain all his days but at the end repented, the Holy One, Blessed be He, accepts him. What is the Scriptural basis for this? "When a wicked one turns from his evil and does justice and charity, by them shall he live."[282] [The phrase "turns from his evil" is superfluous since it is already implied by the fact that the formerly wicked one is now doing justice and charity. Accordingly, the phrase must mean that the wrongdoer regrets his former actions.[283]] Rabbi Yochanan said: And not only that, but all the sins he committed are accounted for him as merits. What is the Scriptural basis for this? "[Sweet smelling] myrrh, aloe and cassia are all your garments... ."[284] [The root of the Hebrew word for "garments" (בגד) also means "betrayal."] All the betrayals you have committed against me have become like myrrh, aloe and cassia.

How can it be that a righteous person who regrets his or her former deeds loses their merit? The Talmud

---

282 Ezekiel 33:19.
283 *P'nei Moshe.*
284 Psalms 45:9.

stated earlier that Hashem does not count an evil thought against a person unless he or she actually sins. In this situation, not only did the person not sin, he did a Mitzvah! How can any subsequent thought be held against him?

*The answer is that there are some exceptions to the rule that Hashem does not count an evil thought against a person. First of all, this is not true with respect to idolatry. God punishes a person even if he or she did not commit an act of idolatry, but merely **thought** about doing so.[285] Secondly, this rule does not apply when the evil thought itself is the sin. Thus, the Mishnah in Sanhedrin declares that there are several categories of people who have no share in the world to come: those who deny that the dead will be resurrected, those who deny that God gave the Torah and heretics.[286] By definition, these sins involve only thought.*

One who is carried away by his or her passions to sin yet still believes in the Torah has a share in the world to come but will be punished for his or her misdeeds. However, this is not the case when one denies the fundamentals of the Jewish religion. Such a person forfeits his or her right to enter the world to come.

The Rambam writes that if someone regrets the Mitzvoth he performed, thinking, "How did I benefit doing them? I only wish that I did not do them," he loses the

---

[285] B.T. *Kiddushin* 40A.
[286] *Sanhedrin* 10:1.

merit of their performance.[287] *Since he says that he sees no benefit in the Mitzvoth he has performed, such a person denies belief in the world to come for if he believed in it surely he would understand that he has benefited enormously from doing Mitzvoth. Although such a sin involves only thought, it is among those exceptional transgressions listed by the Mishnah as causing a person to lose his share in the world to come.*[288]

The Talmud explains that there are two broad categories of repentance: repentance out of fear and repentance out of love.[289] *One may repent because one fears punishment or out of a sense of awe and respect for the majesty of the Creator. However, repentance out of love is much greater. This occurs when one feels such love for the Creator that he cannot bear the thought that anything interferes with his relationship with God. It is repentance out of love which has the power to convert sins to merits.*[290] *One can understand how God accepts the repentance of the wicked and erases or ignores sins, but how can sins be converted to merits as the passage translated here teaches?*

---

[287] *Yad HaChazakah, Hilchoth T'shuva* 3:3.
[288] *Rambam* on *Sanhedrin* 10:1 declares that unless a Jew believes thirteen basic tenets, he or she has no share in the world to come. Among these is belief in reward in the world to come for the performance of *Mitzvoth*. (*Iyun Yaakov* on B.T. *Kiddushin* 40B poses the same question but offers a different solution.)
[289] B.T. *Yoma* 86A-B.
[290] B.T. *Yoma* 86B.

Rabbi Abba bar Kahana declared that, "Greater was the removal of a ring [which King Ahasuerus gave to Haman when he authorized the annihilation of the Jewish people] than forty-eight prophets and seven prophetesses who prophesied for Israel, for all of them could not cause them to return to good whereas removal of a ring caused them to return to good."[291] *Ironically, the prospect of total destruction which on its surface appears evil was actually the very opposite because it goaded Israel to repent.*

When a penitent considers the damage a sin has caused him spiritually by interfering with his relationship with God, he does two things. First, he takes precautions never to sin or even approach sinning again. Second, he strives to perform more Mitzvoth and to do them with greater sincerity so as to compensate for the damage he has done. Because the sins are the catalyst for the penitent to reach ever higher spiritual levels, they actually become merits.

Rabbi Abahu taught that, "In the place where penitents stand [in the world to come], even the completely righteous cannot stand."[292] *One can understand how God may forgive a person who repents, even converting sins to merits, but how is it that he or she can have greater merit than someone who is completely righteous and has never sinned?*

---

[291] B.T. *Megillah* 14A.
[292] B.T. *Brachoth* 34B.

This passage of the Talmud suggests an answer. Ben Heh Heh said, "According to the suffering is the reward."[293] *One who puts more effort into learning Torah and doing Mitzvoth will earn greater reward than one who exerts less effort. Once a person commits a sin, it becomes easier for him to repeat it. Someone who has sinned once may backslide because in the back of his mind he knows that he has done so before. Accordingly, he must exert more effort to refrain from sinning than the perfectly righteous person who has never sinned. Because the sin forces the penitent to exert extra effort to maintain his righteousness, it becomes a source of merit and may earn him greater reward than one who never sinned.*

---

[293] *Pirkei Avoth* 5:22.

Peah 1:1 (Compare *Kiddushin* 40B)

רובי זכיות ומעוטי עבירות, נפרעים ממנו מיעוט עבירות
קלות שעשה בעולם הזה בשביל ליתן לו שכרו משלם לעתיד לבא.
אבל רובי עבירות ומעוטי זכיות, נותנין לו שכר מצות קלות שעשה
בעולם הזה בשביל לפרע ממנו משלם לעולם הבא. אבל הפורק ממנו
עול, והמיפר ברית, והמגלה פנים בתורה, אף על פי שיש בידו מעשים
טובים, נפרעים ממנו בעולם הזה והקרן קיימת לעולם הבא.

If one possesses less sins than merits, retribution is
exacted for the few minor sins he committed in this world
so as to give him a complete reward in the future.
However, if one possesses more sins than merits, they give
him reward for the minor *Mitzvoth* he did in this world so
as to exact complete retribution from him in the world to
come. However, one who breaks off the yoke, one who
nullifies the covenant[294] and one who twists the teachings
of the *Torah*,[295] even though he has good deeds in hand,

---

[294] In *Pirkei Avoth* 3:11, the phrase reads:
והמפר בריתו של אברהם אבינו עליו השלו-ם, referring to someone who
does not circumcise his son or who fails to have himself circumcised
when it was not done for him as a baby. Alternatively, it alludes to a
person who tries to hide his circumcision with cosmetic surgery. (See
Rabbi Pinchas Kehati *ad. loc.*)

[295] In *Pirkei Avoth* 3:11, the phrase reads:
מגלה פנים בתורה שלא כהלכה, meaning "one who reveals aspects of the
Torah contrary to *Halachah*." The expression may also be interpreted
to mean "one who reveals his face in the *Torah*" indicating a brazen
attempt to interpret the *Torah* contrary to tradition. (See Rabbi Pinchas
Kehati *ad. loc.*)

they exact retribution from him in this world while the principal remains for the world to come.

Rabbi Yaakov said, "Reward for a Mitzvah does not exist in this world."[296] If so, how can this passage of the Talmud say that a wicked person is paid for the few Mitzvoth he performed in this world so as to exact full retribution from him in the world to come? In addition, such a policy sounds vindictive. God has no emotions and is certainly not vengeful, so how does this make sense?

One answer involves the overall outlook of the wicked person. Because his basic attitude is one of rebellion against God, it is unlikely that any good deed he does is sincerely motivated. Thus, for example, he may contribute to charity to acquire prestige rather than to fulfill God's will. Because the wicked person does not perform good deeds wholeheartedly, he only merits reward in this world.

Another answer is that a wicked person could argue that if only he had known the tremendous reward that awaits those who do good deeds and the horrible punishment that awaits those who sin, he would have behaved differently. Since reward and punishment do not generally occur in this world, the wicked person did not have a fair opportunity to fully comprehend the consequences of his or her actions. God responds to this objection by rewarding the wicked for their good deeds in

---

[296] B.T. *Kiddushin* 39B.

this world. If they nonetheless continue to pursue their evil course, they have no one but themselves to blame and can be justly punished in the world to come.

A third possibility is that a wicked person may be fully punished in the hereafter for his sins, but then go on to eternal reward.[297] *Because the punishment of the wicked purifies them so that they can enter Paradise, it is not vindictive at all.*

Finally, there is the opinion of Rabbi Yosef Hayyim who states, based upon Kabbalistic tradition, that when the sages say that a person has no share in the world to come, they only mean that he or she is not presently fit for such a share. After they die, such individuals undergo extensive reincarnations until they correct their wrongdoing and merit a place in the world to come.[298]

---

[297] Rabbi Shlomo Sirilio.
[298] *Ben Yehoyada* on B.T. *Sanhedrin* 90A. See below pp. 243-245.

Peah 1:1 (Compare B.T. *Yoma* 38B-39A)

עבודה זרה וגילוי עריות: רבי יונה ורבי יוסי: חד אמר
כקלות וחד אמר כחמורות. מה אנן קיימין? אם כשעשה תשובה, אין
כל דבר עומד בפני בעלי תשובה. אלא כי אנן קיימין באותו שלא
עשה תשובה ומת בייסורין.

Rabbi Yonah and Rabbi Yossi had a dispute
regarding idolatry and sexual immorality. One said they are
like minor sins while the other said they are like severe
sins. [One argued that these are viewed as minor sins for
which an otherwise righteous person may be punished in
this world and go on to enjoy the next world, while the
other contended that these sins are so severe that whoever
does them is judged wicked and must suffer in the hereafter
for them just like one who denies the *Torah*.[299]] How
should we understand this dispute? If the sinner repented,
nothing stands in the way of penitents. Rather we must
understand this dispute as pertaining to one who did not
repent and died amid torments. [One maintains that since
he suffered for his sins in this world, they are atoned even
though he did not repent. The other sage holds that these
sins are too serious for suffering to atone unless
accompanied by repentance.[300]]

---

[299] *P'nei Moshe.*
[300] By way of comparison, B.T. *Yoma* 85B quotes Rabbi Yehudah
HaNassi as saying that *Yom Kippur* atones for sins even if one did not
repent, except for sins of a very serious nature such as rejection of the
Torah.

Rabbi Shlomo Sirilio comments that the issue of whether certain sins rise to the level where they render the one who does them irredeemable applies to bloodshed and evil gossip as well. Due to its abbreviated style, the Talmud omits these two which must be understood by implication.

Peah 1:1

תמן תנינן: אלו שאין להם חלק לעולם הבא: האומר, "אין
תחית המתים," ו"אין תורה מן השמים," ואפיקורס. רבי עקיבא
אומר: אף הקורא בספרים החצונים, והלוחש על המכה ואומר, "...כָּל
הַמַּחֲלָה אֲשֶׁר שַׂמְתִּי בְמִצְרַיִם לֹא אָשִׂים עָלֶיךָ כִּי אֲנִי ה' רֹפְאֶךָ."
(שמות טו:כו) אבא שאול אומר: אף ההוגה את השם באותיות.
הוסיפו עליהן: הפורק עול, והמיפר ברית, והמגלה פנים
בתורה, אין להם חלק לעולם הבא.
הפורק עול: זה שהוא אומר, "יש תורה ואיני סופנה."
המיפר ברית: זה שהוא מושך לו ערלה.
המגלה פנים בתורה: זה שהוא אומר, "לא נתנה תורה מן
השמים." ולא כבר תניתה? האומר, "אין תורה מן השמים." תני רב
חנניה סנתוניא קומי רבי מנא: זה שהוא עובר על דברי תורה
בפרהסיא כגון יהויקים מלך יהודה וחבירו.

Over there we learned in a *Mishnah*:[301] **These do
not have a share in the world to come: One who says
there is no resurrection of the dead or that the *Torah* is
not of Divine origin, or a heretic.**[302] **Rabbi Akiva says:
Also one who studies heretical books, and one who
whispers over a wound, saying, "...all the sickness which
I inflicted in Egypt I shall not inflict upon you for I am
the Lord your Healer."**[303],[304] **Abba Shaul said: Also**

---

[301] *Sanhedrin* 10:1.
[302] The *Talmud* defines a heretic (אפיקורוס) as one who denigrates a
Torah scholar. (B.T. *Sanhedrin* 99B).
[303] Exodus 15:26.
[304] Of course one may pray for a sick person using verses from the

one who pronounces the Tetragrammaton as it is written.

They added upon these: one who breaks off the yoke of the *Torah*, one who nullifies the covenant and one who twists the teachings of the *Torah* have no share in the world to come.

"One who breaks off the yoke of the *Torah*" means one who says "There is a *Torah* but I do not care about it."

"One who nullifies the covenant" means one who stretches the foreskin [so as to cosmetically disguise his circumcision].

"One who twists the teachings of the *Torah*" means one who says, "the *Torah* was not given from Heaven." Was this not already taught in the *Mishnah*: **"One who says...that the Torah is not of Divine origin"**? Rabbi Chananiah of Santhunia recited a *Braitha* before Rabbi Manna: This means one who violates the words of the *Torah* publicly such as Jehoiakim, king of Judea, and his comrades.

Although they did not say that they denied the Torah, the brazen actions of Jehoiakim and his associates showed that they denied it or twisted its teachings.[305] Still,

---

Tanach. Here, however, the *Mishnah* refers to people who spit before reciting a verse. Mentioning God's Name when spitting is highly disrespectful. (B.T. *Sanhedrin* 101A)

[305] It may also be that the *Tanna* is understanding המגלה פנים בתורה to mean "one who shows his face in the *Torah*," i.e., one who brazenly violates the *Torah*. See *Yad HaChazakah, Hilchoth T'shuvah* 3:11.

why does the Talmud single out Jehoiakim? Surely there were many others who disobeyed the Torah publicly.[306]

Public violation of the Torah (חלול השם) is considered the most serious sin a person can commit.[307] *Such desecration by leaders is especially harmful because it induces others to follow their bad example. This may explain why a leader who does so forfeits his share in the world to come.*

Jehoiakim's father was King Josiah about whom the Tanach says, "Like him there was none before him, a king who returned to the Lord with all his heart and with all his soul and with all his strength, according to the law of Moses, and after him none arose like him."[308] *Jehoiakim deserved unusually severe punishment because someone with such a father should have known better than to publicly desecrate the Torah. Moreover, this would tend to make those who observed Jehoiakim's wrongdoing even more likely to imitate him than they might an ordinary leader. If one with such a background could publicly disobey the Torah, how much more so ordinary folk.*

---

[306] See *Shayarei Korban* on J.T. *Sanhedrin* 10:1 asks this question but offers no answer.

[307] B.T. *Yoma* 86A.

[308] II Kings 23:25.

Peah 1:1

רובו זכיות יורש גן עדן. רובו עבירות יורש גיהנם. היה
מעויין, אמר רבי יוסי: "נֹשֵׂא עֲוֹנוֹת" אין כתיב כאן, אלא, "...נֹשֵׂא
עָוֹן... ." (שמות לד:ז) הקדוש ברוך הוא חוטף שטר אחד מן העבירות
והזכיות מכריעות.

אמר רבי אליעזר: "וּלְךָ אֲ-דֹנָי חָסֶד כִּי אַתָּה תְשַׁלֵּם לְאִישׁ
כְּמַעֲשֵׂהוּ." (תהלים סב:יג) ואי לית ליה, את יהב ליה מן דידך. היא
דעתיה דרבי אליעזר, דרבי אליעזר אמר: "וְרַב חֶסֶד" (שמות לד:ו)
מטה כלפי חסד.

רבי ירמיה אמר: רבי שמואל בר רב יצחק בעי: "צְדָקָה תִּצֹּר
תָּם דָּרֶךְ וְרִשְׁעָה תְּסַלֵּף חַטָּאת." (משלי יג:ו) "חַטָּאִים תְּרַדֵּף רָעָה וְאֶת
צַדִּיקִים יְשַׁלֶּם טוֹב." (משלי יג:כא) "אִם לַלֵּצִים הוּא יָלִיץ וְלַעֲנָיִים
[וְלַעֲנָוִים קרי] יִתֶּן חֵן." (משלי ג:לד) "רַגְלֵי חֲסִידָו [חֲסִידָיו קרי] יִשְׁמֹר
וּרְשָׁעִים בַּחֹשֶׁךְ יִדָּמּוּ... ." (שמואל א ב:ט) "כָּבוֹד חֲכָמִים יִנְחָלוּ וּכְסִילִים
מֵרִים קָלוֹן." (משלי ג:לה) וסיגין סיגה ותרעין תרעין?

רבי ירמיה אמר רבי שמואל בר רב יצחק: שומר אדם את
עצמו מן העבירה פעם ראשונה ושניה ושלישית, מכאן ואילך הקדוש
ברוך הוא משמרו. מה טעם? "הֶן כָּל אֵלֶּה יִפְעַל אֵ-ל פַּעֲמַיִם שָׁלוֹשׁ
עִם גָּבֶר. [לְהָשִׁיב נַפְשׁוֹ מִנִּי שָׁחַת לֵאוֹר בְּאוֹר הַחַיִּים.]" (איוב לג:כט-ל)
אמר רבי זעירא: ובלחוד דלא יתיב ליה. מה טעם? "וְהַחוּט הַמְשֻׁלָּשׁ
לֹא לְעוֹלָם יִנָּתֵק" אין כתיב כאן, אלא, "[וְהַחוּט הַמְשֻׁלָּשׁ] לֹא בִמְהֵרָה
יִנָּתֵק." (קהלת ד:יב) אין מטרחת עלוי, מפסק הוא.

ואמר רבי הונא אמר רבי אבהו: הקדוש ברוך הוא אין לפניו
שכחה. הא בשל ישראל נעשה שוכחן. מה טעם? ""...נֹשֵׂא עָוֹן..."
(שמות לד:ז), "נֹשֵׂא" כתיב. וכן דוד הוא אומר, "נָשָׂאתָ עֲוֹן עַמֶּךָ כִּסִּיתָ
כָל חַטָּאתָם סֶלָה." (תהלים פה:ג)

If one possesses mostly merits, he or she inherits Paradise. If mostly sins, he or she inherits *Gehinnom*. If it is perfectly balanced, Rabbi Yossi said: [When Moses begged *Hashem* to forgive the Jews for the sin of the golden calf, he prayed, "...Lord, Lord, merciful and gracious God, patient and Master of kindness and truth. Maintaining kindness for thousands [of generations], lifting iniquity and transgression and sin... ."[309]] "lifting iniquities" is not written here but rather "lifting iniquity." The Holy One, Blessed be He, snatches away one of the records of sin so that the merits tip the balance.

Rabbi Eliezer said: "And Yours, Lord, is kindness for you pay a person according to his deeds."[310] If one does not have sufficient merit, You give him from Yours. [The word "pay" in Hebrew (תשלם) can also mean "complete." Thus, the verse can mean that God completes a person's merits by, so to speak, adding from His own.[311]] This is the opinion of Rabbi Eliezer for Rabbi Eliezer said: "and Master of kindness"[312] means "inclining towards kindness." [According to Rabbi Yossi above, God deletes one sin before a person is judged so that he or she will be judged meritoriously. Rabbi Eliezer, however, contends that even *after* people are judged and it has been

---

[309] Exodus 34:6-7.
[310] Psalms 62:13.
[311] Alternatively, *P'nei Moshe* says that the term "kindness" in the verse implies that God bestows undeserved kindness, crediting people with merit they have not actually earned.
[312] Exodus 34:6.

determined that their merits and demerits are in balance, God tips the scales of justice in their favor.]

Rabbi Yirmiah said that Rabbi Shmuel bar Rav Yitzchak asked: "Charity shall preserve [one who follows] a path of innocence and wickedness shall ruin a sinner."[313] "Evil shall pursue the wicked and good shall reward the righteous."[314] "With scoffers He will cause scoffing and with the humble He will give grace."[315] "The feet of His pious He will guard, but the wicked shall be silent in darkness... ."[316] "The wise shall inherit honor and fools acquire disgrace."[317] Are the fences fortified and the gates locked? [These verses imply that God compels the righteous and the wicked to act as they do, contrary to the Jewish teaching that people have free will.[318]]

Rather, Rabbi Yirmiah said that Rabbi Shmuel bar Rav Yitzchak said: If a person guards himself or herself from sin a first time, a second time and a third time, from then onward the Holy One, Blessed be He, guards the individual from sinning. What is the Scriptural basis for this? "Behold all these God does twice [and] three [times] with a man. To bring back his soul from destruction to

---

[313] Proverbs 13:6.
[314] Proverbs 13:21.
[315] Proverbs 3:34.
[316] I Samuel 2:9.
[317] Proverbs 3:35.
[318] B.T. *Brachoth* 33B quotes Rabbi Chanina that "All is in the hands of Heaven except fear of Heaven."

shine in the light of life."[319] [In view of this teaching, the *Talmud* interprets the verses cited above as referring to those who have already committed themselves to good or evil. Thus, for example, "With scoffers He will cause scoffing and with the humble He will give grace,"[320] refers to individuals who have adopted a course of scoffing or humility. Once people have developed certain routines, God assists them to continue.[321]]

Rabbi Z'eira said: This is provided that he or she does not stray back. What is the Scriptural basis for this? It is not written, "...the three-ply cord never unravels," but rather "...the three-ply cord does not quickly unravel."[322] If it is chafed, it breaks. [Although God helps those who have chosen a positive lifestyle to maintain their course, such assistance does not guarantee that people will not stray, only that they will be less likely to do so.]

[The *Talmud* now digresses to the earlier discussion about how God tips the scales of justice when they are evenly balanced so that people are judged favorably.] Rabbi Huna said in the name of Rabbi Abahu: There is no forgetfulness before the Holy One, Blessed be He, but for Israel He becomes "forgetful." [He overlooks sins.] What is the Scriptural basis for this? The phrase נושא עון which means "bearing iniquity"[323] is written נשא עון [which can

---

[319] Job 33:29-30.

[320] Proverbs 3:34.

[321] *P'nei Moshe.*

[322] Ecclesiastes 4:12.

[323] Exodus 34:6-7.

be read "He bore iniquity." Use of the past tense implies that God does not merely forgive the sin presently, but has entirely "forgotten" it as though it never existed in the first place.[324] So David says, "You bore the sin of Your people; You covered all their sin forever."[325]

*People often wonder how it is possible for God to wipe out a sin. If one person wrongs another, the injured party may forgive the offender, but that does not mean that what happened never occurred. According to the Talmud, however, it appears that Hashem tampers with the scales of justice and actually **erases** sins, making it as though they never happened. How can this be?*

This question becomes stronger when one notes that Adam committed only one sin, yet God did not forgive him and humanity continues to suffer from the effects of that sin down to this very day. If God is as merciful and forgiving as Jewish tradition claims, why did He not pardon Adam? Why did He not tip the scales of justice in Adam's favor? Why is his sin still remembered?

In the case of Adam, the answer is that he had but one commandment to observe and failed to do so. By contrast, Jews have six hundred thirteen commandments with myriads of ramifications. Because the Mitzvoth are so many, Jews have the excuse that they are unable to

---

[324] Also, the term נשא can allude to "*nashah*," (נשה) meaning "He forgot." *P'nei Moshe* and Rabbi Shlomo Sirilio.
[325] Psalms 85:3.

faithfully observe so much. This explains the well-known Talmudic statement that, "The Holy One, Blessed be He, desired to make Israel meritorious. Therefore He increased Torah and Mitzvoth."[326] *By increasing the burden of observance, He left open a loophole whereby those who fall short have an excuse.*[327]

Whether Hashem judges a person to be good or bad can vary depending on what factors He takes into account.[328] *Even if a person does something contrary to what the Torah demands, God may not view it as a violation depending on whether He chooses to find mitigating circumstances to excuse it. In fact, whether God judges a person guilty or innocent may depend upon a multitude of factors, many of which humans may not understand or even be aware of. Accordingly, if a person repents properly, God can view a sin as though it never happened at all because He finds an excuse for it and judges it not to be a sin under the circumstances.*

---

[326] B.T. *Makkoth* 23B.
[327] *Ya'aroth D'vash* II:5.
[328] See Rabbi Eliyahu Dessler, *Michtav MiEliyahu* Part I, Chapter 2.

Peah 2:4 (Compare *Shemoth Rabbah* 47:1 and B.T. *Gittin* 60B)

רבי זעירא בשם רבי אלעזר: "אֶכְתָּב [אֶכְתָּב קרי] לוֹ רֻבֵּי
[רֻבֵּי קרי] תּוֹרָתִי [כְּמוֹ זָר נֶחְשָׁבוּ]." (הושע ח:יב) וכי רובה של תורה
נכתבה? אלא מרובין הן הדברים הנדרשים מן הכתב מן הדברים
הנדרשים מן הפה. וכיני? אלא כיני: חביבין הן הדברים הנדרשים מן
הפה מן הדברים הנדרשים מן הכתב.

רבי יודא בן פזי אומר: "אֶכְתָּב [אֶכְתָּב קרי] לוֹ רֻבֵּי [רֻבֵּי קרי]
תּוֹרָתִי..." (שם שם) אלו התוכחות. אפילו כן, לא "כְּמוֹ זָר נֶחְשָׁבוּ"?
(שם שם)

אמר רבי אבין: אילולי כתבתי לך רובי תורתי, לא כמו זר
נחשבו? מה ביגן לאומות? אלו מוציאין ספריהם, ואלו מוציאין
ספירהם. אלו מוציאין דפתריהן, ואלו מוציאין דפתריהון.

רבי חגי אמר בשם רבי שמואל בר נחמן: נאמרו דברים בפה
ונאמרו דברים שבכתב, ואין אנו יודעין איזה מהן חביב אלא מן מה
דכתיב, "...כִּי עַל פִּי הַדְּבָרִים הָאֵלֶּה כָּרַתִּי אִתְּךָ בְּרִית וְאֶת יִשְׂרָאֵל."
(שמות לד:כז) הדא אמרה אותן שבפה חביבין.

רבי יוחנן ורבי יודן בי רבי שמעון: חד אמר: אם שמרת מה
שבפה ושמרת מה שבכתב, אני כורת אתך ברית ואם לאו, אין אני
כורת עמך ברית. וחרנא אמר: אם שמרת מה שבפה וקיימת מה
שבכתב, אתה מקבל שכר ואם לאו, אין אתה מקבל שכר.

רבי יהושע בן לוי אמר: "עֲלֵיהֶם," "וַעֲלֵיהֶם"; "כָּל," "בְּכָל";
"דְּבָרִים," "הַדְּבָרִים." מקרא, משנה, תלמוד, ואגדה, אפילו מה שתלמיד
ותיק עתיד להורות לפני רבו, כבר נאמר למשה בסיני. מה טעם? "יֵשׁ
דָּבָר שֶׁיֹּאמַר רְאֵה זֶה חָדָשׁ..." (קהלת א:י) משיבו חבירו ואומר לו,
"כְּבָר הָיָה לְעֹלָמִים..." (שם שם)

Rabbi Z'eira in the name of Rabbi Elazar said: "I write for him [Israel] most of my *Torah*, [yet] they are considered as a stranger."[329] [Although God reproves Israel constantly through His prophets, they ignore the reproof as though they are strangers.] Is most of the *Torah* written? [To the contrary, most of the *Torah* was transmitted from generation to generation by word of mouth.] Rather, the verse means that the things which are inferred from the Written *Torah* exceed the things which are inferred from the Oral *Torah*. [There are certain rules for deriving teachings from the Written *Torah* which cannot be applied to the Oral *Torah*. For example, when the *Torah* uses similar words in two different verses, similar *Halachoth* may apply to both (גזרה שוה). This principle does not apply to the Oral *Torah*.] Is this so? [Although certain rules of interpretation do not apply to the Oral *Torah*, surely the overall body of Oral law in which the rabbis infer one thing from another and apply the law to new situations far exceeds the scope of the Written *Torah*.] Rather one must interpret the verse so: The matters which are inferred from the Oral *Torah* are more precious than those inferred from the Written *Torah*. [When the verse says "they are considered as a stranger," it alludes to the fact that strangers (non-Jews) have copied the Written *Torah* and used it to invent their own religions as Rabbi Avin points out below. The Oral *Torah* is more precious

---

[329] Hosea 8:12.

because it has not been subverted in this manner.[330] Moreover, someone who reads the Written *Torah* may misinterpret its contents. By contrast, the Oral *Torah* is transmitted from generation to generation directly by father to son and teacher to pupil, permitting the person teaching it to eliminate any ambiguity or misunderstanding concerning its content.]

Rabbi Yuda ben Pazi says: "I write for him [Israel] most of my *Torah*..."[331] refers to the warnings [in the *Torah* of the dire consequences which will befall the Jews if they fail to observe it. The word רבי, translated here as "most," can also imply "quarrel" or "contention."[332]] Even so, are they not considered as a stranger? [Although *Hashem* gave Israel fair warning regarding the consequences of disobedience, the Jews ignored it.]

Rabbi Avin said: The verse means: If I had written most of the *Torah*, would Israel not have been considered a stranger? What distinguishes Israel from the nations of the world? These produce books and these produce books. These produce scrolls and these produce scrolls. [Non-Jews have copies of the Written *Torah* which they use as the basis for their own religions, but they do not have

---

[330] *Tosafoth* sub verba "*Ithmohee*" (אתמוהי) on B.T. *Gittin* 60B. *BaMidbar Rabbah* 14:9 says that the "Ishmaelites" (Arabs) falsified the Written *Torah* and claimed that they were the true chosen people.
[331] Hosea 8:12.
[332] Rabbi Shlomo Sirilio. He also says that the word רבי alludes to "shooting," as in shooting an arrow, which hints at punishment.

ready access to the Oral *Torah* so it is the latter which distinguishes Jews.]

Rabbi Chaggai said in the name of Rabbi Shmuel bar Nachman: Things were stated verbally and things were stated in writing, but we do not know which of them is more precious except from that which is written, "...for according to these words I have formed with you a covenant and with Israel."[333] Thus the *Torah* declared that the verbal are more precious. [The phrase "according to these words" (על פי הדברים האלה) literally means "by the mouth of these words," alluding to the Oral *Torah*.]

Rabbi Yochanan and Rabbi Yudan of the academy of Rabbi Shimon had different views on how to interpret the verse "...for according to these words I have formed with you a covenant and with Israel."[334] One said: If you preserve that which is oral and preserve that which is written, I will form a covenant with you and if not, I will not form a covenant with you. The other said: If you preserve that which is oral and fulfill that which is written, you will receive a reward and if not, you will not receive a reward. [The Oral *Torah* must be "preserved" because it must be committed to memory. By contrast, the Written *Torah* need merely be "fulfilled."[335] The complete verse reads, "The Lord said to Moses: Write for yourself these words for according to [literally, "by the mouth of"] these

---

[333] Exodus 34:27.
[334] Ibid.
[335] *Vilna Gaon.*

words I have formed with you a covenant and with Israel."[336] One view is that the written and oral segments of the *Torah* are equal since the verse mentions both "write" and "mouth." The other view, however, maintains that the Oral *Torah* is more important because the phrase "by the mouth of these words" (על פי הדברים האלה), alluding to the Oral *Torah*, appears immediately prior to "I have formed with you a covenant and with Israel,"[337] implying that *Hashem's* covenant with the Jewish people derives mainly from the Oral *Torah*.[338]]

Rabbi Yehoshua ben Levi said: [The *Torah* says, "The Lord gave me the two tablets of stone inscribed by the finger of God and upon them is a likeness of all the words which the Lord spoke with you upon the mountain from the midst of the fire on the day of assembly."[339]] Instead of the phrase "and upon them" (ועליהם), the *Torah* could have simply said "upon them," (עליהם). Instead of the phrase "a likeness of all" (ככל), the *Torah* could have simply said "all" (כל). Instead of the phrase "the words" (הדברים), the Torah could have simply said "words" (דברים). These extra letters in the Torah imply that Scripture, *Mishnah*, *Gemara* and *Aggadah*, even that which an advanced student will profess before his master in the future, was already told to Moses at Sinai. What is the Scriptural basis for this?

---

336 Exodus 34:27.
337 *P'nei Moshe.*
338 *P'nei Moshe.*
339 Deuteronomy 9:10.

"There is a thing concerning which [a person] will say, 'See this is new'... ."[340] His friend will answer and say to him, "...[but] it already existed from eternity... ."[341]

One of the cornerstones of the Jewish faith is that both the written and oral elements of the Torah are of Divine origin. If the Oral and Written Torah have equal validity, why did the rabbis of the Talmud think it important to establish which has greater quantity or which is more precious?

The answer is that the Oral Torah consists of two parts: (a) the material God transmitted to the Jewish people at Mount Sinai to explain the Written Torah or to complement the Written Torah; and (b) the "new" material students of the Torah develop as they ponder it and apply it to new situations, deriving one thing from another by using traditional rules of logical deduction. As this passage indicates, such material is not "new" at all, but latent in the Torah God gave the Jews at Mount Sinai.

The information God transmitted to Moses orally at Mount Sinai indeed has equal validity with the Written Torah. However, "new" material which later scholars developed is more precious than the Written Torah because a person's willingness to delve into the Torah to try to understand it more deeply shows his great love for the Torah.

---

[340] Ecclesiastes 1:10.
[341] Ibid.

The Mishnah tells how Rabban Yochanan ben Zakkai used to recount the outstanding traits of his five chief disciples: "Rabbi Eliezer ben Hyrcanus is a waterproofed cistern which does not lose a drop. [He retained all his learning perfectly.] Rabbi Yehoshua ben Chananya: happy is the one who bore him. Rabbi Yossi HaKohen is a pious person. [One who does more than the minimum the Torah requires.] Rabbi Shimon ben Nathanel is one who fears sin. Rabbi Elazar ben Arach is like a spring which surges. [He constantly develops new ideas just as a spring gushes water.]"[342]

The Mishnah continues, "He used to say, 'If all the sages of Israel were in one dish of a balance scale and Eliezer ben Hyrcanus in the other dish, he would outweigh them all.' Abba Shaul said in his name, 'If all the sages of Israel were on one dish of a balance scale and Eliezer ben Hyrcanus with them, while Elazar ben Arach was in the other dish, he would outweigh them all.'"[343]

Each of Rabban Yochanan ben Zakkai's disciples was great in his own way, yet, according to Abba Shaul, he thought it important to stress that Rabbi Elazar ben Arach was the greatest of them all. Rabban Yochanan ben Zakkai would not have praised Rabbi Elazar ben Arach had the latter's superiority been due merely to exceptional intellectual ability. A person's native abilities are God-given and do not reflect any effort on his or her part.

---

[342] *Pirkei Avoth* 2:11.
[343] *Pirkei Avoth* 2:12.

Just as some individuals may be blessed with exceptional eyesight, keen hearing or a muscular physique, so some possess unusual intellectual ability. One does not praise a person for possessing such traits, but for how he or she puts them to use. Hence, Rabban Yochanan ben Zakkai lauded Rabbi Elazar ben Arach because the latter developed his intellectual ability by constantly delving into the Torah to discover new insights. Rabban Yochanan ben Zakkai considered such enthusiasm for Torah study more important than any other trait a person could develop.

A parable for this is as follows: Once a wealthy man had a young son who was very bright but also rather mischievous. The father went to great lengths to try to teach the boy Torah. He hired the best tutors money could buy, but the child did not pursue his studies wholeheartedly, often daydreaming during his lessons. He seemed far more interested in playing than in learning. As he approached Bar Mitzvah age, his father decided to have a serious talk with the boy.

"I will not be able to support you forever," explained the father. "While I would be very glad to have a son who is a Torah scholar, it is clear these matters simply don't interest you. Perhaps a career in something else is more suitable."

It often happens that people do not appreciate something until they lose it. Faced with the possibility that his studies would stop, the young man suddenly grew very serious. He made up his mind to pay attention during his lessons with his tutors. Gradually, he discovered that the subject matter was interesting. Not only did he master the material thoroughly, but he also found himself asking pointed questions about it. Sometimes the questions were so well constructed that the teacher could not immediately answer them. The student would then discuss the topic at length with the tutor until together they came up with what they thought was a suitable answer. After a while, the young man became so enthusiastic about his lessons that he spent a good deal of his own free time making notes and recording all the interesting questions and answers he had discussed with his teachers.

One can well imagine the delight the father felt when he observed the change in his son's attitude. He would certainly have been pleased had his son merely mastered whatever his tutors tried to convey to him. However, his delight at seeing his son enthusiastically pursue his studies far exceeded anything he could have felt had his son merely memorized his teachers' words.

Similarly, God is greatly pleased when Jews study the oral and written parts of the Torah He gave Moses at Mount Sinai. However, He takes even greater pleasure when they become so interested in what the Torah teaches that they wish to delve into it further and further, developing new approaches to understanding it. This is just like a father who takes pride in a son who no longer needs to be prodded to study but enthusiastically seeks to learn.

Peah 3:7

"[וְשָׁלֹשׁ פְּעָמִים בַּשָּׁנָה יֵרָאֶה כָּל זְכוּרְךָ אֶת פְּנֵי הָאָדֹן ה' אֱ-לֹהֵי
יִשְׂרָאֵל]... וְלֹא יַחְמֹד אִישׁ אֶת אַרְצְךָ בַּעֲלֹתְךָ לֵרָאוֹת אֶת פְּנֵי ה'... ."
(שמות לד:כג-כד)

מעשה באחד שהניח את כריו ובא ומצא אריות סובבים אותו.
מעשה באחד שהניח בית של תרנגולים ובא ומצא חתולים
מקורעים לפניו.
חד בר נש שביק ביתיה פתיח ואתא ואשכח הכינה כריכה
על קרקסוי.
רבי פינחס משתעי הדין עובדא: תרין אחין הוון באשקלון.
הוו להון מגורין נוכראין. אמרין, "כדין אילין יהודאין סלקין
לירושלים, אנן נסבין כל מה דאית להון."
מן דסלקין, זימן להם הקדוש ברוך הוא מלאכים נכנסים
ויוצאים בדמותן. מן דנחתון, שלחנון לון מקמן.
אמרו לון, "אן הויתם?"
אמרו לון, "בירושלים."
אמרו לון, "ומאן שבקותון בגו ביתא?"
אמרו, "ולא בר נש."
אמרו, "בריך א-ללההון דיהודאי דלא שבקון ולא שביק להון."

"Three times during the year all your males shall
appear before the Master, the Lord, God of Israel...and no
man shall covet your land when you ascend to appear
before the Lord your God... ."[344] [During Temple times, it
was a *Mitzvah* for every Jewish male to go up to Jerusalem
on *Pesach*, *Shavuoth* and *Sukkoth*. Although this meant

---

[344] Exodus 34:23-24.

leaving the land unguarded and vulnerable to attack, the *Torah* promised that no other nation would invade.]

There was an incident where someone left his grain pile out in the field. When he came back, he found lions surrounding it.

There was an incident where someone left a chicken house unguarded. When he came back, he found cats torn up before it.

One person left his house open. When he came back, he found a snake coiled around the doorlatch [to thwart intruders].

Rabbi Pinchas related this incident: There were two brothers in Ashkelon who had heathen neighbors. The latter said to themselves, "When these Jews go up to Jerusalem, we will seize everything they own."

When they ascended, the Holy One, Blessed be He, arranged angels with their appearance to go in and out. When [the Jews] descended, they sent word of their imminent arrival to their heathen neighbors.

The heathens asked them, "Where were you?"

"In Jerusalem," they answered.

"Who did you leave in the house?"

"Not a soul."

"Blessed is the God of the Jews who did not abandon them and will not abandon them!"

The Torah promises that "...no man shall covet [יחמד] your land when you ascend to appear before the Lord your God...,"[345] *meaning that not only will no one seize your property, but that they will also not desire to do so, yet the story in the above passage tells how heathens desired to steal but were thwarted. Thus, the very story the Talmud cites as fulfillment of the verse appears to contradict it. How does this make sense?*

The last of the Ten Commandments states, "You shall not covet [תחמד] your neighbor's house. You shall not covet your neighbor's wife, his manservant, his maidservant, his ox, his donkey or anything which is your neighbor's."[346] *Many commentators question how a person can fulfill such a commandment. While a person can certainly refrain from stealing something which belongs to someone else, it seems only natural for a person to desire things he or she wants. Rabbi Avraham Ibn Ezra explains that this Mitzvah requires a person to accustom himself to think of other people's belongings as things which are completely out of his grasp. Just as a simple peasant would never realistically expect to marry a wealthy princess or a person of normal intelligence would not expect to attach wings to his arms and fly to the moon, a person should understand that whatever someone else has is granted by Divine wisdom and Divine decree. Taking someone else's belongings is simply outside the realm of*

---

[345] Exodus 34:23-24.
[346] Exodus 20:14.

possibility. While one might initially have a desire for that which belongs to another, the Torah commands him to adopt this attitude so that such desires immediately vanish.[347]

This means that the Hebrew expression ולא יחמד איש, *"no man shall covet" does not mean that there will be no desire whatsoever, but that the desire will be squelched immediately because its fulfillment will appear impossible. That is precisely what happened in the passage translated here. Although the heathens wanted to plunder the property of their Jewish neighbors, their desire immediately evaporated because they believed that it would be impossible to achieve. As far as they knew, their neighbors had never left, or, if they had left, had stationed others to guard their property.*[348]

Rabbi Eliyahu Lopian noted that the Mitzvah of going up to Jerusalem three times a year while leaving the land open to attack is proof of the Divine origin of the Torah. Although the Tanach records numerous instances of complaints and rebellions on the part of the Jewish people, it never mentions a single situation where they claimed that they had obeyed this Mitzvah yet suffered attack from foreigners, clearly a supernatural phenomenon.

---

[347] *Avraham Ibn Ezra* on Exodus 20:14.

[348] *Tanna D'Bei Eliyahu*, chapter 26, says that by obeying the commandment not to covet, Jews merit the fulfillment of the Divine promise that others will not desire their land when they ascend to Jerusalem.

Had people written the Torah, this could never have happened.[349]

---

[349] Rabbi Moshe Heinemann שליט"א heard this from Rabbi Lopian.

Peah 7:3 (Compare B.T. *Kethuboth* 111B and J.T. *Sotah* 1:8)

דלמא: רבי אבהו ורבי יוסי בן חנינא ורבי שמעון בן לקיש
עברו על כרם דורון. אפיק לון אריסא חדא פרסיקא. אכלון אינון
וחמריהון ואייתרון ושערונא כהדין לפיסא דכפר חנניא מחזיק סאה
של עדשים.

בתר יומין, עברון תמן. אפיק לון תרי תלת לגו ידא.

אמרו ליה, "מן ההוא אילנא אנן בעיין."

אמר לון, "מיניה אינון."

וקרון עלוי, "אֶרֶץ פְּרִי לִמְלֵחָה מֵרָעַת יֹשְׁבֵי בָהּ." (תהלים
קז:לד)

אמר רבי חנינא: כד סלקת להכא, נסיבת איזורי ואיזוריה
דברי ואיזוריה דחמרי מקפא בירדתא דחרובתיה דארעא דישראל ולא
מטין. קצת חד חרוב ונגד מלא ידוי דובשא.

אמר רבי יוחנן: יפה סיפסוף שאכלנו בילדותינו מפרסקי
שאכלנו בזקנותינו. דביומוי אישתני עלמא.

אמר רבי חייא בר בא: סאה ארבלית היתה מוציאה סאה
סולת, סאה קמח, סאה קיבר, סאה מורסן, סאה גניינין. וכדון אפילו
חדא בחדא לא קיימא.

רבי חונא בשם רבי אבון: קינמון מאכל עזים הן והיו ישראל
מגדלין אותו.

רבי חונא בשם רבי אבון: שני תמידין שהיו מקריבין בכל יום
היו מרכיבין אותן על גבי גמל ורגליהן נוגעות בארץ.

רבי חונא בשם רב אידי: מעשה באחד שקשר עז לתאינה
ובא ומצא דבש וחלב מעורבין.

רבי אמר לרבי פרידא, "לית את חמי לי ההיא סגולה בגו
כרמך?"

אמר ליה, "אִין."

נפיק, בעי מחמייא ליה. עד דהוא רחוק, צפה ביה כמין תור.

אמר ליה, "לית הדין תורא מחבל כרמך?"

אמר ליה, "הדין תורא דאת סבר, הוא סגולה."

וקרא עליו, "עַד שֶׁהַמֶּלֶךְ בִּמְסִבּוֹ נִרְדִּי נָתַן רֵיחוֹ." (שיר השירים א:יב) בית מקדשא חריב ואת קאים בקשיותך? מיד איתבעין ולא אשכח.

אייתון קומיה תרין פוגלין מבין ריש שתא לצומא רבא והוה אפוקי שמיטתא, והוו בעון טעיניה דגמלא.

אמר לון, "ולית אסור? ולית ספיחיה אינון?"

אמרו ליה, "באיפוקי ריש שתא איזדרעין."

...בעון קומי: מהו הדין דכתיב, "עָבְשׁוּ פְרֻדוֹת תַּחַת מֶגְרְפֹתֵיהֶם..." (יואל א:יז)

אמר לון: תחת שהיינו גורפים דבש, הרי אנו גורפין רקבובית.

מעשה באחד שהיה לו שורה של תאינין ובא ומצא גדר של דבש מקיף אותן. חד בר נש זרע חקלא לפת והוה מקטע ומזבין. מעשה בשועל שבא וקינן בראשה של לפת.

מעשה בשיחין בקלח אחד של חרדל שהיו בו שלשה בדין ונפשח אחד מהם וסיככו בו סוכת יוצרים ומצאו בו שלשת קבין של חרדלי.

אמר רבי שמעון בן חלפתא, "קלח אחד של חרדל היה לי בתוך שלי והייתי עולה בו כעולה בראש התאינה. מעשה באחד שזרע סאה של אפונים ועשת שלש מאות סאין."

אמרו לו, "התחיל קודשא בריך הוא לברכך?"

אמר לון, "אזלון לכון! די אנחת טלא בישא עליה. די לא כן, בכפלא הוות מעבד!"

אמר רבי שמעון בן חלפתא: היה מעשה שאמר רבי יהודא לבנו בסיכנין, "עֲלֵה והביא לנו גרוגרות מן החביות."

עלה והושיט ידו ומצאה של דבש. אמר ליה, "אבא, של דבש

הוא."

אמר ליה, "השקע ידך ואת מעלה גרוגרות."

מעשה שאמר רבי יוסי לבנו בציפורין, "עֲלֵה והביא לנו גרוגרות מן העלייה." עלה ומצא את העלייה צף עליה דבש.

רבי חנניא מזבין דבש דדבוריין והוה ליה דבש דצליין. בתר יומין עברין תמן. אמר לון, "בגין לא מטייעא לכון, הוון ידעין ההוא דובשא (דתאניה) דיהבית לכון, דצליין אינון."

אמרו ליה, "מיניה אנן בעון דו טב לעבידתיה."

ואפריש טמיתיה ובנא בי מדרשא דציפורן.

ראיה אזל לחד אתר ואייתון קומיה כרוב מצמק. אמר לון, "סגין דבש יהבתון ביה."

אמרין ליה, "לא יהבינון ביה. מיניה וביה הוא."

It once happened that Rabbi Abahu, Rabbi Yossi ben Chanina and Rabbi Shimon ben Lakish passed by a vineyard in Doron. A sharecropper brought them one peach. They and their donkey drivers ate from it, and they had some left over. They measured and found it to be as large as a certain kettle in K'far Chananya capable of holding a *Se'ah* of lentils [about eight liters].

After a number of days, they passed there again. The sharecropper brought for them two or three [small] peaches in his hand.

"We desire some from the same tree," they said.

He responded, "These are from it."

They applied to it the verse, "A fruitful land is barren because of the evil of its inhabitants."[350] [The tree

350 Psalms 107:34.

159

which bore such magnificent fruits no longer did so because of the sinfulness of the people who lived there.]

Rabbi Chanina said: When I came up here [to the Land of Israel], I took my belt, my son's belt and my donkey driver's belt to measure the circumference of a carob tree of the Land of Israel but they would not reach. I cut off one carob and my whole hand filled with carob nectar.

Rabbi Yochanan said, "Better were the remnants that we ate in our childhood than the choice fruits that we ate in our old age." He said this because the world changed during his time. [The Land of Israel stopped producing exceptional fruits.]

Rabbi Chiya bar Ba said: A *Se'ah* of Arbelian wheat[351] used to produce a *Se'ah* of fine flour, a *Se'ah* of ordinary flour, a *Se'ah* of coarse meal, a *Se'ah* of bran and a *Se'ah* of husks. Now all the products of a *Se'ah* of wheat do not equal one *Se'ah*.

Rabbi Chuna in the name of Rabbi Avon said: Cinnamon is the food of goats and Israel used to raise it. [Although it later became a rare and expensive spice, at one time cinnamon was so common that the Jews used it for animal fodder.]

Rabbi Chuna in the name of Rabbi Avon said: They used to mount the two *Tamid* offerings which they sacrificed each day on the back of a camel and yet their legs

---

[351] From the town of Arbel. (*P'nei Moshe*) Compare *Pirkei Avoth* 1:7 which quotes Nitai of Arbel.

touched the ground. [The *Tamid* offerings were lambs, but they were so large that their feet touched the ground even when slung over the back of a camel.]

Rabbi Chuna said in the name of Rabbi Iddi: There was an incident where someone tied a goat to a fig tree and came and found fig nectar and milk mixed together.

Rebbi said to Rabbi Prida, "Won't you show me that cluster in your vineyard?" [Rebbi had heard that Rabbi Prida had an unusually large grape cluster in his vineyard.]

"Yes," he answered.

He went out intending to show it to him. When they were at a distance, Rabbi observed what looked like a kind of ox. He said, "Doesn't that ox damage your vineyard?"

"That which you perceive as an ox is the cluster."

Rebbi applied the verse, "'While the king was at his party, my spikenard gave its fragrance.'[352] The Temple is destroyed yet you, vineyard, retain your strength?" [The verse means that while God (the King) has a Temple service (His party), Israel enjoys exceptional bounty (its spikenard exudes fragrance). Once the Temple was destroyed, however, it was no longer appropriate for the vineyard to produce unusual fruits.] Instantly, when they searched for it, it could no longer be found.

They brought before Rebbi two radishes which grew between *Rosh HaShannah* and the Great Fast [*Yom*

---

352 Song of Songs 1:12.

Kippur]. It was after the Sabbatical year and they had the weight of a camel-load.

"Aren't they forbidden?" asked Rebbi. "Aren't they leftovers from the Sabbatical year?"

They answered, "Right after *Rosh HaShannah* we planted them."

...They asked Rebbi: What is the meaning of this which is written, "Wine barrels spoiled under their lids... ."[353]?

He answered: "Instead of our gathering nectar, we gather decay." [The plain meaning of the verse is that disobeying God causes famine. As a result, barrels become moldy and spoiled due to lack of use when there is nothing to fill them.[354] The Hebrew words תחת מגרפתיהם, meaning "under their lids," can also mean "instead of their harvest," hinting at the idea that there was not only a scarcity of food after the destruction of the Temple, but that such scarcity existed instead of the once bountiful harvest.]

There was an incident with someone who had a row of fig trees. He came and found a wall of honey surrounding them. One person planted a turnip field nearby and would cut out congealed fig nectar and sell it. [The fig trees produced so much nectar that it permeated the adjacent field.]

There was an incident where a fox came and built a lair in the head of a turnip.

---

353 Joel 1:17.
354 *Metzudoth David* ad. loc.

There was an incident in Shichin with a stalk of mustard that had three shoots. One of them split apart and they covered a potter's hut with it. Even so, they found three *Kabim* [about four liters] of mustard left in it.

Rabbi Shimon ben Chalafta said, "I had one stalk of mustard on my own property and I used to climb it as one would climb a fig tree. An incident happened where someone planted a *Se'ah* of peas there and it yielded three hundred *Sa'im*."

They said to Rabbi Shimon ben Chalafta sarcastically, "Has the Holy One, Blessed be He, started to bless you?"

"Go away!" he answered. "Bad dew fell upon it [the mustard plant]. Otherwise, it would have produced twice as much!"

Rabbi Shimon ben Chalafta said: There was an incident in Sichnin where Rabbi Yehudah told his son, "Go up to the attic and bring us dried figs from the barrels."

He climbed up, stuck his hand in and discovered nectar. "Father," he said, "this is nectar."

"Sink in your hand further and you will bring up figs." [The figs were so juicy that they produced a deep layer of nectar when they were stored.]

There was an incident in Sepphoris where Rabbi Yossi told his son, "Go up and bring us dried figs from the attic." He went up and found the attic flooded with nectar.

Rabbi Chananya sold bee honey and also owned locust honey.[355] After some time, customers passed there. He told them, "In order not to mislead you, you should know that the honey I am giving you is from locusts."

"That is just what we want because it serves the same function."

Rabbi Chananya then set aside the value of the locust honey and used it to build a study hall in Sepphoris. [This shows how valuable even the locust honey of the Land of Israel was.]

Ra'ayah went to a certain place where they brought before him a ripened cabbage. He said to them, "You gave me a lot of nectar with it."

They responded, "We gave nothing. The nectar comes from itself."

The above passage states that the sacrificial lambs used in the daily Temple service were so huge that even when mounted on the back of a camel, their hooves touched the ground. If, however, the fruits and animals of the Land of Israel literally had the unusual proportions the Talmud describes, then the camels also should have been exceptionally large and the lambs' hooves should not have reached the ground. Accordingly, it appears that the

---

[355] *P'nei Moshe* equates the Aramaic word צלייין with the Hebrew word צרעים and identifies them as locusts based on *Rashi*'s commentary to B.T. *Bekoroth* 7B. Rav Hai Gaon in his commentary to *Machshirin* 6:4, however, says that צרעים are wasps or hornets. Either way, the idea is that this was an inferior grade of honey.

Talmud intended this passage as a metaphor and not necessarily as a literal description of the flora and fauna of the Land of Israel.

The Torah decrees that only land animals which chew their cud and have split hooves are Kosher. It then goes on to specify four creatures which have only one Kosher sign and, therefore, are not Kosher. The pig has a split hoof but does not chew its cud. The camel, Arneveth and Shafan (usually identified as types of hares) chew their cud but do not have split hooves.[356]

The Midrash teaches that these four animals represent four gentile empires which conquered the Land of Israel. The camel is Babylon, the Shafan is Medea, the Arneveth is Greece and the pig is Edom (Rome).[357]

The Midrash goes on to make the point that the outstanding negative characteristic of these non-Kosher animals is hypocrisy. For example, when the pig eats, it sticks out its split hooves as if to show off to the world that it is Kosher. Only upon closer examination does one discover that the pig is not Kosher because it does not chew its cud. Likewise, the Roman nation loudly proclaimed its righteousness while often practicing the very same evils it condemned.[358] Similarly, the camel symbolizes Babylonian King Nebuchadnezzar's penchant for praising

---

[356] Leviticus 11:3-7.
[357] *VaYikra Rabbah* 13:5.
[358] Ibid.

God with his mouth (chewing cud) but carrying out all manner of evil.[359]

The Talmud predicts that when the Messiah arrives, the Roman nation will hypocritically claim that all the grandiose building projects it undertook to maintain control of its empire were actually undertaken solely to help the Jews observe the Torah. The other nations will make similar false claims.[360]

The people who lived during the era of the First Temple committed the three cardinal sins of idolatry, adultery and bloodshed.[361] However, the Prophet Isaiah did not limit himself to pointing out those sins when he criticized Israel before the destruction of the First Temple. Rather, he condemned the hypocrites who spread their hands in prayer and offered many sacrifices, yet whose hands were full of blood and who refused to act justly.[362]

As bad as the three cardinal sins may be, God can hold off punishment if repentance is possible. Repentance, however, requires recognition of wrongdoing and willingness to correct it. A person who sins openly may recognize the wrongfulness of his or her actions but feel overcome by evil impulses. By contrast, hypocrites deceptively present themselves to others as righteous

---

[359] Ibid. See also B.T. *Kiddushin* 49B where Rabbi Yochanan states that Babylon was steeped in hypocrisy.

[360] B.T. *Avodah Zarah* 2B.

[361] B.T. *Yoma* 9B.

[362] Isaiah 1:11-17.

people while sinning privately. They do not have the basic recognition that what they are doing is wrong, so they cannot ever correct it. Moreover, because they observe the Torah publicly but sin privately, they show that they fear people but not God and one who does not fear God cannot repent.[363]

On a more profound level, Kabbalistic tradition refers to evil as Klipah (קליפה), meaning "husk" or "shell." In reality, God exists everywhere and in everything. However, God's presence is hidden and covered over so that people do not perceive it. It is this covering or "husk" which makes evil possible in the world.[364] *This means that hypocrisy, appearing one way on the surface but being something else underneath, represents the very ability of evil to exist. When hypocrisy pervades a society, evil becomes so prevalent that destruction is bound to follow.*

The Talmud states that the second Temple was destroyed as a result of disproportionate hatred (שנאת חנם).[365] *Such hatred is often hidden behind a mask of hypocrisy. King Yannai, himself a Sadducee, told his wife not to fear his enemies the Pharisees, but only*

---

[363] See B.T. *Brachoth* 28B where Rabban Yochanan ben Zakkai blessed his disciples that they fear God as much as they fear flesh and blood. In B.T. *Baba Kama* 79B, he points out that the *Torah* prescribes a harsher punishment for one who steals secretly (גנב) than for one who steals openly (גזלן) because the actions of the former show that he or she fears people but not God.

[364] *Likutei Amarim Tanya*, chap. 22.

[365] B.T. *Yoma* 9B.

hypocrites *"whose deeds are like those of Zimri but who seek the reward of Phinehas."*[366] *Extreme differences between people, even hard feelings, can often be overcome when people are forthright with one another and try to find common ground. However, when people deceive one another about their true feelings, hatred continues to fester to the point where it tears families and communities apart.*

As noted in comments to an earlier passage, during the years leading up to the destruction of the Temple, two brothers who descended from the royal Hasmonean family fought a bitter war for control of the Jewish state. Hyrcanus's forces took control of the Temple while Aristobolus's army laid siege from without. Each day Hyrcanus's soldiers lowered a basketful of money to the enemy who then supplied the lambs necessary for the sacrificial service. A certain old man used Greek philosophy to convince Aristobulus's soldiers that as long as the sacrificial service continued, they would never prevail. The very next day, instead of sending lambs, the soldiers placed a pig in the basket. As it was raised, the pig struck its hoof into the Temple wall, creating a noise that could be heard four hundred parasangs (Persian miles) away.[367]

---

[366] B.T. *Sotah* 22B. Zimri, the prince of the tribe of Simeon, publicly engaged in immoral relations with a Midianite princess. Phinehas slew him and the princess. (Numbers 25:7-8.)

[367] B.T. *Sotah* 49B. A Persian mile equals four Talmudic miles (about four kilometers). See footnote 636 below.

The hypocritical deceit of sending up a basket supposedly loaded with sacrificial lambs but actually bearing a pig was the beginning of the end. Such deceit was aptly represented by the pig, symbol of hypocrisy and of the Roman Empire, and an eerie harbinger of the impending Roman invasion. Such treacherous behavior between brothers also demonstrated the level to which Israel had sunk, a level of disproportionate hatred which left nothing sacred.[368]

The Midrash depicts Israel as a sheep among seventy wolves.[369] *The innocent lamb reflects the ideal nature of a Jew as one who is straightforward and honest just as the Torah calls Jacob, "an honest man" (אִישׁ תָּם).*[370] *In the passage under review, the reference to the lambs covering the camel alludes to the attitude Jews had prior to the destruction of the Temple. So long as Jews maintained the innocent, sincere approach of the lamb, their spiritual superiority over the hypocritical nations of*

---

[368] Hypocrisy played a major role in the destruction of both Temples. Thus, after the downfall of the Second Temple, Rabbi Nathan said that when the Jews hypocritically declared their approval of King Agrippas, they became liable for destruction. Rabbi Elazar said that any congregation which engages in hypocritical flattery suffers exile. (B.T. *Sotah* 41B-42A).

[369] *Pesikta Rabbathai* 9:2 and *Esther Rabbah* 10:11. Also, *Otzar HaMidrashim, Gan Eden V'Gehinnom* 16 says that in Heaven the angel Michael offers the souls of the righteous upon an altar on each Sabbath eve. Hence the righteous are comparable to the sacrificial lambs used in the Temple service.

[370] Genesis 25:27.

the world ensured their survival. In its physical aspects, a lamb is puny compared to a camel, but spiritually it can overwhelm it. Once hypocrisy, deceit and the disproportionate hatred that accompanies them prevailed, the "lamb" became just an ordinary lamb easily outweighed and outclassed by the larger camel.

This passage of the Talmud also hints at the change in attitude among the Jewish people in another way. The Mishnah states that ten miracles took place while the Temple stood. One was that "A man never said to his fellow, 'Space is too scarce for me to lodge in Jerusalem.'"[371] Some commentators explain that indeed space was scarce in Jerusalem when all the men ascended to the Temple, but the miracle was that no one ever complained about it because of their great love for Jerusalem and because of the friendship and brotherhood among them.[372]

So long as Jews showed love and respect for one another, the Temple could stand. Because everyone got along so well and shared what they had, they perceived the

---

[371] *Pirkei Avoth* 5:5.

[372] Rabbi Pinchas Kehati ad. loc., citing *Likutei Bathar Likutei* and *Chatham Sofer*. The idea that a person's **attitude** affects his or her perception is further reflected in the well-known statement: "Who is rich? One who is happy with his or her portion." (*Pirkei Avoth* 4:1). A billionaire may not be happy because he feels he still lacks something. By contrast, a penniless pauper can be happy if he is content with the little he possesses.

fruits to be huge and luscious as the Talmud describes. When selfishness entered the picture and people no longer felt the same affection for one another, the fruits appeared smaller. There was not as much to go around not due to any change in agricultural conditions but because of a change in the attitude of the people which led to the destruction of the Temple.

Peah 8:6

רבי חגיי כד הוה מקים פרנסין, הוה מטעין לון אורייתא,
לומר שכל שררה שניתנה, בתורה ניתנה. "בִּי מְלָכִים יִמְלֹכוּ [וְרֹזְנִים
יְחֹקְקוּ צֶדֶק.] בִּי שָׂרִים יָשֹׂרוּ [וּנְדִיבִים כָּל שֹׁפְטֵי צֶדֶק.]" (משלי
ח:טו-טז) רבי חייא בר בא: מקיים ארכוניי.

רבי אלעזר הוה פרנס. חד זמן, נחית לבייתיה. אמר לון,
"מאי עבדיתון?"

אמרו ליה, "אתא חד סיעא ואכלון ושתון וצלו עלך."
אמר לון, "ליכא אגר טב."

נחת זמן תנינן. אמר לון, "מאי עבדיתון?"
אמרו ליה, "אתא חד סיעא חורי ואכלון ושתון ואקלונך."
אמר לון, "כדון איכא אגר טב."

רבי עקיבא בעין ממניתיה פרנס. אמר לון, "נמלך גו בייתא."
הלכון בתריה. שמעון קליה דימור, "על מנת מקל. על מנת מבזייא."

When Rabbi Chaggai would appoint communal
officers,[373] he would enlighten them with *Torah* to indicate
that all authority is granted by virtue of *Torah* study, as it
says, "Through me kings shall reign and princes legislate
justice. Through me officers and leaders shall rule, all
upright judges."[374] Rabbi Chiya bar Ba explained these
verses to mean that the *Torah* establishes leaders.[375]

---

[373] The word פרנס generally has this meaning. Here the term denotes
those in charge of charity distribution.

[374] Proverbs 8:15-16. *Etz Yosef* says that Rabbi Chaggai actually
handed a *Torah* scroll to each appointee to impress him with this
concept.

[375] *P'nei Moshe.* Rabbi Shlomo Sirilio points out that the term ארכוניי

Rabbi Elazar was a communal leader. One time when he went home, he asked the members of his household, "What has been going on?"

They answered, "One group came along, ate and drank and prayed for you."

He said, "This is not good reward."

He visited a second time and asked the members of his household, "What has been going on?"

"Another group came along, ate, drank and denigrated you."

"Now there is good reward."

The community wanted to appoint Rabbi Akiva as a leader. He told them, "I must consult my wife." His students followed after him and heard a voice which said, "Only accept with the understanding that you may be denigrated and with the understanding that you may be disgraced."

One can understand that a leader must be willing to face the possibility that the decisions he makes may not be popular with the public. However, would it not make more sense for Rabbi Elazar to hope that the community would recognize that he is trying to act in its best interests and support what he is doing? One would think that he would be rewarded for serving the community even if he is

---

(*archos*) is of Greek origin. It is used in modern English to mean "chief" or "leader," as in "arch defender" or "arch villain."

*well-liked, yet Rabbi Elazar appears to say that he can expect reward from Heaven **only** if he is detested.*

Rabbi Moshe Chaim Luzzatto explains that a private person is responsible solely for his or her own acts. A communal leader, however, can be held accountable for whatever goes on in his community.[376] As Moses told the Jewish people, "The Lord was angry with me because of you... ."[377] Moreover, the Talmud teaches that whoever can object when he sees another person doing something wrong but fails to do so, is punished.[378] Perhaps Rabbi Elazar worried that Heaven would judge him for the faults of his community if he failed to rebuke his fellow Jews sufficiently. However, such judgment would only apply if he were a popular leader whose reproof would find willing listeners among the public. If people disliked him, however, he would have the defense that no one would listen to his rebuke. In that case, Rabbi Elazar could receive the reward for leading the community without running the risk of punishment for failing to correct its shortcomings.

---

[376] *Mesilath Yesharim*, chapter 22.
[377] Deuteronomy 3:26.
[378] B.T. *Avodah Zarah* 18A.

Peah 8:7 (B.T. *Kethuboth* 67B and see B.T. *Sotah* 21B)

חד תלמיד מן דרבי היה לו מאתים זוז חסר דינר, והוה רבי
יליף זכי עמיה חד לתלת שני מעשר מסכנין. עבדון ביה תלמידוי
עינא בישא ומלון ליה.

אתא בעי מזכי עימיה. אמר ליה, "רבי, אית לי שיעורא."
אמר, "זה מכת פרושים נגעו ביה." רמז לתלמידיו ואעלוניה
לקפילין וחסרוניה חד קרט וזכה עימיה היאך מה דהוה יליף.

משפחת אנטבילא היתה בירושלים והיתה מתייחסת של ארנן
היבוסי. פעם אחת, פסקו להן חכמים שש מאות ככרי זהב שלא
להוציאן חוץ לירושלים דהוון דרשון, "בִּשְׁעָרֶיךָ," "בִּשְׁעָרֶיךָ," לרבות
ירושלים.

והתני: מעשה בהלל הזקן שלקח לעני בן טובים סוס אחד
להתעמל בו ועבד לשמשו. שוב מעשה באנשי גליל שהיו מעלין לזקן
אחד ליטרא בשר צִיפֳּרִין בכל יום. ואפשר כן? אלא דלא הוה אכיל
עם חורנין.

[The *Mishnah* states that if a person has at least two
hundred *Zuz* (silver coins), he or she is not allowed to
collect the gifts given to the poor such as the tithe which is
distributed during the third and sixth years of the Sabbatical
cycle (מעשר עני). On the other hand, if a person has just
under two hundred *Zuz*, he or she may accept even a large
share of such gifts.]

One disciple of Rebbi had one hundred ninety-nine
Zuz. Rebbi used to give him the tithe of the poor every
three years. His other disciples were jealous, so they made
up the difference of one *Zuz*. [Since the poor student then

had two hundred *Zuz*, he became disqualified from receiving the tithe of the poor.]

When Rebbi came and wanted to contribute to him, the disciple said, "Rebbi, I have the limit."

"The plague of the Pharisees struck this one." [The *Talmud* typically views Pharisees as hypocrites.[379] In this situation, the disciples displayed themselves outwardly as charitable by giving their fellow a *Zuz*, while their true intent was to disqualify him from being able to accept the tithe.] Rebbi signaled to his students who took that man into a shop where they made him a *Karat* coin poorer [by purchasing something] so that he could accept the tithe as he used to.

The family of Antbila was in Jerusalem and had a lineage back to Arnan the Jebusite [upon whose property King David built the altar later used in the Temple].[380] One time, the sages allotted them six hundred talents of gold so as not to cause them to go outside Jerusalem, for they expounded "in your gates" "in your gates" to include Jerusalem. [These descendents of Arnan converted to Judaism. There are several verses in the *Torah* which refer to converts and mention "in your gates." One refers to distribution of the tithe for the poor: "The Levite shall come, for he has no share or inheritance with you, and the convert and the orphan and the widow who are in your

---

[379] J.T. *Brachoth* 9:5 and B.T. *Sotah* 22B.
[380] I Chronicles 21:18-26.

gates and they shall eat and be satisfied... ."[381] Another verse says, "You shall rejoice before the Lord your God, you and your son and daughter, your manservant and your maidservant, and the Levite who is in your gates, the convert, the orphan and the widow who are in your midst in the place which the Lord your God shall choose to make His Name dwell there."[382] The first verse anticipates that converts will live "in your gates," while the second verse teaches that "in your gates" means Jerusalem which is "...the place which the Lord your God shall choose to make His Name dwell there." From this the rabbis concluded that it was important to try to support converts in such a manner that they could continue to live in Jerusalem.[383].]

There is a similar teaching: An incident took place involving Hillel the Elder who bought a horse for a poor person of wealthy background to amuse himself with and a slave to serve him. There was another instance where the people of the Galilee who would provide one old man a pound of poultry every day. Is it possible that they provided such expensive food to their poor? However, he never ate with anyone else. [The townsfolk treated this person separately from their other poor people because he

---

[381] Deuteronomy 14:29.
[382] Deuteronomy 16:11.
[383] *P'nei Moshe* offers a slightly different interpretation using Deuteronomy 16:11 and 16:14. Interestingly, King David paid Arnan six hundred gold shekels for the altar site (I Chronicles 21:25), the same number as the talents of gold the sages allotted his descendants.

had become so pampered before losing his fortune that he could not digest other food.]

The Babylonian Talmud has a somewhat different version of the last section of this passage: "The people of the Galilee bought a pound of meat each day for a poor person of wealthy background. What is unique about that? Rav Huna said, 'It was a pound of poultry meat.' If you want, I'll tell you it was ordinary meat, as Rav Ashi said, 'That was a small town. Each day they would lose their livelihood because of him.'"[384] *Since they could not preserve the meat by refrigeration, they had to slaughter fresh meat each day. Because the town was small, there were not enough customers for whatever that needy person left over, so much of the meat went to waste.*

In accordance with these sections of the Talmud, the Code of Jewish Law rules as a matter of practice that a community must provide a poor person with whatever he or she is normally accustomed to have.[385] *This is consistent with the Jewish point of view that charity (צדקה) entails not only providing for the physical needs of the poor, but commiserating with them as well.*[386] *It is not enough to help a poor person survive on modest means. One must make him feel better by providing him with the type of lifestyle to which he was accustomed.*

---

[384] B.T. *Kethuboth* 67B.
[385] *Shulchan Aruch, Yoreh Deah* 250:1.
[386] B.T. *Baba Bathra* 9B.

Peah 8:8 (Compare *VaYikra Rabbah* 34:10; J.T. *Shekalim* 5:4 and *Kethuboth* 67B-68A)

שמואל ערק מן אבוי. אזל וקם ליה בין תרין צריפין
דמיסכנין. שמע קולהון אמרין, "בהדין אגנטין אנן אכלין יומא דין?
באגנטין דדהבא ובאגניטן דכספא אנן אכלין?"

עאל ואמר קומי אביו. אמר ליה, "צריכין אנו להחזיק טובה
לרמאין שבהם."

דלמא: רבי יוחנן וריש לקיש עלון מיסחין בהדין נימוסין
דטבריא. פגע בון חד מסכן. אמר לון, "זכון בי."

אמרו ליה, "מי חזרון."

מי חזרון, אשכחוניה מית. אמרו, "הואיל ולא זכינין ביה
בחייו, ניטפל ביה במיתותיה."

כי מיטפלון ביה, אשכחון כיס דינרין תלוי ביה. אמרו, "הדא
דאמר רבי אבהו אמר רבי אלעזר: צריכין אנו להחזיק טובה לרמאין
שבהן שאילולי הרמאין שבהן, היה אחד תובע צדקה מן האדם ולא
נותן לו מיד נענש."

אבא בר בא יהב לשמואל בריה פריטין דיהא פליג
למסכינייא. נפק ואשכח חד מסכן אכל קופר ושתי חמר. עאל ואמר
קומי אבוי. אמר ליה, "הב ליה יתיר דנפשיה מרתי."

...רבי זכריה, חתניה דרבי לוי, היו הכל מליזין עליו. אמרו
דלא צריך והוא נסב. כד דמוך, בודקין, ואשכחון דהוה מפליג ליה
לחורנין.

רבי חנינא בר פפא הוה מפליג מצוה בלילייא. חד זמן, פגע
ביה רבהון דרוחין. אמר ליה, "לא כך אולפן רבי, 'לא תסיג גבול
רֵעֲךָ...'"? (דברים יט:יד)

אמר ליה, "ולא כן כתיב, 'מַתָּן בַּסֵּתֶר יִכְפֶּה אָף...'"? (משלי
כא:יד)

והיה מתכפי מיניה וערק מן קמוי.

אמר רבי יונה: "אַשְׁרֵי נוֹתֵן לְדָּל" אין כתיב כאן, אלא,
"אַשְׁרֵי מַשְׂכִּיל אֶל דָּל... ." (תהלים מא:ב) הדא דמסתכל במצוה היאך
לעשותה.

כיצד היה רבי יונה עושה? כשהיה רואה בן טובים שירד
מנכסיו, היה אומר לו, "בני, בשביל ששמעתי שנפלה לך ירושה ממקום
אחר, טול ואת פורע." מן דהוה נסב ליה, אמר ליה, "מתנה."

אמר רבי חייא בר אדא: איתהוו סבין ביומינו. מאן דהוה
יהב לון מבין ריש שתא לצומא רבא הוו נסבון. מן בתר כן, לא הוו
נסבון. אמרי, "דשותן גבן."

נחמיא איש שיחין פגע ביה ירושלמי אחד. אמר ליה, "זכה
עמי חדא תרנגולתא."

אמר ליה, "הילך טומיתא וזיל זבין קופד." ואכיל ומית.
אמר, "בואו וספדו להרוגו של נחמיא!"

נחום איש גם זו היה מוליך דורון לבית חמא. פגע ביה מוכה
שחין אחד. אמר ליה, "זכה עמי ממה דאית גבך."

אמר ליה, "מי חזר."

חזר ואשכחוניה ומית. והוה אמר לקיבליה, "עייַנוהי דחמונך
ולא יהבון ליך יסתמיין. ידים דלא פשטן למיתן לך יתקטעון. רגליים
דלא רהטן מיתן ליך יתברון." ומטתיה כן.

סליק לגביה רבי עקיבא. אמר ליה, "אי לי שאני רואה אותך
כך."

אמר ליה, "אי לי שאני אין רואה אותך בכך."

אמר ליה, "מה את מקללני?!"

אמר ליה, "ומה את מבעט ביסורין?"

רבי הושעיא רבא, הוה רביה דבריה חד סגיה נהורא, והוה
יליף אכל עימיה בכל יום. חד זמן, הוו ליה אורחין ולא מטא מיכול
עימיה. ברומשא סליק לגביה. אמר ליה, "לא יכעס מרי עלי. בגין
דהוה לי אורחין ולא בעית מבזייה איקרייה דמרי. בגין כן, לא אכלית
עמך יומא דין."

180

אמר ליה, "את פייסת למאן דמתחמי ולא חמי. דין דחמי ולא
מתחמי יקבל פיוסך."

אמר ליה, "מנא לך הא?"

אמר ליה, "מרבי אליעזר בן יעקב, דרבי אליעזר בן יעקב על
חד דסגיה נהורא לביתיה. יתב ליה רבי אליעזר בן יעקב לרע מיניה.
אמרון, 'אילולי דהוא בר נש רבא, לא יתב ליה רבי אליעזר בן יעקב
לרע מיניה.' עבדין ליה פרנסה דאיקר.

"אמר להו, 'מהו הכין?'

"אמרו ליה, 'רבי אליעזר בן יעקב יתיב לרע מינך.'

"וצלי עלוי הדא צלותא, 'אתה גמלת חסד למאן דמתחמי
ולא חמי. דין דחמי ולא מתחמי יקבל פיוסך ויגמול יתך חסד.'"

דלמא: רבי חמא בר חנינא ורבי הושעיא הוון מטיילו באילין
כנישתא דלוד. אמר רבי חמא בר חנינא לרבי הושעיא, "כמה ממון
שיקעו אבותי כאן!"

אמר ליה, "כמה נפשות שקעו אבותיך כאן! לא הוון בני נשא
דילעון באורייתא?"

[One time, when Shmuel was young, his father grew
angry with him, so] Shmuel fled from his father. He went
and stood between two huts of poor people. He heard their
voices saying, "With which tableware should we eat today?
Shall we eat with the gold tableware or with the silver
tableware?"

Shmuel went back and repeated this before his
father.

His father said, "We have to be grateful to the
cheaters among them."[387]

---

[387] The *Talmud* will explain why further on.

An incident occurred where Rabbi Yochanan and Resh Lakish went to bathe in the public baths of Tiberias.[388] A beggar met them on the way who said, "Contribute to me."

They answered, "When we return."

When they returned, they discovered that he had died. They said, "Since we did not contribute to him when he was alive, let us care for him in his death [by preparing him for burial]."

While caring for him, they found a purse of *dinarii* on him. They said, "This is what Rabbi Abahu said in the name of Rabbi Elazar: We have to be grateful to the cheaters among them, for if it were not for the cheaters among them, when a beggar would demand charity from a person and the latter not give it, the donor would immediately be punished."[389]

Abba bar Ba gave his son Shmuel coins to distribute to paupers. He went out and found one pauper eating meat

---

[388] Instead of נימוסין, both the Venice edition of 1523 and *VaYikra Rabbah* 34:10 read דימוסין, which may mean "public" from the Greek "*demos*" (as in "democracy," rule of the public) and thus imply a public bath. Alternatively, the word comes from the Greek word "*thermos*," meaning "hot" and, so, refers to a heated bathhouse. Rabbi Shlomo Sirilio, however, had a text that read דיומסין which he interpreted as deriving from the Aramaic word מיסת, meaning "bath."

[389] Actually, Rabbi Yochanan and Rabbi Shimon ben Lakish would not have quoted Rabbi Abahu who belonged to a later generation than they did. It is the ancient editors of the *Talmud* who drew this conclusion and quoted Rabbi Abahu. (*Maharzu* on *VaYikra Rabbah* 34:10).

and drinking wine. He returned and reported it to his father. He told him, "Give him more because his spirit is bitter." [He apparently is used to fine food and should be maintained according to his custom.]...

Everyone used to speak ill of Rabbi Zachariah, the son-in-law of Rabbi Levi, saying that he did not need charity but took it. When he died, they checked and found that he distributed it to others.

Rabbi Chanina bar Papa used to distribute charity at night.[390] [He would avoid embarrassing the poor by dropping off donations when no one could see.] One time the chief of the demons met him and said, "Has not the rabbi taught, 'Do not encroach upon the boundary of your neighbor...'[391]?" [You have no business being out and about during the night which is the domain of demons.]

He responded, "And is it not also written, 'A gift in secret overturns anger...'[392]?"

The demon recoiled and fled from his presence. [The merit of giving charity rendered the demon powerless.]

Rabbi Yonah said: "Happy is one who gives to the poor" is not written here, but rather, "Happy is one who is

---

[390] In the *Talmud*, the term *"Mitzvah"* without further elaboration always means "charity." (*Mashbiach* citing *Rashi* on B.T. *Shabbath* 156A, sub verba *"Tzidkan B'Mitzvoth"* (צדקן במצות)).

[391] Deuteronomy 19:14.

[392] Proverbs 21:14.

discerning to the poor... ."[393]   This refers to one who scrutinizes the *Mitzvah* to see how best to do it.

How did Rabbi Yonah do it? When he would see a person of wealthy background who lost his property, he would say to him, "My son, because I heard that you are due an inheritance from somewhere, take money now and pay me later." Once the person accepted the money, Rabbi Yonah said, "It's a gift." [Someone from a wealthy background would feel uncomfortable accepting charity, so Rabbi Yonah found a shrewd way of giving it.]

Rabbi Chiya bar Adda said: There were elders in our days to whom one would contribute between *Rosh HaShannah* and the Great Fast [*Yom Kippur*] and they would accept it. After that, they would not accept it, saying, "This is our habit." [They were too proud to accept charity during the rest of the year, but agreed to do so during this time to provide their fellow Jews with the opportunity to increase their merit by giving *Tzedakah*.[394]]

Nechemiah of Shichin met a certain Jerusalemite who said to him, "Contribute me a hen."

"Here is its value in money," he told him. "Go buy beef!"

The pauper did so, ate it and died. Nechemiah said, "Come eulogize the one who was killed by Nechemiah!" [The pauper died because he ate something to which he was

---

[393] Psalms 41:2.
[394] Rabbi Moshe Heinemann שליט"א.

unaccustomed.[395] Rabbi Nechemiah felt responsible since he suggested the change in diet.]

Nachum of Gamzu[396] was transporting a gift to his father-in-law's house when a person afflicted with boils confronted him. He said, "Contribute to me from what you have."

Nachum replied, "When I return."

When he returned, he found that the person had died so he said in the presence of the corpse, "The eyes which saw you but did not give you should be stopped up. The hands which did not stretch forth to give you should be cut off. The legs which did not run to give you should be broken."

This curse came true. Rabbi Akiva went up to Nachum and said, "Woe to me that I see you so!"

He answered, "Woe to me that I do not see you so!"

"Why do you curse me!?!"

"Why do you rebel against hardships?" [If God imposed such torments, they must be accepted and it is improper to cry out against them.]

A certain blind man was the teacher of the son of Rabbi Hoshaya the Great. Every day he would give his lessons and then eat with Rabbi Hoshaya. One time, Rabbi

---

[395] See B.T. *Kethuboth* 67B. In B.T. *Kethuboth* 110B, Shmuel says that changing one's eating habits causes intestinal sickness.

[396] He was known as Nachum of Gamzu (גם זו) because no matter what happened, he always used to say, "This too is for the best." (לטובה גם זו) (B.T. *Ta'anith* 21A). In addition, he came from the town of Gimzo. (*Anaf Yosef* on B.T. *Ta'anith* 21A).

Hoshaya had guests, so he did not call the teacher to eat with him. That evening he visited the teacher and said, "Let my master not be angry with me for I had guests and did not wish to sully my master's honor [to have to sit among them]. Therefore, I did not eat with the master today."

"You placated one who is seen but does not see," answered the teacher. "May the One who sees but is not seen accept your placating." [May God respond favorably to your prayers.]

"Where do you get this idea from?"

"From Rabbi Eliezer ben Yaakov, for an incident took place where a blind person entered the house of Rabbi Eliezer ben Yaakov. Rabbi Eliezer ben Yaakov sat below him. Those present said, 'If he were not a great person, Rabbi Eliezer ben Yaakov would not have sat below him,' so they supported him honorably.

"The blind man said, 'What's all this about?'

"They replied, 'Rabbi Eliezer ben Yaakov sat below you.'

"He recited concerning Rabbi Eliezer ben Yaakov this prayer: 'You bestowed kindness to one who is seen but does not see. The One who sees but is not seen should accept your placating and bestow upon you kindness.'"

It once happened that Rabbi Chama bar Chanina and Rabbi Hoshaya were visiting certain synagogues in Lod. Rabbi Chama bar Chanina remarked to Rabbi Hoshaya, "How much money my ancestors sank here!" [They contributed heavily to building the synagogue.]

Rabbi Hoshaya responded, "How many lives your ancestors sank here! Were there not men who toiled in *Torah*?" [Your ancestors would have done better to support poor *Torah* scholars in their studies than to spend their money building lavish synagogues.]

The Talmud teaches that one should be grateful to dishonest beggars because were it not for them, if a donor did not respond to an honest beggar, God would punish him. Such a proposition might justify delaying a contribution to check the legitimacy of the supplicant, but Rabbi Yochanan and Rabbi Shimon ben Lakish delayed contributing to a poor person merely to go to the bathhouse. How does the fact that some beggars are cheats justify what they did?

In addition, the Talmud teaches that "the diligent go early to do a Mitzvah" (זריזין מדקמין למצות). *Thus, for example, Abraham rose early in the morning to go to sacrifice his son Isaac.*[397] *Similarly, although it is meritorious to recite the Shema early in the morning, one does not lose the Mitzvah of saying it in a timely manner unless he procrastinates until after one quarter of the day has elapsed.*[398] *Why should giving charity be an exception to this rule? Why should one who delays contributing deserve punishment as suggested by this passage?*

---

[397] B.T. *Pesachim* 4A.
[398] *Brachoth* 1:2; *Shulchan Aruch, Orach Chaim* 58:1.

The answer to the above questions lies in the ruling of the Rambam that one should not turn away any beggar empty-handed even if all a person contributes is a dried fig.[399]   *As proof he cites the verse, "Let not a pauper return ashamed... ."*[400]

The Talmud views embarrassment as among the worst things that can befall a person.   Hence, it teaches that "one who publicly shames his or her fellow has no share in the world to come" and is viewed "as though he or she committed bloodshed."   Indeed, it is better for one to cast himself into a fiery furnace than to shame another person publicly.[401]   *Moreover, Rav Chisda taught that since the destruction of the Temple, all gates to Heaven are closed except those of mistreatment, meaning to say that ordinary prayers may not be heard but the complaint of one who is shamefully mistreated is heard.*[402]

The Torah views begging as so humiliating that the ancient rabbis incorporated into the grace after meals the prayer "please do not cause us, Lord out God, to need the gifts of flesh and blood."   When Noah sent out the dove to see if the waters of the Flood had receded, the dove

---

[399]   *Yad HaChazakah, Hilchoth Matanoth Aniyim* 7:7 cited by the *Rama* in *Shulchan Aruch, Yoreh Deah* 249:4.

[400]   Psalms 74:21.

[401]   B.T. *Kethuboth* 67B tells how Mar Ukba and his wife used to give charity to a certain person in a clandestine manner.   When the pauper tried to detect them, they hid inside a large oven where Mar Ukva almost burned his feet.

[402]   B.T. *Baba Metzia* 58B-59A.

returned with an olive branch in its beak. Rashi explains that the dove hinted that it would prefer to eat the bitter leaves of an olive tree obtained through the grace of God than to eat food sweet as honey provided by flesh and blood.[403]

According to Kabbalah, God created the universe because He desired to have an object upon which to lavish kindness. If, however, God merely bestowed kindness outright without any effort on the part of the recipients, they would feel shame. In order to be able to bestow kindness upon humanity in a dignified way, God created the system of commandments so that people can "earn" the right to God's kindness.[404]

In light of the above, it is clear that a poor person who is reduced to begging suffers the greatest pain and humiliation imaginable. In addition, one who disgraces such a person may be viewed as acting contrary to the very purpose of having Torah and Mitzvoth which is to avoid shame. Nonetheless, the shame a person feels when reduced to begging is somewhat alleviated if he or she at least receives something in response. If, however, he gets absolutely nothing, not even a dried fig, he has debased himself for no reason and the potential contributor deserves severe punishment for causing unnecessary humiliation to the beggar. This apparently holds true even

---

[403] *Rashi* on Genesis 8:11 citing B.T. *Eruvin* 18B.
[404] Rabbi Moshe Chaim Luzzatto, *Pithchei Chochmah V'Da'ath*, chapter 1.

when one shames a beggar merely by delaying the contribution. Hence, while delay in the fulfillment of other commandments does not warrant punishment, delay in the giving of charity does.

The above only applies, however, if the beggar is definitely entitled to Tzedakah. Because of the cheaters, a potential contributor can argue that when a beggar approaches him, he is only presented with doubtful case of giving Tzedakah (ספק). Only hesitation in giving Tzedakah to one who is definitely in need (ודאי) warrants punishment. Thus, whether one delays to check out the beggar's claim of poverty or whether one delays merely to go to the bathhouse, he is exempt from Divine retribution because he is not necessarily delaying fulfillment of the Mitzvah of Tzedakah.

This raises another issue which many commentators discuss concerning the above Talmudic passage. If it is legitimate to keep a poor person waiting, why did Nachum of Gamzu view what happened when he kept a beggar waiting as such a terrible sin? Indeed, according to the version of this story in the Babylonian Talmud, Nachum did not tell the beggar that he would give him something upon his return, but merely told him to wait until he had a chance to unload something from his donkey to give him.[405] One wonders what more he could have done. For this reason, some commentators say that the text of the Jerusalem Talmud is preferable and that Nachum Ish

---

[405] B.T. *Ta'anith* 21A.

Gamzu was culpable because he made the poor person wait until he returned from his journey and not merely while he unloaded.[406]   *Another explanation suggests that this pauper suffered from a type of bulimia which would have been evident from his appearance.   Thus, Nachum Ish Gamzu was at fault for taking the time to properly open the bags on his donkey rather than immediately tearing them open to feed him.*[407]

These explanations appear problematic.   For one thing, if the pauper was so desperate, perhaps he would have died even if Rabbi Nachum had rendered assistance immediately.   Furthermore, the Talmud specifically states that Nachum of Gamzu was "accustomed to miracles."[408] *It seems unlikely that a person of his stature would make such mistakes.*

The ancient rabbis taught that, "The Heavenly Court brings about good through those who are worthy and they bring about affliction through those who are corrupt."[409]   *Since something bad occurred through Nachum, albeit in an indirect and unavoidable manner, he took it as a sign of personal deficiency.   Just as Heaven holds the righteous to higher standards than it does*

---

[406] *Etz Yosef* on B.T. *Ta'anith* 21A.

[407] Rabbi Yosef Hayyim, *Ben Yehoyada*, on B.T. *Ta'anith* 21A. The *Mishnah* teaches that bulimia is so dangerous that one must feed someone who suffers from it immediately even with non-Kosher food. (*Yoma* 8:6).

[408] B.T. *Ta'anith* 21A.

[409] *Tanna D'Bei Eliyahu Zuta* 7:2.

ordinary folks, the righteous are very demanding of themselves.[410]

This leads, however, to another question. Why did Rabbi Yochanan and Rabbi Shimon ben Lakish react so differently from Rabbi Nachum? They obviously did not think they had done anything wrong or that the death of the pauper was any kind of ill omen even before they discovered that he was a fraud. The distinction may be that in their case, the beggar asked for a monetary contribution. Even if they had immediately granted his request, he would still have had nothing to eat until he bought food. Moreover, the Talmud does not say or imply that this beggar died of starvation. His death may well have resulted from something unrelated to receiving a contribution. In Rabbi Nachum's case, however, the poor man asked for some of the food Rabbi Nachum was transporting to his father-in-law. Since the connection between the delay to render assistance and the death of the beggar was more direct, Rabbi Nachum viewed the mishap as a sign of Divine displeasure.

---

[410] See *Maharsha* on B.T. *Ta'anith* 21A.

Demai 1:3 (Compare B.T. *Chullin* 7A-B, *Devarim Rabbah* 3:3 and J.T. *Ta'anith* 3:1)

רבי אבא בר זבינא בשם רבי זעירא אמר: אֵין הוון קדמאי בני
מלאכים, אנן בני נש, וְאִין הוון בני נש, אנן חמרין.

אמר רבי מנא: בההיא שעתא אמרין, "אפילו לחמרתיה דרבי
פנחס בן יאיר לא אידמינן.

חמרתיה דרבי פנחס בן יאיר גנבונה לסטיי בליליא. עבדת
טמורה גבן תלתא יומין דלא טעמא כלום. בתר תלתא יומין, איתמלכן
מחזרתה למרה. אמרין, "נישלחנה למרה דלא לימות לגבן ותיסרי
מערתא." אפקונה, אזלת וקמת על תרעת דמרה. שוריית מנהקא.

אמר לון, "פתחין להדא עלובתא דאית לה תלתא יומין דלא
טעימת כלום." פתחין לה ועלת לה.

אמר לון, "יהבון לה כלום למיכל תיכל."

יהבין קומה שערין ולא בעית מיכל. אמרו ליה, "רבי, לא בעית
מיכל."

אמר לון, "מתקנין אינן?"

אמרו ליה, "אין."

אמר לון, "וארימתון דמיין?"

אמרו ליה, "ולא כן אילפן רבי, 'הלוקח לזרע לבהמה...פטור מן
הדמאי'?"

אמר לון, "מה נעביד להדא עלבתא דהיא מחמר על גרמה
סגין?"

וארימון דמיין ואכלת.

תרין מסכינין אפקדון תרין סאין דשערין גבין רבי פנחס בן
יאיר. זרעון וחצדון ואעלון. בָּעין מיסב שעריהון. אמר לון, "אייתון
גמליא וחמריא וסבון שעריכון!"

רבי פנחס בן יאיר אזל לחד אתר. אתון לגביה. אמרו ליה,
"עכבריא אכל עיבורן." גזר עליהון וצמתון, שרון מצפצפין. אמר לון,

"ידעין אתון מה אינון אמרין?"

אמרו ליה, "לא."

אמר לון, "אמרו דלא מתקנה."

אמרו ליה, "עורבן?"

וערבון ולא אנכון.

מרגלי מן דמלכא סרקיא נפלת ובלעת חד עכבר. אתא לגבי
רבי פנחס בן יאיר. אמר ליה, "מה אנא חבר?"

אמר ליה, "לשמך טבא אתית."

גזר עליהון וצמתון. חמא חד מגבע ואתא. אמר, "גבי ההן
ניהו." וגזר עלוי ופלטה.

רבי פנחס בן יאיר אזל לחד אתר. אתון לגביה, אמרו ליה,
"לית מבועןמספק לן."

אמר לון, "דילמא לא אתון מתקנן."

אמרו ליה, "עורבן?"

וערבון ומספק להון.

רבי פנחס בן יאיר הוה אזל לבית וועד. אמר
ליה, "גיניי מה את מנע לי מן בית וועדא?" ופליג קומוי ועבר.

אמרו ליה תלמידיו, "יכלין אנן עברין?"

אמר לון, "מאן דידע בנפשיה דלא אקיל לבר נש מן ישראל מן
יומוי יעבור ולא מנכה."

...רבי אמר ליה, "מישגה רבי למיכל עימי ציבחר בטל יומא
דין?"

אמר ליה, "אין." מי נחית, חמא מולוותא דרבי קיימין. אמר,
"כל אילון יהודאי זנין? אפשר דלא חמי סבר אפוי מן כדון!"

אזלין ואמרון לרבי. שלח רבי, בעי מפייסתיה. מטון בי גבי
קרתי. אמר, "בני קרתי, קורבין לי!" ונחתו בני קרתתיה ואקפון עלוי.
אמר לון, "רבי בעי מפייסתיה." שבקוניה ואזול לון.

אמר, "בני דידי קורבין לי!" נחתת אישתא מן שמיא ואקפת
עלוי.

אזלון ואמרון לרבי. אמר, "הואיל ולא זכינן נישבע מיניה
בעלמא הדין, ניזכי נישבע מיניה בעלמא דאתא."

רבי חגי בשם רבי שמואל בר נחמן: מעשה בחסיד אחד שהיה
חופר בורות שיחין ומערות לעוברים ולשבים. פעם אחת היתה בתו
עוברת לינשא ושטפה נהר והוון כל עמא עללין לגביה. בעיין מנחמתיה
ולא קביל עלוי מתנחמה. עאל רבי פנחס בן יאיר לגביה. בעי מנחמתיה
ולא קביל עלוי מתנחמה.

אמר לון, "דֵין הוא חסידכון?"

אמרו ליה, "רבי כך וכך היה עושה כך וכך אידעין."

אמר, "אפשר שהיה מכבד את בוראו במים והוא מקפחו במים?"

מיד נפל קול הברה בעיר: "באת בתו של אותו האיש!"

אית דאמרי בסיכתא איתערית, ואית דאמרי מלאך ירד בדמות
רבי פנחס בן יאיר והצילה.

Rabbi Abba bar Zevina said in the name of Rabbi Z'eira: If our predecessors were like angels, then we are like people and if they were like people, then we are like donkeys.

Rabbi Manna said: At that time, people said, "We don't even resemble the donkey of Rabbi Pinchas ben Yair."

The donkey of Rabbi Pinchas ben Yair was stolen at night by bandits. It remained hidden with them for three days during which time it tasted nothing. After those three days, the bandits decided to return it to its owner. They said, "Let us return it to its owner so that it will not die with us and create a stench in our cave." When they sent it out, it came and stood before the gate of its master and started to bray.

Rabbi Pinchas ben Yair said to his servants, "Open for this poor creature which has not tasted anything for three days." They opened for her and she entered.

The rabbi said, "Give her something to eat!"

They placed barley before her, but she did not want to eat. The servants said, "Rabbi, she does not want to eat."

"Have the tithes been removed properly?"

"Yes."

"Did you remove the doubtful tithe?"[411]

"Did the rabbi not teach us, 'One who buys grain...for an animal...is exempt from the doubtful tithe.'?" [Since taking the "doubtful tithe" is merely an extra precaution because of the possibility that the seller did not tithe properly, the rabbis did not require it for animal feed.]

"What can we do with this poor creature who is so strict on herself?"

They removed the doubtful tithe and the donkey ate.

Two paupers deposited two measures of barley with Rabbi Pinchas ben Yair. He planted them, harvested what grew from them and stored it. When the paupers sought to take their barley, Rabbi Pinchas ben Yair told them, "Bring camels and donkeys to take your barley [because it produced so much]."[412]

---

[411] In *Talmudic* times, one who purchased grain or produce from someone who might not observe the laws of tithing was required to tithe them himself. The tithe so performed was called "*Demai*" (דמאי), a "doubtful tithe."

[412] In *Devarim Rabbah* 3:3, the *Midrash* says that from the faithfulness of a righteous person such as Rabbi Pinchas ben Yair, one

Rabbi Pinchas ben Yair went to a certain place. The townsfolk came to him and said, "Mice eat our grain." He summoned the mice whereupon they gathered and began to squeak. He asked the townsfolk, "Do you know what they are saying?"

"No" they answered.

"They say that your grain is not tithed [so they are entitled to consume it as punishment]."

"Do you guarantee [that the mice will leave our grain alone if we tithe it]?"

He guaranteed them and afterwards the mice caused no harm.[413]

A jewel belonging to the king of Saracen fell and a mouse ate it. The king came to Rabbi Pinchas ben Yair to retrieve it.

"Am I a sorcerer?"[414] asked the rabbi.

"I came because of your good reputation."

Rabbi Pinchas ben Yair summoned the mice whereupon they gathered. He saw one strutting.[415] He

---

can ascertain the faithfulness of God. Just as the rabbi carefully tended the grain so that its owners enjoyed great bounty, so God, in a manner of speaking, invests and reinvests the merit of a *Mitzvah* so that the person who did it eventually receives a manifold reward. (See *Maharzu* ad. loc.).

[413] This translation is based on *Devarim Rabbah* 3:3, but *P'nei Moshe* says that the townsfolk asked Rabbi Pinchas ben Yair to assume the responsibility to tithe their grain, which he did.

[414] The term "Gueber" (חבר) in the text refers to Zoroastrian priests who practiced magic.

[415] The verb מגבע is not found elsewhere in the *Talmud* or *Midrash*.

said, "It is with that one." He commanded and the mouse spit it out.

Rabbi Pinchas ben Yair visited a certain place. The townsfolk came and said to him, "Our spring does not supply enough water for us."

He said, "Perhaps you do not tithe properly."

"Do you guarantee [that if we tithe we will have enough water]?"

He guaranteed them and afterwards the spring supplied them plentifully.

Rabbi Pinchas ben Yair was going to the study hall. The Ginai River had risen [blocking his way]. He said, "Ginai, why do you hinder me from going to the study hall?" It split before him and he passed through.

His students asked, "Can we also pass through?"

"One who is sure about himself that he never in his life denigrated a Jewish person may pass and not be harmed."

...Rebbi said to Rabbi Pinchas ben Yair, "Would the rabbi see fit[416] to join us eating something choice today?"

He answered, "Yes." When he arrived, he observed Rebbi's mules standing. He said to himself, "Do Jews

_____

P'nei Moshe suggests that it derives from the word גבעה meaning "hill" and suggesting that the mouse raised itself up. The Biblical use of the word מגבעות for the hats which the priests wore in the Temple supports this interpretation since it implies a tall hat which projected from the priest's head. (See, e.g., Exodus 28:40).

[416] According to the Venice edition and *P'nei Moshe* the text should read מישגה instead of מישגה.

support all these? Perhaps he shall not see my face from now on!"417

Some people went and reported this to Rebbi who then sent messengers intending to appease him. When they arrived at his town, Rabbi Pinchas ben Yair said to the townsfolk, "Gather round me!" The townsfolk descended and surrounded him [thus preventing the messengers from approaching him].

The messengers told the townsfolk, "Rebbi wants to appease him," so the townsfolk departed and went their way.

Rabbi Pinchas ben Yair said, "My own sons, gather round me!" Fire descended from Heaven and surrounded him.418

The messengers went and reported all this to Rebbi. He said, "Since we did not merit to behold him in this world, we will merit to behold him in the world to come."

Rabbi Chaggai in the name of Rabbi Shmuel bar Nachman said: There was an incident with a certain pious person who used to dig pits, cisterns and wells for passersby [thus providing a convenience for travelers who

---

417 These mules were of a white species known to be dangerous. (See B.T. *Chullin* 7B). The *Halachah* generally forbids Jews to keep dangerous animals. (See B.T. *Baba Kama* 46A and *Shulchan Aruch, Choshen Mishpat* 409:1.)

418 The principal offspring of a righteous person are his or her good deeds. (*Rashi* on Genesis 6:9). *Torah* is compared to fire (Deuteronomy 33:2), so when Rabbi Pinchas ben Yair called upon his sons to surround him, a Heavenly fire descended.

needed water]. One time, his daughter was traveling to marry when the river flooded [seemingly drowning her] and all the people wailed with him [in sympathy]. They sought to console him, but he would not accept their consolation. Rabbi Pinchas ben Yair visited to console him, but he would not accept consolation.

The rabbi said to the townspeople, "Is this your pious one?" [If he were truly pious, believing in the righteousness of God, he would accept consolation.]

They said, "Rabbi, thus and such he used to do, yet thus and such befell him."

He said, "Is it possible that he used to honor his Creator with water, yet He afflicts him with water?"

At once a clamor arose in the town, "The daughter of that man has come!"

Some say she became tangled on a peg [which saved her from being swept away by the flood]. Others say that an angel descended in the image of Rabbi Pinchas ben Yair and saved her.[419]

There are several opinions regarding the nature of Rabbi Pinchas ben Yair's donkey. Etz Yosef says that it was a donkey like any other, but that God prevented it from

---

[419] When someone is saved in the merit of another, the angel which saves him appears in the image of the person whose merit caused the salvation. (*Ahavath Eithan* on *Ein Yaakov, Ta'anith* 24B, sub verba "*Atha Abuha*" (אתא אבוה)).

eating forbidden foods so as to protect the dignity of Rabbi Pinchas ben Yair.[420]

Rabbi Yosef Hayyim, however, says that the donkey was a reincarnation of Ishmael whose soul required rectification because he had committed theft during his lifetime. This would explain why bandits stole the donkey but it refused to eat their food which was either stolen or not properly tithed. (Not giving the tithes to those to whom they belong is a form of theft.)[421]

Rabbi Shneur Zalman of Liadi expresses a third opinion. Rabbi Pinchas ben Yair's donkey was like the primordial animals of the six days of Creation. Adam rectified the spiritual essence of those animals by giving them their Hebrew names. Hence, this donkey had special spiritual qualities which made it sensitive to the spiritual qualities of the food it consumed so that it rejected food which was stolen or not properly tithed.[422]

---

[420] *Etz Yosef* on *Chullin* 7A-B.

[421] *Ben Yehoyada* on *Chullin* 7A-B. See also *Sefer Likutei HaShas (Likutim MiEtz Chaim)*. This presents a slight problem. Based on the *Talmud* and *Midrash*, *Rashi* explains that Ishmael repented later in life. (*Rashi* on Genesis 25:9) If so, why was this reincarnation necessary? The answer may be that his repentance was incomplete. For example, the *Talmud* teaches that one who repents out of fear of punishment rather than love of the Creator must undergo a further purification process. (B.T. *Yoma* 86A). *Ohr HaChaim* on Numbers 23:10 suggests that the donkey was a reincarnation of Bilaam.

[422] *Likutei Torah, Parshath Nasso*, p. 27A. Also see *Sefer Ta'amei HaMitzvoth, Parshath Ekev*.

Why did Rabbi Pinchas ben Yair state that only someone who had never offended another Jew deserved a miracle such as splitting the Ginai River and passing through?

The Midrash says that when the miracle of the splitting of the Reed Sea occurred, the ministering angels objected that the Jews were unworthy of crossing through safely. Only their prayers and the fact that they would eventually accept the Torah at Mount Sinai caused Israel to merit a safe passage.[423] *The Torah says that when the Jews arrived before Mount Sinai, they"...camped there before the mountain."*[424] *Rashi explains that Israel camped there "as one person with one heart,"*[425] *meaning that one reason they merited receiving the Torah was because the entire nation acted as a single unit. This merit also caused the splitting of the Reed Sea.*

To deserve a miracle similar to the splitting of the Reed Sea, a person must have some connection to the original merit the Jewish people had when that occurred. Just as God performed that miracle due to the merit of the nation as a whole unit, God will perform a similar miracle only for someone who can represent the entire nation. If one has offended another Jew, he or she cannot represent the entire nation and such a miracle cannot occur.

---

[423] *Mechilta, BeShalach 6.*
[424] Exodus 19:2.
[425] *Rashi ad. loc. citing the Mechilta.*

Moreover, the very first word of the Torah, "Breishith" (בראשית), "In the beginning...," hints that God created the universe for the sake of Israel which is called "first" or "beginning."[426] *If one wants to alter the laws of nature which were established at Creation, he or she must have merit related to the purpose of Creation.*

Finally, it is almost impossible not to insult or denigrate another person at some point. The Talmud teaches that practically everyone says something tainted with evil gossip daily.[427] *This means that a person would have to exert superhuman effort to never offend anyone else throughout his or her life, an effort beyond the normal bounds of nature. Measure for measure, such a person merits performance of a miracle which goes beyond the normal bounds of nature.*

According to Kabbalistic tradition, water alludes to kindness (חסד).[428] *It makes sense that someone such as Rabbi Pinchas ben Yair who was so meticulous to act kindly and avoid offending others would merit to have the water of a river split for him.*

Rabbi Pinchas ben Yair's attitude about offending other Jews helps to explain another question this passage raises. The Halachah forbids one to own a vicious dog or

---

[426] *Rashi* on Genesis 1:1.

[427] B.T. *Baba Bathra* 164B-165A. Although people may avoid outright derogatory statements, it is practically impossible to avoid saying something which carries negative implications. See above pp. 94-96 and 109.

[428] See, for example, *Tikunei Zohar* 38A.

other dangerous animal which is liable to cause injury.[429]
*The Talmud says that if a white mule kicks someone, the
wound never completely heals.*[430] *If so, how could Rebbi
keep dangerous white mules? The answer must be that
although such an injury is serious, the mules are not
readily prone to kick. Therefore, Rebbi was permitted to
own white mules unlike vicious dogs which are likely to
bite. Even so, Rabbi Pinchas ben Yair could not tolerate
anything that might offend or injure someone else, even if
the chance of such harm is remote.*

---

[429] B.T. *Baba Kama* 46A and *Shulchan Aruch, Choshen Mishpat*
409:1.
[430] B.T. *Chullin* 7B identifies Rebbi's mules as being of this species.

Kilayim 1:7 (*Breishith Rabbah* 5:9)

...וְאָם כן למה נתקללה הארץ? רבי יודן בר שלו-ם אמר: על
ידי שעברה על גזרותיו של הקדוש ברוך הוא. "...תַּדְשֵׁא הָאָרֶץ דֶּשֶׁא
עֵשֶׂב מַזְרִיעַ זֶרַע [עֵץ פְּרִי עֹשֶׂה פְּרִי]... ". (בראשית א:יא). והיא לא עשתה,
אלא, "וַתּוֹצֵא הָאָרֶץ דֶּשֶׁא עֵשֶׂב מַזְרִיעַ זֶרַע לְמִינֵהוּ [וְעֵץ עֹשֶׂה פְּרִי]... ".
(בראשית א:יב).

רבי פינחס אמר: שמחה בציווייה והוסיפה אילני סרק.

על דעתיה דרבי יודן בר שלו-ם, יפה נתקללה הארץ. על
דעתיה דרבי פינחס, למה נתקללה הארץ? כאיניש דאמר, "ליט ביזא
דכן איינק." ואתיא כיי רבי נתן: שלשה נכנסו לדין וארבעה יצאו
מקוללין.

[God commanded, "Let the Earth cause herbs to
sprout forth, grass which produces seed... ."[431] The *Torah*
then says, "The Earth brought forth herbs, grass which
produces seed according to its kind... ."[432] God only
commanded the Earth to sprout grass which produces seed.
He did not use the phrase "according to its kind." Since the
Torah uses that additional phrase to describe what the Earth
actually did, it implies that the Earth did even more than
what God commanded.]

If so, why was the Earth cursed? [After Adam and
Chavah sinned, God said, "...cursed is the land because of
you... ."[433]]

---

[431] Genesis 1:11.
[432] Genesis 1:12.
[433] Genesis 3:17.

Rabbi Yudan bar Shalom said: Because it transgressed the decrees of the Holy One, Blessed be He. The *Torah* says, "...Let the Earth cause herbs to sprout forth, grass which produces seed, fruit trees which produce fruit...,"[434] but she did not do it. Rather, "The Earth brought forth herbs, grass which produces seed according to its kind and trees which produce fruit... ."[435] [The implication of the first verse is that the Earth should grow only fruitbearing trees since it says "*fruit* trees which produce fruit." In the second verse which describes what actually happened, the *Torah* refers only to "trees which produce fruit," hinting that the Earth grew non-fruitbearing trees as well.[436]]

Rabbi Pinchas [disagreed and] said: [The Earth did not do anything wrong.] It rejoiced in its commandment and added non-fruitbearing trees [which people need for construction and other purposes].

According to the opinion of Rabbi Yudan bar Shalom, the Earth deserved to be cursed, but according to the opinion of Rabbi Pinchas, why was the Earth cursed? As a person who might say, "Cursed is the breast which nursed such a person." [God cursed the Earth from which Adam was formed just as a person might curse the breast which nurtured a wicked person.] This accords with that which Rabbi Nathan said: Three went into judgment, but

---

[434] Genesis 1:11.
[435] Genesis 1:12.
[436] *P'nei Moshe.*

four came out cursed. [*Hashem* judged Adam, Chavah and
the serpent, but also cursed the Earth.]

*When God created the universe, He created
spiritual forces which govern it. As the Midrash explains,
"There is not a single blade of grass below which does not
have a spiritual force in Heaven which stimulates it and
instructs it to grow."*[437] *Hence, when God created the
Earth, He created a spiritual force which governs it. This
spiritual force or "angel" has intelligence and a certain
amount of free will.*[438] *Thus, when the Talmud depicts an
inanimate object such as the Earth speaking or acting, it
refers to the spiritual force which guides that object.*

*According to Rabbi Yudan, Hashem cursed the
Earth because it produced non-fruitbearing trees in
addition to fruit-bearing ones. What did the Earth do that
was so terrible?*

*A classic proof that God exists is that the design of
the universe is so complex and intricate that it could not
have come into being by accident, but only at the behest of
an Intelligent Being. This proposition is so persuasive and
widely accepted that philosophers such as Aristotle as well
as theologians of non-Jewish religions have adopted it.*[439]
*By producing trees which do not bear fruit, however, the
Earth made possible the counter-argument that not*

---

[437] *Breishith Rabbah* 10:6.
[438] *Moreh Nevuchim* Part II, chapter 7.
[439] *Moreh Nevuchim* Part II, chapters 19-20.

everything is perfectly designed. Since some trees bear fruit while others do not, people might argue that this is not the best of all possible worlds and perhaps it came about by chance. Hence, the Earth sinned by producing a situation where some could doubt that God created the universe.[440]

Rabbi Pinchas counters that people will be able to understand that non-fruitbearing trees also play an important role in the world. They yield wood for fuel and for constructing buildings and furniture. Hence the Earth did nothing wrong in and of itself but shared the consequences of Adam and Chavah's sinfulness.

There is another way to view the dispute in this passage. Every human being is composed of two elements: physical and spiritual. The Torah teaches that God created the physical body from the ground. The soul comes from

---

[440] According to some opinions, God commanded the Earth not merely to produce fruit trees, but to produce trees the wood of which tasted like their fruit. (*Rashi* on Genesis 1:11). Rabbi Yaakov Moshe Hellin Ashkenazi explains that the Earth thought it fulfilled this order by producing the citron (אתרג) tree which has this attribute. He suggests that the Tree of Knowledge in the Garden of Eden was a citron tree and Adam and Chavah could not resist the temptation to eat from it because of this unique quality. (See B.T. *Brachoth* 40A for other views about the identity of the Tree of Knowledge). If all trees in the Garden had had this quality, they would not have found the Tree of Knowledge so tempting and could have resisted sinning. Accordingly, the Earth caused Adam and Chavah to sin and so was punished along with them. (*Y'dei Moshe* sub verba "*Samkah Da'atah*" (סמכה דעתה) in *Breishith Rabbah* 5:9).

Heaven, the spiritual realm. The physical body follows its nature, desiring physical pleasures, while the soul longs for spiritual pleasures and closeness to Hashem. Rabbi Yudan holds that if the Earth had strictly complied with God's command, then Adam, who was later formed from the Earth, would have been obedient by nature and would not have disobeyed God. Thus, although the Earth may not have intended any evil, it deserved punishment when Adam and Chavah sinned as the source of their impulse to deviate from God's commands.[441]

Rabbi Pinchas disagrees. The Earth did nothing wrong if in its excitement to perform God's will, it went beyond its duty. To the contrary, such enthusiasm should have given Adam and Chavah a positive outlook towards obeying God. Only because it had the misfortune to be associated with the first humans did the Earth suffer.

---

[441] See *Kli Yakar* on Deuteronomy 29:22 who says that God punishes the Earth when people sin because the Earth is the source of humanity's tendency to sin. See below pp. 249-251.

Kilayim 9:3 (*Bresihith Rabbah* 96:5 and 100:2; B.T. *Shabbath* 114A)

תני בשם רבי נתן: כסות היורדת עם אדם לשאול, היא באה
עמו. מה טעמא? "תִּתְהַפֵּךְ כְּחֹמֶר חוֹתָם וְיִתְיַצְּבוּ כְּמוֹ לְבוּשׁ." (איוב
לח:יד)

אנטולינוס שאל לרבי, "מהו 'תִּתְהַפֵּךְ כְּחֹמֶר חוֹתָם...'?"
אמר ליה, "מי שהוא מביא את הדור הוא מלבישו."
רבי יוחנן מפקד, "מלבשוני בְּוָרִידִיקָא, לא חיוורין ולא אוכמין.
אין קמית ביני צדיקייא, לא נבהת. אין קימת ביני רשיעיא לא נבהת.
רבי יאישה מפקד, "אלבשוני חוורין חפיתין."
אמרין ליה, "ומה את טב מן רבך?"
אמר לון, "ומה אנא בהית בעבדאי?"
רבי ירמיה מפקד, "אלבשוני חוורין חפיתין. אלבשוני בנרסיי.
יהבון מסנא ברגליי וחוטרא בידיי ויהבוני על סיטרא. אין אתא משיחא,
אנא מעתד."

It is learned in the name of Rabbi Nathan: The very clothing which descends with a person to the grave returns with him at the time of resurrection. What is the Scriptural source for this? "The image [of a person] shall transform like clay [at death], but they shall arise as they were clothed."[442]

Antoninus[443] asked Rebbi, "What does it mean, 'The image shall transform like clay... .'[444]?"

---

[442] Job 38:14 according to *Rashi*. The last phrase can also refer to the fact that God will clothe the decomposed corpses with flesh.

[443] This is the name in the Romm Vilna edition of *Ein Yaakov*. The

He answered, "The One who revives the generation at the time of the resurrection, He will dress them." [The same God who miraculously revives the dead will miraculously reconstitute their clothing or provide new clothing.[445]]

Rabbi Yochanan ordered that after his death those caring for him should, "Dress me in turquoise,[446] not white and not black. If I arise among the righteous, I won't be embarrassed and if I arise among the wicked, I won't be embarrassed."

Rabbi Yoshayah ordered that after his death, "Dress me in pressed white garments."

His disciples said to him, "Are you then better than your master [Rabbi Yochanan]?"

He answered, "Am I then ashamed of my deeds?"

Talmud tells many stories about the friendship and mutual respect between Rabbi Yehudah HaNassi and the Roman emperor Antoninus. (B.T. *Sanhedrin* 91A-B and *Avodah Zarah* 10B-11A.) According to some opinions, Antoninus converted to Judaism. (J.T. *Megillah* 1:11).

[444] Job 38:14.

[445] *P'nei Moshe* and *HaKothev.*

[446] There are different opinions as to what בורידיקא means. *Korban HaEidah* on J.T. *Kethuboth* 12:3 says it is brown. *Breishith Rabbah* 96:5 has a version that reads דבריקא which *Matnoth Kehunah* interprets as "the color of lightning" (ברק). However, *Etz Yosef* identifies ורידיקא as *T'cheleth* (תכלת), the same blue-green color used in ancient times for one of the strings in the ritual fringes (ציצית). He cites the *Aruch* that this is a Latin word and, indeed, "*viridis*" (ורידיקא) means "green" in Latin. (Compare the modern English word "verdant.")

Rabbi Yirmiah ordered that after his death those caring for him should, "Dress me in pressed white garments. Dress me according to my custom. Put my shoes on my feet and my staff in my hand and place me on my side. When the Messiah comes, I will be ready."

The Talmud discourages inquiry into the particulars of the coming of the Messiah and the resurrection of the dead. The Rambam states that one cannot know the precise details of how these events will occur until they in fact happen.[447] *Nonetheless, the rabbis wanted their disciples to have a firm faith that such events will eventually take place. By ordering their families and followers to dress them in a certain way for burial because God will reconstitute their clothing when He revives them, they demonstrated their unswerving belief in the resurrection of the dead in a concrete way.*[448]

Surely Rabbi Yoshayah's disciples had a valid point when they asked how he could order that he be dressed in white for his burial when his master, Rabbi Yochanan, did not feel worthy to do so. What did he mean by responding as he did? Yismach Yisrael explains that Rabbi Yochanan was sincerely humble, so it made sense for him to make modest burial arrangements. By contrast, Rabbi Yoshayah did not feel that he possessed the same level of sincere humility and that it would be hypocritical to act as though

---

[447] *Yad HaChazakah, Hilchoth Melachim* 12:2.
[448] *P'nei Moshe.*

he did. Thus, when Rabbi Yoshayah said, "Am I then ashamed of my deeds?" what he meant was that he did not feel the same degree of honest humility about his deeds as Rabbi Yochanan did.[449]

Why was Rabbi Yochanan worried about how he might look if resurrected among the wicked? One would think that if he would be resurrected to be judged among the wicked, he would have a lot more to be concerned about than the state of his apparel! In addition, why assume that the wicked will be clothed in black? Perhaps those who bury them will dress them in white or some other color. In addition, one does not always know who is wicked because an outwardly righteous person may sin privately. Hence, even if a custom existed in Talmudic times to dress the wicked in black, the identity of the wicked might often not be known.

In light of the above, it makes sense to say that perhaps Rabbi Yochanan meant to refer to the Mitzvah of wearing ritual fringes (ציציות) which have a turquoise thread (תכלת).[450]

---

[449] *Yismach Yisrael* on *Parshath VaYechi* as cited in *Beurei HaChassiduth LeShas* by Rabbi Yisrael Yitzchak Chassidah (*Mossad HaRav Kook*, Jerusalem, 1975), pp. 68-69.

[450] The tradition of how to produce the turquoise dye for the ritual fringes has been lost since ancient times. During the 1800's, Rabbi Gershon Henoch Leiner (Poland 1839-1890) wrote several treatises concerning the identity of the sea creature from which the dye should be made and claimed to have discovered a method for producing it. The majority of rabbinical opinion, however, does not agree with his findings. Accordingly, most people continue to wear ritual fringes

Rabbi Yochanan taught that even if a person observes but one law of the Jewish religion, he or she will be saved from Gehinnom.[451] *Rabbi Shlomo Ephraim Lunshitz explains that this is so because the Mishnah guarantees that if an individual performs one Mitzvah, it will cause him to perform another Mitzvah.*[452] *Therefore, when a person fulfills a commandment, he or she has the potential to fulfill all the commandments even if such potential has not yet been realized. In particular, the turquoise (תכלת) thread of the ritual fringes (ציצית) represents this concept because the Torah says, "...and you shall see it and you shall remember all the commandments of the Lord... ."*[453] [454] *Accordingly, Rabbi Yochanan's statement that he be buried in turquoise (תכלת) alludes to the commandment of wearing fringes (ציצית) and he meant that he hoped that by the time he died he would merit to fulfill at least one commandment to perfection.*

In the Babylonian Talmud, Rabbi Chiya bar Yosef used a logical argument to prove that God will resurrect the dead in their clothes: "Just as wheat is buried naked yet emerges with several coverings, how much more so the

---

without the turquoise thread. (Rabbi Aryeh Kaplan, *Tzitzith, A Thread of Light*, (National Conference of Synagogue Youth, New York, 1984), pp. 87-95).

[451] B.T. *Sanhedrin* 111A according to *Kli Yakar* on Numbers 15:38.

[452] *Pirkei Avoth* 4:2.

[453] Numbers 15:39.

[454] *Kli Yakar* on Numbers 15:38.

righteous who are buried with their clothing."[455]
*Certainly not every righteous person has been buried fully
clothed. Rather, as Rabbi Yochanan did, Rabbi Chiya bar
Yosef used clothing as a symbol for the Mitzvoth the
righteous perform which cause them to merit
resurrection.*[456]

*Why did Rabbi Yochanan refer to the turquoise
thread of the ritual fringes in such a roundabout manner?
Surely his family and disciples were familiar with the
Hebrew term for turquoise (תכלת). Why did he choose to
issue his instructions using the Latin word "viridis"
(ורידיקא) rather than simply say what he meant?*[457]

*The answer to these questions requires examination
of a Talmudic passage about the turquoise thread. The
Torah says that the purpose of wearing a turquoise thread
is to remind the wearer of all the commandments.*[458] *Rabbi
Meir said: "How is turquoise (תכלת) different from any
other type of color? Because turquoise resembles the color*

---

[455] B.T. *Kethuboth* 111B.

[456] See *Maharal* on B.T. *Kethuboth* 111B who states that the clothing
Rabbi Chiya bar Yosef referred to is of a spiritual nature.

[457] Although the rabbis frequently use foreign words in the *Talmud*
and *Midrash*, they do not normally use them to denote religious articles.
This usage is the equivalent of a rabbi referring to "the black boxes"
instead of saying "*Tefillin.*" In addition, a translation of *Techeleth*
(תכלת) into any other language is inexact and confusing since the word
specifically refers to the color produced by a dye extracted from a
particular species of sea creature, whereas "green," "turquoise" and
"*viridis*" are more general terms.

[458] Numbers 15:39.

of the sea and the color of the sea resembles the color of the sky and the color of sky resembles the color of the Throne of Glory. "[459] *Why does Rabbi Meir describe the special quality of turquoise in such an oblique manner? Why not simply say that turquoise resembles the color of the Throne of Glory? Why mention the sea and the sky?*[460] *The answer is that the true reasons for God's commandments are unknown to humans. Rather, Mitzvoth affect spiritual realms which the human mind can neither perceive nor understand. By describing the symbolism of turquoise in an oblique manner, Rabbi Meir hinted that the spiritual effect of Mitzvoth are indirect and not readily appreciated by humans. This is why the word for turquoise (תכלת) in Hebrew is virtually identical to the word for "purpose" (תכלית). One who gazes at the turquoise thread in the ritual fringes remembers that the true benefit of the Mitzvoth is not directly observable and that their ultimate purpose is a spiritual one.*

This explains why Rabbi Yochanan chose an indirect way of referring to the Mitzvah of wearing turquoise (תכלת) in the ritual fringes. Like Rabbi Meir, he wished to express the underlying idea of this Mitzvah which is to engender a commitment to observe all the other

---

[459] B.T. *Sotah* 17A.
[460] A version of this homily in *BaMidbar Rabbah* 14:3 stretches the series of reminders even further. Turquoise reminds one of grass which reminds one of the sea which reminds one of the sky which reminds one of the colors of the rainbow which reminds one of the Cloud of Glory which reminds one of the Throne of Glory.

Mitzvoth by reminding Jews that even if a Mitzvah does not appear to accomplish anything in the physical world, it accomplishes a great deal in the spiritual realm.

Kilayim 9:3 (B.T. *Kethuboth* 104A; *Breishith Rabbah* 33:3; J.T. *Kethuboth* 12:3)

צפריא אמרין, "מאן דאמר לן, 'רבי דמך,' אנן קטלינן ליה."
אדיק לון בר קפרא. רישיה מכסי. מאנוי מבזעין. אמר לון,
"מצוקים ואראלים תפוסין בלוחות הברית וגברה ידן של אראלים וחטפו
את הלוחות."
אמרין ליה, "דמך רבי?"
אמר לון, "אתון אמריתון." וקרעון. ואזל קלא דקרעון לגו
פפתה, מהלך תלתא מילין.
רבי נחמן בשם רבי מנא: מעשה ניסין נעשו באותו היום. ערב
שבת היתה ונתכנסו כל העיירות להספידו. ואשידרוניה תמני עשרה
כנישן ואחתוניה לבית שריי. ותלה לון יומא עד שהיה כל אחד ואחד
מגיע לביתו וממלא לו חבית של מים ומדליק לו את הנר. כיון ששקעה
החמה, קרא הגבר. שרון מציקין, אמרין, "דילמא דחללינן שבתא."
יצתה בת קול ואמרה להן, "כל מי שלא נתעצל בהספדו של רבי יהא
מבושר לחיי העולם הבא בר מן קצרא." כיון דשמע כן, סליק ליה
לאיגרא וטלק גרמיה ומית. נפק בת קלא ואמרה, "ואפילו קצרא."

The people of Sepphoris said, "Whoever says, 'Rebbi died,' we will kill him." [They said this when Rebbi lay on his deathbed. Although they knew what was about to happen, they loved him so much that they could not bear to hear someone actually utter the bad news.]

Bar Kappara appeared to them with his head covered and his clothing torn [as in mourning]. He said, "Mortals and angels took hold of the Tablets of the Covenant. The hand of the angels conquered and they snatched the Tablets."

They said to him, "Has Rebbi died?"

"You uttered it."

They tore their clothing and the sound of the ripping reached Papatha, a distance of three [*Talmudic*] miles [which equals about three kilometers].[461]

Rabbi Nachman said in the name of Rabbi Manna: Miraculous events took place that day. It was the eve of the Sabbath and all the townsfolk gathered to eulogize Rebbi. The procession made eighteen stops to praise him and brought him down to Beth She'arim for burial. Daylight lingered for them until each and every one reached his home, filled a barrel with water and lit a lamp [in preparation for the Sabbath]. When the sun set, the rooster crowed [indicating that it was already very late[462]]. Everyone began to worry, thinking, "Perhaps we have desecrated the Sabbath." A Heavenly voice emerged and said to them, "Whoever was not lazy about attending the eulogy of Rebbi is destined for life in the World to Come except for a laundryman [who usually visited Rebbi but failed to attend his funeral.[463]]" When he heard this, he ascended the roof, threw himself down and died. A Heavenly voice emerged and said, "And even the laundryman."

---

[461] See footnote 636 below about calculating the length of *Talmudic* miles.

[462] *Etz Yosef* says that the crowing of the rooster showed that it was midnight, but perhaps the *Talmud* simply refers to the crowing which roosters (and most other birds) make when they roost at sundown.

[463] *P'nei Moshe.*

*The Torah forbids suicide which it views as a form of murder[464] and it is widely accepted that one who commits suicide has no share in the world to come.[465] Accordingly, none of the rituals Jews ordinarily perform to honor the dead may be performed for such a person.[466] How, then, could a Heavenly voice assure the laundryman who committed suicide a share in the world to come? The answer appears to be that only **willful** suicide warrants losing one's share in the world to come. If one commits suicide due to insanity, he or she does not forfeit life in the hereafter.[467] The laundryman apparently suffered a kind of insanity, being unduly distraught at not having participated in Rebbi's funeral. Hence, he did not lose his share in the future world.*

---

[464] *Shulchan Aruch, Choshen Mishpat* 420:31 forbids harming oneself.

[465] *Tifereth Yisrael* on *Sanhedrin* 10:2 in note 12 states that he does not know the source for this but hypothesizes that whereas other sinners may repent, one who commits suicide cannot do so because his or her last act is a violation of *Torah* law.

[466] *Shulchan Aruch, Yoreh Deah* 345:1.

[467] *Aruch HaShulchan, Yoreh Deah* 345:4-5.

Kilayim 9:3 (B.T. *Baba Metzia* 85A; *Breishith Rabbah* 33:3; J.T. *Kethuboth* 12:3)

רבי הוה יתיב ליה בציפורין שבע עשרה שנין וקרא על גרמיה,
"וַיְחִי יַעֲקֹב בְּאֶרֶץ מִצְרַיִם שְׁבַע עֶשְׂרֵה שָׁנָה..." (בראשית מז:כח). ויחי
יהודה בציפורין שבע עשרה שנה. ומן גובעין, עבד תלת עשרה שנין
חשש בשינוי. אמר רבי יוסי בי רבי בון: כל אותן שלש עשרה שנה לא
מתה חיה בארץ ישראל ולא הפילה עוברה בארץ ישראל.
ולמה חש שינוי? חד זמן, עבר, חמא חד עיגל מנכס, געה ואמר
ליה, "רבי, שיזבי!" אמר ליה, "לכך נוצרת."
ובסופה איך אינשמת? חמתון קטלין חד קן דעכברין. אמר,
"ארפונון! [טוב ה' לַכֹּל] וְרַחֲמָיו עַל כָּל מַעֲשָׂיו (תהלים קמה:ט) כתיב."
רבי הוה ענוון סגין והוה אמר, "כל מה דיימר לי בר נשא אנא
עביד חוץ ממה שעשו זקני בתירה לזקני, דשרון גרמון מנשיאותיה
ומנוניה. אין סליק רב הונא ריש גלותא להכא, אנא מותיב ליה לעיל
מיניי, דהוא מן יהודה ואנא מבנימין, דהוא מן דכריא ואנא מן נוקבתא."
חד זמן, אעל רבי חייא רובה לגביה. אמר ליה, "הא רב הונא
לברי!" נתכרכמו פניו של רבי. אמר ליה, "ארונו בא."
אמר ליה, "פוק וחמי מאן בעי לך לברי!" ונפק ולא אשכח בר
נש וידע דהוא כעיס עלוי. עבד דלא עליל לגביה תלתין יומין. אמר
רבי יוסי בר בון, "כל אינון תלתין יומין יליף רב מיניה כללא דאורייתא."

Rebbi lived in Sepphoris for seventeen years. He applied to himself the verse, "Jacob lived in the land of Egypt seventeen years... ,"[468] saying, "And Yehudah lived

---

468 Genesis 47:28. After being displaced from the chamber it occupied in the Temple, the *Sanhedrin* moved together with Rebbi to Beth She'arim, Sepphoris and Tiberias. When he became ill, they

in Sepphoris for seventeen years."[469]   Out of these, he
spent thirteen years pained by his teeth. Rabbi Yossi son of
Rabbi Bon said: All those thirteen years no woman giving
birth died throughout the Land of Israel and no pregnant
woman miscarried throughout the Land of Israel.[470]

And why did his teeth pain him? One time as he
was walking, he saw a calf being led to slaughter which
lowed as if to say, "Rebbi, save me!" He remarked, "For
this you were created." [He was punished because of his
insensitivity to the calf's plight.]

In the end how was he cured? He observed people
killing a nest of mice. He said, "Leave them alone! It is
written, 'The Lord is good to all and His mercy is upon all
His creatures.'[471]"

Rebbi was exceedingly humble. He used to say,
"Whatever a person would tell me to do, I would do, except

---

returned him to Sepphoris which had a better climate. (*Rashi* on B.T.
Rosh HaShannah 31B sub verba *"U'MiYavneh L'Usha"*
(ומיבנה לאושא)). He made this statement right before he died, just as
the *Torah* says before Jacob died that he lived seventeen years in Egypt
after moving from the Land of Israel. (*Etz Yosef*).

[469] Rebbi's proper name was Yehudah.

[470] *HaKothev* says that Rebbi's cries of pain from his dental problems
might have disturbed such women, causing death or miscarriage. Not
only did God miraculously prevent this from happening, but He also
prevented all pregnancy-related mishaps so that no one would
erroneously attribute them to Rebbi. *Etz Yosef*, however, says that
Rebbi's suffering protected that generation from many hardships. The
Talmud mentions the benefits to pregnant women by way of illustration.

[471] Psalms 145:9.

what the elders of Batheira did for my ancestor by discharging themselves from the presidency and appointing him." [The Batheira family had served as heads of the *Sanhedrin* but gave up their position in favor of Rebbi's ancestor, Hillel.[472]] "If Rabbi Huna the Exilarch would come up here [from Babylon], I would seat him above me, for he is from the tribe of Judah while I am from the tribe of Benjamin and he is descended from a male line while I am descended from a female line." [The *Torah* decreed that the ruler of the Jewish people should descend from Judah[473] and a person's tribal affiliation is determined through his or her father's lineage.[474] Since Rebbi descended from Judah only on his mother's side, Rabbi Huna had a better claim to the presidency of the *Sanhedrin* than he did.]

One time Rabbi Chiya the Great visited Rebbi. He declared, "Rabbi Huna is outside!" Rebbi's face turned pale [for he thought he would have to fulfill his promise]. "His coffin has arrived," continued Rabbi Chiya.

"Go see who wants you outside!" answered Rebbi.

Rabbi Chiya went outside. When he found no one, he knew that Rebbi was angry with him. He did not visit him for thirty days.[475] Rabbi Yossi bar Bon said: All

---

[472] B.T. *Pesachim* 66A and *Baba Metzia* 85A.

[473] Genesis 49:10.

[474] Numbers 1:2 with commentary of *Rashi*; B.T. *Baba Bathra* 109B.

[475] Ordinarily, one who offended a scholar suffered excommunication for thirty days. (B.T. *Mo'ed Katan* 16A-B).

those thirty days Rav studied the principles of the *Torah* from him.[476]

Rabbi Yehudah HaNassi and the Batheira family had two divergent views on how to select leaders for the Jewish community. The actions of the Batheira family were very noble. When they discovered that Hillel's level of learning surpassed theirs, they stepped down and appointed him head of the Sanhedrin because they held that a leader must be selected according to personal merit, not ancestry. Indeed, there is even an opinion in the Talmud which suggests that there is an advantage to choosing a leader who has questionable lineage because such a person can be reminded of his humble origins if he behaves arrogantly.[477] This may explain why King David's reign succeeded. People could and did remind him that his grandmother Ruth was a Moabitess.[478]

Although it seems logical to select as a leader the person who has the greatest ability, the Halachah follows the opinion of Rabbi Yehudah HaNassi. Thus, the Talmud records that although Rabbi Akiva had seniority and was probably the most talented person available to become president of the Sanhedrin, the sages chose young Rabbi Elazar ben Azariah instead because his lineage went back

---

476 Rav was the nephew of Rabbi Chiya. (*Etz Yosef*).

477 B.T. *Yoma* 22B.

478 B.T. *Yevamoth* 76B-77A.

to Ezra.[479] *Moreover, the Rambam rules that every leadership position in the Jewish community should pass from father to son provided that the son has sufficient wisdom and fear of Heaven to properly carry out the duties of the position.[480] Additionally, the Talmud states that it is forbidden to appoint a leader over the community without first consulting its members.[481] Accordingly, rather than installing the wisest or most talented leaders, the community must select leaders with good lineage and popular support.*

On a practical level, appointing a leader whose ancestors were leaders and who is approved by the community helps promote harmony. Determining who is the best person to fill a position can be tricky, especially when several talented people are available. Rather than get into nasty political fights which can damage the community, it is preferable to install the son of the former leader if that person has sufficient ability to serve.[482] In addition, choosing a leader who has popular approval assures public support and cooperation so that he will be able to govern successfully. Such considerations outweigh any advantage of selecting a more talented person.

---

[479] B.T. *Brachoth* 27B-28A.

[480] *Yad HaChazakah, Hilchoth Melachim* 1:7.

[481] B.T. *Brachoth* 55A.

[482] Along similar lines, the *Talmud* teaches that a priest (כהן) should not relinquish his right to be called up first to read the *Torah* because that would lead to squabbles among the congregants about who should receive that honor. (B.T. *Gittin* 59B).

Spiritually, there is also an advantage to the Halachic method for choosing a leader. The Mishnah teaches that those who toil for the community should do so for the sake of Heaven for the merit of the ancestors of the Jewish people stands eternally by them.[483] In other words, the skill of the leaders is of no actual importance because they are mere tools through whom God acts to guide His people. That being the case, someone who has more meritorious lineage is preferable since his ancestry gives him merit to succeed in his public mission. Furthermore, the merit of a community far exceeds that of a lone individual.[484] Accordingly, when a Jewish leader has popular approval, the merit of the community aids him.

---

[483] *Pirkei Avoth* 2:2.
[484] See, e.g., B.T. *Avodah Zarah* 4B.

Kilayim 9:3 (*Breishith Rabbah* 33:3; B.T. *Baba Metzia* 85B; *Koheleth Rabbah* 9:10; J.T. *Kethuboth* 12:3)

לסוף תלת עשרתי שניא ותלתתוי יומיא, עאל אליהו לגביה
בדמות רבי חייא רובה. אמר ליה, "מה מרי עביד?"

אמר ליה, "חד שיניי מעיקא לי."

אמר ליה, "חמי לה לי."

וחמי לה ליה ויהב אצבעתיה עלה ואינשמת.

למחר, עאל רבי חייא רובה לגביה. אמר ליה, "מה עביד רבי?
האי שינך מה היא עבידה?"

אמר ליה, "מן ההיא שעתא דיהבת אצבעתך עלה, אינשמת."
באותה שעה אמר, "אי לכם חיות שבארץ ישראל! אי לכם
עוברות שבארץ ישראל!" אמר ליה, "אנא לא הוינא."

מן ההיא שעתא הוה נהיג ביה ביקר. כד הוה עליל לבית וועדא
הוה אמר, "יכנס רבי חייא רובה לפנים."

אמר לו רבי ישמעאל בי רבי יוסי, "לפנים ממני?"

אמר לו, "חס ושלו-ם. אלא, רבי חייא רובא לפנים ורבי
ישמעאל בי רבי יוסי לפני לפנים."

רבי הוה מתני שבחיה דרבי חייא רובה קומי רבי ישמעאל בי
רבי יוסי. חד זמן, חמי גו בני ולא איתכנע מן קומי.

אמר ליה, "אהנו דאת מתני שבחיה?"

אמר ליה, "מה עבד לך?"

אמר ליה, "חמתי גו בני ולא איתכנע מן קומי."

אמר ליה, "למה עבדת כן?"

אמר ליה, "ייעול עלי דאין סחית, לא ידעית. בההיא שעתא
אשגרית עינייי בכל ספר תילים אגדה."

מן ההיא שעתא, מסר ליה שני תלמידין דיהלכון עימיה בגין
סכנתא.

רבי יוסי צם תמניי יומין למיחמי רבי חייא רובה ולסופא חמא

ורגזן ידיה וכהו עינוי. ואין תימר דהוה רבי יוסה בר נש זעיר, חד גרדיי
אתא לגבי דרבי יוחנן. אמר ליה, "חמית בחילמי דרקיעא נפל וחד מן
תלמידך סמך ליה."

אמר ליה, "וחכים את ליה?"

אמר ליה, "אין אנא חמי ליה, אנא חכים ליה."

עבר כל תלמידוי קומוי וחכים לרבי יוסה.

רבי שמעון בן לקיש צם תלת מאוון צומין למיחמי רבי חייא
רובה ולא חמתיה. ובסופא שרא מצטער. אמר, "מה הוה לעי באוריתא
סגין מינייי?"

אמרו ליה, "דיבץ תורה בישראל יותר ממך, ולא עוד, אלא
דהוה גלי."

אמר לון, "ולא הוינא גליי?"

אמרין ליה, "את הוית גלי מילף והוא הוה גלי מלפה."

At the end of thirteen years [of Rebbi's sickness described above] and thirty days [that Rabbi Chiya did not visit him], Elijah visited Rebbi in the form of Rabbi Chiya the Great. He said to him, "How is my master doing?"

"One tooth hurts me," he answered.

"Show it to me."

He showed it to Elijah who touched it with his finger and healed it.

The next day, Rabbi Chiya the Great visited Rebbi. He asked him, "How is Rebbi doing? How is your tooth doing?"

He responded, "From the very time you touched your finger to it, it is healed."

At that moment Rabbi Chiya said, "Woe unto you childbearing women of the Land of Israel! Woe unto you pregnant women of the Land of Israel!" [Rebbi's suffering which protected them was gone.] He continued, "I was not here."

From that time, Rebbi treated Rabbi Chiya with special respect [since he realized that Elijah had appeared in his image].[485] When the latter entered the study hall, he said, "Let Rabbi Chiya the Great enter within."

Said Rabbi Yishmael, son of Rabbi Yossi, to him, "Further inside than me?"

"God forbid! Rather, Rabbi Chiya the Great should go inside and Rabbi Yishmael, son of Rabbi Yossi, should be innermost."

Rebbi used to recount the praises of Rabbi Chiya the Great in front of Rabbi Yishmael, son of Rabbi Yossi. One time, Rabbi Yishmael, son of Rabbi Yossi, observed Rabbi Chiya inside the bathhouse, but the latter did not acknowledge him [by rising before him].[486]

Said Rabbi Yishmael, son of Rabbi Yossi, to Rebbi, "Is this the one whose praises you recount?"

"What did he do to you?"

---

[485] When someone is saved in the merit of another, the angel which saves him appears in the image of the person whose merit caused the salvation. (*Ahavath Eithan* on *Ein Yaakov*, *Ta'anith* 24B, sub verba "*Atha Abuha*" (אתא אבוה)).

[486] They were in the vestibule of the bathhouse where people are clothed and it is appropriate to acknowledge others respectfully. (*P'nei Moshe*).

"He saw me inside the bathhouse but did not acknowledge me."

When Rebbi met Rabbi Chiya, he asked him, "Why did you do so?"

"May evil befall me [if I was aware of it]! If I bathed, I do not recall because at that time I was focusing my attention on the *Aggadoth* of the entire Book of Psalms."

From that time, Rebbi provided Rabbi Chiya with two disciples who escorted him because of the danger [that might befall him due to his tendency not to focus on his surroundings when engrossed in *Torah* study].

Rabbi Yossi fasted for eighty days to merit seeing Rabbi Chiya the Great [in a vision after the latter died]. In the end, after he saw him, his hands trembled and his eyes became weak. If you will say that this occurred because Rabbi Yossi was a person of minor standing, it is not so. One weaver came before Rabbi Yochanan and said to him, "I saw in a dream that the sky fell and one of your disciples supported it."

"Do you know him?" asked Rabbi Yochanan.

"If I saw him, I would know him."

All Rabbi Yochanan's disciples filed by him and he recognized Rabbi Yossi.

Rabbi Shimon ben Lakish fasted three hundred fasts to see Rabbi Chiya the Great, yet he did not see him. In the end, he became upset and said, "Did he toil in *Torah* more than me?"

Others said to him, "He spread *Torah* in Israel more than you and not only that, but he exiled himself to do so."

"Did I not go into exile?"

"You exiled yourself to learn, but he exiled himself to teach."

The Babylonian Talmud says that Rabbi Chiya occupies a place in the Heavenly Academy so exalted that one who tries to view it may suffer injury. Moreover, had he and his sons prayed together under the proper conditions, the Messiah would have come. All this greatness resulted from Rabbi Chiya traveling to a village that had no teachers and teaching each of five boys one of the volumes of the Chumash and each of six boys one of the orders of the Mishnah. He then instructed them to teach each other what they had learned.[487]

Certainly Rabbi Chiya's work of disseminating the Torah was admirable, but what made it so outstanding that he was considered greater than so many other sages? There are many rabbis whose students numbered far more than a mere eleven boys. Rabbi Akiva, for example, had twelve thousand pairs of students.[488] *In addition, the Talmud refers to the academy established in Yavneh as a vineyard (כרם ביבנה) because of the rows upon rows of*

---

[487] B.T. *Baba Metzia* 85B.

[488] B.T. *Yevamoth* 62B. According to some accounts, it was twice that number.

scholars who studied there.[489] Moreover, one would assume that the accomplishments of the highly advanced disciples of the rabbis of the Talmud would far outshine those of eleven anonymous boys.

One can surmise the secret of Rabbi Chiya's greatness from the Talmud's description of how he prepared to teach the boys. First he planted flax which he later harvested and wove into nets that he used to trap deer. He slaughtered the deer and gave the meat to poor orphans. He then processed the deer hides into parchment upon which he wrote out the five books of the Torah.[490] Rabbi Chiya's purpose in going to so much trouble was to make sure that this Torah study would be completely for the sake of Heaven, untainted by any personal motives both on his part and on the part of his students. That is why Rabbi Chiya chose untutored youngsters as his pupils. Certainly Rabbi Chiya was qualified to teach the most advanced intellectuals of his time. Such scholarship would have yielded great prestige as those men spread his teachings, but it was just such prestige that he sought to avoid. In addition, such advanced scholars might pursue their studies, at least in part, to gain recognition and possibly as a vehicle to earn a livelihood. Young boys would hardly expect widespread honor for their learning and do not

---

[489] J.T. *Brachoth* 4:1. The *Talmud* there and in B.T. *Brachoth* 28A tells how hundreds of benches had to be added to the academy when Rabbi Elazar ben Azariah was appointed president of the *Sanhedrin*.
[490] B.T. *Baba Metzia* 85B and *Kethuboth* 103B.

typically study with a career in mind. Accordingly, Rabbi Chiya chose them because he wanted both teacher and student to learn Torah purely for its own sake.

For the same reason, Rabbi Chiya specifically chose to teach in a village which had no instructor.[491] *Even in ancient times, just about every Jewish town and village had some kind of school or teacher for its youth.*[492] *In fact, the rabbis placed a ban on any village which did not provide a teacher for its children.*[493] *Only a village where the people had absolutely no respect for Torah study would lack a teacher. Accordingly, neither Rabbi Chiya nor his young pupils could expect to gain recognition for their studies.*

In sharp contrast, Rabbi Shimon ben Lakish specifically exiled himself to a place where there was more Torah learning. Certainly one who is willing to leave family and friends to travel to unfamiliar surroundings for the sake of Torah learning deserves great reward. However, that does not compare to one who enters a hostile environment to establish Torah learning.

There is a famous story that one year, when it was very difficult to obtain a set of the Four Species needed for Sukkoth, the community of Vilna sent out emissaries to acquire such a set for the Vilna Gaon. After much effort,

---

[491] *Rashi* on B.T. *Baba Metzia* 85B sub verba *"VeSalikna LeMatha"* (וסליקנא למתא) says that there were no teachers there.
[492] B.T. *Baba Bathra* 21A.
[493] B.T. *Shabbath* 119B. Some hold that such villages must be destroyed. See *Shulchan Aruch, Yoreh Deah* 245:7.

the emissaries located a set of the Four Species, but the individual who owned them refused to sell them for any price. When he discovered that the buyers sought them for the Vilna Gaon, he agreed to the sale but only on condition that any reward the great rabbi might receive for performing the Mitzvah would belong to him. The emissaries were stunned by this request, but having little choice, they agreed. When they brought the Four Species to the Vilna Gaon they were surprised to find that he reacted with delight.

"All my life I have strived to perform a Mitzvah completely for the sake of Heaven," explained the Vilna Gaon. "Now that I know that the reward for this Mitzvah will not be mine, I shall at last have an opportunity to achieve this goal."

The Vilna Gaon is among the very greatest leaders, if not the greatest leader, of the Jewish people during the past several hundred years. Legends abound concerning his vast erudition as well as his devotion and self-sacrifice for Torah study, yet he believed that he had not reached the pinnacle of success in serving Hashem until this episode took place. Surely this illustrates the great importance of performing Mitzvoth for the sake of Heaven. Such was the greatness of Rabbi Chiya. He achieved ultimate perfection in learning Torah solely for its own sake, untainted by any personal motives.

Kilayim 9:3 (B.T. *Mo'ed Katan* 25A; *Koheleth Rabbah* 9:10; J.T. *Kethuboth* 12:3)

כד דמך רב הונא ריש גלותא, אסקוניה להכא. אמרי, "אן אנן
יהבין ליה?"

אמרין, "נייתיניה גבי רבי חייא רובא דהוא מן דידהון." אמרין,
"מאן בעי מיהב ליה?"

אמר רבי חגיי, "אנא עליל יהיב ליה."

אמרו ליה, "עילתך את בעי דאת גבר סב ואת בעי מיעול מיתב
לך תמן."

אמר לון, "יהבון משיחתא ברגליי ואין עניית, אתון גרשין.

עאל ואשכח תלת דָנֵין: יהודה בני אחריך ואין עוד. חזקיה בני
אחריך ואין עוד. אחריך יוסף בן ישראל ואין עוד.

תלת עינוי מסתכלה. אית אמר ליה, "אָפִיךְ אַפֵּיךְ!"

שמע קליה דרבי חייא רובא אמר לרב יהודה בריה, "נפיש לרב
הונא יתיב ליה!"

ולא קביל עלוי מתיב ליה. אמרין, "כמה דלא קביל עלוי מתיב
ליה, כן זרעיתיה לא פסקה לעולם."

ויצא משם והיה בן שמונים שנה ונכפלו לו שניו.

When Rabbi Huna the Exilarch died, they brought him up here [to the Land of Israel]. They said, "Where shall we bury him?"

They answered, "Let us place him next to Rabbi Chiya the Great since he is one of theirs [i.e., a fellow Babylonian]. Who wants to put him there?"

Rabbi Chaggai said, "I will enter and put him there."

"You seek a pretext to go since you are an old man and wish to enter and be buried there."

"Tie a rope around my legs so that if I am detained you can pull me out."

He entered and found these three [being praised]:[494] Yehudah my son, after you there is no other as great. Chizkiah my son, after you there is no other as great. After you, Joseph son of Israel, there is no other as great. [Rabbi Chiya's two sons, Yehudah and Chizkiah, were buried with him.]

Rabbi Chaggai lifted his eyes to look, but Rabbi Chiya said, "Turn your face!"

He heard the voice of Rabbi Chiya the Great say to Rabbi Yehudah, his son, "Make room for Rabbi Huna to settle himself!"

---

[494] The word דנין appears to mean "these," being the plural of דין, "this." *P'nei Moshe*, however, suggests that the word means "discussing," from דן, meaning "to judge." Thus, the three righteous men were being "discussed" in a laudatory manner, presumably by a Heavenly voice (בת קול). Alternatively, he says that the word should be רנין, from the word רינה meaning "song," indicating that praises were being sung about these three people. *Korban HaEidah* on J.T. *Kethuboth* 12:3 says that perhaps Rabbi Chiya and his sons were "considering" (דנין) whether to permit Rabbi Huna to be buried with them. Alternatively, he suggests that the text should read ארונין, meaning that Rabbi Chaggai entered and found three coffins. *Ben Yehoyada* on B.T. *Baba Metzia* 85B, however, suggests that Rabbi Chaggai did not hear anything, but found three inscriptions in the cave. The text in B.T. *Mo'ed Katan* 25A has "גני," meaning "sleeping," i.e., the three were lying in repose.

Rabbi Huna, however, did not agree to settle himself [by taking space from Rabbi Chiya's son].[495] They said in Heaven, "Just as he did not agree to settle himself [between Rabbi Chiya and his sons], so his progeny shall not cease forever."[496]

When Rabbi Chaggai emerged from there, he was eighty years old and his years were doubled [in the merit of having helped bury Rabbi Huna].

Why does the Talmud mention Joseph when it discusses the burial arrangements of Rabbi Chiya and his sons? Rabbi David Fraenkel points out that the Babylonian Talmud reckons Rabbi Chiya and his sons to be as great as Abraham, Isaac and Jacob.[497] Since Joseph followed the latter in greatness, he is mentioned here.[498]

Rabbi Yosef Hayyim, however, suggests that Rabbi Chiya and Joseph had similar spiritual qualities.[499] This

---

[495] *P'nei Moshe.*

[496] Just as Rabbi Huna did not intrude upon the relationship between Rabbi Chiya and his sons, so measure for measure, God allowed nothing to interrupt the line of his descendents. (*Korban HaEidah* on J.T. *Kethuboth* 12:3) Rabbi Chaim Vital teaches that a father transmits part of his soul to his sons. (*Sha'ar HaGilgulim, Hakdamah* 10). This may explain the importance of not interfering in their relationship.

[497] B.T. *Baba Metzia* 85B.

[498] *Korban HaEidah* on J.T. *Kethuboth* 12:3 sub verba "*Achareicha Yosef*" (אחריך יוסף).

[499] *Ben Yehoyada* on B.T. *Baba Metzia* 85B. Based on the writings of the *Arizal*, he suggests, alternatively, that Rav Hamnuna Sabba was buried in the same cave and that the reference to Joseph really alludes

makes sense because the Talmud stated earlier that Rabbi Chiya was greater than Rabbi Shimon ben Lakish in that he exiled himself to teach Torah rather than merely to learn it. Joseph also faced a very different form of exile than that of his brothers. They went into exile because the famine in the Land of Canaan forced them to purchase provisions in Egypt. Joseph, however, did not descend to Egypt for his own benefit. As Joseph himself explained to his brothers, "What you planned for me as evil, God planned for good, in order to do as [I am doing] this day, to give life to a large people."[500] *Joseph viewed his role in the grand scheme of things as a sort of vanguard who prepared the way for the Jewish people to survive the Egyptian exile.*

Joseph served as a trailblazer for the Jewish people not only physically, but spiritually as well. His experience of facing and overcoming the temptation to assimilate into Egyptian society set an example for the Jews who followed him, giving them the spiritual strength to resist such temptation.[501] *Just as Joseph faced and overcame a hostile environment, maintaining Jewish standards of ethical behavior in the face of Egyptian depravity, so Rabbi Chiya went to a place desolate of Torah learning and reversed the situation by educating its youth. Thus, the*

---

to him.

[500] Genesis 50:20.

[501] The deeds of the ancestors of the Jewish people influence later generations. See, for example, *Breishith Rabbah* 48:7 and *VaYikra Rabbah* 29:1. See also *Kether Shem Tov* 256.

spiritual qualities of these two great men were virtually identical.

Kilayim 9:3 (B.T. *Kethuboth* 111A; *Breishith Rabbah* 96:5)

כתיב, "וַיִּקְרְבוּ יְמֵי יִשְׂרָאֵל לָמוּת וַיִּקְרָא לִבְנוֹ לְיוֹסֵף וַיֹּאמֶר לוֹ אִם נָא מָצָאתִי חֵן בְּעֵינֶיךָ שִׂים נָא יָדְךָ תַּחַת יְרֵכִי וְעָשִׂיתָ עִמָּדִי חֶסֶד וֶאֱמֶת אַל נָא תִקְבְּרֵנִי בְּמִצְרָיִם. וְשָׁכַבְתִּי עִם אֲבֹתַי] וּנְשָׂאתַנִי מִמִּצְרַיִם וּקְבַרְתַּנִי בִּקְבֻרָתָם... ." (בראשית מז:כט-ל).

יעקב, כל הָן דהוא, מה הוא מנכי? רבי לעזר אמר: דברים בגב. רבי חנינא אמר: דברים בגב. רבי יהושע בן לוי אמר: דברים בגב.

מהו דברים בגב? רבי שמעון בן לקיש אמר: "אֶתְהַלֵּךְ לִפְנֵי ה' בְּאַרְצוֹת הַחַיִּים." (תהלים קטז:ט) והלא אין "אַרְצוֹת הַחַיִּים" אלא צור וחברותיה וקיסרין וחברותיה, תמן זולת תמן שובעא? רבי שמעון בן לקיש משום בר קפרא: ארץ שֶׁמֵּתֶיהָ חיין תחילה לימות המשיח. ומה טעם? "[כֹּה אָמַר הָאֵ-ל ה' בּוֹרֵא הַשָּׁמַיִם וְנוֹטֵיהֶם רֹקַע הָאָרֶץ וְצֶאֱצָאֶיהָ] נֹתֵן נְשָׁמָה לָעָם עָלֶיהָ [וְרוּחַ לַהֹלְכִים בָּהּ.]" (ישעיה מב:ה).

אלא מעתה רבותינו שבגולה הפסידו? אמר רבי סימיי: מחליד הקדוש ברוך הוא לפניהן את הארץ והן מתגלגלין כנודות וכיון שהן מגיעין לארץ ישראל, נפשן חוזרות עליהן. ומה טעם? "[לָכֵן הִנָּבֵא וְאָמַרְתָּ אֲלֵיהֶם כֹּה אָמַר אֲ-דֹנָי ה' הִנֵּה אֲנִי פֹּתֵחַ אֶת קִבְרוֹתֵיכֶם וְהַעֲלֵיתִי אֶתְכֶם מִקִּבְרוֹתֵיכֶם עַמִּי וְהֵבֵאתִי אֶתְכֶם אֶל אַדְמַת יִשְׂרָאֵל.] ...וְנָתַתִּי רוּחִי בָכֶם וִחְיִיתֶם וְהִנַּחְתִּי אֶתְכֶם עַל אַדְמַתְכֶם [וִידַעְתֶּם כִּי אֲנִי ה' דִּבַּרְתִּי וְעָשִׂיתִי נְאֻם ה'.]" (יחזקאל לז:יב,יד).

It is written, "The time for Israel to die drew close and he called to his son Joseph and said to him, 'If I have found favor in your eyes, place your hand beneath my thigh and do for me kindness and truth: Do not bury me in

Egypt. When I lie with my fathers, carry me from Egypt and bury me in their gravesite.'... ."[502]

Jacob wherever he might be, what does he lose? [Why did he care so much about where he would be buried?]

Rabbi Lazar said: Secret matters. Rabbi Chanina said: Secret matters. Rabbi Yehoshua ben Levi said: Secret matters.

What are secret matters? Rabbi Shimon ben Lakish said: "I shall walk before the Lord in the land of the living."[503] Isn't it true that there are no lands of the living except Tyre and its vicinity and Caesarea and its vicinity, for there goods are cheap and there goods are plentiful? [It is unlikely that the Psalm refers to the "good life" available in these places. What, then, is meant by the "land of the living?"] Rabbi Shimon ben Lakish in the name of Bar Kappara explains: A land whose dead will be resurrected first in the days of the Messiah. What is the Scriptural basis for this? "Thus said God, the Lord who created the heavens and extended them, who laid out the Earth and that which grows from it, He who gives a soul to the people upon it and a spirit to those who walk on it."[504] [The term "the Earth" (הארץ) refers to the Land of Israel, so the verse indicates that those buried there will benefit first when

---

[502] Genesis 47:29-30.
[503] Psalms 116:9.
[504] Isaiah 42:5.

Hashem infuses a soul and spirit into people to resurrect them.[505]

But if so, have our masters in the Diaspora lost out? [Will the righteous scholars buried outside the Land of Israel not merit to be among the first to be resurrected?] Rabbi Simai said: The Holy One, Blessed be He, drills the land before them and they roll through it like waterskins. Once they reach the Land of Israel, their souls return to them. What is the Scriptural basis for this? "Therefore prophesy and say unto them, 'Thus says the Lord God: Behold I shall open your graves and raise you from your graves, my people, and I shall bring you to the Land of Israel. ...I shall place My spirit in you and you shall live and I shall guide you upon your land and you shall know that I am the Lord, I have spoken and I have performed, says the Lord.'"[506] [The sequence of the verses suggests that God will raise the people from their graves, bring them to the Land of Israel and then, afterwards, revive them by placing His spirit in them.]

Why did the rabbis refer to Jacob's request that he be buried in the Land of Israel as "secret matters?" Why not simply explain outright that Jacob meant that those buried elsewhere will have to roll beneath the ground? A simple answer might be to say that the expression "דברים בגב" *should be translated literally as "matters*

[505] *P'nei Moshe.*
[506] Ezekiel 37:12 and 14.

within," meaning "matters under the ground" which the Talmud then defines.

All the classic commentators, however, interpret "דברים בגב" to mean "secret matters" as translated here. Accordingly, perhaps the explanation is that resurrection itself is a "secret matter." The Torah does not mention resurrection explicitly even though it is a crucial tenet of Judaism. Instead, resurrection is known only from statements in the Prophets and Writings, and by inference.[507] In addition, logic dictates that there must be a hereafter because, although the Torah promises reward to its adherents, many who observe it do not receive a reward in this world. An afterlife could exist, however, without the dead coming back to life. Hence, resurrection itself may be the "secret matter" to which the Talmud refers because one would not conclude that it will take place based upon logical reasoning alone and the Torah does not explicitly mention it. Furthermore, as explained below, rolling underground to reach the Land of Israel is a secret mystical concept.[508]

The passage under consideration proclaims that those buried in the Land of Israel will be resurrected ahead of those buried elsewhere. The rabbis of the Babylonian Talmud, however, have a dispute as to whether those buried outside the Land of Israel will be resurrected at all.

---

[507] See B.T. *Sanhedrin* 91B-92A for examples of the many indirect allusions to this doctrine in the *Torah*.
[508] *Maharsha* on B.T. *Kethuboth* 111A.

Like the Jerusalem Talmud, the Babylonian Talmud concludes that whoever merits resurrection will roll underground to the Land of Israel.[509]

According to the view of the Jerusalem Talmud that those outside the Land of Israel will have a later resurrection, why was Jacob so concerned about being buried in the Land of Israel? What would be so terrible about being resurrected later? Moreover, all the sages agree that the righteous must roll beneath the ground to reach the Land of Israel where they will then be resurrected. As long as Hashem is making miracles such as drilling subterranean tunnels and reviving the dead, why not have angels carry the righteous to the Land of Israel or provide some other supernatural means of transport? For that matter, what special connection is there between the Land of Israel and the resuscitation of the dead? Surely, Hashem could perform this miracle anywhere in the world.

The answer is that the resurrection of the dead is not a miracle at all. When God created the world, He intended that people should live forever. Only because Adam and Chavah sinned did death come into the world.[510] *In the end of days, sin will not exist and the world will return to its original pristine state in which death did not exist.*[511] *A natural consequence of this will be that those already dead will come to life.*[512]

---

[509] B.T. *Kethuboth* 111A.

[510] Genesis 3:19.

[511] Rabbi Chanina ben Dosa once located the den of a poisonous

God swore that the Land of Israel would belong to the descendents of Abraham, Isaac and Jacob.[513] Accordingly, it is only natural that all Jews should live there. Once again, however, human misconduct interfered with the natural order of the universe and when the Jews sinned, they were driven into exile. This, too, will eventually be rectified in the end of days when Hashem will reveal Himself to all humankind and sin will disappear. Thus, the advent of the Messiah and return of all Jews to their homeland are not a miraculous events. Rather, they are merely the natural outcome of the elimination of sin just as the revival of the dead is the natural result of the elimination of sin. Therefore, the resurrection will take place in the Land of Israel.

The Mishnah lists three kings who will not participate in the world to come: Jeroboam, Ahab and Menasseh.[514] The Talmud cites another source, however,

---

lizard which had killed several people. He placed his foot over the lizard's hole. The lizard emerged, bit the rabbi and died. Rabbi Chanina ben Dosa then carried the lizard to town and announced, "My sons, it is not the lizard which kills, but sin that kills." When there is no sin, there is no death.

[512] Some authorities hold that the resurrection is not a miracle for another reason: The *Zohar* says that, "the Holy One, Blessed be He gazed into the *Torah* and created the world," (*Zohar* II, 161B) meaning that He, so to speak, used the *Torah* as a blueprint for creating the universe. Since resurrection of the dead is alluded to in the *Torah*, it is not a miracle, but a natural phenomenon.

[513] Genesis 50:24; Exodus 13:5.

[514] *Sanhedrin* 10:2; B.T. *Sanhedrin* 90A. The expression "world to

which states that everyone will have a share in the world to come, including these three kings.[515] *Rabbi Yosef Hayyim resolves this contradiction by explaining the Mishnah to mean that although wicked people will not merit resurrection because of the sins they committed during their lifetimes, they will undergo repeated reincarnations until they rectify those sins. Thus, ultimately, everyone will participate in the resurrection of the dead.*[516] *This cycle of reincarnations is called "gilgulim" (גלגולים) in Hebrew, literally "rollings."*

Each person enters the world for the purpose of doing things which will accomplish something in the spiritual realm. If a person sins and therefore fails to accomplish his mission, he must be reincarnated until he achieves the goal God has designated for him. Jacob succeeded in fully accomplishing his personal mission in the world and required no further reincarnations.[517] *However, in addition, to each person's specific spiritual mission, there is an overall rectification the universe must undergo for the final redemption to take place. The Patriarchs managed to rectify most of the spiritual damage which Adam caused and which brought death into the*

---

come" in this context refers to the resurrection whereas in other passages it refers to the spiritual realm where a person's soul resides after his or her death.

[515] B.T. *Sanhedrin* 104B-105A.

[516] *Ben Yehoyada* on B.T. *Sanhedrin* 90A. See above p. 131.

[517] *Yalkut Reuveni, Parshath VaYechi* 15.

world.[518] *Nonetheless, the final rectification will not occur until the end of days. The Talmud refers to that spiritual rectification as "rolling (גלגולים) under the Earth," a rectification similar to the reincarnations (גלגולים) of each individual.*

Rabbi Chaim Vital explains at great length that the series of reincarnations a person must endure are highly unpleasant.[519] *The ultimate rectification which will occur at the end of days will also entail much suffering. The sages will be severely persecuted,*[520] *impudence and disrespect will be rampant,*[521] *and warfare of an unprecedented nature will take place.*[522] *Once the final rectification happens, sin and its effects will disappear so that all Jews, both living and dead, will return to the Land of Israel where the dead will come back to life. By being buried in the Land of Israel, Jacob sought to avoid the torments of the final rectification.*

---

[518] *Perush HaRamchal Al HaTorah* on Exodus 6:4. Rabbi Luzzatto states that Jacob achieved the most in repairing the damage done by Adam.

[519] *Sha'ar HaGilgulim, Hakdamah* 22.

[520] B.T. *Kethuboth* 112B.

[521] B.T. *Sanhedrin* 97A.

[522] B.T. *Brachoth* 13A.

Kilayim 9:3 (J.T. *Kethuboth* 12:3)

רבי ברכיה שאל לרבי חלבו, רבי חלבו שאל לרבי אימי, רבי
אימי שאל לרבי אלעזר, רבי לעזר שאל לרבי חנינה, ואית דאמרין רבי
חנינה שאל לרבי יהושע בן לוי: אפילו כגון ירבעם בן נבט וחביריו?
אמר ליה: "גָּפְרִית וָמֶלַח שְׂרֵפָה כָל אַרְצָהּ... ." (דברים כט:כב).
אמר רבי ברכיה: מה, "הן שאל להן והן שאל להן?" לא שמעינן מינה
כלום!

מיי כדון? כיון שנשרפה ארץ ישראל, נעשה בהן מידת הדין.

תני בשם רבי יהודה: שבע שנים עשת ארץ ישראל נשרפת.
הדא הוא דכתיב, "וְהִגְבִּיר בְּרִית לָרַבִּים שָׁבוּעַ אֶחָד... ." (דניאל ט:כז).
כותים שבה מה היו עושים? מטליות מטליות והיתה נשרפת.

כתיב, "וְאַתָּה פַשְׁחוּר וְכֹל יֹשְׁבֵי בֵיתֶךָ תֵּלְכוּ בַּשֶּׁבִי וּבָבֶל תָּבוֹא
וְשָׁם תָּמוּת וְשָׁם תִּקָּבֵר [אַתָּה וְכָל אֹהֲבֶיךָ אֲשֶׁר נִבֵּאתָ לָהֶם בַּשָּׁקֶר.]
(ירמיה כו:ו). רבי אבא בר זמינא אמר רבי חלבו ורבי חמא בר חנינא:
חד אמר: מת שם ונקבר שם יש בידו שתים. מת שם ונקבר כאן יש
בידו אחת. וחרנה אמר: קבורה שבכאן מכפרת על מיתה שלהן.

Rabbi Berachya asked Rabbi Chelbo, Rabbi Chelbo
asked Rabbi Immi, Rabbi Immi asked Rabbi Elazar, Rabbi
Elazar asked Rabbi Chanina, and some say Rabbi Chanina
asked Rabbi Yehoshua ben Levi: Does this apply even to
Jeroboam son of Nebat and his comrades? [Jeroboam was
king of the Ten Tribes of Israel while King Solomon's son,
Rehoboam, reigned over Judah and Benjamin. Jeroboam
feared that his subjects might be influenced to switch their
allegiance to Rehoboam when they obeyed the Biblical
commandment to ascend three times a year to Jerusalem
which was in Rehoboam's kingdom. To prevent this,

Jeroboam and his associates introduced an idolatrous cult among the people.[523] The *Talmud* questions whether people guilty of such a grievous sin will nonetheless be resurrected just because they happen to be buried in the Land of Israel.]

He answered him: "Sulphur and salt, a burning of all her land... ."[524]

Rabbi Berachyah said: What use is "they asked them and they asked them?" In the end we learn nothing from it! [How does the verse answer the question?]

What indeed is the answer? Since the Land of Israel was burned, a measure of justice was done to them. [When the land was burned, so were the wicked people buried there. Such punishment atoned for their sins, so that they can participate in the resurrection.[525]]

It was taught in the name of Rabbi Yehudah: For seven years the Land of Israel was burning. Thus it is written, "He shall form a mighty covenant with the nobles for one septenary... ."[526] What did the Samaritans there do? [When the Assyrians conquered the Land of Israel, they tried to prevent rebellion by exiling the native Jews to other places and importing foreign non-Jews.[527] When the

---

[523] I Kings 11:29-12:33.

[524] Deuteronomy 29:22.

[525] *P'nei Moshe.*

[526] Daniel 9:27.

[527] II Kings 17:23-24. These Gentiles came from several areas, especially Kutha, and so are called *Kuthim* (כותים) in the *Talmud*. Since they settled in the province of Samaria (שומרון), they are also called

Babylonians conquered the Land of Israel later on, they too had a policy of exiling the native people, but permitted the foreign Samaritans to remain. If the land burned for seven years, how could those foreigners plant crops and survive?] It was burning patch by patch. [The land burned bit by bit so that, at any given time, part remained arable. The Samaritans raised crops on those parts of the land which were not burning.[528]]

It is written, "And you, Pashchor, and all who dwell in your house shall go into captivity; you shall come to Babylon and there you shall die and there you shall be buried, you and all your friends to whom you have falsely prophesied."[529] Rabbi Abba bar Zamina said that there is a dispute between Rabbi Chelbo and Rabbi Chama bar Chanina. One said: If he died there and was buried there, he has two sins [one for living outside the Land of Israel and the other for being buried there]. If he died there but was buried here [in the Land of Israel], he has one sin [for living outside the Land of Israel]. The other said: Burial

---

Samaritans.
[528] *Korban HaEidah* on J.T. *Kethuboth* 12:3. The *Shayarei HaKorban*, however, raises the point that it would be inappropriate for the righteous who were buried in the Land of Israel to be burned as well. Accordingly, he suggests that some patches of land were not burned at all and that the text should read, "What did the righteous (כשרים) there do?" rather than, "What did the Samaritans (כותים) there do?"
[529] Jeremiah 20:6.

here atones for their death. [Burial in the Land of Israel
atones for the sin of not living there.]

*The Talmud states in this passage that after the
Jews sinned and were exiled, the Land of Israel burned.
Rabbi Shlomo Ephraim Lunshitz asks: Why is the land
stricken when the Jewish people sin? He answers that the
Earth is the root cause of sin. God made Adam's body
from earth and then infused it with a soul. The soul itself is
pure and not inclined to sin. The body, however, derives
from the Earth and, so, is drawn after material desires
which lead to sin.[530] This is why when the generation of
the Flood sinned, the Torah says, "The Lord saw the Earth
and behold, it was defiled... ."[531]*

*The Talmud teaches that "fire is one-sixtieth of
Gehinnom."[532] After a righteous person dies, he or she
enters Paradise. Sinners, however, go to Gehinnom where
they are purified of their sins and afterwards enter
Paradise. Rabbi Elisha ben Abuya was a sage who turned
heretic during the second century C.E. After his death, his
disciples realized that he had been so wicked that he was
ineligible to enter even Gehinnom! After his chief pupil,
Rabbi Meir, died, smoke rose from Rabbi Elisha ben
Abuya's grave signifying his admission into Gehinnom.[533]*

---

[530] *Kli Yakar* on Deuteronomy 29:22. See above pp. 207-208.

[531] Genesis 6:12.

[532] B.T. *Brachoth* 57B.

[533] B.T. *Chagigah* 15B.

Thus, fire represents the spiritual purification of the soul in Gehinnom.

If a person succeeds in avoiding sin in this world, he or she elevates the physical, earthen body so that it can share with the soul in the reward of resurrection. However, if an individual sins, the body requires purification. Fire is the one natural occurrence which utterly destroys whatever comes into contact with it. Fire also converts a substantial portion of the matter it consumes from solid or liquid form into gas, symbolizing conversion from the physical to the spiritual. Wicked people such a Jeroboam can participate in the resurrection after their corpses are burned because the complete destruction of a wicked person's physical body permits later reconstitution with the soul in a purified state.

This concept of purifying the earth by fire may explain why the Hashem required an earthen altar in the Temple. All sacrifices which people brought to the Temple were either wholly or partly burned on the altar, a process which separated the physical from the spiritual.

The Torah itself alludes to this concept by using the term sulphur (גפרית) in connection with the burning of the Land.[534] The ג in the word גפרית, "sulphur," may be exchanged with a כ because they belong to a group of letters which are formed by the same parts of the mouth and have a similar sound.[535] The Hebrew root "Kaper"

---

[534] Deuteronomy 29:22.
[535] Rabbi Yom Tov Lipman Heller in *Tosafoth Yom Tov* on *Challah*

(כפר) *means "atonement," hinting that the burning of the Land provides atonement.*

A similar idea is suggested by Hashem's command to Noah to build an ark specifically out of gopher (גפר) wood and to cover it with pitch (כפר).[536] *When the Flood destroyed the world, Noah and his family became completely separated from the Earth by riding above the raging waters in the ark. This separation purified them from the sin which engulfed and destroyed the rest of humankind just as, metaphorically, fire separates the physical from the spiritual.*

The word "Kofer" (כפר) also means deny: an atonement denies sin and erases it. To do so, the physical aspect of a person must be erased. This occurred when the bodies of Jeroboam and his comrades were burned.

2:5 sub verba "*Ve'Kafsha*" (וקפשה) says that letters which one forms in similar ways by, for example, touching the tongue to the front teeth ("dentals") or by parting the lips ("labials") may be interchanged. In addition, the *Targum Yonathan ben Uziel* on Deuteronomy 29:22 translates the word גפרית as כובריתא.

[536] Genesis 6:14.

Kilayim 9:3 (B.T. *Sukkah* 53A; J.T. *Kethuboth* 12:3)

רבי יונה בשם רבי חמא בר חנינה: ריגליי דְבַּר נשא ערבתיה
למיקמתיה כל הָן דהוא מתבע. כתיב "וַיֹּאמֶר ה' מִי יְפַתֶּה אֶת אַחְאָב
וְיַעַל וְיִפֹּל בְּרָמֹת גִּלְעָד?... ." (מלכים א כב:כ). וימות בתוך ביתו ולא
תמן.

אליחורף ואחיה תרין איסקבטירייי דשלמה. חמא מלאך מותא
מסתכל בון וחריק בשינוי. אמר מלה ויהבון בחללא. אזל (ונסתון)
[ונסבון] מן תמן. אתא, קאים ליה, גחיך לקבליה.

אמר ליה, "ההיא שעתא הויתא איחרוק בשינייך וכדון את
גחיך לן?"

אמר ליה, "רחמנא אמר דינסב לאליחורף ואחיה מן חללא
ואמרית, 'מאן יהיב לי אילין לְהָן דאישתלחית מיסבינין?' ויהב בליבך
למיעבד כן בגין דנעביד שליחותי."

אזל ואיטפל בון זמן תמן.

תרין ברויי דרבי ראובן בר איסטרובילוס תלמידוי דרבי. חמא
מלאכה דמותא מסתכל בון וחרק בשינוי ואמר, "נגלינון לדרומה. שמא
הגלות מכפרת." אזל (ונסתון) [ונסבון] מן תמן.

Rabbi Yonah in the name of Rabbi Chama bar
Chanina said: A person's legs are his guarantors to bring
him to where he is wanted. [Things will work out so that a
person reaches the place where he or she is destined to die.]
It is written, "The Lord said, "Who will entice Ahab so that
he will go up and fall [in battle] at Ramoth Gilead?... ."[537]
Why not let him die in his house rather than there? [This
proves that "a person's legs are his guarantors." Naboth

---

[537] I Kings 22:20.

owned a vineyard adjacent to King Ahab's palace which the king coveted. The king demanded that Naboth sell him the vineyard, but the latter refused. When King Ahab complained to his wife about it, she had false witnesses accuse Naboth of blasphemy. After Naboth's execution, Ahab seized the vineyard.[538] The prophet Elijah then informed Ahab that "...in the place where the dogs lapped the blood of Naboth, the dogs shall lap up your own blood."[539] *Hashem* then lured Ahab into a battle with Aram, even sending him false prophets who assured him of victory, so that he would die in the place predicted.]

Elihoreph and Ahijah were two scribes of King Solomon.[540] He saw the angel of death gazing upon them and gnashing his teeth. He said a special word and put them in midair [where he thought the angel could not reach them]. The angel went and seized them from there, then came and stood laughing before King Solomon.

Said the king, "Earlier you were gnashing your teeth and now you laugh?"

---

[538] I Kings 21:1-16.

[539] I Kings 21:19.

[540] See I Kings 4:1-3. The term איסקבטירייי in the text here is written איסקריטורי in J.T. *Kethuboth* 12:3 which *Korban HaEidah* explains means "scribe" (secretary) in Latin. Since the *Tanach* itself calls these men סופרים, it is unclear why the *Talmud* does not use that term and, instead, borrows a Latin word. Perhaps the editors wanted to convey the idea that these were not merely scribes, but also King Solomon's confidential advisers, consistent with the original meaning of the word "secretary" which derives from "secret."

The angel of death replied, "The Merciful One said to take Elihoreph and Ahijah from midair, so I said to myself, 'Who will put them there for me that I may proceed to take them?' God put it into your heart to do so in order for my mission to be fulfilled."

King Solomon went and arranged their burial.[541]

The two sons of Rabbi Reuven bar Istrobilos were disciples of Rebbi. He [Rebbi] observed the angel of death gazing upon them and gnashing his teeth, so he said, "I will send them to the south. Perhaps exile atones sin." The angel went and seized them from there [since that is where they were destined to die].

Why does the Talmud use the case of Ahab as proof that a person must die in a predestined place? The prophet Elijah specifically informed Ahab that he would die in the same location where Naboth had been executed.[542] The wording of the verse indicates that God wished to kill Ahab in a way that would show that He was punishing him for his treatment of Naboth.[543] If Ahab died in a specific location because of Elijah's prophecy and Hashem's desire

---

[541] The editors of the Romm Vilna edition note that the words זמן תמן do not appear in the Rome manuscript. The version of this text in J.T. *Kethuboth* 12:3 reads מן תמן, meaning that King Solomon arranged their burial "from there."

[542] I Kings 21:19.

[543] God always treats people "measure for measure," rewarding them in ways which reflect their good deeds and punishing them in ways which reflect their sins. (B.T. *Sanhedrin* 90A).

to punish him there, how can the editors of the Talmud infer that everyone else must die in a predestined place?

As Elijah told Ahab, Hashem always makes the punishment fit the crime (מדה כנגד מדה). To have others murder Ahab just as he murdered Naboth would have satisfied this principle without the murder occurring in a particular location. Accordingly, the rabbis of the Talmud concluded that there must be a need for a person to die in a particular place.

The question remains: Why should it matter where a person dies? One can understand the difference between dying in the Holy Land and elsewhere as discussed in the Talmudic passages above,[544] but why should it matter beyond that where one dies?

A punishment must resemble a sin so that it can effectuate atonement. When a person sins, he creates spiritual damage to himself and the universe. Punishment which mirrors the sin repairs that damage. The punishment of death, however, atones for all sin in general.[545] When a person sins, he or she interferes with the life force of the universe because rebelling against God cuts off the Divine life force which constantly flows into the world. Measure for measure, death atones for that wrongdoing because the person who "killed" the universe is killed.

---

[544] See above pp. 240-251.
[545] B.T. *Yoma* 86A, J.T. *Yoma* 8:7, B.T. *Shavuoth* 8B.

Each physical point in the universe corresponds to a point in the spiritual universe.[546] For instance, just as there is a physical Jerusalem, there is also a celestial Jerusalem.[547] Likewise, the tribes, as well as each individual Jew, had particular plots of land assigned to them in the Land of Israel because the spiritual realm corresponding to each plot also corresponded to the spiritual composition of the person to whom it was assigned. That is why if a Jew sold his land, the buyer had to return it in the jubilee year.[548] Specific people have a spiritual connection to specific locations. Since death causes atonement, it must occur in a specific place to rectify the spiritual damage associated with that physical location.

---

[546] *Zohar* II, 15B states that for whatever *Hashem* created in Heaven, He created something corresponding to it on Earth.
[547] B.T. *Ta'anith* 5A.
[548] Leviticus 25:10, 13.

Kilayim 9:3 (Compare B.T. *Kethuboth* 111A)

עולא נחותא הוה אידמך תמן, שרי בכי.

אמרין ליה, "מה לך בכי? אנן מסקין לך לארעא דישראל."

אמר לון, "ומה הנייה לי? אנא מובד מרגליתי גו ארעא

מסאבתא. לא דומה הפולטה בחיק אמו לפולטה בחיק נכריה."

רבי מאיר הוה אידמך ליה באסייא. אמר, "אימורין לבני ארעא

דישראל, 'הא משיחכון דידכון.'" אפילו כן, אמר לון, "יהבי ערסי על גיף

ימא. כתיב, 'כִּי הוּא עַל יַמִּים יְסָדָהּ וְעַל נְהָרוֹת יְכוֹנְנֶהָ.'" (תהלים כד:ב).

שבעה ימים סובבין את ארץ ישראל: ימא רבא, ימא דטיבריא, ימא

דסמכו, ימא דמילחא, ימא דחולתא, ימא דשליית, ימא דאפמיא. והא

איכא ימא דחמץ? דיקלטינוס הקוה נהרות ועשאו.

כתיב, "[וּמִבָּמוֹת הַגַּיְא אֲשֶׁר בִּשְׂדֵה מוֹאָב רֹאשׁ הַפִּסְגָּה] וְנִשְׁקָפָה

עַל פְּנֵי הַיְשִׁימֹן." (במדבר כא:כ) . אמר רבי חייא בריא: כל מי שהוא

עולה להר ישימון ומצא כמין כברה בים טיבריא, זו היא בורה של מרים.

אמר רבי יוחנן: שערונה רבנין והיא היא מכוונא כל קביל

תרעא מציעיא דכנישתא עתיקתא דסרונגין.

רבי בר קירייא ורבי לעזר הוון מטיילין באיסטרין. ראו ארונות

שהיו באין מחוצה לארץ לארץ. אמר רבי בר קירייא לרבי לעזר, "מה

הועילו אילו? אני קורא עליהם, '...וְנַחֲלָתִי שַׂמְתֶּם לְתוֹעֵבָה,' (ירמיה ב:ז)

בחייכם, '...וַתָּבֹאוּ וַתְּטַמְּאוּ אֶת אַרְצִי...' (שם שם) במיתתכם."

אמר ליה, "כיון שהן מגיעין לארץ ישראל הן נוטלין גוש עפר

ומניחין על ארונן, דכתיב, '...וְכִפֶּר אַדְמָתוֹ עַמּוֹ.'" (דברים לב:מג)

Ulla, the one who descends, [so called because he used to travel frequently from the Land of Israel to Babylonia], approached death there [in Babylonia] and began to weep.

His acquaintances said, "Why do you cry? We will carry you up to the Land of Israel."

He replied, "What benefit is that to me if I lose my soul in an unclean land? One cannot compare discharging it into the lap of one's mother with discharging it into the lap of a stranger."

Rabbi Meir was dying in Asia. He said, "Tell the people of the Land of Israel, 'Your anointed one is here!'" [In other words, those attending him should make arrangements to transport his body to the Land of Israel.]

Even with this precaution, he said to them, "Put my coffin on the seashore for it is written, 'For He founded it upon the seas and upon the rivers He established it.'"[549] Seven seas surround the Land of Israel: The Great Sea [Mediterranean], the Sea of Tiberias [Galilee], the Sea of Samchu,[550] the Sea of Salt [Dead Sea], the Sea of Chultha, the Sea of Shilayath[551] and the Sea of Apamaya.[552] [If it would not come about for Rabbi Meir to be buried in the Land of Israel, it would still help to be buried by the

---

[549] Psalms 24:2.

[550] Located north of the Sea of Galilee. See B.T. *Baba Bathra* 74B where it is called Sibchi סיבכי.

[551] In B.T. *Baba Bathra* 74B these last two are called the "Sea of *Chilatha*" (חילתא) and the "Sea of *Chilath*" (חילת). *Chilatha* means "valley" in Aramaic, but it is not clear which valley might be meant. *Chilath* means "reed" in Hebrew, perhaps referring to a swampy area.

[552] This is the cave of Pameas or Paneas which is source of the Jordan River. See B.T. *Baba Bathra* 74B. It is described as one of the boundaries of the Land of Israel in Numbers 34:11 according to *Targum Yonathan ben Uziel*.

seashore since the Land of Israel is surrounded by seven seas.[553]]

But is there not also the Sea of Chemetz? Diocletian[554] channeled several rivers together and made it. [Since it was a manmade lake, it cannot be listed among the bodies of water which form the border of the Land of Israel.]

It is written, "And from the heights to the valley which is in the field of Moab near the top of the summit which looks out before the desert."[555] Said Rabbi Chiya Barya: Whoever ascends Mount Yeshimon[556] and finds a rock resembling a type of sieve in the Sea of Tiberias [the Sea of Galilee], this is the well of Miriam. [Numbers 21:16-20 describes the journeys upon which the well of Miriam accompanied the Jewish people. The verses end with a reference to the desert, "Yeshimon" (ישימון) in Hebrew. Rabbi Chiya Barya explains that one can still find the well at its final stopping point near Mount Yeshimon.]

Rabbi Yochanan said: The disciples surveyed it and it is aligned with the center gate of the ancient synagogue of

---

553 *P'nei Moshe*. *HaKothev*, however, says that Rabbi Meir wanted his coffin placed on the seashore even after his body arrived in the Land of Israel.
554 A Roman emperor who lived from 245 to 313 C.E.
555 Numbers 21:20.
556 *P'nei Moshe* identifies this as Mount Carmel based on B.T. *Shabbath* 35A.

Serongin. [Thus, whoever wants to view it may visit the synagogue and do so.[557]]

Rabbi Bar Kirya and Rabbi Elazar were traveling in the street. They observed coffins coming from outside the Land of Israel to the Land of Israel. Rabbi Bar Kirya said to Rabbi Elazar, "What does this benefit them? I apply to them the verse, '...and My inheritance you considered an abomination'[558] during your lives, '...and you come and defile My land...'[559] at your death." [Much of the merit of living in the Land of Israel is related to fulfillment of those *Mitzvoth* which one can perform only there. Since one cannot perform *Mitzvoth* after he or she dies, what use is it to be buried there?[560]]

He answered, "Once they reach the Land of Israel, they take a clod of earth and place it on their coffins, as it is written, '...His Land atones His people.'[561]" [Burial in the Land of Israel reflects the strong, albeit unfulfilled, desire of the deceased to live there and so causes atonement.[562] As the *Talmud* says elsewhere, whenever one wants to perform a *Mitzvah* but cannot due to circumstances beyond his control, it is considered as though he did it.[563]]

---

[557] *P'nei Moshe.*

[558] Jeremiah 2:7.

[559] Ibid. Rabbi Bar Kirya reverses the order in which these phrases appear in Jeremiah to produce this homily.

[560] *HaKothev.*

[561] Deuteronomy 32:43.

[562] *HaKothev.*

[563] B.T. *Brachoth* 6A.

Rabbi Shimon bar Yochai taught that Hashem gave three special gifts to the Jewish people which entail hardships: Torah, the Land of Israel and the world to come.[564] *Hardship plays a role in acquiring Torah knowledge because one must reject worldly pursuits if he wishes to invest sufficient time and effort into his studies to succeed. Hardship applies to the Land of Israel in the sense that a person should not desire to live there for the worldly purpose of enjoying the bounty for which the Land is praised, but to perform the special Mitzvoth which apply there. Finally, one acquires the world to come through hardship because the difficulties one confronts in this world atone for one's sins so that he or she can merit the world to come.*[565]

In addition to the fact that Torah, the Land of Israel and the world to come are all acquired through hardship, there are other special connections between them. Torah has a special relationship to the Land of Israel as the Tanach says, "For from Zion shall go forth Torah and the word of the Lord from Jerusalem."[566] *The sages taught that the air of the Land of Israel makes one smart*[567] *and that there is no Torah like the Torah of the Land of Israel.*[568] *This is reflected by the Talmud's teaching in the*

---

[564] B.T. *Brachoth* 5A.
[565] *Maharsha* on B.T. *Brachoth* 5A.
[566] Isaiah 2:3 and Michah 4:2.
[567] B.T. *Baba Bathra* 158B.
[568] *VaYikra Rabbah* 13:5.

above passage that the Land of Israel is surrounded by seven seas since Torah is compared to water.[569]   *In addition, there are seven sections to the Torah if "It was when it traveled... "*[570] *(ויהי בנסע) is counted as a separate book.*[571]

The future resurrection also has a special relationship to the Land of Israel because those buried there will be revived first when it happens.[572]   *Also, there is a spiritual Jerusalem which corresponds to the earthly Jerusalem*[573] *and the entrance to Gehinnom is located in the Land of Israel.*[574]   *Moreover, whoever treads four cubits in the Land of Israel is assured a share in the world to come.*[575]

Ulla and Rabbi Meir wished to unite all three of these special gifts which are acquired through hardship. They themselves were superior Torah scholars who, upon death, were sure to have a share in the world to come. By insisting on burial in the Land of Israel, they gained the third element.

---

[569] *Derech Eretz Zuta* 8.

[570] Numbers 10:35-36.

[571] B.T. *Shabbath* 116A says that this passage may be considered as an independent book of the Pentateuch.

[572] *Breishith Rabbah* 74:1 and see above pp. 239-240.

[573] B.T. *Ta'anith* 5a.

[574] B.T. *Sukkah* 32B.

[575] B.T. *Kethuboth* 111A. This applies only if one did so intending to fulfill the *Mitzvah* of living in the Land of Israel. See *P'nei Yehoshua* ad. loc.

Shevi'ith 4:7 (compare B.T. *Kethuboth* 112A-B)

רבי יוסי בן חנינא מנשק לכיפתא דעכו. "עד כה היא ארעא
דישראל." רבי זירא עבר ירדנא במנוי. רבי חייא בר בא מתעגל בהדא
אליסוס דטבריא. רבי חייא רבא מתקל כיפי. רבי חנניא מתקל גושייא.
לקיים מה שנאמר, "כִּי רָצוּ עֲבָדֶיךָ אֶת אֲבָנֶיהָ וְאֶת עֲפָרָהּ יְחֹנֵנוּ." (תהלים
קב:טו).

Rabbi Yossi ben Chanina used to kiss the stones of
Acco, saying, "Until here is the border of the Land of
Israel." Rabbi Zera crossed the Jordan while wearing his
clothing.[576] [He was so anxious to enter the Land of Israel
that when he reached the Jordan River, he did not search for
a ferry or bridge, but swam across without even removing
his clothing.] Rabbi Chiya bar Ba used to roll around in the
dust of Tiberias.[577] Rabbi Chiya the Great used to weigh
the stones [of the Land of Israel]. Rabbi Chanania used to
weigh the clods [of earth of the Land of Israel]. [The rabbis
could tell whether they had reached the Land of Israel by
feeling the weight of its stones or clods of earth.[578]] So

---

[576] *Mareh HaPanim.*

[577] *Mathanoth Kehunah* on *VaYikra Rabbah* 19:4 explains אליסים to
mean something which has been pulverized to the point where it is
unusable, i.e., dust. The present translation is consistent with the
version of this passage in B.T. *Kethuboth* 112B which says that Rabbi
Chiya bar Gamda rolled in the dust. *P'nei Moshe*, however,
understands אליסוס here to refer to a certain district in Tiberias. Perhaps
it was an area of the city which had been destroyed (pulverized) or
abandoned, and thus acquired this name.

[578] *P'nei Moshe.*

they fulfilled that which is written, "For Your servants have desired its stones and its dust they have cherished."[579]

During his younger years, the Baal Shem Tov conducted himself as though he were a simple, unlearned Jew, hiding his true greatness from the world. One time, he put on his Tefillin in an unusual way to fulfill certain Kabbalistic requirements. His brother-in-law did not know that the Baal Shem Tov was a great Torah scholar and Tzaddik, so he chastised the Baal Shem Tov for wearing his Tefillin in a manner which he thought contrary to the Halachah. When the Baal Shem Tov refused to change his manner of putting on Tefillin, his brother-in-law decided to haul him in front of the local rabbi who would properly rebuke this "ignorant" Jew for his behavior. When the Baal Shem Tov entered the study of the local rabbi, he touched the Mezuzah, but did not kiss it. The rabbi, who was a righteous man, detected a spiritual glow when the Baal Shem Tov entered the room. Realizing whose presence he was in, he rose from his place. The two men spoke privately for awhile. During the conversation, the rabbi asked the Baal Shem Tov why he had touched the Mezuzah but failed to kiss it. The Baal Shem Tov explained that the Mezuzah had a defect which rendered it ritually unfit. The rabbi checked the Mezuzah and discovered that the Baal Shem Tov was right.

---

[579] *Psalms* 102:15.

This story, and many others like it, show that great people have a sensitivity to spiritual matters which others do not. For this reason, the rabbis of the Talmud could hold a stone or clod of earth and tell by the feel of it whether it came from the Land of Israel.

Commentators explain that the rabbis perceived the stones of the Land of Israel as "heavier" than those of other places.[580] This is because the Torah is more closely associated with the Land of Israel than with other places and Torah is compared to stone as the verse says, "Are not My words like fire, says the Lord, and like a hammer shattered by a rock?"[581] Just as a hammer breaks into many slivers when it strikes a stone which is harder than it is, so a Scriptural verse may be broken into many interpretations.[582] Furthermore, Rabbi Akiva once said that the words of the Torah are as hard as iron[583] because mastering the Torah requires many, many years of intense toil.

The Tanach also says about the Land of Israel that, "...its stones are iron... ."[584] Rabbi Abba said that this phrase actually refers to Torah scholars because the words "its stones" in Hebrew (אבניה) can be interpreted to mean "its builders" (בוניה).[585] Torah scholars must be hard as

---

580 *P'nei Moshe.*

581 Jeremiah 23:29.

582 B.T. *Sanhedrin* 34A according to *Tosafoth* ad. loc.

583 *Avoth D'Rabbi Nathan* 6:2.

584 Deuteronomy 8:9.

585 B.T. *Ta'anith* 4A. *Torah* scholars are called "builders" because

iron, that is, persistent in their learning. Accordingly, the stones and earth of the Land of Israel appeared heavier to the sages of the Talmud than those of other lands because of the special relationship between the Land of Israel and the Torah.[586]

---

they build upon the principles of the *Torah* which they study, applying those principles to each situation which arises, or because they supervise and build up the spiritual life of the communities they serve.
[586] See *Maharal* on B.T. *Kethuboth* 112A-B.

Shevi'ith 4:8

אמר רבי יונה: כתיב, "זַיתִים יִהְיוּ לְךָ בְּכָל גְּבוּלֶךָ וְשֶׁמֶן לֹא
תָסוּךְ] כִּי יִשַּׁל זַיתֶךָ." (דברים כח:מ). חד לתלת מאה וארבעין קיים בה.
אמר רבי יונה: כתיב, "אַל תִּירְאוּ בַּהֲמוֹת שָׂדַי כִּי דָשְׁאוּ נְאוֹת
מִדְבָּר כִּי] עֵץ נָשָׂא פִרְיוֹ..." (יואל ב:כב). מגיד שלא נשא פריו בעולם הזה.
"...תְּאֵנָה וָגֶפֶן נָתְנוּ חֵילָם." (שם שם). מגיד שלא נתנו חילם בעולם הזה.
אמר רבי יונה בשם רבי חמא בר חנינא: המת בשבע שני גוג,
אין לו חלק לעתיד לבא. סימנא: דאכיל פרוטגמיא אכיל משתיתא.
שמע רבי יוסי ואמר: ויאות? עד כדון אית תותבה לעלמא
דאתי!

Rabbi Yonah said: It is written, "You will have
olive trees throughout your borders but you will not smear
[yourself with oil] because your olive trees will drop [their
fruit prematurely]."[587] One olive out of three hundred forty
will survive. [This is one of the curses which the *Torah*
says will befall the Jewish people if they abandon their
faith. The numerical value of the Hebrew word for "drop"
(ישל) equals three hundred forty.]

Rabbi Yonah said: It is written, "Do not fear,
animals of the field, for the habitations of the desert have
sprouted grass, for the tree has borne its fruit... ."[588] This
means that the trees did not bear fruit in this world. "...the
fig tree and grapevine have given forth their strength"[589]

---

[587] Deuteronomy 28:40.
[588] Joel 2:22.
[589] Ibid.

means that they did not give forth their strength in this world. [This verse contains a prophetic prediction of the final redemption which will be so complete that not only will it apply to humans, but even animals will find relief.[590] The verse hints that the quality and quantity of the fruits of the Messianic era will be so much greater than at present that it will be as though the trees never bore fruit in the past.]

Rabbi Yonah said in the name of Rabbi Chama bar Chanina: One who dies during the seven years of Gog will have no share in the future to come. An analogy for this is that one who eats at the engagement party also eats at the wedding feast.[591] [It was customary in *Talmudic* times for a young groom's friends to contribute to his wedding

---

[590] *Gei Chizayon* by Rabbi Meir Leibush Malbim on Joel 2:22.

[591] *P'nei Moshe* understands the word פרוטגמיא in this text to refer to the wedding feast for a couple who have never before been married, from the Greek "*protos*," meaning "first" (as in the English word "*proto*type") and "*gamos*," meaning "marriage" (as in the English word "poly*gamy*"). *Ma'arecheth HeAruch*, however, understands this word as a variation of the word פרקמטיא, meaning "merchandise." The text would then mean that one who lives during the time of Gog has "consumed his merchandise" and so has nothing left for the future. (The *Talmud* and *Midrash* sometimes substitute the letter ק for ג, and vice versa, in Greek and Latin words, because the sounds of these two letters are similar. In this case, the text would be using the Greek word "*pragmatikos*" which means "businessman" and from which the English word "pragmatic," meaning "practical" or "business-minded" is derived.)

expenses. Typically, one who contributed to the party would attend.[592]

Rabbi Yossi heard this and said: Is this right? If so, it would be a refutation of the world to come!

This passage of the Talmud reflects the principle that Hashem's mercy far outstrips His wrath. As punishment for disobeying the Torah, He causes fruit trees to fail, but the future reward will be so great that it will be as though the trees never yielded anything to begin with.

After the arrival of the Messiah, the peoples of the world, led by Gog and his nation, Magog, will attack the Jews only to be miraculously defeated through God's intervention.[593] The rabbis of the Talmud taught that "reward for a Mitzvah does not exist in this world."[594] Accordingly, Rabbi Chama bar Chanina cannot mean that people who witness the war of Gog and Magog literally have no share in the world to come. He merely meant that the great pleasure the righteous will feel at their triumph over the forces of evil will approach that of the world to come.

---

592 *P'nei Moshe* citing *Baba Bathra* 9:4.
593 Ezekiel, chapters 38-39. The numerical value of "Gog and Magog" (גוג ומגוג) equals seventy corresponding to the seventy basic nationalities of the world. (*Kithvei HaAri, Likutei Torah* on *Parshath Shemoth*, sub verba, *V'Yakam Melech Chadash.*) Accordingly, "Gog and Magog" allude to an alliance of all gentile nations.
594 B.T. *Kiddushin* 39B.

Rabbi Yossi, however, disagreed and held that not even the awesome events of the Messianic era can rival the reward which awaits the righteous in the world to come.

This dispute may parallel a disagreement between Rabbi Yochanan and Shmuel recorded in the Babylonian Talmud. Rabbi Yochanan taught that the Messianic era will include many miraculous events while Shmuel held that the only difference between that time and the present will be the elimination of gentile oppression.[595]

Perhaps Rabbi Chama bar Chanina maintains that great miracles will take place after the arrival of the Messiah. Accordingly, one who witnesses them is as though he consumed his share in the world to come.

Rabbi Yossi, however, holds that the Messianic era will involve a spectacular military victory, but nothing miraculous. Accordingly, it cannot be said to even remotely compete with the reward awaiting the righteous in the world to come.

---

[595] B.T. *Brachoth* 34B.

Shevi'ith 4:8 (Compare B.T. *Brachoth* 64A and B.T. *Sanhedrin* 91B)

רבי יונה בשם רבי חייא בר אשי: עתידין הן חבידין להתייגע
מבתי כנסיות לבתי מדרשות. מה טעם? "יֵלְכוּ מֵחַיִל אֶל חָיִל יֵרָאֶה אֶל
אֱ-לֹהִים בְּצִיּוֹן." (תהלים פד:ח).

Rabbi Yonah said in the name of Rabbi Chiya bar Ashi: In the future the scholars will trouble themselves to move from the synagogues to the study halls. What is the Scriptural basis for this? "They go from strength to strength, [their multitude] will appear before God in Zion."[596] [An earlier verse says, "Happy are those who sit in Your house; they shall yet praise You forever."[597] The use of the future tense suggests that the righteous will pray and study *Torah* even after they are resurrected.[598]]

Several commentators understand Rabbi Yonah as referring to the spiritual world to which a person's soul goes after his or her death. However, once a person dies, he or she is exempt from further performance of the Mitzvoth,[599] so how does it make sense to talk about someone praying or studying Torah?

---

[596] Psalms 84:8 according to *Rashi* ad. loc.
[597] Psalms 84:5.
[598] B.T. *Sanhedrin* 91B.
[599] J.T. *Kilayim* 9:3 and *Tosefta Shabbath* 18:11.

Rabbi Yosef Hayyim suggests that although people do not do Mitzvoth after death, they do still learn Torah![600] *Rabbi Eliezer Waldenburg offers a different answer: After a scholar dies, he can still rise to higher spiritual levels when his disciples recite his teachings.*[601]

The context of the passage under review, however, indicates that it refers to the future resurrection of the dead rather than the spiritual world to which a person's soul goes immediately after death.[602] *Rabbi Eliyahu Dessler wrote that after the resurrection of the dead, people will still have an evil inclination but that it will be highly attenuated, like the evil inclination of Adam and Chavah before they sinned. Accordingly, people will perform Mitzvoth at that time, but the spiritual level of such activities will be much higher than what it is today because the temptation to disobey or to be lax will be greatly reduced.*[603] *Nonetheless, it is never possible for anyone to*

---

[600] *Ben Yehoyada* on B.T. *Brachoth* 64A.

[601] *Tzitz Eliezer*, Vol. XVIII, Chapter 64. B.T. *Yevamoth* 96B-97A says that when a student recites his deceased master's teachings, it causes the latter's lips to move in the grave, a figurative way of saying that the master's position in the spiritual world is elevated. (See *Torah From Jerusalem*, Vol. I, pp. 51-52.)

[602] This is also how the *Talmud* interprets "Happy are those who sit in Your house, they shall yet praise You forever." (Psalms 84:5) in B.T. *Sanhedrin* 91B.

[603] Rabbi Eliyahu Dessler, *Michtav Me'Eliyahu*, Vol. II, Part II, pp. 147-148.

fully comprehend God. Therefore, even in the future, scholars will have to continue studying the Torah.[604]

---

[604] Rabbi Avraham Chaim of Zlotchow as cited in *Beurei HaChassiduth LeShas* by Rabbi Yisrael Yitzchak Chassidah (*Mossad HaRav Kook*, Jerusalem, 1975), pp. 65-66.

Shevi'ith 4:8 (Compare B.T. *Sanhedrin* 110B-111A)

מאימתי קטני ישראל חיין? רבי חייה רובה ורבי שמעון ברבי:
חד אמר משיולדו וחד אמר משידברו. מאן דאמר משיולדו, "יָבֹאוּ וְיַגִּידוּ
צִדְקָתוֹ לְעַם נוֹלָד כִּי עָשָׂה." (תהלים כב:לב). מאן דאמר משידברו, "זֶרַע
יַעַבְדֶנּוּ יְסֻפַּר לַה' לַדּוֹר." (תהלים כב:לא).

תני בשם רבי מאיר: מֶשׁהוּא יודע לענות "אמן" בבית הכנסת.
מה טעם? "פִּתְחוּ שְׁעָרִים וְיָבֹא גוֹי צַדִּיק שֹׁמֵר אֱמֻנִים." (ישעיה כו:ב).
תמן אמרי: משימולו. "[עָנִי אֲנִי וְגֹוֵעַ מִנֹּעַר] נָשָׂאתִי אֵמֶיךָ
אָפוּנָה." (תהלים פח:טז).

ורבנן דהכא אמרין: משיולדו. "וּלְצִיּוֹן יֵאָמַר אִישׁ וְאִישׁ יֻלַּד בָּהּ
וְהוּא יְכוֹנְנֶהָ עֶלְיוֹן." (תהלים פז:ה).

רבי אלעזר אומר: אפילו נפלים. מה טעם? "...וּנְצוּרֵי יִשְׂרָאֵל
לְהָשִׁיב..." "...וּנְצִירֵי יִשְׂרָאֵל לְהָשִׁיב... ." (ישעיה מט:ו).

From when do Jewish minors merit resurrection?
Rabbi Chiya the Great and Rabbi Shimon ben Rebbi each
expressed a view. One said that it is once they are born
while the other said it is once they start to speak. The one
who said that it is once they are born concludes so from the
verse, "They shall come and tell His righteousness to a
nation which is born for [so] He has done."[605] The one
who said that it is once they start to speak concludes so
from the verse, "Seed [of Israel] shall serve Him; it shall
speak of the Lord to [the next] generation."[606] [The verse
in Psalms immediately preceding these two says that

---

[605] Psalms 22:32.
[606] Psalms 22:31.

Hashem will not resurrect the wicked.[607] The *Talmud* therefore understands these verses as referring to resurrection as well.]

It is taught in the name of Rabbi Meir: [A Jewish minor merits resurrection] once he knows to respond *"Amen"* in the synagogue. What is the Scriptural basis for this? "Open the gates and let enter a righteous nation which keeps faith."[608] [The term "keeps faith" (שומר אמונים) in Hebrew may be read "which says '*Amens*'" (שאומר אמן).[609]]

There [in Babylonia] they say: Once they are circumcised, as it says, "I am poor and afflicted from youth; I have born Your fear firmly."[610] [The expression "poor and afflicted" may refer to circumcision, a painful operation a Jew must endure as a "youth." *Rashi*, however, says that "Your fear" refers to circumcision while the Hebrew term for "afflicted" (גוע) is used in the *Tanach* to refer to the death of the righteous. Hence, one who has undergone circumcision merits to be considered among the righteous who die and are later resurrected.[611]]

The rabbis here [in the Land of Israel] say: Once they are born, as it says, "And to Zion it will be said, 'Each man who will be born in it, He will establish it on

---

607 See *Targum Yonathan ben Uziel* on Psalms 22:30.
608 Isaiah 26:2.
609 B.T. *Sanhedrin* 110B.
610 Psalms 88:16.
611 *Rashi* on B.T. *Sanhedrin* 110B sub verba *"Oni Ani"* (עני אני).

high.'"[612] [The *Talmud* appears to understand the verse to mean that "He," God, will establish the soul of each person born in Zion, i.e., every Jew, "on high," meaning at the time of the resurrection.]

Rabbi Elazar says: Even stillborns are destined for resurrection. What is the Scriptural basis for this? The phrase, "...and to cause the besieged [ונצורי] of Israel to return..." should be understood to mean, "and to cause those formed [ונצירי] of Israel to return... ."[613] [The word "ונצירי" is actually written in the verse, but when read, it is pronounced "ונצורי."]

Rabbi Yisrael Eisenstein presents a question raised by the Y'feh Mareh: What is the significance of knowing at what point a child is subject to resurrection? As a rule, the Talmud only deals with issues that have current practical application, not theoretical ones which apply to the future Messianic era. Whatever will happen in the future is up to God and not for people today to conjecture about.[614]

Rabbi Eisenstein answers that there is indeed a practical side to this inquiry. If a baby dies before being circumcised and circumcision is a prerequisite to resurrection, then the baby should be circumcised before he is buried. According to those who say that the baby merits

---

[612] Psalms 87:5.

[613] Isaiah 49:6.

[614] B.T. *Sanhedrin* 51B with *Tosafoth* sub verba "*Hilchatha L'Meshicha*" (הלכתא למשיחא).

resurrection without circumcision, this ritual need not be performed.[615] *In actual practice, the Shulchan Aruch indeed rules that a baby who dies before he is circumcised should be circumcised and given a name.*[616] *Presumably, Rabbi Eisenstein would add that according to the view that a baby merits resurrection once he knows to say "Amen," it is important to try to teach children this response as soon as they can speak.*

Actually, however, the question of the Y'feh Mareh may have a simpler answer. The Talmud does not address theoretical questions concerning the era of the resurrection which have nothing to do with people living today. For example, suppose a woman's husband dies and she remarries. The Talmud does not discuss which husband she will be married to at the time of the resurrection as such theoretical matters have no importance today. However, the Talmud frequently discusses the future redemption to give hope, encouragement and consolation to the Jewish people. For instance, the Talmud teaches that in the future farmers will be able to grow a new crop of grain each month and trees will bear a new crop of fruit every two months.[617] *Similarly, the Midrash declares that in the future, the Jewish people will attain a spiritual level far greater than that of the ministering angels.*[618] *The*

---

[615] *Amudei Yerushalayim.*
[616] *Shulchan Aruch, Yoreh Deah* 263:5.
[617] J.T. *Shekalim* 6:2.
[618] *BaMidbar Rabbah* 20:20.

Talmud further describes how God will provide a delightful banquet and beautiful dwellings for the righteous in the future. In addition, He will decorate the restored Jerusalem with huge jewels.[619] *In this way, despite the downtrodden position Jews may find themselves in during the long period of their exile, they do not despair because they think about the glorious future. Although these teachings have no Halachic significance, the Talmud records them to comfort the Jewish people.*

In the same way, the passage of the Talmud translated here consoles those who have suffered the loss of a young baby or a miscarriage by pointing out that babies and fetuses will merit resurrection. As a case in point, a young man whose mother suffered several miscarriages once consulted Rabbi Moshe Feinstein about that tragedy. Rabbi Feinstein consoled him by telling him that after the future resurrection, he will merit to have righteous brothers and sisters who have never sinned.[620] *Thus, the Talmud records the dispute of the rabbis concerning this issue not because the answer matters Halachically, but because the discussion provides comfort and encouragement to those who are bereaved.*

The Mishnah says, "All Israel has a share in the world to come, as it says, 'Your people are all righteous, they shall surely inherit land; a creation of My planting,

---

[619] B.T. *Baba Bathra* 75A and *Pesikta Rabbathai* 31:4.
[620] *Igroth Moshe, Yoreh Deah* III, Responsa 138.

the work of My hands in which I glory.[621]*"[622]* *God created all Jews with the potential to share in the world to come. True, some plants grow and develop to a much greater extent than others, but all possess the same basic characteristics. So, too, even a baby, or according to some opinions, a fetus, has this potential.*

One of the basic tenets of the Jewish religion is that people are rewarded according to their actions. Why, then, should a fetus or baby merit resurrection? One possible answer is that babies will be resurrected as part of the reward of the Patriarchs and Matriarchs. A parent always wants his or her children to be happy and successful. Thus, God will resurrect even those who lack merit not for their own sake, but as a reward to the righteous ancestors of the Jewish people.

A person cannot be resurrected without studying Torah or helping others to do so.[623] *This is why the rabbis state that an angel teaches each Jewish baby the entire Torah while it resides in its mother's womb. When the baby emerges, the angel strikes it on the mouth and causes*

---

[621] Isaiah 60:21.

[622] *Sanhedrin* 10:1. Righteous non-Jews also have a share in the world to come. (See B.T. *Sanhedrin* 105A and *Yad HaChazakah, Hilchoth Melachim* 8:11.).

[623] See B.T. *Brachoth* 17A which says that women who are not learned merit a share in the world to come because they assist their sons and husbands to learn *Torah.*

it to forget what it learned.[624] *God makes sure that even a fetus learns Torah so that it will merit resurrection.*[625]

This may explain the different opinions expressed in the Talmud. According to one view, a baby merits resurrection immediately upon conception since at that time he already starts learning Torah. Another view requires that the baby be born and, thus, have completed his studies. Yet another opinion is that the baby must be circumcised because both the Torah and circumcision are called "covenants." Other rabbis hold that the baby must start to speak, thus having the ability to study Torah and regain what he has forgotten. Finally, one of the sages held that the baby be able to answer "Amen" in the synagogue, putting his preliminary knowledge of Torah to practical use.

---

[624] B.T. *Nidah* 30B.

[625] *Midrash Othioth Rabbi Akiva HaShalem* says that the angel Metatron spends three hours each day teaching *Torah* to stillborns and children who died very young.

Shevi'ith 6:1

אמר רבי אלעזר: מאליהן קיבלו עליהן את המעשרות. מה
טעם? "וּבְכָל זֹאת אֲנַחְנוּ כֹּרְתִים אֲמָנָה וְכֹתְבִים וְעַל הֶחָתוּם שָׂרֵינוּ לְוִיֵּנוּ
כֹּהֲנֵינוּ." (נחמיה י:א).

מה מקיים רבי אלעזר, "...וְאֶת בְּכוֹרֵי בָקָרֵינוּ וְצֹאנֵינוּ [לְהָבִיא
לְבֵית אֱ-לֹהֵינוּ לַכֹּהֲנִים הַמְשָׁרְתִים בְּבֵית אֱ-לֹהֵינוּ]" (נחמיה י:לו)? מכיון
שקיבלו עליהן דברים שלא היו מחוייבים עליהן, אפילו דברים שהיו
מחוייבים עליהן העלה עליהן כאילו מאליהן קבלו עליהן.

מה מקיים רבי יוסי בר רבי חנינא, "וּבְכָל זֹאת..." (נחמיה י:א)?
מכיון שקיבלו עליהן בסבר פנים יפות, העלה עליהן הכתוב כאילו
מאיליהן קבלו עליהן.

[When Joshua led the Jews into the Land of Israel,
they became liable to observe those *Mitzvoth* which apply
only there, such as tithing crops. The sages disagree as to
whether the obligation to fulfill such commandments
resumed after the Jews returned from the Babylonian exile.
Rabbi Yossi bar Chanina says that the original Biblical
obligation went back into place while Rabbi Elazar says
that these commandments only applied because of a
rabbinical decree.]

Said Rabbi Elazar: On their own, they accepted
upon themselves the tithes. [The Jews only observed them
due to a rabbinical decree.] What is the Scriptural source
for this? "Despite all this, we form and write an agreement,
and our officers, Levites and priests sign upon it."[626]

---

[626] Nehemiah 10:1.

[Although the Jews suffered many hardships upon returning to the Land of Israel from Babylonia, they voluntarily pledged to observe the *Torah*. The verses which follow this one mention those *Mitzvoth* associated with the Land, such as tithing. Rabbi Elazar takes this to mean that the Jews undertook to perform those commandments although not obligated to do so by the *Torah* itself.]

How does Rabbi Elazar interpret [the following verse which appears in the same section of the *Tanach*]? "...and the firstborn of our cattle and our sheep to bring to the house of our God to the priests who serve in the house of our God."[627] [The *Mitzvah* to give the firstborn offspring of sheep and cattle to the *Kohanim* applies even outside the Land of Israel. Since the verse mentions this *Mitzvah* along with the *Mitzvoth* that apply only in the Land of Israel, it implies that the obligation to obey such commandments derived from the *Torah* and not merely from the rabbis.] Because they accepted things upon themselves which were not obligatory, Scripture views them as having voluntarily accepted upon themselves even those things which were obligatory upon them.

How does Rabbi Yossi bar Chanina [who says the Biblical obligation to tithe resumed when the Jews returned from Babylonian exile] understand the verse [quoted above], "Despite all this, we form and write an agreement, and our officers, Levites and priests sign upon it?"[628]

---

[627] Nehemiah 10:37.
[628] Nehemiah 10:1.

Since they accepted the *Mitzvoth* upon themselves graciously, Scripture views it as though they voluntarily accepted them.

> *Both Rabbi Elazar and Rabbi Yossi bar Chanina held that it is more meritorious to perform Mitzvoth voluntarily than to do so because one is commanded. The Babylonian Talmud also expresses this view. The Torah says that God "...does not show favoritism nor take a bribe."[629] The ministering angels asked how God can show partiality to Israel, as the Torah says, "May the Lord favor you and grant you peace?"[630] God answered that He could hardly do otherwise in light of the fact that whereas He only commanded Jews to recite grace after a meal which fully satisfies one's appetite, the sages instituted its recitation even after eating a piece of bread as big as an egg or as big as an olive.[631] Since Jews do more than is commanded of them, they merit that God go beyond the letter of the law and show special favor towards them.*
>
> *Elsewhere, however, the Talmud teaches that one who is commanded to do a Mitzvah is greater than one who performs it voluntarily.[632] The reason for this is that it is the nature of the evil inclination to be rebellious,[633] people having a natural aversion to being forced to do things. The*

---

[629] Deuteronomy 10:17.
[630] Numbers 6:26.
[631] B.T. *Brachoth* 20B.
[632] B.T. *Kiddushin* 31A, *Avodah Zarah* 3A.
[633] See *Tosafoth* ad. loc.

same person who views his or her work as grinding drudgery may exert substantial effort at recreational activities. In addition, Hashem decreed certain commandments because of the spiritual effect they have. One who performs a Mitzvah voluntarily does not accomplish the same thing spiritually as one who is commanded.[634]

Rabbeinu Nissim explains that these passages of the Talmud do not really contradict one another. It is true that a private person who assumes the responsibility upon himself to perform a Mitzvah does not receive as great a reward as one who is commanded to perform it because his evil inclination does not tempt him to be lax or because he does not accomplish the same thing spiritually as one who is commanded. However, the Torah authorized the sages to issue decrees which Jews must obey.[635] *Therefore, when the rabbis ordained recitation of grace after eating only a small quantity of bread, it counts as though the Jews were commanded to do so.*

In the passage under consideration, although Rabbi Elazar and Rabbi Yossi bar Chanina disagree as to whether the Mitzvoth associated with the Land of Israel were Biblically required after the Jews returned from the Babylonian exile, they both agree that a rabbinical decree which shows the great love Jews have for the Mitzvoth would cause them to have greater merit.

---

[634] *Maharal, Chiddushei Aggadoth* on B.T. *Kiddushin* 31A.
[635] *Drashoth HaRan, HaDrush HaChamishi.*

Shevi'ith 6:1 (Compare B.T. *Eruvin* 63A)

רבי חייא בשם רב הונא: תלמיד שהורה אפילו כהלכתא, אין
הוראתו הורייה.
תני: תלמיד שהורה הלכה לפני רבו חייב מיתה.
תני בשם רבי אליעזר: לא מתו נדב ואביהו אלא שהורו בפני משה רבן.
מעשה בתלמיד אחד שהורה לפני רבי אליעזר רבו. אמר
לאימא שלו-ם אשתו, "אינו יוצא שבתו." ולא יצא שבתו עד שמת.
אמרו לו תלמידיו, "רבי, נביא אתה?"
אמר להן, "לא נביא אנכי ולא בן נביא אנכי, אלא כך אני
מקובל שכל תלמיד המורה הלכה בפני רבו חייב מיתה."
תני: אסור לתלמיד להורות הלכה בפני רבו עד שיהיה רחוק
ממנו י"ב מיל כמחנה ישראל... כהדא רבי תנחום בר חייא הוה בְּחֵפָה
והוון שאלין ליה והוא מורה, שאלין ליה והוא מורה. אמרין ליה, "ולא
כן אולפן רבי שאסור לתלמיד להורות הלכה לפני רבו עד שיהא רחוק
ממנו י"ב מיל כמחנה ישראל? והא רבי מנא רבן יתיב בציפורין!"
אמר לון, "ייתי דלא ידעית!" מן ההיא שעתה, לא הורי.

Rabbi Chiya in the name of Rav Huna said: A student who renders a decision, even if it accords with the *Halachah*, his ruling is no ruling.

A *Braitha* teaches: A student who makes a *Halachic* ruling in the presence of his master deserves death.

It was learned in the name of Rabbi Eliezer: Nadab and Abihu did not die except because they ruled in front of Moses, their master.

There was an incident with a certain student who ruled in front of Rabbi Eliezer, his master. Rabbi Eliezer said to Imma Shalom, his wife, "He will not last the week." And, indeed, the week did not pass before he died.

His disciples said to him, "Rabbi, are you a prophet?"

"I am not a prophet nor am I the son of a prophet," he answered. "However, I have it as a tradition that any student who renders a *Halachic* decision in the presence of his master deserves death."

A *Braitha* teaches: It is forbidden for a student to render a *Halachic* decision in the presence of his master until he is distant from him twelve miles[636] like the encampment of Israel [in the Sinai desert]... as with Rabbi Tanchum bar Chiya who was in Haifa and they repeatedly asked him questions and he repeatedly made rulings. They asked him, "Did not the master instruct us that it is forbidden for a student to make a *Halachic* ruling in the presence of his master until he is distant from him twelve miles like the encampment of Israel and here Rabbi Manna, our master, resides in Sepphoris?"

He answered, "I swear that I did not know!" From that moment on, he did not issue *Halachic* rulings.

---

[636] *Talmudic* miles consisted of two thousand cubits each. Opinions as to how long a cubit is in modern measurements range from one and a half to two feet (45 to 60 centimeters). That would make a *Talmudic* mile about three thousand to four thousand feet (900 to 1,200 meters). (See *Aids to Talmud Study*, Rabbi Aryeh Carmell, 4th Revised Edition (Feldheim, New York, 1980), p. 74.). The *Talmud* calculated that an average person could walk one such mile in about eighteen minutes. (*Chochmath Adam, Klal* 30:9.).

One would think that it would be highly desirable to have as many people as possible teaching the laws of the Torah. Why does the Talmud view a student who renders Halachic rulings in the presence of his master, even correct rulings, so severely?

The Talmud tells how a non-Jew once approached Shammai and asked to convert to Judaism on condition that he only require him to accept the Written Torah but not the Oral Torah. Since both the written and oral parts of the Torah are of Divine origin, Shammai rejected the potential convert. The same person went to Hillel who agreed to his condition. Hillel began the Gentile's conversion training by teaching him the Hebrew alphabet. When the Gentile arrived the following day for his next lesson, Hillel pointed to the letter Aleph and said, "This is Tav."

"But yesterday you taught me that this is Aleph!" protested the non-Jew.

"Now you see the point," explained Hillel. "Didn't you rely on me to teach you the alphabet in the first place? Just as you have to rely on rabbinic tradition even to know which letters are which, you have to rely on rabbinic tradition to understand the Torah."

Realizing that Hillel was right, the non-Jew agreed to accept all of the Torah and convert properly.[637]

From this story one can see the profound importance of respecting the rabbis. Without a reliable

---

[637] B.T. *Shabbath* 31A.

chain of tradition that leads back to Mount Sinai, people today would not know an Aleph from a Tav and the entire Jewish religion would collapse. By making a Halachic ruling in the presence of his instructor, a disciple shows that he wishes to rely on his own expertise rather than that of his master. Such an attitude gives the impression that people are free to interpret the teachings of the Torah as they see fit rather than strictly according to tradition. For this reason, one who makes even a correct Halachic ruling without the permission of his master deserves punishment.

Shevi'ith 6:1   (*VaYikra Rabbah* 17:6; compare *Devarim Rabbah* 5:14)

אמר רבי שמואל: שלש פרסטיניות שלח יהושע לארץ ישראל
עד שלא יכנסו לארץ. מי שהוא רוצה להפנות יפנה, להשלים ישלים,
לעשות מלחמה יעשה.

גרגשי פינה והאמין לו להקדוש ברוך הוא והלך לו לאפריקי.
"עַד בֹּאִי וְלָקַחְתִּי אֶתְכֶם אֶל אֶרֶץ כְּאַרְצְכֶם..." (מלכים ב יח:לב). זו
אפריקי.

גבעונים השלימו. "...וְכִי הִשְׁלִימוּ יֹשְׁבֵי גִבְעוֹן אֶת יִשְׂרָאֵל... ".
(יהושע י:א)

שלושים ואחד מלך עשו מלחמה ונפלו.

Rabbi Shmuel bar Nachman[638] said: Joshua sent three edicts[639] to the Land of Israel before the Jews entered. [They said:] Whoever wants to depart may depart, whoever wants to make peace may make peace, and whoever wants to wage war may do so.

The Girgashites departed. They believed the Holy One, Blessed be He, and took off to Africa. "Until I come

---

[638] *Ein Yaakov* has the name this way instead of "Rabbi Shmuel" as in the Romm Vilna edition.

[639] *P'nei Moshe* and *Ein Yaakov* have the word here as "פרסטיגיות." *P'nei Moshe* says it means the same as פריסתקא, "a royal edict." The term *"peri"* or *"para"* in Greek means "around," while *"steichein"* means "go," so a *"parastichy"* would be a letter which "circulates around." According to the Romm Vilna text which reads "פרסטיניות," perhaps the end of the word derives from the Greek *"stellein"* meaning "to send," again indicating a letter which is "sent around."

and take you to a land like your land... ."[640] This means
Africa. [The verse refers to an offer made by Rabashakeh,
a general of the Assyrian army, to repatriate the Jews.
Since he was referring to Africa, the *Talmud* infers that part
of Africa is similar to the Land of Israel and that the
Girgashites moved there as a reward for believing God.]

The Gibeonites made peace [as the verse says,]
"...and that the inhabitants of Gibeon made peace with
Israel... ."[641]

Thirty-one kings made war and fell.

*The Torah required the Jews to offer peace to the
Canaanite nations which inhabited the Land of Israel
before invading. Had the Canaanites agreed to pay taxes,
provide labor for public works and observe the seven
Noahide commandments, then a peace treaty would have
been concluded.*[642] *Accordingly, in his last letter, Joshua
was not really offering the Canaanites to make war, but
merely informing them that the Jews were prepared for war
if necessary.*

*The Tanach records how the Gibeonites, a
Canaanite nation, used worn out clothing and moldy food
to disguise themselves as a people which came from
another land far away. Joshua and the Elders made a
peace treaty with them, swearing not to harm them. When*

---

[640] II Kings 18:32.
[641] Joshua 10:1.
[642] *Yad HaChazakah, Hilchoth Melachim* 6:1-4.

the Jews discovered that they had been tricked, they did not kill the Gibeonites because of the oath they had made.[643]

The Rambam, among others, asks: If Joshua sent letters offering to make peace, why did the Gibeonites perpetrate this deception? Also, if the Torah required the Jews to offer peace to the Canaanites, why does the Tanach suggest that if not for the oath which the Jewish leaders made, they would have killed the Gibeonites?[644]

The answer to these questions is that the Jews were only to offer peace at a time when they had some assurance that the response would be sincere. Once the Jews crossed the Jordan River to enter the Land of Israel, its Canaanite inhabitants would have become so overwhelmed by fear that they would have agreed to abandon idolatry just to save their lives. That could lead to a dangerous situation where they would resume their idolatrous practices later on and be a harmful influence on their Jewish neighbors. The Gibeonites decided to accept peace only after the Jews crossed the Jordan and knew that Joshua's offer no longer remained open.[645]

---

[643] Joshua 9:3-27.

[644] *Yad HaChazakah, Hilchoth Melachim* 6:5.

[645] *Me'Am Loez* on Joshua 9:1-2.

Shevi'ith 9:1 (Compare B.T. *Shabbath* 33B-34A and *Breishith Rabbah* 79:6)

רבי שמעון בן יוחי הוה עבר בשמיטתא וחמי חד מלקט שביעית. אמר ליה, "ולית אסור? ולאו ספיחין אינון?"
אמר ליה, "ולא את הוא מתירן?"
אמר ליה, "ואין חביריי חלוקין עלי?" קרא עליו, "...וּפֹרֵץ גָּדֵר יִשְׁכֶנּוּ נָחָשׁ. (קהלת י:ח). וכן הוות ליה.

רבי שמעון בן יוחי עביד טמיר במערתא תלת עשר שנין, ב"מערת חרובין דתרומה," עד שהעלה גופו חלודה. לסוף תלת עשר שנין, אמר, "לֵינָה נפיק חמי מה קלא עלמא?"

נפיק ויתיב ליה על פומא דמערתא. חמא חד צייד צייד ציפרין, פרס מצודתיה. שמע ברת קלא אמרה, "דִימוֹס," ואישתיזבת ציפור. אמר, "ציפור מבלעדי שמיא לא יבדא. כל שכן בר נשא." כד חמא דשדכן מילייא, אמר, "ניחות ניחמי בהדין דימוסין דטבריא."

אמר, "צריכין אנו לעשות תקנה כמו שעשו אבותינו הראשונים. וַיִחַן אֶת פְּנֵי הָעִיר,' (בראשית לג:יח), שהיו עושין איטלוסן ומוכרין בשוק." אמר, "נידכי טבריא."

והוה נסב תורמסין ומקצץ ומקליק וכל הָן דהוה מיתא, הוה טייף וסליק ליה מן לעיל.

חמתיה חד כותי. אמר, "לֵינָא אזל מפלי בהדין סבא דיהודאי?" נסב חד מית, אזל ואטמריה הָן דדכי. אתא לגביה רבי שמעון בן יוחי. אמר ליה, "לא דכית אתר פלן? איתא ואנא מפיק לך מן תמן." צפה רבי שמעון בן יוחי ברוח הקודש שנתנו שם. אמר, "גזור אני עליך העליונים שירדו ועל התחתונים שיעלו!" וכן הוית ליה.
מי עבר קומי מגדלא, שמע קליה דספרא אמר, "הא בר יוחי מדכי טבריא!"
אמר ליה, "ייבא עלי אם לא שמעתי שטבריא עתידה להיטהר.

אפילו כן לא הימנין הוית!"
מיד נעשה גל של עצמות.

[The *Torah* forbids Jews to cultivate the Land of
Israel during the Sabbatical year. However, some crop
growth occurs on its own. The *Mishnah* teaches that Rabbi
Shimon bar Yochai permitted the use of such growth except
in the case of cabbage. The majority of sages, however,
forbade harvesting and using aftergrowth altogether.]

Rabbi Shimon bar Yochai was traveling during the
Sabbatical year when he saw someone gathering crops
which had sprouted during that year. He said, "Is it not
forbidden? Are they not aftergrowth?"

Replied the man, "Aren't you the one who permits
them?"

"Don't my colleagues disagree with me?"
[Whenever there is a dispute, the *Halachah* goes according
to the majority, so, although Rabbi Shimon bar Yochai
disagreed with the other rabbis, when it came to matters of
practice, he ruled according to their opinion.] Rabbi
Shimon bar Yochai applied to him the verse, "...and a snake
will bite one who breaches a fence."[646] And so it was [that
a snake bit the offender]. [The *Torah* itself permits the use
of crops which grow on their own during the Sabbatical

---

[646] Ecclesiastes 10:8. A snake is the proper vehicle to punish one who
breaches the fences erected by the sages to protect Jewish observance
since it was a snake which first enticed Adam and Chavah to breach
Hashem's commandment. (*VaYikra Rabbah* 26:2).

year. The rabbis, however, forbade the use of such aftergrowth to prevent violations of the laws against cultivating or storing crops grown during that year. The *Torah* both authorizes and commands the rabbis to make such "fences" to guard its laws.[647]]

[When a careless person repeated a derogatory remark Rabbi Shimon bar Yochai made about the Roman government, the rabbi was forced to flee for his life.[648]] Rabbi Shimon bar Yochai hid in a cave for thirteen years, in the "cave of the sacred carobs,"[649] until his body developed sores. [To preserve their clothing, Rabbi Shimon and his son would bury themselves in sand up to their necks while they studied *Torah*, only wearing their clothing during prayer. This caused their bodies to develop sores and lesions.[650]] At the end of thirteen years, he said,

---

[647] See, for example, the *Rambam's* introduction to the *Mishnah*. For further discussion of this topic, see Volume I of *Torah from Jerusalem*, pp. 29-32.

[648] B.T. *Shabbath* 33B.

[649] The cave got this name after Rabbi Shimon bar Yochai and his son lived there for thirteen years miraculously sustained by the fruit of a carob tree which grew there. (*P'nei Moshe*). The word "תרומה" used in this text comes from the word "רום" and, denoting something "lifted" because the *T'rumah* gift which Jews gave to the *Kohanim* was "lifted" and removed from the rest of the crop. This "uplifting" was also spiritual as evidenced by the fact that *T'rumah* acquires an elevated *Halachic* status whereby only *Kohanim* may eat it and must do so in a state of ritual purity. The carob tree in the cave was not literally *T'rumah*, but obviously "uplifted" or "sacred," because it grew there by dint of a miracle.

[650] B.T. *Shabbath* 33B.

"Should I not go out to see what news there is in the world?"

He emerged and sat himself at the mouth of the cave. He observed a hunter trapping birds by spreading a net. He heard a Heavenly voice say, "Clemency," whereupon the bird escaped. He remarked, "If a bird cannot be trapped contrary to the will of Heaven, how much more so a human being."

When he saw that matters had quieted down [and that he was no longer a wanted man], he said, "Let us go down and see the bathhouses of Tiberias." [The word "דימוס" in Greek means "clemency," while the word "דימוסין" means "bathhouse,"[651] so Rabbi Shimon bar Yochai understood the Heavenly voice as hinting to him that he was safe to emerge from the cave and that he should visit the bathhouses of Tiberias.]

---

[651] *Rashi* and *Tosafoth* on B.T. *Avodah Zarah* 16B say that דימוס was the name of a Greek deity and that the word means "mercy." The Greek goddess Themis was indeed supposed to be the goddess of law and justice. It appears from the *Talmudic* text there that the name of the goddess was invoked whenever a gentile judge declared an accused innocent. Thus, the word came to mean "mercy" or "clemency." The word דימוסין in Greek meant "bathhouse," probably from the word, "*thermos*," meaning "hot." Hot water was such an outstanding feature of ancient bathhouses that B.T. *Brachoth* 60A records a special prayer one should recite to seek protection from the heat. In addition, *Mussaf HeAruch* states that the word תורמסר found in J.T. *Ma'aser Sheni* 1:1 means "bathhouse attendant." Greek and Latin loan words often appear with slight variations in sundry Jewish texts.

He further said, "We should make a improvement as our first ancestors did. [Concerning Jacob, the *Torah* says,] '...and he encamped before the city,'[652] meaning that they made shops and sold things in the marketplace. [The term ויחן, "he encamped," can also mean "he acted graciously."[653] Thankful that he had just escaped from Laban and Esau, Jacob acted graciously when he arrived in Shechem by building shops. This was an act of kindness either because there were not enough shops or because Jacob and his sons sold goods cheaply in them.[654]] Let us purify Tiberias." [There were areas around the city where the precise location of gravesites had been forgotten. This caused great inconvenience for *Kohanim* who had to walk far out of their way to avoid the possibility of ritual defilement.[655]]

Rabbi Shimon bar Yochai took lupines, cut them, and scattered them over the area. Wherever there was a corpse, it would float and bulge up.

A certain Samaritan observed him. He said to himself, "Why don't I go have some fun with this Jewish elder?" He took a corpse and hid it where Rabbi Shimon bar Yochai had purified. Then he went to Rabbi Shimon

---

[652] Genesis 33:18.

[653] *Rashi* sub verba "*Tiken LaHem*" (תיקן להם) on B.T. *Shabbath* 33B. *Rashi* also suggests that the word ויקן which starts the next verse means "he improved," having the same root as the word תיקון.

[654] The text in *Breishith Rabbah* 79:6 adds the word "cheaply."

[655] B.T. *Shabbath* 33B-34A.

bar Yochai and said, "Didn't you purify such and such a place? Come and I will produce a corpse from there."

Rabbi Shimon bar Yochai realized by means of a spirit of holiness [a type of prophecy] that the Samaritan had placed it there. He declared, "I decree upon you above to descend and upon those below to rise up!" [The wicked Samaritan should descend to the grave while the corpse should rise.] And so it happened to him.

When Rabbi Shimon bar Yochai passed before a tower, he heard the voice of a scribe saying [sarcastically], "Here is Bar Yochai who purified Tiberias!"

The rabbi responded, "May evil befall me if I have not heard that in the future Tiberias will be purified. Even so, you do not believe me!" [Evidently, there was a tradition that ritual impurity would be removed from Tiberias at some point. Thus, the scribe was not merely skeptical of Rabbi Shimon bar Yochai, but of rabbinic tradition in general.]

Immediately the scribe became a pile of bones.

The Talmud explains that when a person is saved from a dangerous predicament, he or she should show thanks by doing something for the benefit of the general public. What does one thing have to do with the other?

Rabbi Yosef Hayyim explains that when Hashem performs a miracle for someone, He usually reduces that person's reward in the world to come.[656] *God does not*

---

[656] B.T. *Shabbath* 32A.

diminish such a person's merit, however, if he or she shows special kindness towards others. In this case, Rabbi Shimon bar Yochai did not reside in Tiberias, nor was he a Kohen. Accordingly, the improvement he made for the city was a completely unselfish and unusual act of kindness. Measure for measure, God rewarded Rabbi Shimon by keeping his merit intact, something not normally done.[657]

A question remains. Why did Rabbi Shimon bar Yochai choose to remove ritual impurity from the environs of Tiberias as opposed to some other form of public service?

The Babylonian Talmud explains that when Rabbi Shimon bar Yochai left the cave, he met his father-in-law, Rabbi Pinchas ben Yair. Together they visited a bathhouse where Rabbi Pinchas ben Yair began to cry when he observed the sores and lesions which had developed on Rabbi Shimon bar Yochai due to his stay in the cave. Rabbi Shimon bar Yochai pointed out that had his body not been reduced to that condition, he would not have achieved the spiritual level that he did. Before entering the cave, when Rabbi Shimon bar Yochai raised a question, Rabbi Pinchas ben Yair gave twelve answers to it. After the ordeal of the cave, when Rabbi Pinchas ben Yair raised a question, Rabbi Shimon bar Yochai would offer twenty-four answers.[658] *In addition, Rabbi Shimon bar Yochai became*

---

[657] *Ben Yehoyada* on B.T. *Shabbath* 33B.
[658] B.T. *Shabbath* 33B.

the foremost master of Kabbalah (Jewish mystical tradition) and the originator of the Zohar.

By remaining in the cave for thirteen years with his son and later re-emerging into the world, Rabbi Shimon bar Yochai had an experience similar to resurrection. This is hinted at by the carob tree since the Hebrew word for "carob" (חרוב) also means "destroyed."[659] Rabbi Shimon bar Yochai's situation was equivalent to one destroyed and removed from the world but later reborn. This is further suggested by the numerical value of the word "carob" (חרוב) which equals that of "strength" (גבורה), alluding to the revival of the dead as found in the second blessing of the Amidah called "the strength of the rains" (גבורות גשמים) which praises Hashem for reviving the dead.

Rabbi Moshe Chaim Luzzatto wrote that when the dead return to life in the future, they will be on a high spiritual level not presently possible because the soul will be fully revealed in the body.[660] In a similar manner, Rabbi Shimon bar Yochai experienced a unique spiritual development as a result of his ordeal in the cave. Undergoing an experience similar to resurrection gave Rabbi Shimon bar Yochai the spiritual power to perform miracles resembling revival of the dead. Wishing to use this special power to help the community and to allude to

---

[659] Furthermore, carob is not the type of fruit one would think could sustain a person for years. It is hard and not very nourishing. The version of this story in *Breishith Rabbah* 79:6 adds that these were dried out carobs.

[660] *Derech Hashem* 1:3:13.

his resurrection-like experience, he chose to purify Tiberias by causing the corpses of the dead to rise and be identified.[661]

This also clarifies why Rabbi Shimon bar Yochai chose to use lupines as the medium to perform the miracle rather than something else. A righteous person cannot perform a miracle out of nothing. Rather, he or she must choose some physical object upon which the miracle can take effect.[662] *Rabbi Shimon bar Yochai probably chose lupines because the Talmudic word for them,* תורמוסין, *resembles the words* דימוס *(clemency) and* דימוסין *(bathhouse) which played a prominent role in his salvation.*[663] *Furthermore, the Talmud states that lupines must be cooked seven times to become edible,*[664] *hinting at the resurrection of the dead when God will remove the sun from its sheath and it will glow seven times brighter than it does today,*[665] *so lupines were an appropriate medium for*

---

[661] Rabbi Shimon bar Yochai's son, Rabbi Elazar, who lived with him in the cave, also gained a power akin to that of resurrection. After he died, he remained in an attic unburied for many years during which time he rendered *Halachic* decisions. (B.T. *Baba Metzia* 84B).

[662] For example, Elisha performed a miracle of filling many utensils with oil from one small cruise rather than simply filling them out of nothing. (*Me'Am Loez* on II Kings 4:2).

[663] See note 651 above.

[664] B.T. *Shabbath* 74A-74B. This may explain why they were referred to by the Greek word "*thermos*" which means "hot."

[665] Isaiah 30:26 according to *Metzudoth David*. Others hold that the sun will glow 7^3 (three hundred forty-three) times what it does today. (*Rashi* ad. loc.).

performing a miracle which corresponded to the resurrection.[666]

Along these lines, one can understand the seemingly harsh punishment which befell those who challenged Rabbi Shimon bar Yochai's ability to miraculously identify the dead of Tiberias. The Rambam lists resurrection as one of the thirteen fundamental doctrines every Jew must believe.[667] *Those who denied Rabbi Shimon bar Yochai's ability to perform a miracle akin to resurrection were close to denying resurrection itself and, therefore, punished.*

The Talmud teaches that Hashem will reconstitute the bodies of the deceased from a bone in the spine called the "luz."[668] *Just as one of the people who doubted Rabbi Shimon bar Yochai's miraculous powers thereby cast doubt on the resurrection which will emanate from a bone, so he was punished by becoming a pile of bones.*

The Talmud's description of the punishments which befell those who mocked Rabbi Shimon bar Yochai are not meant literally, however. Rabbi Nachman of Breslau explains that the Hebrew word for "pile" (גל) also means "reveal," while the word for "bone" (עצם) also means "essence." Rabbi Shimon bar Yochai revealed the essence

---

[666] *Ben Yehoyada* on B.T. *Shabbath* 34A points out that the seven-fold cooking of lupines is reminiscent of the seven day period of ritual purification required when one is contaminated by contact with the dead, another connection between lupines and Rabbi Shimon bar Yochai's purification of Tiberias.

[667] *Perush HaMishnayoth* on *Sanhedrin* 10:1.

[668] *Breishith Rabbah* 28:3.

of the scribe's sin to him, the spiritual damage created by his scoffing. There can be no greater punishment for a person than to see for himself the spiritual damage a sin has caused.[669] *Likewise, when Rabbi Shimon bar Yochai decreed upon the Samaritan that "you above descend and those below rise up," he made the same type of revelation.*

---

[669] *Likutei Moharan* 98 as cited in *Beurei HaChassiduth LeShas* by Rabbi Yisrael Yitzchak Chassidah (*Mossad HaRav Kook*, Jerusalem, 1975), pp. 60.

T'rumoth 8:3 (Compare *VaYikra Rabbah* 5:6 and *Pesikta D'Rav Kahana* 11:9)

חד איתתא הוות רחמנא מצוותא סגיא. חד זמן, סליק גבה חד
מיסכן. יהבת קומוי מיכול. כי אכל, ארגשת בעלה. איסלק יהבתיה גו
עיליתא. יהבת קומי בעלה דייכיל. אכל, נם ודמך ליה. אתיא חיוויא,
אכל מן מה דהוה קומיה. והוה מסתכל ביה. מן דאיתער, קם, בעי
מיכול מן מה דהוה קומיה. שרי ההוא דעיליתא מילולי ביה.
הדא אמרה ישן מותר?

בריך הוה.

ואין אסור משום יחוד? מכיון דלא חשיד על הדא, לא חשיד
על הדא. "כִּי נָאֵפוּ וְדָם בִּידֵיהֶן ... ." (יחזקאל כג:לז).

מעשה בטבח אחד בציפורין שהיה מאכיל ישראל נבילות
וטריפות. פעם אחת, שתה יין בערב שבת ועלה לגג ונפל ומת והיו
כלבים מלקקים בדמו. אתון, שאלו לרבי חנינא, "מהו מידמיתי מן
קמיהון?"

אמר לון, "כתיב, '...וּבָשָׂר בַּשָּׂדֶה טְרֵפָה לֹא תֹאכֵלוּ לַכֶּלֶב
תַּשְׁלִכוּן אֹתוֹ.' (שמות כב:ל). וזה היה גוזל את הכלבים ומאכיל את
ישראל." אמר לון, "ארפונון דמדידהון אינון אכלין."

מעשה בחסיד אחד שהיה מגלגל בגילוי יין. פעם אחת, לקה
בדלקת וראו אותו יושב ודורש ביום הכפורים וצלוחית של מים בידו.

חד בר נש איגלי לה גרב דחמר. אזל בערובא צומא רבא
למישפכיניה. חמתיה חד. אמר ליה, "הביה לי נשתייה."

אמר ליה, "לאו מגלי הוא?"

אמר ליה, "הביה לי ומרי דצומא ליקום."

לא איספק משתייה עד דאיתחלחל.

...כתיב, "בִּרְצוֹת ה' דַּרְכֵי אִישׁ גַּם אוֹיְבָיו יַשְׁלִם אִתּוֹ." (משלי
טז:ז). רבי אומר: זה הכלב. ורבי יהושע בן לוי אומר: זה הנחש.
רעייא חלבון חלב ואתא חיוויא ואכל מיניה והוה כלבא

מסתכל ביה. כד אתון ייכלון, מישרי נבח בהון ולא אתבוננון. בסופה
אכיל ומית.

חד בר נש עביד תום שחיק גו בייתיה ואתא חיויא דטור ואכיל
מיניה והוי חיויא דבית מסתכל ביה. אתון בני בייתיה מיכל מיניה.
מישרי מתרתר עליהון עפר ולא אתבוננון וקלק גרמיה גוויה.

חד בר נש זמין חד רבן ואייתיב כלבא גביה.

אמר ליה, "ביזיון אנא חייב לך?"

אמר ליה, "רבי, טיבו אנא משלם ליה. שביין עלון לקרתא.
עאל חד מינהון בעא מינסב איתתי ואכל ביציו."

[The *Mishnah* teaches that one may not consume
wine, water or milk which have been left uncovered
because a snake may have drunk from them and left behind
its venom.[670] The rabbis of the *Talmud* have a dispute as
to whether this prohibition applies when a person is
sleeping nearby, since in that circumstance, perhaps a snake
would not approach.[671]]

A certain woman loved *Mitzvoth* greatly. One time,
a certain beggar visited her. She served him food. While
he ate, she detected her husband approaching. [Since her
husband did not approve of helping the poor,] she took the
beggar and hid him in the attic. She set out food for her

[670] *T'rumoth* 8:4.
[671] B.T. *Avodah Zarah* 30A rules that the danger exists even when the
food or drink is left out in front of someone who is asleep. *Shulchan
Aruch, Yoreh Deah* 116:1, however, concludes that one need not worry
about using uncovered food or drink in modern times because snakes do
not commonly live around people. Others maintain that the prohibition
still applies today. (See *Pithchei Teshuvah* ad. loc.).

husband who ate and dozed off. A snake came and ate from the food that was set out before the sleeping man. The hidden beggar observed this. When the husband awakened, he got up and wanted to eat from the food which was before him. The beggar in the attic started to speak [to warn him of the danger].

Does this incident mean that food and drink left out in the presence of one who is sleeping are permitted? [To the contrary, one sees that snakes do contaminate food and drink even in the presence of a sleeping person.]

[This particular snake] was accustomed [to being around people, having lived in a hole in the wall of the house, whereas snakes in general would be afraid to venture near a sleeping person.[672]]

Yet is not the husband prohibited to cohabit with his wife due to seclusion? [A man may not continue to live with a woman suspected of adultery. Although no direct proof of an illicit relationship existed, the fact that this

---

[672] *P'nei Moshe. Maharam de Lonzano*, however, interprets the word "בריר" to mean "wrapped up." The husband had wrapped himself in a sheet so that the snake did not realize he was there. Had he been visible, the snake would not have approached him. The *Vilna Gaon* offers a third view. He says that the text should not read "ברין הוה," but rather "בור הוה," meaning, "he was a boor." The *Talmud* would be saying, "This incident proves that food and drink left exposed in the presence of someone sleeping is permitted since the husband wanted to eat it." The response would be, "You cannot conclude anything from the fact that the husband wanted to eat the food because he was an ignorant boor who did not know or care about the prohibition."

woman hid with the beggar, or had been alone with him, should warrant a separation.]

Since the beggar was not suspected of [bloodshed], he was not suspected of [adultery]. "For they have committed adultery and blood is upon their hands... ."[673] [An adulterer would not warn his paramour's husband about a life-threatening danger because he would prefer for the husband to die so that he could pursue the relationship. Since the beggar warned the husband not to eat from the food the snake had contaminated, the husband could assume that the beggar had not violated his wife.[674]]

There was an incident with a certain butcher in Sepphoris who used to feed Israel non-Kosher meat.[675] One time, he drank wine on the Sabbath eve, ascended a roof, fell off and died. Dogs were lapping up his blood. The townsfolk came and asked Rabbi Chanina, "Is it permissible to move him away from them [although handling a corpse on the Sabbath is usually forbidden]?"

Answered the rabbi, "It is written, '...meat torn in the field you shall not eat; to the dog you shall throw it.'[676]

---

[673] Ezekiel 23:37.

[674] B.T. *Nedarim* 91B according to *Tosafoth* sub verba "*Mayim Genuvim*" (מים גנובים).

[675] The term נבילות in the text means animals which have not had proper ritual slaughter, while טריפות are animals which have one of eight conditions which indicate that they will die within the next twelve months. (*Shulchan Aruch, Yoreh Deah* 29:1).

[676] Exodus 22:30.

This person stole from the dogs and fed Israel. Leave them be, for they eat what is rightfully theirs."[677]

There was an incident with a certain pious person who ridiculed the danger of exposed wine. One time, he was stricken with fever and they saw him sitting and lecturing on *Yom Kippur* with a flask of water in his hand. [Consumption of wine contaminated with venom had made him ill. He soothed the fever by placing the flask on his body to cool himself.[678]]

A certain person had a barrel of wine which had been left exposed. He went to spill it out on the eve of the Great Fast [*Yom Kippur*]. Someone who saw him said, "Give it to me to drink."

"Has it not been exposed?" cautioned the other.

"Give it to me and the Master of the Fast will stand by me."

He no sooner drank from it than he went into convulsions. [A person must take proper precautions against danger and not rely on miracles for protection.[679]]

...It is written, "When the Lord is pleased with a man's ways, even his enemies make peace with him."[680]

---

677 According to *Halachah*, the townsfolk certainly had to move the corpse to protect it from the dogs even on the Sabbath. The rabbi simply meant that the butcher got his just deserts. (*Amudei Yerushalayim Tinyana*).
678 *P'nei Moshe*.
679 Ibid. See B.T. *Pesachim* 64B.
680 Proverbs 16:7.

Rebbi said: This refers to the dog. Rabbi Yehoshua ben Levi said: This refers to the snake.

A snake came along and drank from milk which some herdsmen had drawn. A dog observed this. When they came to eat, it started to bark at them, but they did not understand, so in the end he ate it and died [sacrificing his life to protect his masters].[681]

A certain man prepared ground garlic inside his house. A mountain snake came and ate from it while a snake which lived in the house looked on. When the members of the household came to eat from it, the household snake started to drop dirt on them, but they did not understand, so it threw itself upon it.

A certain man invited over a certain rabbi and seated a dog next to him.

Said the rabbi, "Do I warrant such a disgrace from you?"

"I am repaying him for a favor, Rabbi," he answered. "Marauders entered this town. One came in here seeking to seize my wife, so the dog bit him in his privates."

The Mishnah which serves as the basis of this Talmudic passage lists three liquids one must not leave

---

[681] This translation is supported by the version of this story in *Pesikta D'Rav Kahana*, Section 11 sub verba "*Birtzoth*" (ברצות) which adds that the herdsmen buried the dog and erected a gravestone for it. *P'nei Moshe*, however, says that the herdsmen drank the milk and died.

*uncovered for fear that a snake will poison them: wine,
water and milk.*[682] *The Midrash identifies three verses of
the Tanach as the bases for this Halachah:*[683] *Water
should be covered, as it says, "[Give praise] to Him who
spreads the earth upon the water... ."*[684] *Milk should be
covered, as it is recorded, "[Sisra said to Yael,] ... 'Give me
a little water to drink for I am thirsty.' She opened the
goatskin of milk, gave him to drink, and covered it."*[685]
*Wine should be covered, as it says, "...every goatskin is full
of wine."*[686]

*Why does the Midrash use these Biblical verses as
the source for this Halachah? One would have expected
the Midrash to cite verses which caution Jews to guard
their health and to avoid dangerous situations. That the
Midrash refers to verses which have nothing to do with any
health hazard suggests that the sages based the injunction
against consuming uncovered water, milk or wine upon
other considerations as well.*

*The Torah calls the serpent which seduced Adam
and Chavah to sin the "...most deceptive of all the beasts of
the field... ."*[687] *The primordial snake, which is identical*

---

[682] The *Talmud* adds a few other foods to the list such as ground
garlic.
[683] *Midrash Tehilim* on Psalms 136:6.
[684] Psalms 136:6.
[685] Judges 4:19.
[686] Jeremiah 13:12.
[687] Genesis 3:1.

to the evil inclination,[688] *had a special power to craftily deceive people. Hashem had merely commanded Adam and Chavah not to eat from the Tree of Knowledge.*[689] *The snake, however, said, "...Did not God say, 'Do not eat from any tree in the garden'?"*[690] *In this way, the serpent misrepresented himself as a pious friend who wished to promote obedience to Hashem. True, God had forbidden only one tree, he explained, but you should not eat from any of them to avoid violating the prohibition. By blurring the distinction between what was permitted and what was forbidden and by pretending to wish to act beyond the letter of the law, the snake succeeded in beguiling Chavah.*[691]

Torah is the antidote to the deception of the evil inclination, the snake's poison, because Torah study gives a person the ability to distinguish clearly between what is permitted and what is forbidden. As the Talmud states, "The Holy One, Blessed be He, told Israel: I created the evil inclination and I created Torah as its antidote. If you study Torah, you will not be yielded up to its control."[692]

The Talmud says that Torah is compared to water, milk and wine. One can only preserve these three liquids in

---

humble containers such as earthenware, but if they are stored in silver or gold vessels, they spoil. So, too, the Torah can only reside with a humble person.[693]

To understand the Torah correctly, a student must grasp it on its own terms without twisting its meaning or trying to superimpose his own ideas upon it, and certainly without trying to introduce foreign, non-Jewish philosophies into its teachings. Only one who is humble can accept the Torah on its own terms. Thus, the Torah which resembles wine, milk and water in that it must be studied with humility, must be covered and protected from the pernicious venom of the snake, the tendency to twist and pervert its teachings.

This concept applies especially when Jews are in exile. The word for "exile" in Hebrew (גלות) has the same root as "revealed" or "uncovered" (גלוי) because when Jews are in exile, they are exposed to the culture of the people among whom they find themselves. Jews must take care to see that foreign influences do not contaminate their Torah learning.

This insight also answers an interesting question about the passage under consideration. Why does the Talmud refer to someone who mocked the danger of leaving wine, milk and water exposed as "pious?" One would think the sages would describe such a person in quite a different way. However, this shows precisely the extent of the power of the evil inclination. The Torah defines

---

[693] B.T. *Ta'anith* 7A.

"piety" (חסידות) as going beyond the letter of the law.[694] *A person may do more than is strictly required of him for a positive reason such as the fear that he will accidentally violate the Halachah unless he removes himself a step further from that which is prohibited. On the other hand, he may simply be showing off, so that apparently pious acts are actually a sham. In the passage under consideration, the "pious" person evidently had a reputation for acting beyond the letter of the law. Unknown to the public, however, he did so with impure motives. As a result, eventually he went astray.*[695]

The reason that the problem of snakes contaminating wine, water and milk is not widespread today is that just as the level of spirituality has declined, so has the level of impurity. Thus, for example, just as there is no longer prophecy, so, too, demons are no longer prevalent. There is a correlation between the spiritual and physical worlds. Just as spiritual impurity has declined, so has the prevalence of snakes, the symbols of impurity, invading human living space.

The Talmud teaches that a person does not sin unless a spirit of folly enters him or her.[696] *If a sinner*

---

[694] *Rambam, Shemoneh Perakim*, chapter 4.

[695] This clarifies the *Talmud's* teaching that the *Torah* can be an elixir of life or an elixir of death. (B.T. *Yoma* 72B). The word elixir (סם) hints that when the *Torah* is misused and its teachings perverted, it becomes a tool of Samael (סמא-ל), the guardian angel of Esau and the forces of evil, an elixir of death.

[696] B.T. *Sotah* 3A.

would stop to think carefully about the effects of his sin, he would refrain. As the Mishnah says, "Contrast the transitory loss caused by a Mitzvah against its eternal reward and the transitory benefit of a sin against its eternal loss...and you will not come into the grip of sin."[697] The snake represents a type of impulsive behavior, acting without thinking things through. That is why the snake pushed Chavah against the Tree of Knowledge when she hesitated to touch it.[698]

Rashness or boldness, however, is not always a negative trait. The Mishnah teaches that one who is shy cannot learn because he or she will not be willing to ask questions for fear of embarrassment.[699] Going a step further, the Talmud relates how several students clandestinely observed their teachers' activities in the bathroom or bedroom. Such impertinent behavior was justified because the students needed to learn the Halachoth associated with every aspect of daily life.[700]

The Midrash says that while the other tribes debated about which should enter the Reed Sea first, Nahshon ben Aminadab went ahead and jumped in.[701] The name Nahshon (נחשון) alludes to the snake (נחש) and, so, to

---

[697] *Avoth* 2:1.
[698] *Rashi* on Genesis 3:4.
[699] *Avoth* 2:5.
[700] B.T. *Brachoth* 62A.
[701] *Midrash Tehillim* on Psalms 76.

capricious behavior, the difference being that this was capricious behavior for a good purpose. [702]

This explains why the Talmud says that the person who drank exposed wine on Yom Kippur eve was punished. At first glance, it seems admirable that he relied on God to protect him from possible poisoning. The point of the Talmud, however, is that it is only admirable to act rashly in conformity with Torah principles. One such principle is not to rely on miracles to save one from a dangerous situation. [703]

Dogs also symbolize the evil inclination. [704] *The Tanach identifies the outstanding negative trait of dogs as impudence.* [705] *The Zohar compares the wicked nation of Amalek to an insolent dog because it dared to challenge the Jewish people at a time when all other nations feared to do so.* [706] *Likewise, the Talmud says that the generation which*

---

[702] Another example of rash behavior which was good is that of Phinehas who killed Zimri, the prince of the tribe of Simeon, while the latter was having illicit relations with a Midianite woman. The *Halachah* does not require an individual to take this type of action and Phinehas faced the danger not only that Zimri might defend himself, but that the entire tribe of Simeon might seek revenge. Had Phinehas stopped to consider matters more carefully, he may have refrained. However, this was an instance of engaging in rash behavior for the sake of Heaven. (Numbers 6-8).

[703] B.T. *Pesachim* 64B.

[704] *Tikunei Zohar* 60A.

[705] Isaiah 56:11.

[706] *Zohar* II, 65A.

precedes the coming of the Messiah will have a face like a dog's, meaning that insolence will abound.[707]

Before entering the Promised Land, the Jewish people sent twelve spies, one from each tribe, to survey the situation. Moses prayed for Joshua and changed his name from Hosea [הושע] to Joshua [יהושע] in the hope that its increased resemblance to God's Name would prevent him from joining the evil counsel of the other spies who returned and maligned the Land of Israel.[708] The only other spy who did not disparage the Land of Israel was Caleb, yet Moses did not change his name or pray that he not be influenced by the other spies. The reason Moses had to seek special protection for Joshua is that the latter was unusually humble.[709] As noted above, humility is a good trait because it permits a person to learn the Torah in an accepting way, without twisting its meaning. However, there is also a downside to humility in that one who is humble can be influenced by wicked people.[710] For example, King Saul permitted his soldiers to convince him to spare the flocks of the Amalekites, contrary to Torah law which required their destruction.[711] The Prophet Samuel criticized King Saul and declared him unfit to establish a

---

[707] B.T. *Sotah* 49B. B.T. *Beitzah* 25B also says that dogs are impudent.

[708] *Rashi* on Numbers 13:16, citing *BaMidbar Rabbah* 16:9.

[709] *Targum Yonathan ben Uziel* ad. loc.

[710] Rabbi Nosson Scherman, *Artscroll Chumash*, (Mesorah Publications, Ltd., New York, 1994), p. 800.

[711] I Samuel 15:15.

royal dynasty, saying, "...even if you are small in your own eyes, are you not the head of the tribes of Israel...?"[712]

Caleb, on the other hand, was a bold, independent-minded person as suggested by his Hebrew name (כלב) which means "dog." He used this trait of impudence and rashness to stand up for what was right. After the other spies incited the people to rebel against Moses, it was Caleb who stood up to them, silenced the raucous mob, and said, "...let us rise and inherit it [the Land], for we can surely overcome it."[713]

The Babylonian Talmud states: "Why are heathens contaminated? Because they did not stand at Mount Sinai. At the time when the snake cohabited with Chavah, he defiled her. As to Israel which stood at Mount Sinai, their defilement ceased. Heathens, who did not stand at Mount Sinai, their defilement did not cease."[714] *The Talmud explains that Hashem offered the Torah to all the nations of the world. Each nation found some aspect of the Torah which it felt incapable of observing, but when God offered the Torah to the Jewish people, they said "we will do and we will listen,"*[715] *meaning that they accepted the Torah unconditionally, immediately agreeing to obey it and later study its contents.*[716] *The good capriciousness which*

---

[712] I Samuel 15:17.
[713] Numbers 13:30.
[714] B.T. *Shabbath* 145B-146A.
[715] Exodus 24:7.
[716] B.T. *Avodah Zarah* 2B and B.T. *Shabbath* 88A-B.

played a role in the acceptance of the Torah counteracted the bad capriciousness of the primordial snake.

The Talmud teaches that if the snake had not been cursed, each Jew would have two snakes as servants.[717] The power of the snake would have been harnessed for positive purposes, allowing people to act quickly to serve Hashem. Along these lines, the Midrash teaches that the Messiah, who will be a descendent of Nahshon, will restore six things which were taken from Adam when the latter sinned.[718] Nachshon's act of using folly or rashness for serving Hashem helped rectify the error of Adam and Chavah. The final rectification of their sin will take place with the advent of the Messiah.[719]

The above passage of the Jerusalem Talmud tells how a snake and two dogs risked their lives to protect their masters, thereby illustrating the principle that under the right circumstances, bold daring can be used for good.

Yalkut Reuveni states that the shape of the letter נ represents Satan (שטן),[720] meaning that the deceptive trickery of the evil inclination is symbolized by the crooked נ. In the era of Messiah, however, the crookedness will be corrected and the power of the evil inclination used for good. That the final נ in Satan (שטן) is straight reflects the idea that, in the end, the power of the Satan will become

---

[717] B.T. *Sanhedrin* 59B.

[718] *BaMidbar Rabbah* 13:12.

[719] The word for "Messiah" in Hebrew (משיח) has the same numerical value as the word for "snake" (נחש).

[720] Sub verba "*Nachash*" (נחש).

straightened out. As the Tanach says, "the twisted shall become straight."[721] At the time of the future redemption, the power of impudence and capriciousness represented by the snake and the dog will be used only for good. May that time arrive speedily.

---

[721] Isaiah 40:4.

T'rumoth 8:4

עולא בר קושב, תבעתיה מלכותא. ערק ואזיל ליה ללוד גבי
רבי יהושע בן לוי. אתון ואקפון מדינתא. אמרו להן, "אין לית אתון
יהבון ליה לן, אנן מחרבין מדינתא."

סלק גביה רבי יהושע בן לוי ופייסיה ויהביה לון. והוה אליהו,
זכור לטוב, יליף מתגלי עלוי ולא אתגלי. וצם כמה צומין ואיתגלי עלוי.

אמר ליה, "ולמסורות אני נגלה?"

אמר ליה, "ולא משנה עשיתי?"

אמר ליה, "וזו משנת החסידים?"

Ulla bar Koshev was sought by the gentile
government [which wanted to kill him]. He fled to Lod to
Rabbi Yehoshua ben Levi. The king's men came and
surrounded the city. They said, "If you do not surrender
him to us, we will destroy the city."

Rabbi Yehoshua ben Levi approached him,
persuaded him about the matter, and they turned him over.
Elijah, of blessed memory, who used to reveal himself to
Rabbi Yehoshua ben Levi, stopped revealing himself.
Rabbi Yehoshua ben Levi fasted many fasts until Elijah
revealed himself.

The Prophet said, "Should I reveal myself to
informers?"

"Did I not do as the *Mishnah* instructs?" he
answered. [The *Mishnah* teaches that if heathens tell a
group of women, "Give us one of you to defile and if you

refuse, we will defile all of you," they must risk the defilement of all and not turn anyone over to the enemy.[722] The *Talmud* explains that this *Mishnah* addresses only a general demand that Jews surrender one of their number, but when heathens seek a specific person, it is permitted to turn the person over.[723]]

"Is this the *Mishnah* of the pious?" [Although the *Halachah* is so, it is not what a righteous person would do.[724]]

Why does the Talmud distinguish between a demand to surrender someone in general and a demand for a specific person? When heathens threaten to destroy an entire community unless it turns over a specific person, that person will be killed one way or another, either by being surrendered or by dying with the rest of the community. Therefore, the community is not deemed to be doing anything to harm such a person if it agrees to the demand. However, if heathens order a Jewish community to yield

---

[722] *T'rumoth* 8:12.

[723] *Rama* on *Shulchan Aruch, Yoreh Deah* 157:1 rules this way as a matter of practical *Halachah*. However, he points out that several authorities hold that it is only permitted to turn over someone who is also liable for the death penalty under Jewish law.

[724] *Rambam* in *Yad HaChazakah, Hilchoth Yesodei HaTorah* 5:5 writes that one should not teach that it is permitted to turn someone over to heathens even though the *Halachah* is so. Rabbi Shabbethai Cohen adds that the community can only do this as a last resort after it has exhausted all efforts to bribe the enemy or otherwise avoid doing so. (*Sifthei Kohen*, note 15, on *Shulchan Aruch, Yoreh Deah* 157:1).

one of its members at random, it is the community which is singling out the victim and causing the death. This it may not do.[725] *Nonetheless, it is permissible for a person to volunteer to surrender himself to the enemy. The Talmud declares that the spiritual realm such a person occupies is so exalted that no one else can stand there.*[726]

---

[725] Rabbi Moshe Heinemann שליט"א.

[726] Ibid., citing *Rashi* on B.T. *Ta'anith* 18B sub verba *"BiLudkia"* (בלודקיא).

T'rumoth 8:4

רבי אימי איתצד בסיפסיפה.

אמר רבי יונתן, "יכרך המת בסדינו."

אמר רבי שמעון בן לקיש, "עד דאנא קטיל, אנא מתקטיל.
אנא איזיל ומשיזיב ליה בחיילא." אזל ופייסון ויהבוניה ליה.

אמר לון, "ואתון גבי סבון והוא מצלי עליכון."

אתון גבי רבי יוחנן. אמר לון, "מה דהוה בלבכון איעבד ליה,
יתעבוד לון, ימטא לההוא עמא." לא מטון אֶפִּיפַסִירוּס עד דאזלון
כולהון.

זעיר בר חנינא איתצד בספסיפה. סלק רבי אמי ורבי שמואל
מפייסה עלוי. אמרה להון זנביה מלכותא, "יליף הוא ברייכון עבד לכון
ניסין."

מעשוקין ביה, עלל חד סרקיא טעין חד ספסר. אמר להון,
"בהדא ספסירא קטיל בר נצר ליה לאחוי!" ואישתיזיב זעיר בר חנינא.

רבי יוחנן אמר, "איקפח בעלי קנייה!" סליק לבית וועדא והוה
רבי שמעון בן לקיש שאיל ליה והוא לא מגיב, שאיל ליה והוא לא מגיב.

אמר ליה, "מהו הכין?"

אמר ליה, "כל האיברים תלויין בלב והלב תלוי בכיס."

אמר ליה, "ומהו כן?"

אמר ליה, "ומהו את כן?" אמר ליה, "איקפחת בעלי קנייה."

אמר ליה, "חמי לי זויתה."

נפיק, מחוי ליה. חמיתון מן רחוק ושרי מצלצל. אמרין, "אין
רבי יוחנן הוא, יסב פלגא."

אמר לון, "חייכון, כולה אנא נסיבו!" ונסיב כולה.

Rabbi Immi was trapped in a deadly situation.[727]

---

[727] *P'nei Moshe* understands סיפסיפה to imply a deadly situation from

Said Rabbi Yochanan[728], "Let the dead be wrapped in his shroud." [He was resigned to Rabbi Immi's death, having given up hope of rescuing him.]

Rabbi Shimon ben Lakish said, "Either I will kill or be killed. I will go rescue him by force." He went and appeased the abductors who released Rabbi Immi to him.

Rabbi Shimon ben Lakish told the captors, "Come to our elder that he may pray for you."

They came to Rabbi Yochanan who said, "May that which was in your hearts to do to Rabbi Immi befall you." They did not make it to Epiphasyrus[729] before they were all taken captive.

Z'eir bar Chanina was trapped in a deadly situation. Rabbi Ami and Rabbi Shmuel went to plead on his behalf. The Terror of the Kingdom[730] said [sarcastically], "Your Creator is accustomed to performing miracles for you!"

---

the root ספה which means "extermination." The word could, however, be related to ספסף which is used in the *Mishnah* to mean "removing hair." (*Nazir* 6:3). In that case, the text means that Rabbi Immi was captured in some sort of "removal" operation, i.e., a kidnaping.

[728] The editors of the Romm Vilna edition note a manuscript from Rome which identifies the rabbi here as Rabbi Yochanan rather than Rabbi Yonathan. This appears to fit in better with the rest of the text.

[729] Rabbi Yochanan lived in Tiberias which is in the northern part of the Land of Israel. (B.T. *Avodah Zarah* 58A and J.T. *Brachoth* 57B). Epiphasyrus (אפיפסירוס), as the end of the name suggests, is probably a town or region near the Syrian border. Thus, the abductors had not even reached the border, a short distance from Rabbi Yochanan, when they were captured.

[730] The word לזנב means "to attack" (Deuteronomy 25:18), so זנביה מלכותא would mean "one who attacks the kingdom," an

325

While they spoke, a certain Arab Saracen entered bearing a scimitar. He said to them, "With this scimitar Bar Netzar killed The Terror of the Kingdom's brother." [Bar Netzar was a rival robber chieftain and this was a threat to murder The Terror of the Kingdom.[731] In the confusion,] Z'eir bar Chanina escaped.

Said Rabbi Yochanan, "I've been robbed by hoodlums!" He went up to the academy. Rabbi Shimon ben Lakish repeatedly greeted him but he did not respond.

Said Rabbi Shimon ben Lakish, "What's all this about?"

"All the limbs are dependent upon the heart and the heart is dependent upon the purse."

"Is that true?"

"Is it not true for you?" [Wouldn't you be upset at a great financial loss?] "I've been robbed by hoodlums."

"Show me the direction of their escape."

Rabbi Yochanan went out and showed him. Rabbi Shimon ben Lakish spied them in the distance and started shouting at them. They said, "If Rabbi Yochanan is involved, let him take back half."

"By your lives," declared Rabbi Shimon ben Lakish, "I am seizing it all!" He took it all back.

Why did Rabbi Yochanan become so upset about a robbery? One would normally expect a great sage to have

---

appropriate nickname for a murderous bandit.
[731] *P'nei Moshe.*

little concern for worldly matters. This is especially puzzling in light of the fact that the Talmud tells how Rabbi Yochanan had several children who died. He used to console others who suffered misfortune by showing them a small bone and saying, "This is the bone of my tenth son."[732] *How could any financial loss upset a man who withstood such adversity?*

Rabbeinu Nissim uses an analogy to explain. An untutored onlooker cannot distinguish between a good doctor and a bad one. Just as a good doctor uses certain medicines and therapies, a bad doctor does the same. The distinction is that the good doctor uses them in the proper amounts, at the proper times and to treat the proper symptoms, while a bad doctor does not. The same holds true with serving Hashem. Everyone eats, but a righteous person does so after concentrating on reciting a blessing and with the intention to use the energy he or she gets from eating to serve God.[733] *Far from being materialistic, Rabbi Yochanan was upset because he lost the opportunity to use the stolen money for holy purposes.*[734]

---

[732] B.T. Brachoth 5B according to *Tosafoth* sub verba "*Ve'Ha'amar Rabbi Yochanan*" (והאמר רבי יוחנן).

[733] *Drashoth HaRan, HaDrashah HaShlishi.*

[734] The same principle applies when the *Talmud* says that when Jacob was traveling back to the Land of Israel from Padan Aram, he crossed the Jabbok River. Later, he returned to fetch some small earthenware containers he had forgotten. (*Rashi* on Genesis 32:25 citing B.T. *Chullin* 91A.) Jacob was concerned about elevating spiritually whatever physical objects he owned.

Another possible answer emerges from a story told about Rabbi Chaim of Volozhin, the premier disciple of the Vilna Gaon. One time, the rabbi became terribly distraught upon discovering that he had lost five rubles.

"Why are you so upset about this relatively minor loss?" asked his family members and associates in astonishment.

"I am not concerned about the five rubles themselves," responded the rabbi, "but unless I committed some sin, this would not have happened. The thought that I have done something wrong distresses me."

Perhaps Rabbi Yochanan, too, was concerned not about the financial loss itself, but about the implication of such a loss, namely, that he had somehow done something amiss.[735]

Rabbi Akiva taught, and the accepted Halachah is, that a person's own life takes priority over his fellow's.[736] *Accordingly, a person may not risk his or her own life to save someone else. How, then, could Rabbi Shimon ben Lakish say "Either I will kill or be killed" and risk his life for Rabbi Immi? Not only that, but he even risked his life just to save Rabbi Yochanan's money! Perhaps Rabbi Yochanan's financial loss affected him so greatly that he was in danger of dying. That would explain why he told Rabbi Shimon ben Lakish that, "All the limbs are*

---

[735] Rabbi Moshe Heinemann שליט"א, based on a story he heard about Rabbi Chaim of Volozhin from Rabbi Aharon Kotler.
[736] B.T. *Baba Metzia* 62A.

dependent upon the heart and the heart is dependent upon the purse." Even so, how was Rabbi Shimon ben Lakish permitted to risk his life this way?

The Talmud relates that Rabbi Shimon ben Lakish was scholar who became an outlaw until Rabbi Yochanan convinced him to repent.[737] Apparently, Rabbi Shimon ben Lakish was so skilled in the field of banditry that he had complete confidence he could overcome any thugs who opposed him. For this reason, he was not really risking his life.

The masters of Kabbalah teach that the highest achievement a person can have is to "change darkness to light," converting that which is normally evil to good.[738] Just as light appears brightest when it emerges from darkness, so the highest good emerges when transformed from evil. Rabbi Shimon ben Lakish achieved this by putting his skills as an outlaw to use to rescue Rabbi Immi and to retrieve Rabbi Yochanan's property.

---

[737] B.T. *Baba Metzia* 84A according to *Tosafoth* sub verba "*Ee Hadart*" (אי הדרת).

[738] *Likutei Amarim Tanya*, Part I, chapter 36.

T'rumoth 8:4 (Compare *Breishith Rabbah* 63:8)

דיקלוט חזירא, מחוניה טלייא דרבי יהודא נשיאה. איתעבד
מלך. נחת לְפַמְיָיס. שלח כתבין בתר רבנן, "תיהוון גבי במפקי שובתא
מיד." אמר ליה לשלוחיה, "לא תתן להון כתבין אלא בערובתא עם
מטמעי שמשא."

ואתא שליחא גבהון בערובתא עם מטמעי שמשא והוה רבי יודן
נשיאה ורבי שמואל בר נחמן נחתין למיסחי בדימוסין דטבריא. אתא
אנטיגריס גבהון ובעי רבי יודן נשייא למינזף ביה. אמר ליה רבי שמואל
בר נחמן, "ארפי ליה! לנסיון הוא מתחמי."

אמר לון, "מה רבנן עבדין?"

תנון ליה עובדא. אמר לון, "סחון, דברייכון עביד ניסין."

במפקי שובתא, טעין יתהון ואעיל יתהון. אמרו ליה, "הא רבנן
לבר."

אמר, "לא יחמון אפיי עד דאינון סחיין." הוה ההיא בי בני
אזייה שבעה יומין ושבעה לילוון. נפק ואנצח קדמיהון ועללון וקמון
ליה קדמיהון. אמר לון, "בגין דברייכון עביד לכון ניסין, אתון מבזין
מלכותא."

אמרין ליה, "דיקלוט חזירא בזינן. דיקליטיאנוס מלכא לא
בזינן."

ואפילו כן, לא מכסי לא ברומי זעיר ולא בחבר זעיר.

The younger students of Rabbi Yehudah Nessiah
used to beat Diocletian the pigkeeper. When Diocletian
became king, he descended to Pameas [a cave which is the
source of the Jordan River some distance from Tiberias, the
town where the rabbi lived].[739] He sent letters to the rabbis

---

[739] *P'nei Moshe* and *Matanoth Kehunah* on *Breishith Rabbah* 63:8.

commanding them, "Be with me immediately after the Sabbath!" He told his messenger, "Only deliver the letters to them on Friday afternoon near sunset." [Delivering the order near the onset of the Sabbath would make it impossible for the rabbis to travel to Pameas before the Sabbath and there would not be enough time to get there after the Sabbath. Failure to obey his command would give Diocletian an excuse for exacting revenge against them].[740]

After the messenger came to them near sunset [and delivered the message], Rabbi Yudan Nessiah[741] and Rabbi Shmuel bar Nachman went down to bathe in the bathhouses of Tiberias. Antigeras [a demon who haunted bathhouses[742]] came to them. Rabbi Yudan Nessiah wanted to reprimand him, but Rabbi Shmuel bar Nachman

---

[740] Ibid.

[741] Yudan is a shortened form of Yehudah. *P'nei Moshe* and the version of this text in *Breishith Rabbah* say that the sage of our text is Rabbi Yehudah HaNassi. However, Diocletian was born in 234 C.E., more than forty years after Rabbi Yehudah HaNassi died. In addition, this passage identifies the rabbi in question as a contemporary of Rabbi Shmuel bar Nachman who lived during or shortly after the time of Rabbi Yochanan, a period about one hundred years after Rabbi Yehudah HaNassi flourished. Accordingly, the protagonist of this story must have been Rabbi Yehudah Nessiah II (240 C.E. to 305 C.E.). See Meir Holder, *History of the Jewish People*, (Mesorah Publications, New York, 1986) pp. 163-164.

[742] *P'nei Moshe* understands this to be a proper name. According to *Maharzu* on *Breishith Rabbah* 63:8, however, אנטיגריס refers to a type of demon generally. The text there has the word as ארגיניטון, similar to the modern English "argonaut," a sea explorer.

said to him, "Let him alone! He has appeared to perform a miracle."

"Why are the rabbis upset?" asked Antigeras.

They explained the predicament.

"Wash up [for the Sabbath]," he said. "Your Creator does miracles."

On Saturday evening, the demon carried them and brought them [to Pameas]. Servants told Diocletian, "The rabbis are outside."

"They shall not behold my countenance until they bathe," he replied.

There was a certain bathhouse which had been heated for seven days and seven nights [at the order of Diocletian, to make it unbearably hot].[743] The demon went and cooled it for the rabbis. They entered and presented themselves before the king who said, "Because your Creator performs miracles for you, you scorn the crown!"

"We disgraced Diocletian the pigkeeper," they answered, "but Emperor Diocletian we have not scorned."

Even so, one should not humiliate a lowly Roman or a lowly Gueber[744] [since all people were created by God

---

[743] *P'nei Moshe.*

[744] Guebers were Zoroastrian priests who persecuted Jews. (See B.T. *Gittin* 16B-17A and *Kiddushin* 72A). *Mareh HaPanim*, however, citing a similar dictum in B.T. *Pesachim* 113A, understands חבר as "rabbinical student." Although a slighted rabbinical student would not exact revenge, one who scorns him will suffer severe humiliation after he achieves greatness because he will end up having to learn from him. (*Ben Yehoyada* ad. loc.). Alternatively, scorning a *Torah* scholar is a

and therefore deserve respect.[745]   Moreover, one never knows what position such people may eventually occupy.]

Ben Azzai used to say: "Do not scorn any person and do not be astonished at anything, for there is no person who does not have his or her hour and there is no thing which does not have its place."[746]   Along similar lines, King Solomon said, "One who scorns a thing will be injured by it... ."[747]

Tales abound throughout classical Jewish literature which stress the importance of not scorning people because one never knows how events may unfold. For example, the Midrash tells how a ship sank leaving just one survivor, a Roman who made it to shore stark naked. When he asked the local Jewish inhabitants for assistance, they refused, ridiculing him and saying that they hoped the same would befall all Romans. Rabbi Elazar ben Shamua took the Roman in, fed and clothed him, gave him a purse of coins and gave him a ride to help him get home. That same Roman was later appointed Caesar. In his new position, he sought to destroy the province whose people had treated

---

serious offense for which *Hashem* exacts retribution even if the scholar is young.

[745]   Rabbi Moshe Heinemann שליט״א. The *Rambam* stressed the importance of treating all people decently in imitation of God, as King David said, "The Lord is good to all and His mercies are upon all his creations." (Psalms 145:9) (*Yad HaChazakah, Hilchoth Avadim* 9:8).

[746]   *Pirkei Avoth* 4:3.

[747]   Proverbs 13:13.

him meanly and mocked him. The people sent Rabbi Elazar ben Shamua to appease him with a large bribe. When he saw the rabbi who had helped him, he prostrated himself before him, annulled the decree and gave the rabbi handsome gifts.[748]

The Midrash tells how King David once questioned why God created mentally unstable people who wander about disgracing themselves. God answered, "By your life, you shall have need of it!"[749] *When King Saul wrongly accused David of rebellion and pursued him, David fled to the enemy kingdom of Gath. Some people there recognized him as the one who slew Goliath and reported it to King Achish. To hide his identity, David pretended to be mentally unstable.*[750]

Why should this be so? Why would Hashem create a law of nature which requires that one who scorns someone or something be injured by it or have need of it? The answer is that God is perfect and created the world in a perfect way, although human beings do not understand how the world is perfect because they view it from their

---

[748] *Koheleth Rabbah* 11:1.

[749] *Midrash Tehilim* 34.

[750] I Samuel 21:11-16. Similarly, the *Talmud* teaches that one who treats clothing disrespectfully will not benefit from it. (B.T. *Brachoth* 62B). The *Tanach* tells how David hid in a cave where King Saul entered to go to the bathroom. David cut off a piece of the king's garment. (I Samuel 24:3-4). As a result, the *Tanach* reports that many years later, "King David was elderly, abundant in days; and they covered him with clothing but he was not warm." (I Kings 1:1).

limited perspective. Not only does one who mocks others have a mean, defective character, but his or her actions imply that God's creation is not perfect. By their deeds, such people are saying, in effect, "If the world is perfect, why does it contain pigkeepers and other lowly people?" God causes matters to develop in a way whereby these people will see the error of such thinking.

Ma'aseroth 3:4

דלמא: רבי זעירא ורבי אבא בר כהנא ורבי לוי הוון יתבין
והוה רבי זעירא מקנתר לאילין דאגדתא וצוח להון, "ספרי קיסמי."

אמר ליה רבי בא בר כהנא, "למה את מקנתר לון? שאל ואינון
מגיבין לך."

אמר ליה, "מהו דין דכתיב, 'כִּי חֲמַת אָדָם תּוֹדֶךָ שְׁאֵרִית חֲמֹת
תַּחְגֹּר.'?" (תהלים עו:יא).

אמר ליה, "'כִּי חֲמַת אָדָם תּוֹדֶךָ בעולם הזה, שְׁאֵרִית חֲמֹת תַּחְגֹּר
לעולם הבא.'"

אמר ליה, "או נימר כִּי חֲמַת אָדָם תּוֹדֶךָ בעולם הבא, שְׁאֵרִית
חֲמֹת תַּחְגֹּר בעולם הזה.'"

אמר רבי לוי, "כשתעורר חמתך על הרשעים, צדיקים רואין מה
את עושה להן והן מודין לשמך."

אמר רבי זעירא, "היא הפכה והיא מהפכה. לא שמעינן מינה
כלום. ירמיה בני, אזל צור צור דוקניתא דהיא טבא מן כולם!"

One time, Rabbi Z'eira, Rabbi Abba bar Kahana
and Rabbi Levi were sitting together. Rabbi Z'eira was
criticizing certain masters of *Aggadah*, calling their work
"sorcerers' books" [because the Scriptural interpretations
they contained were, in his opinion, ill-conceived].

Rabbi Ba[751] bar Kahana told him, "Why do you
criticize them? Ask how to interpret a verse and they will
respond properly."

---

[751] Ba (בא) is an abbreviated form of Abba (אבא).

"What is the meaning of this which is written, 'When you are angry at humanity, thanks are Yours that the remnant of anger You withhold.'[752]?"

Answered Rabbi Abba bar Kahana, "When a person acknowledges You for anger in this world, You withhold the remnant of Your anger in the world to come." [When a person suffers in this world but thanks *Hashem* for it, acknowledging his shortcomings and repenting, he merits that *Hashem* withhold further punishment in the world to come.[753]]

"Or we could say," responded Rabbi Z'eira, "'When anger engulfs a person in the world to come, he acknowledges God; the remnant of His anger is restrained in this world.'" [When God punishes the wicked after death, they acknowledge their wrongdoing, whereas God limits their punishment in this world.[754] Rabbi Z'eira's complaint is that those who interpret verses in a homiletic fashion do not get at their true meaning because such homilies can be flipped around so that a verse can be read in two opposite ways, as he has just shown.]

Rabbi Levi offered another interpretation of the verse: "When You arouse Your anger against the wicked, the righteous recognize what You do for them and acknowledge Your Name."

---

[752] Psalms 76:11.

[753] *Etz Yosef.*

[754] B.T. *Eruvin* 19A says that the wicked acknowledge God's justice when they are punished in *Gehinnom*. (*P'nei Moshe*).

Said Rabbi Z'eira, "It switches and switches yet again. We cannot infer anything from it. Rather, Yirmiah, my son, go tie up the pruning shears soundly for that is better than anything!" [Rather than using "pruning shears" to cut up verses and reinterpret them as the *Aggadists* do, stick to the plain meaning of the text. Another interpretation: Rabbi Yirmiah had asked Rabbi Z'eira a *Halachic* question concerning pruning shears immediately prior to this passage. Rabbi Z'eira was instructing Rabbi Yirmiah to stick to the study of straightforward *Halachoth* such as that rather than get involved in the study of *Aggadoth* which is so imprecise. [755]]

What was Rabbi Z'eira's complaint? Surely he cannot mean that it is forbidden or undesirable to interpret verses. The Talmud states that one of the rewards a person will receive for giving charity is to have sons who are "masters of Aggadah."[756] In addition, the Talmud praises Rabban Yochanan ben Zakkai as one who left no area of Torah study untouched, including Aggadoth,[757] indicating that the study of Aggadoth is admirable. Finally, in other sections of the Talmud, Rabbi Z'eira himself offers homiletic interpretations of various verses.[758] What, then, bothered him so much in this passage?

---

[755] *Vilna Gaon.*

[756] B.T. *Baba Bathra* 9B-10A.

[757] B.T. *Sukkah* 28A.

[758] See, for example, *Torah From Jerusalem*, Vol. I, p. 305. Also, B.T. *Brachoth* 55B and *Makkoth* 10A.

In general, it is forbidden to write down the Oral Torah. However, intense persecution of the Jewish people during Talmudic times caused the leading rabbis to fear that unless they committed it to writing, it would be entirely forgotten. The Babylonian Talmud rules that not only may one record Halachoth, but that it is also permitted to write down Aggadoth.[759]

Rabbi Yehoshua ben Levi disagreed with this ruling, holding instead that one who writes down Aggadoth has no share in the world to come. In addition, one who ponders such works deserves to be burned and one who listens to them being expounded receives no reward.[760]

Rabbi David Fraenkel explains that Rabbi Yehoshua ben Levi agrees it is necessary to write down Halachoth because, otherwise, people may commit serious sins. However, that does not apply in the case of Aggadoth which usually have no direct practical implications.[761] Radbaz concurs and points out that the Talmud records that Rabbi Yehoshua ben Levi himself studied Aggadoth. However, the Aggadoth contain many esoteric mysteries. Putting the Aggadoth into written form allows them to reach a wide audience which may not properly appreciate or understand them. By contrast, when a teacher conveys

---

[759] B.T. *Gittin* 60A.
[760] J.T. *Shabbath* 16:1.
[761] *Korban HaEidah* on J.T. *Shabbath* 16:1.

Aggadoth orally, he may clarify any issues which his students raise.[762]

Rabbi Tzvi Hirsch Chajes disagrees. He writes that Rabbi Yehoshua ben Levi maintained that the original prohibition against writing down the Oral Torah applied only to Halachoth, not Aggadoth. Even so, there is a problem with writing down Aggadoth because if a fire breaks out on the Sabbath it would be forbidden to rescue them. This means that one who commits Aggadoth to writing may be viewed as though he burned them, God forbid.[763]

Rabbi Z'eira approved Aggadic teaching in general. However, he agreed with the view of Rabbi Yehoshua ben Levi that writing down Aggadoth is prohibited for one reason or another. Accordingly, he called such books the work of "sorcerers," a term suggesting disapproval to the point where he held that those who write them are wicked wrongdoers. Rabbi Z'eira was especially concerned that writing down Aggadic material which offered conflicting interpretations of Biblical passages might cause confusion among those who study it.[764]

---

[762] Responsa, Part IV, chapter 232.

[763] *Mavoh HaTalmud*. See, however, *Sofrim* 16:10 which says that although it is forbidden to write down *Aggadoth*, one must save such writings from fire on the Sabbath.

[764] Rabbi Z'eira might agree that publishing *Aggadoth* in contemporary times is permitted because of the difficulty people have memorizing material. See Responsa *Be'er Sheva*, chapter 43.

Ma'aser Sheni 4:6 (Compare *Breishith Rabbah* 68:12; B.T. *Brachoth* 55B-56B)

הרי שהיה מצטער על מעותיו של אביו. נראה לו בחלום, "כך
וכך הם ובמקום פלוני הם."
אתא עובדא קומי רבנין. אמרין, "דברי חלומות לא מעלין ולא
מורידין."
רבי יונה בעי, "מצטער וחמי ואת אמרת הכין?!?"
אמר רבי יוסי, "לא מסתברא דלא בההוא דלא מצטער וחמי?
ברם הכא כמה דבר נש הוי, הוא חלים."
אמר רבי אבין, "מאן דעבד יאות עבד כרבי יוסי."

[During the first six years of the Sabbatical cycle, the *Torah* requires Jews to give one-tenth of their crop to the Levites. Of the remaining crop, Jews must separate one-tenth during the first, second, fourth and fifth years to be eaten only in Jerusalem. If one does not wish to transport the produce of this second tithe (מעשר שני) to Jerusalem, he may redeem it for coins which he then takes to Jerusalem and uses to buy food. In this passage, someone knew that his father had made the redemption before he died. He sought to discover where his father had hidden the coins so that he could take them to Jerusalem and spend them there as required.]

A certain person was troubled about the second tithe coins of his father. He appeared to him in a dream and said, "Such and such an amount they were and they are in such and such a place."

This matter came before the rabbis who said, "The words of a dream do not make better nor do they make worse." [One cannot rely on dreams to make *Halachic* rulings. Therefore, even if you find the coins in the amount and location described in the dream, you need not assume that they are the missing second tithe coins.]

Rabbi Yonah asked, "He was troubled and had a vision, yet you rule this way?!?" [Why refuse to rely on the dream when there seems to be a reasonable basis for doing so?]

Rabbi Yossi answered, "Wouldn't it be more logical to say that one who was *not* troubled and saw a dream could rely on it? [People often dream about matters which trouble them, so a dream is reliable only if one who was not disturbed about a matter nonetheless dreamed about it.] However, in this case, whatever a person contemplates [while awake,] he dreams about."

Said Rabbi Abin, "He acts properly who acts in accordance with Rabbi Yossi." [A person should rely on his dreams if they do not deal with matters he was thinking about while awake.]

A popular folk story tells how the people of a certain town were struggling to find a replacement for their beloved rabbi who had died recently. The town was blessed with many learned men, several of whom were exceptional scholars. After the town council carefully considered the qualifications of each candidate, several factions emerged, each offering cogent reasons for supporting the installation of its particular choice for the position. In the ensuing weeks, the members of the council had many heated debates, but no group was able to convince the others that its candidate was the best. Finally, one of the Torah scholars who sought the position asked to address the council.

"Gentlemen," he said, "I had a dream last night in which our late rabbi appeared and told me that you should appoint me as his successor."

The meeting was abuzz as the members of the town council discussed this new development. Then, an elderly Jew banged on the table and demanded quiet. "We have had quite a bit of discussion among ourselves during the past few weeks concerning whom we should appoint as our new rabbi," he explained. "Your qualifications are certainly impressive, but the decision belongs to us. If the old rabbi wanted us to appoint you as his replacement, he should have appeared to us in a dream, not to you!"

This amusing story points out the wisdom of the rabbis in refusing to make Halachic decisions based on the content of dreams. Even assuming the absolute honesty of the person reporting the dream, too many factors such as what a person experienced while awake and his or her subconscious desires may influence its content.

Ma'aser Sheni 4:6 (Compare *Eicha Rabbah* 1:14-18; *Breishith Rabbah* 68:12 and 89:8; B.T. *Brachoth* 55B-56B)

חד בר נש אתא לגבי דרבי יוסי בן חלפתא. אמר ליה, "חמית בחילמאי מיתמר לי, 'איזיל לקפודקָיָא ואת משכח מדלא דאבוך.'"

אמר ליה, "אזל אבוי דההוא גברא לקפודקָיָא מן יומוי?" אמר ליה, "לא."

אמר ליה, "איזל מני עשר שריין גו בייתך ואת משכח מדלא דאבוך [תחות] קפא דקוריא."

חד בר נש אתא לגבי דרבי יוסי בר חלפתא. אמר ליה, "חמית בחילמאי לבוש חד כליל דזית."

אמר ליה, "דאת מתרוממא לבתר יומין."

אתא חד חורן, אמר ליה, "חמית בחילמאי לבוש כלילא דזית." אמר ליה, "דאת מלקי."

אמר ליה, "להthe הוא גברא אמרת דאת מתרוממא ולי אמרת דאת מלקי?!?"

אמר ליה, "ההוא הוה בנציא ואת בחבטיא."

חד בר נש אתא לגבי דרבי ישמעאל בי רבי יוסי.

אמר ליה, "חמית בחילמאי משקא זיתא משח."

אמר ליה, "תיפח רוחיה דההוא גברא! לאימיה הוא חכים!"

חד בר נש אתא לגבי רבי ישמעאל בי רבי יוסי. אמר ליה, "חמית בחילמאי עיני נשקה חבידתה."

אמר ליה, "תיפח רוחיה דההוא גברא! לאחתיה הוא חכים!"

חד בר נש אתא לגבי רבי ישמעאל בי רבי יוסי. אמר ליה, "חמית בחילמאי אית לי תלתא עיינין."

אמר ליה, "תנודין את עביד. תרתין עיניך ועיניה דתנודרא."

חד בר נש אתא לגבי רבי ישמעאל בי רבי יוסי. אמר ליה, "חמית בחילמאי אית לי ארבעה אודנין."

אמר ליה, "מלוי את. תרתי אודניך ותרתי אודני דגרבא."

344

חד בר נש אתא לגבי רבי ישמעאל בי רבי יוסי. אמר ליה,
"חמית בחילמאי ברייתא ערקין מן קומי."

אמר ליה, "דאת מייתי איזייא וכל עמא ערקין מן קדמך."

חד בר נש אתא לגבי רבי ישמעאל בי רבי יוסי. אמר ליה,
"חמית בחילמאי לביש חד פינקס דתרי עשר לוחין."

אמר ליה, "איסטווא דההוא גברא אית בה תרי עשר מרקען."

חד בר נש אתא לגבי רבי ישמעאל בי רבי יוסי. אמר ליה,
"חמית בחלמאי בלע חד כוכב."

אמר ליה, "תיפח רוחיה דההוא גברא! יהודאי קטל דכתיב,
'...דָּרַךְ כּוֹכָב מִיַּעֲקֹב... '" (במדבר כד:יז).

חד בר נש אתא לקמיה דרבי ישמעאל בי רבי יוסי. אמר ליה,
"חמית בחילמאי כרמיה דההוא גברא מסיק חסין."

אמר ליה, "חמריה דההוא גברא מיפוק בסיס ואת מינסב חסין
וצבע כבסין."

חד בר נש אתא לגבי דרבי ישמעאל בי רבי יוסי. אמר ליה,
"חמית בחילמאי מיתמר לי הכין: 'זרק אצבעתך נחת.'"

אמר ליה, "הב לי אגראי ואנא אמר לך."

אמר ליה, "חמית בחילמאי מיתמר לי הכין: 'תיהוי נפח
בפומך.'"

אמר ליה, "הב לי אגראי ואנא אמר לך."

אמר ליה, "חמית בחלמאי הכין: 'זקיף אצבעך.'"

אמר ליה, "לא אמרית לך הב לי אגרי ואנא אמר לך? כד
דאיתמר לך הכין נחת, דילפָּא בחיטך. כד איתמר לך הכין, אינפחן. כד
איתמר לך הכין, צמחין."

חד כותיי אמר, "אנא איזול מפלי בהדין סבא דיהודאי." אתא
לגביה. אמר ליה, "חמית בחילמאי ארבעה ארזין וארבע שיקמין,
מקניתא אדרא תורתא וההוא גברא יתיב מדרך."

אמר ליה, "תיפח רוחיה דההוא גברא! לית הדין חלם! אפילו
כן לית את נפיק ריקן. ארבעתי ארזי ארבעתי שיטתיה דערסא. ארבע

שיקמין ארבעתי כורעתא דערסא. מקניתה מרגלתא. אדרא דרא
דתיבנא. תורתא אצבעתא. וההוא גברא יתיב מדרך. וההוא גברא
רביע בגויה לא חיי ולא מיית."
וכן הוות ליה.
חדא איתא דאתיא לגבי רבי ליעזר. אמרה ליה, "חמית
בחילמאי תיניתא דביתא מיתברא."
אמר לה, "דאת מולד בר דכר." אזלה וילדה בר דכר.
בתר יומין, אזלה בעיא ליה. אמרין לה תלמידוי, "לית הוא
הכא." אמרין לה, "מה את בעיא מיניה?"
אמרה לון, "חמית ההיא איתתא בחלמאי תיניתא דבייתא
מיתברא."
אמרין לה, "דאת מוליד בר דכר ובעלה דההיא איתתא מיית."
כד אתא רבי ליעזר, תנון ליה עובדא. אמר לון, "קטלתון נפש!
למה? שאין החלום הולך אלא אחר פתרונו שנאמר, 'וַיְהִי כַּאֲשֶׁר פָּתַר
לָנוּ כֵּן הָיָה... .'" (בראשית מא:יג).
אמר רבי יוחנן: כל החלומות הולכין אחר פתרוניהון חוץ מן
היין. יש שותה יין וטוב לו יש שותה יין ורע לו. תלמיד חכם שותה
וטוב לו. עם הארץ שותה ורע לו.
חד בר נש אתא לגבי רבי עקיבה. אמר ליה, "חמית בחילמאי
רגלי קטינא."
אמר ליה, "דמועדא מייתי ולית מיכל קופד."
אתא חד חורן לגביה. אמר, "חמית בחלמאי רגלי מסובלא."
אמר ליה, "מועדא מייתי ואית לך קופד סגי."
חד תלמיד מן דרבי עקיבה הוה יתיב ואפוי משניין. אמר ליה,
"מהו כן?"
אמר ליה, "חמית בחילמאי תלת מילין קשיין. באדר את מיית
וניסן לית את חמי ומה דאת זרע לית את כנש."
אמר ליה, "תלתיהון טבין אינון. בהדרא דאורייתא את
מתרוממא וניסין לית את חמי. ומה דאת זרע, לית את כנש. מה דאת

מוליד, לית את קבר."

A certain person came to Rabbi Yossi ben Chalaftha. He said, "I saw in my dream that they told me, 'Go to Kappadokia[765] and you will find the treasure of your father.'"

He asked him, "Did your father ever travel to Kappadokia during his lifetime?"

"No."

"Go count ten rafters inside your house and you will find the treasure of your father beneath the chief rafter." [The word Kappadokia alludes to two Latin words: "*cappa*," meaning "head" or "chief," as in the English word "capital," and "*deka*," meaning "ten," as in the English word "decade."[766]]

A certain man came to Rabbi Yossi ben Chalaftha. He said, "I saw in my dream that I was wearing a wreath of olive branches."

"It means that you will be elevated eventually," explained the rabbi. Another person came and said, "I saw in my dream that I was wearing a wreath of olive branches."

"It means that you will be beaten."

"That person you said would be elevated, but to me you say, 'You will be beaten!?!'"

---

765 The name of the town could also be spelled "Cappadocia" in English.
766 B.T. *Brachoth* 56B.

"That person dreamed during the season of blossoming, but you dreamed during the season of beating." [Farmers used to beat the olive trees at harvest time to cause the ripe olives to fall to the ground.]

A certain person came to Rabbi Yishmael ben Rabbi Yossi and told him, "I saw in my dream oil smeared on a olive."

"May your bones be blasted! You had relations with your mother!" [Oil is the product of olives, so a vision of an olive smeared with oil alludes to this.[767]]

A certain person came to Rabbi Yishmael ben Rabbi Yossi and told him, "I saw in my dream that one of my eyes touched the other."

"May your bones be blasted! You had relations with your sister!" [Just as a person's two eyes are set in the same face, so a brother and sister come from the same source.[768]]

A certain person came to Rabbi Yishmael ben Rabbi Yossi and told him, "I saw in my dream that I had three eyes."

"Your business is making ovens. Two eyes are your own while the third is the eye of the oven." [Artisans used to fashion ovens of clay with a circular shape and a hole at the top which was called an "eye."[769]]

---

[767] *P'nei Moshe.*
[768] Ibid.
[769] Ibid.

A certain person came to Rabbi Yishmael ben Rabbi Yossi and told him, "I saw in my dream that I had four ears."

"Your business is filling wine jugs. Two ears are your own while the other two are the handles of a jug." [The handles of a wine jug were referred to as its "ears."]

A certain person came to Rabbi Yishmael ben Rabbi Yossi and told him, "I saw in my dream that everyone was fleeing from me."

"You are going to bring thorn branches and all the people will flee from before you."

A certain person came to Rabbi Yishmael ben Rabbi Yossi and told him, "I saw in my dream that I was dressed in a ledger with twelve folios."

"Your platform has twelve rungs [i.e., a ladder] leading to it."[770]

A certain person came to Rabbi Yishmael ben Rabbi Yossi and told him, "I saw in my dream that I swallowed a star."

---

[770] The translation here follows *P'nei Moshe. Mathanoth Kehunah* on *Eichah Rabbah* 1:14, however, understands the word איסטווא to mean a worn out garment, so he would read this sentence as, "Your worn out garment has twelve patches." As mentioned earlier, people often dream about the things they think about during the day. Thus, people who engage in a trade may dream about something symbolic of that trade, someone who has pangs of conscience about immoral activity may dream of that, and someone who worries about the condition of his clothing may dream of that.

"May your bones be blasted! You murdered a Jew, as it is written, '...a star shall arise from Jacob... .'[771]" [Jews are compared to stars.]

A certain person came to Rabbi Yishmael ben Rabbi Yossi and told him, "I saw in my dream that my vineyard produced horseradish."

"Your wine will have such sweetness that you will have to take horseradish and dip it into the cups."

A certain person came to Rabbi Yishmael ben Rabbi Yossi and told him, "I saw in my dream that they told me thus: 'Cast your finger down'."

"Pay me my fee and I will tell you [what the dream means]."

[The person did not pay the requested fee, but returned a short time later and said,] "I saw in my dream that they told me thus: 'Blow with your mouth'."

"Pay me my fee and I will tell you."

[Again, the person did not pay, but returned on another occasion and said,] "I saw in my dream [that they told me thus]: 'Your finger has become stiff'."

"Didn't I tell you to pay me my fee and I would tell you? When they told you to cast your finger down, it meant that a seepage of water had descended into your wheat. When they told you to blow with your mouth, it meant that the wheat became swollen [from the water]. When they told you that your finger became stiff, it meant that the wheat became rotten." [Perhaps fingers symbolize

---

[771] Numbers 24:17.

wheat because they are thin and long like wheat. Casting down alludes to water which always flows downward.[772] The Hebrew word "*Nafach*" (נפח) which means "to blow" also means "swollen."]

A certain Samaritan said to himself, "I will go have some fun with this Jewish elder." He appeared before Rabbi Yishmael ben Rabbi Yossi and said, "I saw in my dream four cedars and four sycamores, rows of foot cushions, and I sat upon them going to the bathroom."

"May your bones be blasted! This dream never existed! Even so, you shall not go empty-handed. Four cedars represent the four pieces of a bedframe. Four sycamores represent the four legs of a bed. The foot cushion is the lower board [upon which the bed is set]. The cushion material is a mattress of straw. The rows are the settings [upon which straps were interlaced to support the mattress]. You will sit there and go to the bathroom. You will crouch inside it neither alive nor dead." [You will become bedridden so that you will have to go to the bathroom while remaining in bed.]

And so it happened to him.

A certain woman came to Rabbi Eliezer. She said, "I saw in my dream that the cross-piece of the doorframe of the house broke."

"It means that you will give birth to a male child." [The Hebrew word for "breaking" (שבר) has the same root

---

[772] *P'nei Moshe.*

as the word for "birthing stool" (משבר).[773] The Hebrew word for "building" (בנין) resembles the word for "son" (בן).[774]] She went and gave birth to a male child.

After some time, she came seeking Rabbi Eliezer. His disciples said, "He is not here. What do you want from him?"

"I saw in my dream that the cross-piece of the doorframe of the house broke."

They told her, "You will give birth to a male child and your husband will die." [Perhaps the doorframe alluded to the husband because he provided support for the household by going out through the doorway to work.]

When Rabbi Eliezer came, his disciples related the incident to him. He said, "You have killed a person! Why so? Because a dream is not fulfilled except according to its interpretation, as it says, [when Pharaoh's butler told him about Joseph's ability to interpret dreams], 'And it was just as he interpreted for us, so it was... .'[775]"

Rabbi Yochanan said: All dreams are fulfilled according to their interpretations except for wine. Some envision drinking it and it is good, while some envision drinking it and it is bad. A scholar envisions drinking and it is good for him, while an uneducated person envisions drinking and it is bad for him. [Grapevines symbolize the

---

[773] P'nei Moshe.

[774] Rabbi David Luria on Breishith Rabbah 89:8.

[775] Genesis 41:13.

Jewish people.[776] Accordingly, their appearance in a dream can represent different things for different members of the community. Wine may help a scholar study better by refreshing him and permitting him to view a subject from a different perspective.[777] On the other hand, drinking wine tends to reinforce an ignorant person's deficient behavior as King Solomon said, "One drunk with wine is a scoffer and he who is drunk cries out; whoever blunders in it shall not become wise."[778]]

A certain person came to Rabbi Akiva and told him, "I saw in my dream that my leg was small."

"The holiday will arrive," replied the rabbi, "and you will not eat meat." [The Hebrew word for "leg" (רגל) also means "holiday."]

Someone else came to him and said, "I saw in my dream that my leg was thick."

"The holiday will arrive and you will have much meat."

One student of Rabbi Akiva was sitting with his face contorted. "Why do you look so?" asked the rabbi.

"I saw in my dream three harsh things. I was told, 'In [the month of] *Adar* you will die. [The month of] *Nissan* you will not see. What you plant you will not gather.'"

---

[776] *Zohar* I, 238A.
[777] B.T. *Baba Bathra* 12B.
[778] Proverbs 20:1.

"These are three good things. With the majesty of the *Torah* you shall be exalted. [With a slight change in spelling, the word "*Adar*" (אדר) can be read as "*Haddar*" (הדר), meaning "majesty." The *Talmud* says that one can attain greatness in *Torah* learning only if he is willing to "kill himself over it."[779] That is why the dream referred to death.] You will not see miracles. [The word *Nissan* (ניסן) means "miracles." When God performs miracles for a person, He may reduce his or her merit.[780] Accordingly, it is a blessing when one does not experience miracles.] And that which you plant you shall not gather. What you give birth to, you shall not bury."

When a person sleeps, part of his or her soul ascends to the upper spiritual realms where it perceives various matters such as what may happen in the future. When the soul communicates this information back to the person, he or she does not have the means to fully comprehend such lofty spiritual concepts. Instead, the person's imagination becomes stimulated so that he or she sees a dream. How an individual perceives this spiritual information may be influenced by what the person thought about during the day or by his or her body chemistry. For this reason, all dreams have some worthless content.[781]

---

[779] B.T. *Brachoth* 63B.
[780] B.T. *Shabbath* 32A.
[781] *Derech Hashem* 3:1:6; *Etz Chaim*, Gate 50, Chapter 10; *Zohar* I 183A.

The concept that dreams are fulfilled according to the way in which they are interpreted is the subject of controversy among the commentators. According to many, only certain gifted people can interpret dreams. When the Talmud says that dreams follow the way in which they are interpreted, it does not mean that anyone who wishes to interpret a dream can do so. Instead, the dream has certain valid meanings which can only take effect if someone expresses them verbally. When Rabbi Eliezer criticized his students for killing a man in the above passage, he did not mean that they could have interpreted the dream differently. Rather, had they simply remained silent, the dream would not have come to fruition.[782] As Rav Chisda said, "Any dream which is not interpreted is like a letter which is not read."[783]

Other authorities hold that dreams are indeed fulfilled because of the way in which they are interpreted. Rabbi Avraham Ibn Ezra raises an interesting question about this view, however. When Joseph was imprisoned with Pharaoh's butler and baker, they wanted their dreams interpreted. Joseph said, "Do not solutions belong to God?"[784] This implies that dreams are Divinely inspired premonitions. Indeed, the Babylonian Talmud calls dreams "one-sixtieth of prophecy."[785] If so, how can an

---

[782] *Akeidath Yitzchak,* Gate 29.
[783] B.T. *Brachoth* 55A.
[784] Genesis 40:8.
[785] B.T. *Brachoth* 57B.

interpretation change them? Because of this problem, Rabbi Avraham Ibn Ezra suggests that the view that dreams are fulfilled in accordance with the way in which they are interpreted is a "lone opinion" upon which one cannot rely.[786]

It is difficult to understand Rabbi Ibn Ezra's position. The passage translated above repeatedly states that dreams are fulfilled in accordance with how they are interpreted without mention of any opposing view. The Babylonian Talmud also does not mention a dispute on this point. To the contrary, it relates that there were twenty-four dream interpreters in Jerusalem each of whom interpreted a dream of Rabbi Banaah differently and each interpretation came true.[787]

Still, Rabbi Ibn Ezra's question remains. How can something akin to prophecy change based on human interpretation and what did Joseph mean by saying that the deciphering of dreams belongs to God?

Perhaps the answer is that prophecies can also yield different results depending upon how they are interpreted. For example, Hashem told Abraham that his descendents would be slaves in a foreign land for four hundred years.[788] *In reality, the Jews were slaves in Egypt for only two hundred ten years. Because God desired to*

---

[786] Rabbi Avraham Ibn Ezra on Genesis 40:8. *HaKothev* on B.T. *Brachoth* 55A-56B adopts this position as well.
[787] B.T. *Brachoth* 55B.
[788] Genesis 15:13.

hasten the redemption, He counted the four hundred years as starting from the birth of Isaac.[789]

Jonah prophesied that "...in another forty days Nineveh will be overturned...."[790] That phrase could have two meanings, however. It could mean that Nineveh would be destroyed just as Sodom and Gomorra were "overturned."[791] However, it could also mean that the citizens of Nineveh would be "overturned" in their behavior from evil to good and the calamity averted. The latter interpretation prevailed.[792]

The Tanach records how King Josiah sent his top advisors to seek counsel from the prophet Huldah.[793] The Talmud asks why the king chose her when Jeremiah, a prophet of greater stature, was available. The answer is that "women are merciful,"[794] meaning that although both Jeremiah and Huldah could prophesy, a woman would present the prophecy in a more compassionate form which God, in turn, would fulfill.

Rabbi Moshe Chaim Luzzatto explains that because prophecy is a supernatural phenomenon, it may contain things which appear contradictory to humans who can only understand natural occurrences.[795] For example, Hashem

---

[789] *Shir HaShirim Rabbah* 2:21 and *Rashi* on Genesis 15:13.
[790] Jonah 3:4.
[791] Genesis 19:25.
[792] *Derech Hashem* 3:4:7.
[793] II Kings 22:12-14.
[794] B.T. *Megillah* 14B.
[795] *Da'ath Tevunoth*, Section 190.

said the words "Observe" (שמור) and "Remember" (זכור) simultaneously when He gave the commandment to keep the Sabbath even though it is not possible for humans to utter two words simultaneously.[796] *Likewise, at the Giving of the Torah, Jews prophetically "saw" thunder, a concept which ordinarily makes no sense.*[797] *Just as prophecy can be the subject of apparently contradictory interpretations, so dreams which are a low form of prophecy may be interpreted in contradictory ways. This would explain why dreams often contain contradictory or illogical material and events which could never occur in real life.*

The Shulchan Aruch appears to rule according to the view that dreams become reality depending on how one interprets them. If one is worried about a dream, he or she should appear before three friends and say, "I saw a good dream." The friends should then say, "It is good and it should be good. May the Merciful One make it good. May it be decreed upon you seven times from Heaven that it be good and it shall be good." They then recite certain verses from the Tanach.[798] *Similarly, if one does not remember the contents of a dream, he or she should recite a special prayer during the priestly blessings asking God to strengthen the dream if it was a good one and to rectify it if it was a bad one.*[799] *Although such procedures do not*

---

[796] B.T. *Rosh HaShannah* 27A.

[797] Exodus 20:16 with *Rashi's* commentary.

[798] *Shulchan Aruch, Orach Chaim* 220:1 based on B.T. *Brachoth* 55B.

[799] *Shulchan Aruch, Orach Chaim* 130:1 based on B.T. *Brachoth*

entail specific dream interpretation, their purpose is to try to ensure that whatever positive interpretation a dream may have should apply.

In light of the above, it appears that when Joseph said that interpretation of dreams belongs to God, he meant that many interpretations could apply and whether he would be inspired to construct a good or bad one was up to God. Alternatively, God would decide whether to fulfill Joseph's interpretation or another one.

The Zohar presents a hybrid view on the subject. All dreams contain both true and false material.[800] There is only one true interpretation a dream can have, namely the one God intended. However, if someone interprets a dream according to the false material it contains, that interpretation will come about. This happens because dreams are a highly inferior form of prophecy which can be controlled by what people say.[801]

Rabbi Ovadiah Yosef cites several recent authorities who hold that people today need not worry about dreams because the skill for deciphering them is by and large lost. In addition, as with certain other supernatural phenomena such as demons, "whoever is concerned about them, they are concerned about him, but whoever is not concerned about them, they are not

---

55B.
[800] B.T. *Brachoth* 55A mentions this as well.
[801] *Zohar* I, 183A.

concerned about him."[802] *Accordingly, a person who sees a troublesome dream on the Sabbath should not fast to avert its evil consequences as people once did.*[803]

The Babylonian Talmud strongly criticizes Bar Hedya, a dream interpreter who demanded money for his services and offered negative interpretations if his demands were not met.[804] *How, then, could Rabbi Yishmael ben Rabbi Yossi demand a fee for interpreting dreams? Certainly he would not interpret a dream negatively just because he did not receive payment.*

The Babylonian Talmud praises Rabbi Yishmael ben Rabbi Yossi for being very strict about the prohibition against a judge taking bribes.[805] *A sharecropper used to bring Rabbi Yishmael ben Rabbi Yossi a basket of fruits every Friday as partial payment for his rent. One time, he brought the basket on Thursday. When the rabbi asked his sharecropper why he had deviated from his normal routine, he answered, "I have a court case today, so I figured that while I'm on my way, I would bring this for the Master." Rabbi Yishmael ben Rabbi Yossi refused to accept the fruits and refused to participate in judging the case. As he*

---

[802] B.T. *Pesachim* 110B. Most authorities take this to mean that because the spiritual level of humankind has deteriorated, supernatural occurrences such as demons and prophetic dreams no longer exist and only affect those who worry about them unduly.

[803] *Yechaveh Da'ath*, Part IV, Responsa 24 sub verba "*Omnam Rainu*" (אמנם ריאנו).

[804] B.T. *Brachoth* 56A-B.

[805] B.T. *Makoth* 24A.

listened to the parties discussing their dispute before the other judges, he found himself thinking of arguments the sharecropper might present to win, whereupon he said, "Blasted are the souls of those who accept bribery! I did not accept the fruits and had I accepted them, I would have merely taken what is anyway rightfully mine, yet even so, I find myself influenced. How much more so those who accept bribes!"[806]

The Zohar states that a Kohen should not utter the priestly blessings unless he gets along well with the congregation. Furthermore, the blessings can only be fulfilled when the Kohen who says them does so with a benevolent attitude towards the congregation.[807]

During the priestly blessings, Jews pray that their dreams should portend good.[808] *This suggests that interpreting a dream is similar to giving a blessing. In the passage under consideration, Rabbi Yishmael ben Rabbi Yossi wanted to ensure that he would give a good interpretation to the dream. While he denounced accepting a bribe or anything approaching a bribe when it came to deciding a court case, it is proper and even commendable to accept payment or favors so that one will be in a good mood and sincerely offer a good interpretation of a dream.*

---

[806] B.T. *Kethuboth* 105B.

[807] *Zohar* III 147B.

[808] *Shulchan Aruch, Orach Chaim* 130:1 based on B.T. *Brachoth* 55B.

361

This would especially apply to Rabbi Yishmael ben Rabbi Yossi who himself was a Kohen.[809]

In addition, it is possible that Rabbi Yishmael ben Rabbi Yossi realized that the crop damage to which the petitioner's dream alluded was already in progress. To ensure that a positive interpretation would apply, Rabbi Yishmael ben Rabbi Yossi knew that the person who had the dream would need a special merit. Accordingly, perhaps he requested payment so that he could give the money to charity and so create merit for the petitioner.[810]

---

[809] *Tanchuma Devarim, Shoftim* 8.
[810] Rabbi Yishmael ben Rabbi Yossi held that the wealthy people of the Land of Israel were granted success in the merit of tithing. *(B.T. Shabbath 119A)*.

Ma'aser Sheni 5:1 (Compare B.T. *Sanhedrin* 109A; *Breishith Rabbah* 27:3)

...אמר רבן שמעון בן גמליאל: במה דברים אמורים?
בשביעית, [אבל בשאר שני שבוע הלעיטהו לרשע וימות]...
חברייא אמרי: יאות אמר רבן שמעון בן גמליאל וקשיא על
דרבנין. לא ביום הוא מציין ולא בלילה הוא גונב?
אמר לון רבי מנא: מביום, כיי דאמר רבי חנינא, "חָתַר בַּחֹשֶׁךְ
בָּתִּים יוֹמָם חִתְּמוּ לָמוֹ לֹא יָדְעוּ אוֹר." (איוב כד:טז). "...מִיּוֹמָם חִתְּמוּ
לָמוֹ..." כך היו אנשי דור המבול עושין: היו רושמין באפכולסמין ובאין
וגונבים בלילה.
כך דרשה רבי חנינא בציפורין. איתעביד תלת מאה חתירין
בתים.

[The *Mishnah* instructs farmers to mark off trees which are immature (ערלה) or in their fourth year (רבעי)[811] so that passersby will not accidentally eat their fruits.] **...Rabban Shimon ben Gamliel said: When does this apply? During the Sabbatical year [when farmers must leave their fields open to the public and may not claim ownership of their produce]. However, during the rest of the years of the Sabbatical cycle, stuff the wicked one and let him die! [Since anyone entering a farmer's fields during the other six years of the Sabbatical cycle**

---

[811] The *Torah* forbids Jews to eat fruits produced during the first three years of a tree's life when they are immature (ערלה). Fruits which grow during the fourth year (רבעי) may be eaten only in Jerusalem. The *Tannaim* disagree as to whether the latter restriction applies only to vineyards or to all fruit trees. (B.T. *Brachoth* 35A).

**to take fruits would be stealing, it is simply too bad for
him if he ends up eating something forbidden.]...**

...*Gemara*:   The colleagues of the academy said:
What Rabban Shimon ben Gamliel said is sensible, but
there is a difficulty with what the rabbis said. Wouldn't the
farmer do the marking during the day while the thief steals
at night? [Rabban Shimon ben Gamliel holds that honest
people do not have to go out of their way to protect thieves.
However, even if honest people would do so, as those who
disagree with him maintain, it would not help because
thieves normally come at night and will not see the
markings, so making them is a waste of time.[812]]

Rabbi Manna answered them: From during the day,
similar to that which Rabbi Chanina said: "He breached in
the darkness houses; [during] daytime they marked them,
they did not know light."[813]   "...[during] daytime they
marked them..." Thus did the people of the generation of
the Flood do: They would mark with balsam and come to
steal at night. [The thieves knew where valuables were
hidden in their victims' homes, but did not have the nerve
or prowess to break in during daytime. Therefore, they
marked the location with highly aromatic balsam so that
when they came sneaking around at night they could detect
the location of the valuables by the smell.[814] By contrast,

---

[812] *Melecheth Shlomo* on *Ma'aser Sheni* 5:1.
[813] Job 24:16.
[814]   According to the Babylonian *Talmud*, the thieves would ask
unsuspecting people to store balsam for them. The victims would store
the balsam near their precious belongings and the thieves used the scent

when it came to stealing produce from a field, they were not afraid of being detected so they would generally come during the day. Thus, they would see the markings and refrain from eating immature or fourth year fruits.[815]]

Rabbi Chanina recited the foregoing homily [about the generation of the Flood] in Sepphoris. [That night,] three hundred break-ins took place. [The homily gave the thieves new ideas about how to conduct their business, causing a rash of break-ins.]

The Rambam rules in accordance with the view of Rabban Shimon ben Gamliel that honest people need not worry about the spiritual welfare of thieves.[816] However, the Torah says, "...do not place a hazard before the blind...,"[817] meaning, among other things, that a person should not facilitate the commission of a sin. For example, a person should not give non-Kosher food to a Jew whom he or she knows will eat it. How is it that this prohibition does not apply in this case? How is it permissible to trip up another Jew, albeit a thief, by letting him eat non-Kosher food?

The Talmud declares that, ironically, "A thief calls out to the Merciful One at the entrance of the tunnel [he uses to break into his victim's home]."[818]   Before

---

to trace the location of those valuables. (B.T. *Sanhedrin* 109A).

[815] *P'nei Moshe.*

[816] *Yad HaChazakah, Hilchoth Ma'aser Sheni* 9:7.

[817] Leviticus 19:14.

[818] B.T. *Brachoth* 63A in certain editions of *Ein Yaakov.*

*committing his crime, the thief prays for success.
Unfortunately, there are people who do not observe the
prohibition against stealing yet scrupulously observe other
commandments.*[819] *If a thief realizes that he may end up
eating something forbidden, he may refrain from stealing.
Accordingly, rather than tripping him up, failing to mark
off the forbidden trees will actually discourage him from
stealing.*

*Alternatively, one is only considered liable for
tripping up others if he or she directly provides prohibited
food to another. Merely leaving something out which
another could take without permission does not violate this
commandment. According to this view, the expression
"stuff the wicked one" is not literal, but only means that
one need not go out of one's way to prevent a sinner from
compounding his or her sin.*[820]

*Why did Rabbi Chanina recite the teaching about
the generation of the Flood publicly? The Mishnah
instructs judges to, "Take care with your words lest the
parties learn from them to lie."*[821] *If a judge suggests that
a certain claim or a certain set of facts will yield certain
results, the litigants may be tempted to alter their*

---

[819] Possibly these people intend to eventually pay back what they steal
and assume that such intention excuses their wrongdoing.
(*Encyclopedia Talmudith*, Vol. 9, sub verba "*Haleetaihu LeRasha
VeYamuth*" (הלעיטהו לרשע וימות), citing *Chavoth Yair*, Responsa 142.).
[820] *Encyclopedia Talmudith*, Vol. 9, sub verba "*Haleetaihu LeRasha
VeYamuth*" (הלעיטהו לרשע וימות), citing *Chazon Ish, Demai* 8:9.
[821] *Pirkei Avoth* 1:9.

testimony. Why, then, did it not occur to Rabbi Chanina that he might cause this problem?

The Babylonian Talmud says that this story happened to Rabbi Yossi and that when people complained to him, he said, "How was I to know that thieves would come?" In other words, a rabbi would not normally suspect that thieves would attend his lecture.[822]

---

[822] *Ben Yehoyada* on B.T. *Sanhedrin* 109A.

Ma'aser Sheni 5:2 (Compare *Eichah Rabbah* 3:3)

הדא פליגא על נָקֵיי. נְקֵיי הוה שמש במגדל וצבעייא. בכל
ערובת שובא מן דהוה עביד קנדילוי, הוה סליק שבת בבית מקדשא
ונחית ומדליק לון. ואית דאמרין ספר הוה. בכל ערובת שובתא, הוה
סליק פשט סדרוי לבית המקדש ונחית שבת בבייתיה.
טרטידוי דמהלול הוה סליק שבית לגו בית מקדשא ולא הוה
בר נש קרץ לתאינייא קדמוי מיניה.
בנות צָפּוֹרֵי הוון סלקין שבתין בגו בית מקדשא ולא הוה בר
נש קרץ לתאינייא קדמוי מינהון.
בנות לוד היו לשות עיסתן ועולות ומתפללות ויורדות עד
שלא יחמיצו. חד בר נש הוה קאים רדי. פסקת תורתיה קומוי. הוות
פריא והוא פרי, פריא והוא פרי עד דאשתכח יהיב בבבל.
אמרו ליה, "אימת נפקת?"
אמר לון, "יומא דֵין."
אמרין, "בהיידא אתיתא?"
אמר לון, "בדא."
אמרין ליה, "איתא חמי לון!"
נפק בעי מיחמייא לון ולא חכים בהיידא דא.
מכלל דפליגא. אפילו תימר לית הוא פליגא. מחילות היו
ונגנזו. הדא הוא דכתיב, "גָּדַר דְּרָכַי בְּגָזִית נְתִיבֹתַי עִוָּה." (איכה ג:ט).

[When farmers raise fruit trees in the Land of Israel,
the crop of the fourth year (רבעי), must be transported to
Jerusalem and eaten there. The *Torah*, however, permits
farmers to redeem such fruits with coins, take the coins to
Jerusalem and buy food there. The *Mishnah* explains that
the rabbis decreed that any fruits grown within a day's
journey of Jerusalem should not be redeemed, but, rather,

brought to Jerusalem to make fruits plentiful there. The *Mishnah* goes on to identify four cities which are a day's journey from Jerusalem in different directions.]

The *Mishnah* [which states that Lod lies a day's journey from Jerusalem] contradicts Nikkai. Nikkai was a beadle in Dyers' Tower[823] [a town near Lod]. Every Sabbath eve he would fix the candles, ascend to the Temple to prepare for the Sabbath and descend to light them. Some say he was a schoolteacher. Every Sabbath eve he would ascend to lay out the children's review work in the Temple, then descend and spend the Sabbath at his home. [One way or another, Nikkai clearly lived less than a day's journey from Jerusalem.]

Tartiroy of Mahalul would ascend to spend the Sabbath in the Temple, yet there was not a soul who harvested a fig before him [on Saturday night. Mahalul was apparently located near Lod, but it could not have been far from Jerusalem if Tartiroy could do this.]

The women of Sepphoris used to ascend to spend the Sabbath in the Temple, yet there was not a soul who harvested figs before them.[824]

The women of Lod would knead their dough, ascend to pray and return before it became leavened.

---

[823] *Breishith Rabbah* 79:6 and other passages of *Midrash Rabbah* have מגדלא דצבעייא or similar readings rather than מגדל וצבעייא which appears in the Romm Vilna text.

[824] Sepphoris is in the north of the Land of Israel about eighty kilometers from Jerusalem.

A certain man was plowing when his cow broke loose. It ran and he chased after it. It ran further and he chased after it until he found himself arrived in Babylon.

The people there said to him, "When did you set out?"

"This very day," he replied.

"Upon which route did you come?"

"Upon this one."

"Come show us!"

He went out wanting to show them but could not discern which route [he had taken].

[All of the above] shows that the *Mishnah* is contradicted.

You could even say that it is not contradicted. There were subterranean passages which have become hidden. Thus it is written, "He obstructed my paths with cut stone, my lanes He twisted."[825] [When *Hashem* permitted foreign enemies such as the Babylonians and Romans to conquer the Land of Israel, He withdrew all of the Land's special qualities. Hence, paths which once permitted quick and easy passage through the Land were blocked and twisted.[826]]

How would subterranean passages have permitted people to travel so quickly?

---

[825] Lamentations 3:9.

[826] *Matanoth Kehunah* on *Eichah Rabbah* 3:3, sub verba "*Gadar D'rachai*" (גדר דרכי).

The Talmud teaches that the Holy Ark was located at the precise center of a room that was twenty cubits by twenty cubits, yet one who measured from any wall to the Holy Ark found a distance of ten cubits, meaning that, miraculously, it took up no space.[827] *This occurred because that which is holy is above and beyond the usual confines of the physical world.*

Along similar lines, the Babylonian Talmud states that 600,000 cities occupied a certain mountain in the Land of Israel before the destruction of the Temple. Ulla remarked that he had visited that site and it could not hold 600,000 sticks, let alone 600,000 cities. The Gemara explains that the Land of Israel is called "a majestic land."[828] *The Hebrew word for "majestic" (צבי) also means "deer." Just as a deerskin removed from a deer shrinks and will no longer fit around its carcass, so the Land of Israel shrank after its rightful inhabitants were exiled.*[829]

Based on the above, it appears that the Land of Israel was wide and spacious on its surface prior to the destruction of the Temple to accommodate the Jews who lived there. However, the Land had compressed dimensions underneath its surface, resembling a kernel of maize which is narrow near the cob but bulges outward.

---

[827] B.T. *Megillah* 10B and *Baba Bathra* 99A.
[828] Jeremiah 3:19; Daniel 11:16 and 11:41.
[829] B.T. *Gittin* 57A.

Thus, people could travel short distances below ground which turned out to be vast distances on the surface.

According to the Babylonian Talmud, even the surface dimensions of the Land of Israel have changed since the destruction of the Temple. Originally, the distance between Jerusalem and the border of the Land was thirty-two parasangs (Persian miles)[830] because people could travel along a direct route. The distance grew considerably greater after the destruction of the Temple because people had to travel by means of a circuitous route.[831] Traveling through underground tunnels would have permitted people to proceed more quickly because they could travel in even more of a straight line from one point to another.

---

[830] About 128 kilometers. See footnote 636 above.
[831] B.T. *Rosh HaShannah* 23B.

Ma'aser Sheni 5:5

רבי הונא בר אחא בשם רבי אלכסנדרא: בוא וראה כמה גדול
כוחן של עושי מצוה שכל "השקפה" שבתורה ארורה וזה בלשון ברכה.
אמר רבי יוסי בן חנינא: ולא עוד, אלא שכתוב בו, "היום הזה."
תניי יומא.

רבי יודה בן פזי פתח בה: "אָבוֹא בִגְבֻרוֹת אֲ-דֹנָי ה' [אַזְכִּיר
צִדְקָתְךָ לְבַדֶּךָ]." (תהלים עא:טז).

כתיב, "וַיֹּאמֶר אֵלֶּה שְׁנֵי בְנֵי הַיִּצְהָר הָעֹמְדִים עַל אֲדוֹן כָּל
הָאָרֶץ." (זכריה ד:יד). רבי אבהו אמר: אתפלגון רבי יוחנן ורבי שמעון בן
לקיש. חד אמר אלו שהן באין בטרוניא לפני הקדוש ברוך הוא. וחרנא
אמר אלו שהן באין מכח המצות ומעשים טובים לפני הקדוש ברוך הוא.

[The *Torah* requires Jews to make gifts of certain portions of their agricultural produce. On the last day of Passover in the third and sixth years of the Sabbatical cycle, the *Torah* commands Jewish farmers to recite a prayer in which they acknowledge that they have distributed the agricultural gifts as required. The prayer ends off, "Observe from Your holy habitation, from Heaven, and bless Your people, Israel, and the land which You gave us as You swore to our forefathers, a land flowing with milk and honey."[832]]

Rabbi Huna bar Acha in the name of Rabbi Alexandra said: Come and see how great is the power of those who perform commandments, for every expression of "observe" (השקפה) in the *Torah* denotes curse whereas this

---

832 Deuteronomy 26:15.

is an expression of blessing. [The *Torah* used the term "observe" (השקפה) when God destroyed Sodom and Gomorrah,[833] and when He drowned the Egyptian army,[834] but uses it here to invoke *Hashem's* blessing.]

Rabbi Yossi ben Chanina said: Not only that, but it is written, "on this day," [in the following verse][835] meaning that the blessings [earned through *Mitzvah* observance] are repeated daily.

Rabbi Yudah ben Pazzi commenced a discourse on this topic: "I come with strength, Lord God, recalling Your unique righteousness."[836] [In the merit of performing the commandments, *Hashem* changes the usual negative implication of the term "observe" (השקפה) to a positive one. Similarly, this verse praises God for converting "strength" (גברות), a term which denotes harsh judgment, to something positive.[837]]

It is written, "...These are the two anointed ones which stand before the Lord of all the Earth."[838] [Zachariah had a prophetic vision during which he saw olive trees, one on each side of the candelabrum that stood in the Temple. An angel explained to him that these stood for the High Priest and the King, each of whom was

---

[833] Genesis 18:16 and 19:28.
[834] Exodus 14:24.
[835] "On this day, the Lord your God commands you to perform these statutes... ." (Deuteronomy 26:16).
[836] Psalms 71:16.
[837] *P'nei Moshe.*
[838] Zachariah 4:14.

initiated into office by anointment with olive oil.[839]] Rabbi Abahu said: Rabbi Yochanan and Rabbi Shimon ben Lakish argued about the interpretation of this verse. One said that they [the High Priest and the King] came with complaints before the Holy One, Blessed be He [that He restore their greatness]. The other said that they came through the power of *Mitzvoth* and good deeds before the Holy One, Blessed be He.

Rashi on the Tanach comments that the phrase "two anointed ones" (שני בני היצהר) hints at the two instincts (יצרים) people have: the good inclination and the evil inclination. When Jews obey the Mitzvoth and study Torah, they convert the evil inclination to good.[840] *God always rewards people measure for measure, so when an individual obeys a commandment and overcomes the natural impulses which tempt him to disobey, He reverses the usual course of the world for him, changing that which is evil to good. Thus, a term such as "observe" (השקיפה) which normally connotes punishment can allude to blessing.*

*The above Talmudic passage states that **all** Mitzvoth have the power to convert evil to good. If so, why did the Torah single out tithing as the one Mitzvah which requires a declaration alluding to this? Why not make a similar declaration for every Mitzvah?*

---

839 *Rashi* on Zachariah 4:14 and see *BaMidbar Rabbah* 14:12.
840 Ibid.

The end of the passage which cites a verse about the King and the High Priest suggests an answer. A primary function of the King was to enforce laws between a person and his or her neighbor, while the function of the High Priest was to perform the Temple service, thereby fulfilling Mitzvoth associated with the relationship between humanity and God.[841] *This shows that whoever wishes to merit the blessing of having harsh judgment converted to benevolent blessing must fulfill* **both** *the commandments which affect the relationship between a person and his or her fellows and those which affect the relationship between humanity and God.*

This is why the Torah commanded the recitation of this formula specifically with respect to tithing. All commandments come from God and thus reflect a person's relationship to the Creator. Likewise, all commandments have something to do with the relationship between people and their fellows.[842] *With other Mitzvoth, this dual function may not be readily apparent, but with tithing it is. On the one hand, some tithes must be given to the Levites and the poor and thus are related to the inter-relationship between people. On the other hand, certain laws apply to tithes which pertain to a person's obligation to obey God. For example, one may not eat his or her produce without*

---

[841] *Malbim* on Zachariah 4:14.

[842] See, for example, B.T. *Shabbath* 31A where Hillel stated that the *Torah* could be summed up with the maxim, "What is hateful to you, do not do to your fellow."

first removing the tithes. Thus, tithing is a Mitzvah which has rules which affect both a person's relationship to others and his or her relationship to God. Therefore, it symbolizes the power to convert punishment to reward more than any other Mitzvah.

Ma'aser Sheni 5:5 (Compare B.T. *Brachoth* 17B and B.T. *Chullin* 86A)

רב הוה ליה כיתן ולקת.

...לא כן אמר רבי אמי מְשֵׁם רבי שמעון בן לקיש: משעלו מן הגולה לא לקת פשתן ולא החמיץ יין ונתנו עיניהם בזכות רבי חייא הגדול ובניו.

ורב כהדא: "שִׁמְעוּ אֵלַי אַבִּירֵי לֵב הָרְחוֹקִים מִצְּדָקָה." (ישעיה מו:יב). רבי אבהו אמר: איתפלגון רבי יוחנן ורבי שמעון בן לקיש. חד אמר שכל באי עולם באין בצדקה ואלו באין בזרוע. וחרנא אמר שכל טובות ונחמות הבאות לעולם בזכותן והן אינן נהנין מהן כלום. כגון מר זוטרא דמצלי על חורנין ומתעני ועל נפשיה לא מתעני.

Rav owned flax which was ruined [by a worm infestation].

...Did not Rabbi Ami say in the name of Rabbi Shimon ben Lakish: Once they [the pious Jews of Babylonia] ascended [to the Land of Israel] from the exile, flax was never ruined and wine never soured for they relied upon the merit of Rabbi Chiya the Great and his sons.[843]

As for Rav, the following verse applies: "Listen to me stout-hearted ones who are distant from charity."[844] Rabbi Abahu said: Rabbi Yochanan and Rabbi Shimon ben Lakish disagree about the meaning of this verse. One says that all who pass through the world pass through by

---

[843] Rav was Rabbi Chiya the Great's nephew, so surely his flax should have been protected. (*P'nei Moshe*).
[844] Isaiah 46:12.

means of charity whereas these pass through by means of their might. [The general run of humanity does not deserve to exist, but people such as Rabbi Chiya and his sons exist due to their exceptional merit. Hence, everyone else survives by the grace of God while these "stout-hearted ones" need not rely on "charity."] The other says that all the good and comfort which come into the world are in their merit, but they do not benefit from such beneficence at all. [The merit of righteous people such as Rav protected the flax and wine of others, but not their own.] An example of this is Mar Zutra who prayed for others and was answered, but was not answered [when he prayed for] himself.

Why should it be that great people can help others but not themselves? One would think that if they can successfully assist others who lack merit, they should certainly be capable of assisting themselves.

One answer is that when flax and wine do not spoil or suffer from pests, it is a supernatural occurrence which resembles a miracle. When Hashem performs a miracle for someone, He reduces that person's merit.[845] *Hashem does not wish to reduce the merit of the righteous, so He performs the miracles they request for others, but not the miracles they request for themselves.*

Another reason Tzaddikim are unable to help themselves is that for a person to successfully petition God

---

[845] B.T. *Shabbath* 32A.

on behalf of others, he or she must be totally selfless.[846] *A true leader is so devoted to the people that he is unaccustomed to praying on his own behalf or thinking of his own needs. Since the righteous person offers sincere prayers for others, those are answered, but because the same people do not think much of their own needs, they do not pray as sincerely on their own behalf.*

A related point is that since the righteous possess a strong faith that everything that God causes to happen is for the best, they find it difficult to sincerely ask for anything for themselves and their prayers go unanswered.

The Mishnah teaches that one should always try to view others favorably and assume that their behavior is well-intentioned.[847] *A righteous person cultivates this trait to the extent that he or she normally views others as worthy people who do not deserve punishment. Accordingly, he or she prays for others wholeheartedly and effectively. By contrast, Tzaddikim possess great modesty, thinking that perhaps they deserve punishment, and so do not pray with the same devotion on their own behalf.*[848]

According to tradition, when Jews go into exile, the Divine Presence goes with them, as the Tanach says, "...I am with him during trouble... ."[849] *When Jews suffer, God, so to speak, suffers with them. Despite the anguish*

---

[846] *No'am Elimelech, Likutei Shoshanah.*
[847] *Pirkei Avoth* 1:6.
[848] See *Yismach Moshe,* end of *Parshath T'rumah* for a similar idea.
[849] Psalms 91:15 and see *BaMidbar Rabbah* 7:10.

that the exile causes God, His Wisdom has decreed that He not liberate His Divine Presence unless and until the Jewish people repent. Once they do so wholeheartedly, He will redeem both them and the Divine Presence. Kabbalistic tradition refers to this concept as "He who is imprisoned cannot release Himself."[850]

The goal of every Jew is to imitate the ways of Hashem. As the verse says, "In all your ways know Him... ."[851] *Likewise, the Talmud teaches, "Just as He is gracious and merciful, so you be gracious and merciful."*[852] *A great Tzaddik who is among the leaders of his or her generation achieves this goal to perfection. Thus, just as, metaphorically, Hashem does not redeem Himself from exile because he is so devoted to the Jewish people, a righteous person who resembles Him cannot free himself from his own difficulties for the same reason. Only the repentance of the Jewish masses can save their leaders. Along these lines, the Babylonian Talmud reports that Rabbi Yochanan saved others from illness but could not save himself because "He who is imprisoned cannot release himself."*[853]

---

[850] *Tikunei Zohar* 21B-22B.
[851] Proverbs 3:6.
[852] B.T. *Shabbath* 133B.
[853] B.T. *Brachoth* 5B.

Bikkurim 2:1 (Compare B.T. *Mo'ed Katan* 28A)

דתני: המת לחמשים שנה מת בהיכרת; לחמשים ושתים, זו
היא מיתת שמואל הנביא; לששים, מיתה האמורה בתורה; לשבעים,
מיתה של חיבה; לשמונים, מיתה של זָקְנָה; מכאן ואילך, חיי צער.
מה חמית מימר מת לחמשים מת בהיכרת? כתיב, "אַל תַּכְרִיתוּ
אֶת שֵׁבֶט מִשְׁפְּחֹת הַקְּהָתִי מִתּוֹךְ הַלְוִיִם. וְזֹאת עֲשׂוּ לָהֶם וְחָיוּ וְלֹא יָמֻתוּ..."
(במדבר ד:יח-יט). עשו להם דבר של תקנה שלא יזונו עיניהם מבית
קדש הקדשים. וכתיב, "וְלֹא יָבֹאוּ לִרְאוֹת כְּבַלַּע אֶת הַקֹּדֶשׁ וָמֵתוּ."
(במדבר ד:כ). וכתיב, "וּמִבֶּן חֲמִשִּׁים שָׁנָה יָשׁוּב מִצְּבָא הָעֲבֹדָה [וְלֹא יַעֲבֹד
עוֹד]." (במדבר ח:כה).

רבי אבין בריה דרבי תנחום בר טריפון שמע לה מן הכא: "יְמֵי
שְׁנוֹתֵינוּ בָהֶם שִׁבְעִים שָׁנָה [וְאִם בִּגְבוּרֹת שְׁמוֹנִים שָׁנָה]..." (תהלים צ:י).
צא מהן עשרים [שנה] שאין בית דין של מעלן עונשין וכורתין. נמצאתָ
אומר המת לחמשים [שנה] מת בהיכרת.

לחמשים ושתים, מיתת שמואל הנביא. רבי אבא בריה דרבי
פפי רבי יהושע דסיכנין בשם רבי לוי: "בְּכָל עֶצֶב יִהְיֶה מוֹתָר וּדְבַר
שְׂפָתַיִם אַךְ לְמַחְסוֹר." (משלי יד:כג). חנה, על ידי שריבתה בתפילתה,
קיצרה בימיו של שמואל, שאמרה, "...וְיָשַׁב שָׁם עַד עוֹלָם." (שמואל א
א:כב). והלא אין "עוֹלָמ" של לוי אלא אלא חמשים שנה דכתיב, "וּמִבֶּן
חֲמִשִּׁים שָׁנָה יָשׁוּב מִצְּבָא הָעֲבֹדָה [וְלֹא יַעֲבֹד עוֹד]." (במדבר ח:כה). והיי
דלון חמשין ותרתי? אמר רבי יוסי בר רבי בון: ושתים שגמלתו.

לששים מיתה האמורה בתורה. רבי חזקיה בשם רבי יעקב בר
אחא: כתיב, "[וַיִּשְׁמַע ה' אֶת קוֹל דִּבְרֵיכֶם וַיִּקְצֹף וַיִּשָּׁבַע לֵאמֹר.] אִם
יִרְאֶה אִישׁ בָּאֲנָשִׁים הָאֵלֶּה הַדּוֹר הָרָע הַזֶּה אֵת הָאָרֶץ הַטּוֹבָה אֲשֶׁר
נִשְׁבַּעְתִּי לָתֵת לַאֲבֹתֵיכֶם.] (דברים א:לד-לה). הגע עצמך שיצא ממצרים
בן עשרים שנה ועוד עשה במדבר ארבעים שנה ומת. נמצאתָ אומר
המת לששים מיתה האמורה בתורה. וכתיב, "תָּבוֹא בְכֶלַח אֱלֵי
קָבֶר..." (איוב ה:כו).

לְשִׁבְעִים [שָׁנָה], מִיתָה שֶׁל חִבָּה [דִּכְתִיב], "יְמֵי שְׁנוֹתֵינוּ בָהֶם שִׁבְעִים שָׁנָה... ." (תהלים צ:י). לִשְׁמוֹנִים, מִיתָה שֶׁל זִקְנָה, שֶׁנֶּאֱמַר, "...וְאִם בִּגְבוּרֹת שְׁמוֹנִים שָׁנָה." (תהלים צ:י). וכן ברזילי אָמַר לדוד, "...כַּמָּה יְמֵי שְׁנֵי חַיַּי... בֶּן שְׁמֹנִים שָׁנָה אָנֹכִי הַיּוֹם הַאֵדַע בֵּין טוֹב לְרָע... ." (שמואל ב יט:לו).

אֵפֶר חֲמִשִּׁים וְעָשָׂה דָבָר שֶׁהוּא בְּהִיכָּרֵת, אֲבָל רַב חֲדֵי? אֵפֶר שִׁתִּין וְעָשָׂה דָבָר שֶׁהוּא בְּעָוֹן מִיתָה, אֲבָל חֲדֵי?

תְּנִי: רַבִּי חֲנִינָא בֶּן אַנְטִיגְנוֹס אוֹמֵר: זָקֵן שֶׁאָכַל אֶת הַחֵלֶב, וְכִי מִי מוֹדִיעֵנוּ שֶׁהוּא בְּהִיכָּרֵת, כִּהְדָא דְּתַנְיָא, "אוֹ שֶׁחִיּלֵל אֶת הַשַּׁבָּת בְּהִיכָּרֵת?" אֶלָּא כֵינִי: הַמֵּת לְיוֹם אֶחָד, מִיתָה שֶׁל זַעַם; לִשְׁנַיִם מִיתָה שֶׁל בֶּהָלָה; לִשְׁלֹשָׁה מֵת בַּמַּגֵּפָה.

תָּנֵי רַבִּי חֲלַפְתָּא בֶּן שָׁאוּל: מֵת בְּאֶחָד, בִּשְׁנַיִם, בִּשְׁלֹשָׁה, [מֵת] בְּהִיכָּרֵת. לְאַרְבָּעָה, לַחֲמִשָּׁה, מִיתָה הַדּוּפָה. לְשִׁשָּׁה, מִיתַת דֶּרֶךְ הָאָרֶץ. לְשִׁבְעָה, מִיתָה שֶׁל חִבָּה. מִכָּאן וְאֵילָךְ, מֵת בְּיִיסּוּרִים.

מַה חֲמִית מֵימַר מֵת לִשְׁלֹשָׁה יָמִים, מֵת בַּמַּגֵּפָה? חִילְפַּיי, בַּר בְּרֵיהּ דְּרַבִּי אַבָּהוּ, אָמַר: שְׁמָעִית קָלֵיהּ דְּרַבִּי דָּרֵשׁ, "וַיְהִי כַּעֲשֶׂרֶת הַיָּמִים וַיִּגֹּף ה' אֶת נָבָל וַיָּמֹת." (שמואל א כה:לח). תָּלָה לוֹ הַקָּדוֹשׁ בָּרוּךְ הוּא שִׁבְעַת יְמֵי אֶבְלוֹ שֶׁל שְׁמוּאֵל שֶׁלֹּא יִתְעָרֵב אֶבְלוֹ עִם הַצַּדִּיק וְעָשָׂה עוֹד שְׁלֹשָׁה יָמִים וּמֵת בַּמַּגֵּפָה.

רַבִּי חַגַּי בְּשֵׁם רַבִּי שְׁמוּאֵל בַּר נַחְמָן: "לַעֲשֶׂרֶת יָמִים" אֵין כְּתִיב כָּאן, אֶלָּא "כַּעֲשֶׂרֶת הַיָּמִים." תָּלָה לוֹ הַקָּדוֹשׁ בָּרוּךְ הוּא עֲשָׂרָה יָמִים כַּעֲשֶׂרֶת יָמִים שֶׁבֵּין רֹאשׁ הַשָּׁנָה לְיוֹם הַכִּיפּוּרִים שֶׁמָּא יַעֲשֶׂה תְשׁוּבָה וְלֹא עָשָׂה.

A *Braitha* teaches: One who dies at fifty years, dies of excision; at fifty-two, this is the death of Samuel the Prophet; at sixty is the punishment of death mentioned in the *Torah*; at seventy is a death of belovedness; at eighty is a death of elderliness; from there onward is a life of pain.

Why did the *Tanna* say that one who dies at fifty dies of excision? It is written, "Do not excise the tribe of the families of the Kohathi from the midst of the Levites. This you shall do for them that they shall live and not die... ,"[854] meaning, make for them something beneficial [i.e., a partition] that their eyes not feast upon the Holy of Holies. It is further written, "They shall not come to see when he [Aaron] stores away the Holy [utensils] and they will [not] die."[855] It is further written, "And from the age of fifty years [the Levite] shall retire from the corps of the [Temple] service and he shall no longer serve."[856] [The Levites retired at the age of fifty, so any of them who violated the prohibition against gazing at the Holy of Holies must have been under that age. Since the *Torah* warns that their punishment is the untimely death of excision, excision must entail death before the age of fifty.]

Rabbi Avin, the son of Rabbi Tanchum bar Trifon derived it from here: "The days of our years number seventy years; if with strength, eighty years... ."[857] Deduct from these the twenty years during which the Heavenly Tribunal does not punish or excise. You will find yourself saying that one who dies at fifty years dies of excision. [If a person's ideal lifespan is eighty years, then he or she should live sixty years beyond the first twenty which do not

---

854 Numbers 4:18-19.
855 Numbers 4:20.
856 Numbers 8:25.
857 Psalms 90:10 according to *Metzudoth David*.

count for purposes of Divine punishment. Half of sixty is thirty, so one who dies before the age of fifty has not lived out half of that portion of his life during which he is subject to punishment. Thus, a death before age fifty is one of excision.[858] As the *Tanach* says, the wicked "...shall not attain half their days... ."[859]]

[The above *Braitha* taught that] at fifty-two, this is the death of Samuel the Prophet. Rabbi Abba, son of Rav Pappi, quoted Rabbi Yehoshua of Sichnin in the name of Rabbi Levi: "With all toil there will be an advantage, but a word of the lips [will yield] only loss."[860] Hannah, by virtue of prolonging her prayer, shortened the days of Samuel [her son], for she said, "...may he dwell there forever (עַד עוֹלָם)."[861] Is not the "forever" (עוֹלָם) of a Levite but fifty years as is written, "And from the age of fifty years [the Levite] shall retire from the corps of the [Temple] service and he shall no longer serve."[862] [A strict interpretation of this would mean that Samuel should have lived only fifty years.] How do they come to fifty-two? Rabbi Yossi bar Rabbi Bon said: The two years during which she weaned him [were not included].[863]

---

858 *Tosafoth HaRosh* on B.T *Mo'ed Katan* 28A.
859 Psalms 55:24.
860 Proverbs 14:23.
861 I Samuel 1:22.
862 Numbers 8:25.
863 See *Torah From Jerusalem*, Vol. I, pp. 117-120 for a discussion of Hannah's prayer.

[The above *Braitha* taught that] at sixty is the punishment of death mentioned in the Torah. Rabbi Chizkiah said in the name of Rabbi Yaakov bar Acha: It is written [concerning the spies who brought back an evil report about the Land of Israel], "The Lord heard the sound of your words and grew angry and swore, saying, 'If a man among these men, this evil generation, shall see the good land which I have sworn to give to your fathers.'"[864] Consider for yourself the case of one who left Egypt at the age of twenty years, lived in the desert forty years, and then died. You will find yourself saying that when one dies at sixty years, this is the punishment of death mentioned in the *Torah*. [The decree of death caused by the incident of the spies did not apply to those under twenty nor to those over sixty.[865] During the forty years in which the Jews wandered through the desert, a certain number died each year on the ninth of Av until no one was left from those who had sinned.[866] Rabbi Yaakov bar Acha holds that those who had attained the age of sixty are the ones who died each year.][867] It is further written, "You shall come to

---

[864] Deuteronomy 1:34-35.

[865] B.T. *Baba Bathra* 121B.

[866] *Eichah Rabbah, Hakdamah* 33.

[867] The *Torah* says, "In this desert shall your corpses fall and all your enumerations according to your number from twenty years old and above who complained against Me." (Numbers 14:29). The phrase "your enumerations according to your number" (פקדיכם לכל מספרכם) refers to the censuses taken in the desert and suggests that the deaths took place in the same order in which the Jews were counted during those censuses. Presumably, as a matter of respect, the elders were

the grave in your prime... ."[868] [The Hebrew word בכלח, meaning "in your prime" has a numerical value of sixty.[869]]

[The above *Braitha* taught that] at seventy is a death of belovedness, as it is written, "The days of our years number seventy years... ."[870] [The *Braitha* further taught that] at eighty is a death of elderliness, as it says, "...if with strength eighty years... ."[871] And so Barzillai said to David, "...How many are the days of the years of my life...I am eighty years old today. Can I distinguish between good and evil?..."[872] [An earlier verse says, "Barzillai was very elderly, eighty years old...,"[873] so a death at eighty is one of elderliness.]

---

counted before the younger men. Hence, when God made this decree, the eldest died first.

[868] Job 5:26 according to *Metzudoth Tzion.*

[869] All the standard commentators on the *Tanach* interpret כלח to mean "old age," so this verse should read, "You shall come to the grave in old age... ." According to that rendering, however, death at age sixty would be a natural end to life, not a punishment. Indeed, *Ein Ya'akov* references an alternative reading of this passage in B.T. *Mo'ed Katan* 28A that sixty is an age at which people commonly die. That reading also appears in *Yalkut Shimoni, Iyov* 5, paragraph 899. Several *Midrashim*, however, explain כלח as alluding to "moisture" or "freshness" (לח or לחלוחית). (*Breishith Rabbah* 79:1; *Yalkut Shimoni, Breishith* 33, paragraph 133). Accordingly, it is translated here as "in your prime," consistent with the idea that death at sixty is premature.

[870] Psalms 90:10 according to *Metzudoth David.*

[871] Ibid.

[872] II Samuel 19:36.

[873] II Samuel 19:33.

If one passed fifty years and did something which warrants excision, shall he or she indeed greatly rejoice? If one passed sixty and did something which is a sin warranting death, shall he or she indeed greatly rejoice?

It is taught that Rabbi Chanina ben Antigonos said: If an elder ate forbidden fat, who will inform him that he is liable to excision, as we have learned, "or if he desecrated the Sabbath, that he will die through excision?"[874] Rather, it is thus: Whoever dies after one day suffers a death of fury; after two days, a death of chaos; after three days, a death of plague.

It is taught that Rabbi Chalafta ben Shaul said: Whoever dies after one, two or three days, dies of excision; after four or five days is an abrupt death; after six days is a standard death; after seven days is a death of belovedness. From there onward is a death of torment.

Why does the *Tanna* say that death after three days is a death of plague? Chilfai, the grandson of Rabbi Abahu, said: I heard the voice of Rebbi expound, "It was after ten days that the Lord plagued Nabal and he died."[875] The Holy One, Blessed be He, allowed him the seven day mourning period for Samuel so as not to intermingle his mourning period with that of a righteous person. He granted another three days and Nabal died by a plague.

Rabbi Chaggai said in the name of Rabbi Shmuel bar Nachman: "ten days" (לעשרת ימים) is not written here,

---

[874] *Avel Rabbathai* 3:10.
[875] I Samuel 25:38.

but "*like* ten days" (כעשרת הימים). The Holy One, Blessed be He, allowed him ten days like the ten days between *Rosh HaShannah* and *Yom Kippur*, supposing that he would repent but he did not do so.

A common question is why many people who are known to have committed sins involving excision or death at the hands of Heaven nonetheless do not die prematurely or in a sudden manner as described in this passage.

The Ramban maintains that there are three types of excision. If a person who committed a sin punishable by excision had more merits than sins, he or she will die prematurely as indicated in this passage. Having thus expiated the sin, such a person then goes on to his or her reward in Paradise. One whose sins outweigh his or her merits, however, may live to old age in comfort. After death, however, his or her soul will suffer spiritual punishment in Gehinnom.[876] *Such spiritual punishment is far worse than any possible physical punishment, but is of limited duration.*[877] *Those whom the Mishnah enumerates as having no share in the world to come, such as heretics,*[878] *suffer a third form of excision: eternal punishment in Gehinnom. Such people may also live a long*

---

[876] *Sha'ar HaGemul*, chapter 7.
[877] Ibid., chapter 8. *Ramban* states that such wicked people never attain the same spiritual reward as the righteous, however.
[878] *Sanhedrin* 10:1.

time if they have performed some good deed during their lives.

Rabbi Shneur Zalman of Liadi offers a different approach. Hashem imposed these punishments when the Temple stood and the Divine Presence dwelled among Israel. In those times, a Jew's body received its life-force through his or her Godly soul. If a person committed a sin which damaged the soul, it also affected the body and thus could cause physical death as well. After the destruction of the Temple, the Divine Presence no longer manifests itself among Israel to the same degree, so the body receives its life-force from a much lower spiritual source just as animals and plants do.[879] As a result, sinners can live to old age without dying in the manner described in this section of the Talmud.[880]

A third possible explanation also has to do with the spiritual level of the Jewish people in modern times. The punishments described in the Torah such as excision and death at the hands of Heaven apply only when one sins deliberately but not if one sins accidentally, even if the accident resulted from negligence. As an example, if one performed a forbidden labor on the Sabbath because he did not realize that such activity is forbidden or because he forgot that it was the Sabbath, he does not suffer the

---

[879] Everything in the universe has spiritual source which sustains it as the *Midrash* explains, "There is not a single blade of grass below which does not have a spiritual force in Heaven which stimulates it and instructs it to grow." (*Breishith Rabbah* 10:6).

[880] *Igereth HaTeshuvah*, chapter 6.

punishment of excision. Likewise, if a Jewish baby was captured and raised among non-Jews, he is not punished for his failure to observe the Torah. This is true even if such a person later grew up, learned that he or she was Jewish and witnessed the life-style of other Jews.[881]

In Temple times, Jews lived on a higher spiritual level and appreciated the serious nature of Mitzvah observance. They lived in communities by themselves, separated to a large degree from outside influences. They also observed the Temple service in all its glory because they ascended to Jerusalem at least three times each year. Jewish courts had authority over the day to day life of the people. By contrast, the broad range of outside influences to which people are now exposed sometimes leads them astray, making that which is forbidden appear not only attractive, but even right. As a result, even a person who deliberately violates Torah law is not viewed by Hashem as though he or she did so purposely and punishments which might otherwise apply do not.[882]

---

[881] *Rambam, Yad HaChazakah, Hilchoth Shegagoth* 2:6 and *Hilchoth Mamrim* 3:3.

[882] The term "excision" (כרת) also suggests that the offender is cut off from the rest of the Jewish people. This would apply when a person does something which distinctly separates him from the rest of the Jewish nation. At a time when Jews are on a low spiritual level, however, the transgression cannot have that effect.

Bikkurim 3:3   (Compare B.T. *Kiddushin* 32B-33B; B.T. *Kethuboth* 62B; B.T. *Horayoth* 13B)

ולא כן תני: "מִפְּנֵי שֵׂיבָה תָּקוּם וְהָדַרְתָּ פְּנֵי זָקֵן... ." (ויקרא יט:לב). מה קימה שאין בה חסרון כיס, אף הידור שאין בה חסרון כיס. שנייא היא הכא שהיא אחת לקיצים.

רבי יוסי בי רבי בון בשם רבי חונא בר חייא: בא וראה כמה גדול כוחן של עושי מצוה, שמפני זקן אין עומדין ובפני עושי מצות עומדין.

אמר רבי יוסי בי רבי בון: אילין דקיימין מן קומי מיתא לא מן קומי מיתא אינון קיימין לון אלא מן קומי אילין דגמלים ליה חסד.

עד כמה אדם צריך לעמוד מפני זקן? שמעון בר בא בשם רבי יוחנן: פַּעֲמָיִם ביום. רבי לעזר אומר: פעם אחת ביום. לא כן תני: רבי שמעון בן אלעזר אומר: מִנַּיִן לזקן שלא יטריח? תלמוד לומר, "מִפְּנֵי שֵׂיבָה תָּקוּם וְהָדַרְתָּ פְּנֵי זָקֵן וְיָרֵאתָ מֵאֱ-לֹהֶיךָ אֲנִי ה'." (ויקרא יט:לב).

על דעתיה דרבי יוחנן, ניחא. על דעתיה דרבי לעזר, לא יקום כל עיקר. רבי יעקב בר אחא בשם רבי לעזר: דלא יחמי סייעתא דסבין ועבר קומיהון בגין דיקומון לון מן קמוי.

כשם שהן חלוקים כאן, כך הן חלוקים בשאילת שלו-ם.

רבי חזקיה רבי חנינא בריה דרבי אבהו בשם רבי אבדומא דמן חֵיפָה: לזקן, ד' אמות עבר [לפניו], ישב לו. כהן גדול, משהוא רואהו ועד שהוא נכסה ממנו. מה טעמו? "וְהָיָה כְּצֵאת מֹשֶׁה אֶל הָאֹהֶל יָקוּמוּ כָּל הָעָם וְנִצְּבוּ אִישׁ פֶּתַח אָהֳלוֹ וְהִבִּיטוּ אַחֲרֵי מֹשֶׁה עַד בֹּאוֹ הָאֹהֱלָה." (שמות לג:ח).

תרין אמוראים, חד אמר לשבח וחד אמר לגנאי. מאן דאמר לשבח, מיחמי צדיקא ומזכי. ומאן דאמר לגנאי, חזי שקיה, חזי כרעין, "אכיל מן יהודאי, שתי מן יהודאי. כל מדליה מן יהודאי."

...אמר רבי לעזר: אין התורה עומדת מפני בנה.

שמואל אמר: אין עומדים מפני חבר.

רבי הילא, רבי יעקב בר אידי הוון יתיבין. עבר שמואל בר בא וקמו לון מן קמוי. אמר לון, "תרתיי גבכון. חדא שאיני זקן וחדא שאין התורה עומדת מפני בנה."

אמר רבי זעירא: רבי אחא מפסיק וקאים, דו חשש כהדין תנייא דתני: כותבי ספרים, תפילין ומזוזות מפסיקין לקריאת שמע ואין מפסיקין לתפילה. רבי חנניא בן עקביה אומר: כשם שמפסיקין לקריאת שמע, כך מפסיקין לתפילה ולתפילין ולשאר מצותיה של תורה.

חזקיה בר רבי, מן דהוה לעי באורייתא כל צורכיה, הוה אזל ויתיב ליה קומי בית ועדא בגין מיחמי סבין ומיקם ליה מן קומיהון.

יהודה בר חייה הוה יליף סליק ושאל בשלמיה דרבי ינאי חמוי מערב שבת לערב שבת והוה יתיב ליה על אתר תלי בגין מיחמוניה ומיקם ליה מן קומיהון.

אמרין ליה תלמידיו, "לא כן אילפן רבי, 'לזקן ד' אמות?'" אמר לון, "אין ישיבה לפני סיני."

חד זמן, עני מסיק. אמר, "לית אפשר דיהודה ברי משני מנהגיה." אמר, "לית אפשר דלא יגיעון יסורים בההוא גופא צדיקא. מסתברא שאין לנו יהודה ב"ר."

רבי מאיר חמי אפילו סב עם הארץ ומיקם ליה מן קמוי. אמר, "לא מַגָּן מאריך ימים."

רבי חנינא מחי מאן דלא קאים מן קמוי והוה אמר ליה, "מי בעיתא מבטלה דאורייתא?"

אמר רבי סימון: אמר הקדוש ברוך הוא, "מִפְּנֵי שֵׂיבָה תָּקוּם וְהָדַרְתָּ פְּנֵי זָקֵן וְיָרֵאתָ מֵּאֱלֹהֶיךָ אֲנִי ה'.' (ויקרא יט:לב). אני הוא שקיימתי עמידת זקן תחילה."

כשהנשיא נכנס, כל העם עומדים מפניו ואין רשות לאחד מהן לישב עד שיאמר להן, "שבו!" אב בית דין שנכנס עושין לו שורות. רצה, נכנס בזו. רצה, נכנס בזו. חכם שנכנס, אחד עומד ואחד יושב ואחד עומד ואחד יושב עד שמגיע וישב לו במקומו.

393

רבי מאיר הוה יליף סלק לבית וועדא והוון כל עמא חמיין ליה
וקיימין לון מן קומי. כד שמעון ההן תניא תני, בעון למיעבד ליה כן.
כעס ונפק ליה. אמר לון, "שמעתי שמעלין בקודש ולא מורידין."

[The *Mishnah* teaches that when a group of
individuals approached Jerusalem bearing first-fruit
offerings, they sent a messenger ahead to announce their
arrival. The leading priests and Levites, as well as those in
charge of maintaining the Temple, would go out to greet
them. Artisans, too, would interrupt their work to welcome
the procession.]

Have we not learned: "From before the aged you
shall rise and you shall honor the presence of the
elder... ."[883] Just as rising does not involve financial loss,
so honoring should not involve financial loss. [The *Torah*
only requires a person to show respect for elders in ways
which do not entail monetary loss. In the case of greeting
people who were bringing first-fruits to the Temple, why
does the *Mishnah* require artisans to interrupt their work
and, so, lose money?] It is different here because it is once
in a great while. [People encounter elders on an almost
daily basis so the *Torah* does not require interrupting one's
work to honor them. By contrast, bringing the first fruits

---

[883] Leviticus 19:32. The term "elder" includes a scholar of any age.
Young scholars are called "elders" because they have acquired wisdom
which befits older people. (*Me'Am Loez* ad. loc.).

was an annual event, so interrupting one's work entailed no special hardship.[884]

Rabbi Yossi, son of Rabbi Bon, in the name of Rav Chuna bar Chiya, said: Come and observe how great is the power of those who perform commandments. Before an elder they do not stand, but before those who perform commandments they stand.

Rabbi Yossi, son of Rabbi Bon, said: Those who rise before a funeral procession do not rise for the sake of the deceased, but for those who bestow him kindness. [According to *Halachah*, whoever sees a funeral procession must accompany it at least four cubits out of respect for the deceased.[885] Such honor, however, is not exclusively for the deceased but for those occupied with the *Mitzvah* as well.]

To what extent must a person rise before an elder? Shimon bar Ba in the name of Rabbi Yochanan said: Twice each day. Rabbi Lazar says: Once each day. Have we not learned thus: Rabbi Shimon ben Elazar said: From

---

[884] This translation is consistent with the majority of commentators. *Rambam* in his commentary on the *Mishnah*, however, states that artisans must interrupt their work for those who bring the first fruits because more honor must be given to a large group of people than to an individual. Therefore, he may read this text as, "It is different, for over here [with a scholar], he is but one, whereas [those who bear the first fruits] are many." B.T. *Kiddushin* 33A suggests another reason for this differentiation: By honoring and greeting those who bore the first fruits, the Jerusalemites encouraged them in this *Mitzvah*, thereby ensuring that they would continue to perform it in future years.

[885] *Shulchan Aruch, Yoreh Deah* 343:1 and 361:3.

where is it known that an elder should not trouble others to rise before him? The *Torah* says, "From before the aged you shall rise and you shall honor the presence of the elder and you shall fear your God, I am the Lord."[886] [The *Tanna* understands the end of the verse as applying to the elders who must fear God and not abuse the privilege the *Torah* grants them to receive honor.]

According to the opinion of Rabbi Yochanan, it is well. [If an elder passes, one rises before him no more than twice each day so as not to render him more honor than one does for God for whom he recites *Shema* twice a day.[887]] According to the opinion of Rabbi Lazar, however, one should not rise at all. [If he holds that elders should avoid troubling others to rise, why do so at all?] Rabbi Yaakov bar Acha, in the name of Rabbi Lazar, explained: This means that the elder should not observe a group of others and deliberately pass in front of them so that they rise for him. [While it is incumbent upon those who see an elder to rise before him once each day, the elder himself should avoid troubling others to do so.]

Just as they [Rabbi Yochanan and Rabbi Lazar] disagree on this, so they disagree about greetings. [Rabbi Yochanan says that a disciple must greet his master twice daily while Rabbi Lazar says he need only do so once.[888]]

---

886 Leviticus 19:32.
887 B.T. *Kiddushin* 33B.
888 *P'nei Moshe.*

Rabbi Chizkiah quoted Rabbi Chanina, son of Rabbi Abahu, in the name of Rabbi Avduma of Haifa: Once an elder passes four cubits away from him, he may reseat himself. For a High Priest [one must rise] once one sees him and until he is no longer visible to him. What is the Scriptural basis for this? "It was when Moses went to the Tent [of Meeting], all the people rose and stood, each man at the entrance of his tent, and they gazed after Moses until his arrival at the Tent."[889] [Moses served as High Priest during the dedication of the Tabernacle.[890]]

Two *Amoraim* have opposing interpretations of the foregoing verse, one as praise, the other as criticism. He who interprets it as praise says that they gazed at a righteous person and gained merit. He who interprets it as criticism says that they gazed at his shins and they gazed at his feet, thinking, "He ate from the Jews and drank from the Jews. All his wealth is from the Jews." [Upon observing Moses's healthy gait, the people improperly thought to themselves that he had taken advantage of his position.[891]]

...Rabbi Lazar said: The *Torah* does not rise before her son. [If one is learning *Torah*, he should not rise when

---

[889] Exodus 33:8.

[890] *Yalkut Shimoni, VaYikra*, paragraph 518.

[891] According to the version of this text in *Ein Yaakov*, the people suspected Moses of immoral activity. When he separated from his wife to communicate with *Hashem*, scoffers insisted that no man can forego female companionship. (*Etz Yosef*).

his master enters since that would show disrespect for what he is learning.[892]]

Shmuel said: They do not rise before a colleague. [The obligation to rise for a sage does not apply to fellow scholars.]

Rabbi Hilla and Rabbi Yaakov bar Iddi were sitting. Shmuel bar Ba passed and they stood up before him. He told them, "Two indiscretions have you committed. For one thing, I am not an elder [but only your colleague] and for another, the *Torah* does not rise before its son [so you should not have interrupted your study to rise]."

Rabbi Z'eira said: Rabbi Acha interrupted and stood, for he took into account the view of the *Tannaim* who learned: Those who write *Torah* scrolls, *Tefillin* and *Mezuzoth* interrupt their work for the reading of *Shema*, but do not interrupt for prayer. Rabbi Chananya ben Akavyah says that just as they interrupt for the reading of *Shema*, so they interrupt for prayer and for [putting on] *Tefillin* and for all the other commandments of the *Torah*. [Rabbi Acha took into account this last opinion.]

When Chizkiah bar Rebbi had studied his fill of *Torah* [and needed a break], he would go and sit before the academy so that he could see the elders [going in and out] and rise before them.[893]

---

892 *P'nei Moshe* based, evidently, on B.T. *Kiddushin* 33B. However, *Torathan Shel Rishonim* citing *Hagahoth Maimuni*, understands this expression to mean that a master should not rise before his disciple even if that disciple is very learned.

893 B.T. *Brachoth* 28A reports that Rabbi Zera also did this.

Yehudah bar Chiya used to go up and inquire after the welfare of Rabbi Yannai, his father-in-law, every Sabbath eve. Rabbi Yannai used to sit in a certain place waiting so that he could see him and rise before him.

His students asked Rabbi Yannai, "Did not the master teach us: 'One rises when an elder arrives within four cubits'?"

He told them, "There is no sitting before Sinai." [The Jewish people prepared themselves for three days prior to the giving of the *Torah* at Mount Sinai. So, too, Rabbi Yannai felt he should prepare to receive Yehudah bar Chiya, an exceptional scholar.[894]]

One time, he delayed going up. Rabbi Yannai said, "It is not possible that my son Yehudah should change his custom." He continued, "It is not possible that torments do not plague that righteous body. Probably we no longer have the illustrious Yehudah!"[895]

When Rabbi Meir saw even an unlearned elder, he would rise before him. He explained, "It is not for nothing that he lived long." [Every old person must acquire some

---

[894] B.T. *Kethuboth* 62B adds that Rabbi Yannai knew when Rabbi Yehudah bar Chiya was approaching because a pillar of fire preceded him.

[895] *P'nei Moshe* understands the abbreviation ב"ר in the text to mean ברבי. Although this term means "son of Rebbi" in most places, that would not make sense here. *Rashi* on B.T. *Chullin* 11B sub verba "*Ve'Hatanya B'rabbi*" (והתניא ברבי) explains that the term ברבי refers to "a great one of his generation." B.T. *Kethuboth* 62B states that Rabbi Yannai's statement caused Yehudah bar Chiya to die since a dire prediction can serve as an opening for the Satan to accuse.

knowledge and experience over the course of his lifetime, making him worthy of respect.[896]]

Rabbi Chanina would strike whoever did not rise before him, saying, "Do you wish to disregard a Biblical commandment?"

Rabbi Simon said: The Holy One, Blessed be He, said, "From before the aged you shall rise and you shall honor the presence of the elder and you shall fear your God, I am the Lord,"[897] meaning, "I am the One who fulfilled the commandment of standing for an elder first." [When Abraham went to greet his three angelic visitors, the Divine Presence, so to speak, rose and waited for him.[898]]

When the president of the Jewish people enters, all the people rise before him and not one of them has permission to sit until he tells them, "Be seated!" When the Head of the Court enters, they form rows for him. He may enter through any of them he wishes. When a scholar enters, each person whom he passes stands and then sits until he reaches his place and is seated.

Rabbi Meir was accustomed to ascend to the academy where all the people would see him and rise

---

[896] B.T. *Kiddushin* 33A reports that Rabbi Yochanan would rise before elderly non-Jews for the same reason. *Shulchan Aruch, Yoreh Deah* 244:1 explains that this applies to someone seventy years old or older. *Rama* adds that one should show respect for elderly people who are not scholars only if they are decent people and not wicked.

[897] Leviticus 19:32.

[898] *Matanoth Kehunah* on *VaYikra Rabbah* 35:3 based on *Breishith Rabbah* 49:7.

before him. When they heard certain *Tannaim* reciting the above teaching [that when a scholar enters each person stands and then sits], they wanted to do so for him. He grew angry and left. He said to them, "I have heard that one increases in holiness but does not decrease." [Once you commenced treating me with a certain level of respect, you must maintain that level and not reduce it.]

Rabbi Ovadiah Yosef rules that standing for the wife of a rabbi is appropriate as a mark of respect for her husband, although not necessarily a strict Halachic requirement. One must, however, rise for an elderly woman who is seventy or older in the same way he or she would for a man. In addition, one must rise for a woman who is learned in the Torah or who is one's teacher.[899]

The passage under consideration stresses the importance of the Mitzvah to rise before elders. Fulfillment of this commandment is so important that Chizkiah bar Rebbi went out of his way to wait at the entrance to the academy so that he could rise for the sages as they entered and exited. Rabbi Yannai, himself a great scholar, looked forward to the visits of Rabbi Yehudah bar Chiya with great anticipation, hoping to fulfill this Mitzvah. The Talmud states that God Himself set an example in this regard by showing respect for Abraham. It seems inconsistent, then, that the elders themselves should avoid having people rise for them. Would it not make more sense

---

[899] *Yechaveh Da'ath*, Part III, Chapter 72.

for the elders to try to appear before others to give them the opportunity to fulfill this important Mitzvah?

Perhaps the answer is related to the dispute in this passage about how the Jews viewed Moses. According to one opinion, they stood respectfully watching him and were rewarded. According to another opinion, they observed Moses and suspected him of abusing his position. True, a sage could deliberately walk in front of others to give them the opportunity to fulfill the Mitzvah of honoring him. However, that might lead people to suspect that he is doing so for his own honor. Rather than produce a Mitzvah, it might lead to a sin. It is preferable for elders to avoid such a situation.

Bikkurim 3:3

רבי זעירא הוון בעיין ממניתיה ולא בעי מקבל עלוי. כד שמע
ההן תנייא תני, "חכם חתן נשיא, גדולה מכפרת," קביל עליה ממניתיה.
חכם, "מִפְּנֵי שֵׂיבָה תָּקוּם וְהָדַרְתָּ פְּנֵי זָקֵן... ." (ויקרא יט:לב). מה
כתיב בתריה? "וְכִי יָגוּר אִתְּךָ גֵּר בְּאַרְצְכֶם לֹא תוֹנוּ אתו." (ויקרא
יט:לג). מה הגר מוחלין לו על כל עונותיו, אף חכם שנתמנה, מוחלין לו
על כל עונותיו.
חתן, "וַיֵּלֶךְ עֵשָׂו אֶל יִשְׁמָעֵאל וַיִּקַּח אֶת מַחֲלַת בַּת יִשְׁמָעֵאל...לוֹ
לְאִשָּׁה." (בראשית כח:ט). וכי מַחֲלַת שמה? והלא בָּשְׂמַת שמה? אלא
שנמחלו לו כל עונותיו.
נשיא, "בֶּן שָׁנָה שָׁאוּל בְּמָלְכוֹ... ." (שמואל א יג:א). וכי בן שנה
היה? אלא שנמחלו לו כל עונותיו כתינוק בן שנה.

They wanted to appoint Rabbi Z'eira [to a certain
position], but he did not want to accept. When he heard
certain *Tannaim* reciting, "As to a scholar, a groom and a
president, prominence atones their sins," he accepted the
appointment.

[The *Talmud* now explains why prominence atones
for sin.] As for a scholar, the *Torah* says, "From before the
aged you shall rise and you shall honor the presence of the
elder... ."[900] What is written after that? "When a convert
shall dwell with you in your land, do not mistreat him."[901]
Just as they forgive all the sins of a convert, so they forgive
all the sins of a scholar who is appointed. [The sins of a

---

900 Leviticus 19:32.
901 Leviticus 19:33.

convert are forgiven because he or she assumes a completely new identity upon conversion.]

As for a groom, the *Torah* says, "And Esau went to Ishmael and took Mahalath, daughter of Ishmael,...for himself as a wife."[902] Was her name Mahalath? Was not her name Basemath? Rather, all his sins were forgiven. [A later verse in the *Torah* which lists Esau's wives mentions "Basemath, daughter of Ishmael,"[903] but not Mahalath, so the two must be identical. Her real name was Basemath, but the *Torah* calls her Mahalath from the Hebrew root מחל which means "forgive," to hint that God forgives a person's sins when he or she marries.]

As for a president, the *Tanach* says, "Saul was one year old upon his coronation... ."[904] Was he indeed one year old?!? Rather, all his sins were forgiven so that he was like a one year old baby. [The same applies to the president of the Jewish people.]

Several commentators point out that Esau had married a number of wives, yet it is only concerning Basemath that the Talmud says the marriage caused atonement for all his sins. The Torah says that Esau married this daughter of Ishmael because, "Esau saw that the women of Canaan were unsatisfactory in the eyes of

---

[902] Genesis 28:9.
[903] Genesis 36:3.
[904] I Samuel 13:1.

Isaac, his father."[905]   *Since Esau took into account his father's displeasure with his first wives and sought to repent, the marriage atoned for his sins.*[906]   *This shows that one gains atonement when one marries only if the marriage is for the purpose of fulfilling the Mitzvah of creating a Jewish family and not for other purposes, such as money.*

Why should one who accepts a communal appointment or marries have all his sins forgiven? Why is the fulfillment of these commandments more meritorious than the fulfillment of others?

The Talmud teaches that, "Whoever prays for his or her comrade and needs the same thing will be answered first."[907]   *Likewise, "whoever bestows mercy upon other human beings, they will bestow mercy upon him or her from Heaven."*[908]   *When a person acts only in his personal capacity, he thinks only of his own needs.   Once one accepts a communal position or marries, however, he no longer considers only his own personal aspirations but must look out for the welfare of others as well.   It is the merit of undertaking to think of others that causes atonement.*[909]

---

[905] Genesis 28:8.

[906] *Etz Yosef* and *HaKothev.*

[907] B.T. *Baba Kama* 92A.

[908] B.T. *Shabbath* 151B.

[909] The same concept applies to converts. The *Talmud* proclaims that members of the Jewish people are distinguished by three traits: They are merciful, they are self-conscious about sin and they extend kindness

Bikkurim 3:3 (Compare B.T. *Sanhedrin* 7B)

רבי מנא מיקל לאילין דמתמניי בכסף. רבי אימי קרא עליהון,
"...אֱלֹהֵי כֶסֶף וֵאלֹהֵי זָהָב לֹא תַעֲשׂוּ לָכֶם." (שמות כ:כ).
אמר רבי יאשיה: וטלית שעליו כמרדעת של חמור.
אמר רבי שיין: זה שהוא מתמני בכסף, אין עומדין מפניו ואין
קורין אותו "רבי," והטלית שעליו כמרדעת של חמור.
רבי זעירא וחד מן רבנן הוון יתיבין. עבר חד מן אילין
דמיתמני בכסף. אמר יתיה דמן רבנין לרבי זעירא, "נעביד נפשין תניי
ולא ניקום לון מן קמוי."
תירגם יעקב, איש כפר נבורייא: "הוֹי אֹמֵר לָעֵץ הָקִיצָה עוּרִי
לְאֶבֶן דּוּמָם הוּא יוֹרֶה... ." (חבקוק ב:יט). יודע הוא יורה? "...הִנֵּה הוּא
תָּפוּשׂ זָהָב וָכֶסֶף..." (שם שם). לא בכספייא איתמני? "וְכָל רוּחַ אֵין
בְּקִרְבּוֹ." (שם שם). לא חכים כלום! הוי אומרים, "בעיתון ממנייה." "וַה׳
בְּהֵיכַל קָדְשׁוֹ הַס מִפָּנָיו כָּל הָאָרֶץ." (חבקוק ב:כ). הא רבי יצחק בר לעזר
בכנישתא מדרתא דקיסרין.

Rabbi Manna made light of those who were
appointed because of money [i.e., who bought their
positions]. Rabbi Immi applied to them the verse, "...gods
of silver and gods of gold do not make for yourselves."[910]

Rabbi Yoshayah said: The cloak upon such a
person is like a saddle upon a donkey. [Those who
assumed positions of authority in the community wore a

---

to others. Whoever has such traits is fit to join Israel. (B.T. *Yevamoth*
79A) By undertaking to behave mercifully and show kindness to
others, converts, too, merit that their sins be forgiven.
[910] Exodus 20:20.

distinctive cloak.[911] For one who purchased such a position, however, the cloak bore no more significance than a saddle upon a donkey.]

Rabbi Shayin said: One who is appointed because of money, we do not stand before him and do not call him "rabbi," and the cloak which is upon him is like a saddle upon a donkey.

Rabbi Z'eira and one of the rabbis were sitting when someone who had been appointed because of money passed. That rabbi said to Rabbi Z'eira, "Let us busy ourselves with reciting [*Tannaitic* teachings so as to create a pretext] and not rise before him."

[In ancient times, the community used to appoint an individual with a strong voice to repeat what the president of the Jewish people said so that everyone present could hear it.] Yaakov, the man from the village of Nevorya [was such an interpreter. One time, the people appointed an unworthy person to be president because of his wealth. When the interpreter bent down to hear what the person would say, the latter was silent. Thereupon, Yaakov on his own] interpreted the verse, "Woe [to one who] says to [an idol of] wood, 'Awake!' To a mute stone, 'Arouse!' Shall he teach?..."[912] [means], "Does he know how to teach?"

---

[911] See, for example, B.T. *Baba Metzia* 85A. In addition, the judges would wrap themselves up in their cloaks when hearing a case. (*Shulchan Aruch, Yoreh Deah* 8:2 based on B.T. *Shabbath* 10A). In most communities it is still customary for rabbis, especially those who are authorized to act as judges, to wear special garments.
[912] Habakuk 2:19.

"...Here he is mired in gold and silver..."[913] [means], "Was he not appointed through money?" "...yet there is no spirit [of wisdom] in his midst!" [means], "He is not wise at all! Woe to those who say, 'We want to appoint him!'" [The next verse in the *Tanach* says,] "The Lord is in His holy sanctuary; be desolate before Him all the Earth!"[914] [God will visit severe punishment upon those who make such appointments.[915]] [If you want to appoint a worthy person,] Behold Rabbi Yitzchak ben Lazar is in the synagogue in the gate of Caesarea.[916]

The Mishnah says, "All who work with the community should work with them for the sake of Heaven, for the merit of their ancestors assists them and their righteousness abides forever."[917] If it is not the efforts of the leaders that make a community successful, then why should it matter whether they bought their positions? Moreover, the Talmud instructs that a person should always occupy himself with Torah and Mitzvoth even if not for proper motives because by doing so for selfish motives, he or she will come to do so for proper ones.[918] Thus, for example, it is permissible for a person to donate money to

---

913 Ibid.

914 Habakuk 2:20.

915 *Rashi* on B.T. *Sanhedrin* 7B, sub verba "*VaHashem BiHeichal*" (וה' בהיכל).

916 *Beurei HaGra* based on B.T. *Sanhedrin* 7B.

917 *Pirkei Avoth* 2:2.

918 B.T. *Pesachim* 50B.

charity to acquire prestige because eventually he or she will learn to do so for the sake of the commandment itself. Why should this principle not apply to communal leaders?

The Mishnah teaches that the merit of the community causes its leaders to succeed.[919] *For this reason, they **must** perform their work for the sake of Heaven, meaning, in this case, for the sake of the community. The fact that one who purchased a position may eventually act for proper motives does not matter if, in the meantime, his actions are not supported by the merit of the community.*

It is important to note that the Talmud only forbids using money to purchase a position, i.e., bribery. There is nothing wrong with a community selecting as a rabbi or judge a Torah scholar who also happens to be rich.[920] *In fact, it may be preferable to do so as such a person may be less likely to accept a bribe because he already has his own money.*

---

[919] *Pirkei Avoth* 2:2.
[920] *Pithchei Teshuvah,* note 2 on *Shulchan Aruch, Choshen Mishpat* 8:1.

Bikkurim 3:3

שמעון בר ווא, הוה כד מסקים, ואיתמנון דקיקין מיניה והוא
לא איתמני. שמעון בר ווא הוה בקי במרגליתא, בכל מיליה, ולא הוה
ליה עיגיל מיכלי והוה רבי יוחנן קרי עלוי, "...כִּי לֹא לַקַּלִּים הַמֵּרוֹץ וְלֹא
לַגִּבּוֹרִים הַמִּלְחָמָה וְגַם לֹא לַחֲכָמִים לֶחֶם... ." (קהלת ט:יא). אמר, "כל מי
שאינו מכיר מעשיו של אברהם, יכיר מעשיו אבותיו של זה."
שמעון בר ווא, הוה כד מסקום, ושלח ליה רבי אבהו חדא
איגרא ויהב ליה מן סיבתיה בגוה.
"בגין אילין סבתא, קום אתהלך לארעא דישראל. מי יגלה
עפר מעיניך רבי יוחנן? אבהו ריגלותיה, איתמני. שמעון דמעפריא, לא
איתמני!"

When Shimon bar Vava was poor,[921] lesser people
were appointed [to communal positions] and he was not
appointed. He was an expert in pearls and many other
matters, yet he did not have a loaf of bread to eat. Rabbi
Yochanan used to apply to him the verse, "...for the race is
not to the swift, nor the battle to the mighty, and also not
bread to the wise... ."[922] He further remarked, "Anyone
who is not familiar with the deeds of Abraham may become
familiar through the deeds of the ancestors of this one."
[Rabbi Yochanan expressed surprise at the lack of success
Shimon bar Vava suffered. Although he had expertise in a

---

921 *P'nei Moshe* says that מסקים is equivalent to מסכן, "poor."
Maharam de Lonzano, however, had a text which read בדמסקוס,
meaning that Shimon bar Vava resided "in Damascus."
922 Ecclesiastes 9:11.

number of profitable trades, he could not earn a living. In addition, his ancestors were as righteous as Abraham, yet their merit did not help him because wealth depends not on merit but on "luck."[923]]

When Shimon bar Vava was poor, Rabbi Abahu sent him a letter in which he gave him a present out of the savings of his old age.[924]

Said Shimon bar Vava, "Because of these elders [such as Rabbi Abahu], I will arise and go to the Land of Israel. Who will uncover the dust from your eyes, Rabbi Yochanan? Abahu who was your least distinguished student was appointed a leader, while Shimon who was among your outstanding ones was not appointed!"[925]

The Babylonian Talmud tells how Rabbi Yochanan found his disciple, Rabbi Elazar, weeping. "Why are you

---

[923] *HaKothev.* God predetermines what challenges each person will face during life, including whether he or she will succeed financially.

[924] The word סב in Aramaic means "old," so the term מסיבתיה appears to have this meaning. It is also possible that the reference is to a stipend the community used to provide for elderly rabbis. *P'nei Moshe* explains that, ordinarily, Rabbi Shimon bar Vava would not be willing to accept charity, so Rabbi Abahu clarified in the letter that the gift was to cover the expense of coming to the Land of Israel, figuring that Rabbi Shimon bar Vava would not refuse funds offered to help perform a *Mitzvah.* Alternatively, *Mashbiach* suggests that Rabbi Abahu had arranged a rabbinical appointment for Rabbi Shimon bar Vava.

[925] *P'nei Moshe* understands the last part of this statement, "Who will uncover your eyes..." as having been said by Rabbi Abahu, not Rabbi Shimon bar Vava.

crying?" he inquired. "...If it is because of [lack of]
sustenance, not everyone merits two tables [i.e., success in
this world as well as in the next]."[926] Although Rabbi
Elazar was an outstanding scholar and very righteous,
whether a person succeeds financially depends not on merit
but on predestination (מזל). The Talmud even tells how
God Himself explained to Rabbi Elazar that it was part of
the grand design of the universe that he suffer poverty.[927]
Why, then, did Rabbi Yochanan express surprise at the
circumstances of Rabbi Shimon bar Vava? Was not his
lack of success Divinely ordained in the same way as Rabbi
Elazar's?

Although a person's financial status is
predetermined, substantial merit can cause it to change.
Rabbi Shimon bar Vava had especially meritorious
ancestors. The Talmud states that it is not usual for a
person to be afflicted through the very thing he or she used
for a Mitzvah. Thus, Rabbi Pinchas ben Yair was surprised
that someone who provided water for wayfarers would lose
his daughter in a flood.[928] Rabbi Yochanan said that the
deeds of Rabbi Shimon bar Vava's ancestors resembled
those of Abraham whose outstanding trait was generosity.
It would be strange if the descendant of people who
behaved generously would suffer poverty. Even so, this
was Rabbi Shimon bar Vava's predetermined lot in life.

---

[926] B.T. *Brachoth* 5B.
[927] B.T. *Ta'anith* 25A.
[928] See above pp. 198-199.

Bikkurim 3:6 (Compare *Megillah* 27A)

תני: המוכר ספר תורה של אביו אינו רואה סימן ברכה לעולם.
וכל המקיים ספר תורה בתוך ביתו, עליו הכתוב אומר, "הוֹן וָעֹשֶׁר בְּבֵיתוֹ
וְצִדְקָתוֹ עֹמֶדֶת לָעַד." (תהלים קיב:ג).

It is learned: One who sells his father's *Torah*
scroll will never see a sign of blessing [from the proceeds].
Concerning whoever maintains a *Torah* scroll in his home,
Scripture says, "Riches and wealth are in his home and his
righteousness stands forever."[929]

*It is a Mitzvah for each Jew to write his own Torah
scroll.   Therefore, one who has his own scroll might
assume that it is acceptable to sell the one he inherited
from his father, but this is not true.   Jewish law prohibits
the sale of a Torah scroll except to provide funds for three
purposes: (a) to marry; (b) to study Torah; (c) to provide
one's essential needs if he or she is poverty-stricken.   The
above passage warns that even when it is permissible to
sell a Torah scroll, one who does so will not see a blessing
from the proceeds.[930]*
*At first glance, there does not appear to be any
particular connection between maintaining a Torah scroll
in one's home and the verse, "Riches and wealth are in his*

---

[929] Psalms 112:3.
[930] *Etz Yosef.*

home and his righteousness stands forever."[931] *How does this verse apply to the Mitzvah of keeping a Torah scroll more than to any other Mitzvah? The Me'Am Loez explains that there are certain forms of charity which do not entail giving anything away. One such act of generosity is to keep a Torah scroll or other holy writings. Others can use such items without in any way diminishing them. Since there is no actual expenditure, the "riches and wealth" remain in the person's home while he gains eternal merit.*[932]

May we always act in ways which earn eternal merit!

תם ונשלם בעזרת הא–ל יתברך שמו

---

[931] Psalms 112:3.
[932] *Me'Am Loez* on Psalms 112:3. See B.T. *Kethuboth* 50A.

BIBLIOGRAPHY AND GLOSSARY[*]

Aggadah: Rabbinical interpretations of the text of the **Tanach** and related material which discusses the philosophical, theological and ethical aspects of the Jewish religion. (Plural = **Aggadoth**).

Ahavath Eithan: Commentary on **Ein Yaakov** by **Rabbi Avraham ben Yehudah leib** of Minsk, author of a set of novellae entitled **Maskil L'Eithan**. (Russia, 1788-1848).

Akeidath Yitzchak: Philosophical commentary on the **Torah** written by **Rabbi Yitzchak Aramah**. (Spain and Italy, 1420-1494).

Albo, Rabbi Yosef: Author of **Sefer HaIkarim** ("The Book of Principles"), a work which discusses the fundamental tenets of the Jewish faith. (Spain, late 1300's to early 1400's).

---

[*] The author has gone to great effort to try to ensure the accuracy of the biographical data provided here. However, the reader needs to be aware that in some instances historians differ as to when a given individual was born or died. Due to changing borders and the tendency of prominent rabbis to serve several different communities during their lifetimes, there may also be differences of opinion about where they lived. This problem is compounded by the fact that a town or region was called different names in different languages. The English spelling of the names of most individuals is also uncertain because they are translations or transliterations from Hebrew. In addition, surnames came into use at different times in different locations, so a rabbi may be identified differently by different sources.

Amidah: A prayer Jews recite at least three times each day. During weekdays, the **Amidah** prayer consists of eighteen blessings. The word "**Amidah**" in Hebrew means "standing" because, if possible, one must stand while reciting it.

Amoraim: Sages who lived in the period after the **Mishnah** was reduced to writing. The debates of the **Amoraim** concerning the meaning of the **Mishnah** were reduced to writing in the sixth century C.E. as the **Gemara**. The **Mishnah** consists of the teachings of an earlier generation of sages called **Tannaim**.

Amudei Yerushalayim: Commentary on the Jerusalem **Talmud** by **Rabbi Yisrael Eisenstein** (Europe, 19th century) first published as part of his work **Amudei Esh** and later incorporated into the edition of the Jerusalem **Talmud** published by the Romm publishing house in Vilna during the early 20th century.

Amudei Yerushalayim Tinyana: Revised commentary on the Jerusalem **Talmud** by **Rabbi Yisrael Eisenstein** (Europe, 19th century) which was in manuscript form until published by the Romm publishing house in Vilna during the early 20th century.

Anaf Yosef: Commentary on **Ein Yaakov** and various collections of **Midrashim** by **Rabbi Chanoch Zundel ben Yosef**. (Poland, died 1867).

Arizal: Acronym for **Rabbi Yitzchak Luria**, the foremost **Kabbalist** of the late Middle Ages. **Rabbi Luria** was born in Poland in 1534 and died in the Land of Israel in 1572.

Aruch HaShulchan: An extensive recapitulation of the **Shulchan Aruch** with much added material by **Rabbi Yechiel Michal Epstein** (Belorussia, 1829-1908).

Arvei Nachal: **Chassidic** commentary on the **Torah** by **Rabbi David Shlomo Eibenschutz**. (Born in Russia; died in Land of Israel in 1812).

Avel Rabbathai: A set of **Braithoth** dealing with **Halachoth** which pertain to mourning. It is also euphemistically called **Mesecheth Simachoth**, "The Tractate of Celebrations." (The editors of the Romm Vilna edition of the Babylonian **Talmud** printed it in the same volume as **Avodah Zarah** together with several other collections of **Braithoth**.)

Avoth D'Rabbi Nathan: An expanded version of **Pirkei Avoth** written by **Rabbi Nathan** (Babylonia, 2nd century C.E.) and his disciples.

Avraham Chaim of Zlotchow, Rabbi: **Chassidic** master who was a student of the **Maggid of Mezeritch**, the chief disciple of the **Baal Shem Tov**. (Poland, 1750-1816).

Baal Shem Tov: Founder of the **Chassidic** movement which stresses joy and enthusiasm in serving **Hashem**. His real name was **Rabbi Yisrael ben Eliezer**, but he came to be known as the "**Baal Shem Tov**," meaning "Master of the Good Name," because of his knowledge of the esoteric wisdom of the **Kabbalah**. He lived in Poland from 1698 to 1760.

BaMidbar: The Book of Numbers. **BaMidbar Rabbah** is the portion of the **Midrash Rabbah** on the Book of Numbers.

Bar Mitzvah: A term that means "one is obligated to perform **Mitzvoth**." As a rule, Jewish boys become obligated to perform all commandments when they attain the age of thirteen. **Bath Mitzvah** is the feminine form of **Bar Mitzvah**. However, the **Torah** requires girls to observe the commandments when they attain the age of twelve. No ceremony is necessary for boys or girls to become obligated to obey the **Torah** when they reach these ages.

Be'er Sheva: Set of responsa written by **Rabbi Yissachar Dov Eilenberg**. (Poland, 1570-1623).

Ben Yehoyada: A comprehensive commentary on **Aggadic** material written by **Rabbi Yosef Hayyim** of Baghdad (1832-1909).

Be'urei HaChassiduth Le'Shas: Anthology of comments on the **Talmud** by **Chassidic** masters compiled by contemporary **Rabbi Yisrael Yitzchak Chassidah** of Israel.

Be'urei HaGra: Commentary on the Jerusalem **Talmud** by **Rabbi Eliyahu Kramer**, known as the **Vilna Gaon**. (Lithuania, 1720-1797).

Braitha: A teaching of the **Tannaim** which was not included in the **Mishnah**. **Rabbi Chiya** (Land of Israel, 3rd century C.E.) edited these teachings. (Plural = **Braithoth**)

Breishith: The Book of Genesis. **Breishith Rabbah** is the portion of the **Midrash Rabbah** on the Book of Genesis.

Carmell, Rabbi Aryeh: Contemporary scholar, author and teacher who lives in Israel.

Chaim of Volozhin, Rabbi: Chief disciple of the **Vilna Gaon (Rabbi Eliyahu Kramer)**. (Lithuania, 1749-1821).

Challah: When a Jew prepares dough for baking, he or she must take a portion and donate it to a **Kohen** (priest). That portion is called **Challah**.

Chametz: Dough which has been permitted to rise for more than eighteen minutes. Jews are forbidden to eat or even own such dough or leaven during the Passover holiday.

Chanoch Zundel ben Yosef, Rabbi: Commentator who wrote extensively on **Ein Yaakov** and various collections of **Midrashim** (Poland, died 1867) under the names **Etz Yosef** and **Anaf Yosef**.

Chajes, Rabbi Zvi Hirsch: Rabbi who penned scholarly comments on virtually the entire Babylonian **Talmud**. He wrote a lengthy introduction to **Ein Yaakov** called **Mavoh HaAggadoth**. (Poland, 1805-1855).

Chavah: Eve.

Chaver, Rabbi Yitzchak Isaac: Disciple of **Rabbi Chaim of Volozhin**, he flourished in Lithuania in the early nineteenth century.

Chavoth Yair: Responsa written by **Rabbi Yair Chaim Bachrach**. (Germany, 1638-1702).

Chidushei Aggadoth: Commentary on the **Aggadic** material of the **Talmud** by **Rabbi Shmuel Eliezer Eidels** of Poland. (1555-1632).

Chidushei Gaonim: An anthology of commentaries published in the Romm Vilna edition of **Ein Yaakov**. (The anonymous compilers were commissioned by the publisher.)

Chochmath Adam: A codification of Jewish law by **Rabbi Avraham Danziger**. (Lithuania, 1748-1820).

Choshen Mishpat: Section of the **Shulchan Aruch** written by **Rabbi Yosef Karo** who lived from 1488-1575 and died in the Land of Israel containing laws concerning business and financial matters.

Chumash: Pentateuch.

Culi, Rabbi Yaakov: The originator of **Me'Am Loez**, an extensive anthology of **Midrashic** material on the **Tanach**. **Rabbi Culi** died before completing this huge project which other scholars later finished. He flourished in Turkey from 1689 to 1732.

Da'ath Tevunoth: A philosophical treatise by **Rabbi Moshe Chaim Luzzatto** (born in Italy, 1707, died in the Land of Israel, 1746) cast as a dialog between the soul and the intellect.

Degel Machneh Ephraim: Biblical commentary by the **Chassidic** master **Rabbi Moshe Chaim Ephraim** of Sudylkov, 1746-1790.

Derech Eretz Zuta: Collection of **Tannaitic** teachings called **Braithoth** which were not included in the **Mishnah**.

Derech Hashem: Kabbalistic/philosophical work written by **Rabbi Moshe Chaim Luzzatto** who was born in Italy in 1707 and died in the Land of Israel in 1746.

Dessler, Rabbi Eliyahu Eliezer: Author of the ethical treatise called "**Michtav MiEliyahu.**" (Russia and Great Britain, 1891-1954).

Devarim: The Book of Deuteronomy. **Devarim Rabbah** is the portion of the **Midrash Rabbah** on the Book of Deuteronomy.

Dinar (plural: **dinarim** or **dinarii**): A silver coin commonly used in **Talmudic** times. Four **dinarim** equaled the value of the silver **shekel** referred to in the **Tanach**. The **Talmud** sometimes refers to the **dinar** as a **Zuz**.

Drashoth HaRan: Compilation of sermons and essays by **Rabbeinu Nissim** (1290-1375) who is known by the acronym **HaRan**.

Eichah Rabbah: Section of **Midrash Rabbah** on the Book of Lamentations.

Ein Yaakov: A collection of **Aggadic** material compiled by **Rabbi Yaakov Ibn Chaviv** who lived in Spain and Turkey from 1445-1516.

Eisenstein, Rabbi Yisrael: Author of **Amudei Yerushalayim**, a commentary on the Jerusalem **Talmud**. (Europe, 19th century).

Elimelech of Lizensk: Chassidic master who authored the Biblical commentary, **No'am Elimelech**. (Poland, 1717-1787).

Encyclopedia Talmudith: A compilation of material on Talmudic topics arranged in alphabetical entries like an encyclopedia. This project was initiated in Israel by **Rabbi Shlomo Yosef Zevin** (1890-1978) with the first volume being published in 1947. About twenty-five volumes have been published so far.

Esther Rabbah: The portion of the **Midrash Rabbah** on the Book of Esther.

Ettinger, Rabbi Mordechai Zev: Author of a commentary on the Jerusalem **Talmud** entitled **Gilyon HaShas**. (Poland, 1804-1863).

Etz Chaim: A **Kabbalistic** work by **Rabbi Chaim Vital** based on the teachings of the **Arizal**.

Etz Yosef: Commentary on **Ein Yaakov** and various **Midrashic** collections by **Rabbi Chanoch Zundel ben Yosef**. (Poland, died 1867).

Feinstein, Rabbi Moshe: Former dean of **Yeshiva Tifereth Jerusalem**, a major institution of **Torah** learning in New York, **Rabbi Feinstein** was considered by many to be the leading **Halachic** authority in North America in his time. He authored responsa entitled **Igroth Moshe**. (Born 1895, Russia; died 1986, United States).

Fraenkel, Rabbi David: Author of the **Korban HaEidah** commentary which gives a basic explanation of the Jerusalem **Talmud** and the **Shayarei Korban** commentary which delves into more complex issues raised by the Jerusalem **Talmud** (Germany, 1707-1762).

Gehinnom: Hell.

Gei Chizayon: Commentary on the Twelve Minor Prophets by **Rabbi Meir Leibush Malbim**.

Gilyon HaShas: Commentary on the Jerusalem **Talmud** by **Rabbi Mordechai Zev Ettinger**. (Poland, 1804-1863).

Hagahoth Maimuni: Brief comments in note form on the **Rambam's Yad HaChazakah** written by **Rabbi Meir HaKohen** of Rothenburg (13th century).

Hai Gaon, Rav: Last major head of the ancient Babylonian academy in Pumbeditha who authored many responsa and who is widely quoted by later Medieval authorities. (Died 1038.)

HaKothev: Commentary of **Rabbi Yaakov Ibn Chaviv** published with his collection of **Aggadic** material called **Ein Yaakov**.

Halachah (plural = **Halachoth**): Jewish law. Such laws may be ritual in nature, addressing the relationship between people and God, or civil in nature, addressing the relationship between a person and his or her fellows.

Hashem: God.

Hayyim, Rabbi Yosef: Popularly known as "**Ben Ish Chai**" after his most popular work, **Rabbi Hayyim** flourished in Baghdad from 1832-1909. He wrote two commentaries on **Aggadic** material: **Ben Yehoyada** and **Sefer Benayahu**.

Heinemann, Rabbi Moshe: Major contemporary scholar and expert in Jewish law of the present generation. (Baltimore, Maryland).

Heller, Rabbi Yom Tov Lipman: Author of the commentary on the **Mishnah** known as **Tosafoth Yom Tov** (Vienna, Prague, Poland, 1579-1654).

Ibn Ezra, Rabbi Avraham: Biblical commentator and scholar of Hebrew grammar. (Spain, 1089-1164).

Ibn Chaviv, Rabbi Yaakov: Editor of the **Ein Yaakov** anthology of **Aggadoth** who lived in Spain and Turkey from 1445-1516.   **Rabbi Ibn Chaviv** also wrote a commentary on the **Ein Yaakov** anthology called **HaKothev**.

Igereth HaTeshuvah: Letter by **Rabbi Shneur Zalman of Liadi** (Russia, 1745-1812) to his followers on the topic of repentance, published with **Likutei Amarim Tanya**.

Igroth Moshe: Set of responsa written by **Rabbi Moshe Feinstein** (Born 1895, Russia; died 1986, United States).

Isserles, Rabbi Moshe: Popularly known as the **Rama**, he flourished in Poland from 1530-1572.   he is most famous for his glosses on the **Shulchan Aruch**.

Iyun Yaakov: Commentary on the **Ein Yaakov** collection of **Aggadoth** by **Rabbi Yaakov Reischer** (Prague, 1670-1733).

Kabbalah: Secret Jewish mystical tradition. Although the general outlines of this tradition are available to the public at large, its details are known only to a select few students who have received them orally from their masters.

Kaddish: Aramaic prayer praising God which is recited several times throughout each of the three daily services.

Kavod HaBayith: Commentary on portions of **Ein Yaakov** by **Rabbi Shimon Wolf ben Yaakov** of Pintshuv (published in 1707 in Hamburg, Germany) cited in **Chidushei Gaonim**.

Kaplan, Rabbi Aryeh: A renowned **Torah** scholar and author who translated numerous Jewish texts into English, including **Sefer HaBahir**, **Sefer Yetzirah** and **Derech HaShem**. (United States, 1935-1983).

Kashruth: Jewish dietary laws.

Kedushath Levi: **Chassidic** commentary on the **Torah** by **Rabbi Levi Yitzchak of Berditchev** (Ukraine, circa 1740-1810).

Kehati, Rabbi Pinchas: Author of a comprehensive modern commentary on the **Mishnah** called **Mishnayoth M'vuaroth**. Born in Poland in 1910, he moved to Israel where he died in 1976.

Kether Shem Tov: A collection of teachings of **Rabbi Yisrael Baal Shem Tov**, founder of the Chassidic movement. The teachings were gleaned from the works of his disciple, **Rabbi Yaakov Yosef** of Polnoye (died c. 1784), by **Rabbi Aharon Cohen** of Apta.

Kithvei HaAri: An extensive collection of teachings of the **Arizal** compiled by his disciple, **Rabbi Chaim Vital** (Land of Israel and Syria, 1543-1620).

Kli Yakar: Commentary to the **Torah** by **Rabbi Ephraim Shlomo Lunshitz** (Poland, 1550-1619).

Kohen: Member of the priestly class who descended from Moses's brother, Aaron. (Plural: **Kohanim**)

Kohanim: Members of the priestly class who descended from Moses's brother, Aaron.

Koheleth Rabbah: The portion of **Midrash Rabbah** on the Ecclesiastes.

Korban HaEidah: Commentary on the Jerusalem **Talmud** by **Rabbi David Fraenkel** (Germany, 1707-1762). **Korban HaEidah** gives a basic explanation of the Jerusalem **Talmud**. **Rabbi Fraenkel** also wrote **Shayarei Korban** which delves into more complex issues.

Kotler, Rabbi Aharon: Founder of the famous **Beth Medrash Govoha yeshiva** in Lakewood, New Jersey and pioneer in establishing advanced **Torah** study in the United States (1892-1962).

Levi Yitzchak of Berditchev: **Chassidic** master who authored **Kedushath Levi**, a commentary on the **Torah**. (Ukraine, circa 1740-1810).

Likutei Amarim Tanya: A **Chassidic** work which discusses a wide range of theological issues written by **Rabbi Shneur Zalman of Liadi**, founder of the Lubavitch **Chassidic** dynasty who lived from 1745 to 1812.

Likutei Moharan: A collection of the teachings of the **Chassidic** master, **Rabbi Nachman** of Breslov (Ukraine, 1772-1810) compiled by his disciple, **Rabbi Nathan** of Nemerov, in 1808.

Lopian, Rabbi Eliyahu: Major rabbinic authority and exponent of the **Mussar** movement, a movement founded by **Rabbi Yisrael Lipkin (Salanter)** to promote the study and practice of Jewish ethical teachings. (Poland and Israel, 1876-1970).

Lulav: Palm frond which Jews wave during the holiday of **Sukkoth**.

Lunshitz, Rabbi Ephraim Shlomo: Author of a popular commentary on the **Torah**. (Poland, 1550-1619).

Luria, Rabbi David: Author of scholarly notes and glosses on **Talmud** and **Midrashim**. (Lithuania, 1798-1855).

Luzzatto, Rabbi Moshe Chaim: Author of numerous **Kabbalistic** and philosophical works including "**Derech Hashem**" and "**Da'ath Tevunoth**." He was born in Italy in 1707 and died in the Land of Israel in 1746.

Maamar HaNefesh: One of a series of **Kabbalistic** writings by **Rabbi Menachem Azariah** of Fano (Italy, 1548-1620).

Ma'arecheth HeAruch: The **Aruch** was a seminal work on Hebrew lexicography written by **Rabbi Nathan ben Yechiel** (Rome, 1035-1110). The **Ma'arecheth HeAruch** published in the Romm Vilna edition of the Jerusalem **Talmud** contains excerpts from the **Aruch** which help explain words or phrases in the text. The editors also added material from the **Mussaf HeAruch**, a supplement written by **Rabbi Benjamin Mussafia**.

Maharal: Acronym for **Rabbi Yehudah Loewy**, 1526-1609, who was chief rabbi of Prague. Among his many works is an extensive commentary on the **Aggadoth** of the Babylonian **Talmud**.

Maharam de Lonzano: Acronym for **Rabbi Menachem de Lonzano**, an expert lexicographer who wrote a commentary on the Jerusalem **Talmud**. (Land of Israel, 16th to 17th century).

Maharsha: Acronym for **Rabbi Shmuel Eliezer Eidels** of Poland, 1555-1632.

Maharzu: Acronym for **Rabbi Zev Wolf Einhorn** of Vilna (died 1862) who wrote an extensive commentary on the **Midrash Rabbah**.

Malbim: Acronym for Rabbi *M*eir *L*aibush *b*en *Y*echiel *M*ichael. (Poland, 1809-1879).

Maor VeShemesh: **Chassidic** commentary on the **Torah** by **Rabbi Kalonymus Kalman Epstein** of Krakow, Poland. (died 1823).

Marei HaPanim: Commentary on the Jerusalem **Talmud** by **Rabbi Moshe Margolies** of Amsterdam. In contrast to **P'nei Moshe**, a commentary by the same author, **Marei Panim** delves into complex **Talmudic** problems.

Matnoth Kehunah: Commentary on **Midrash Rabbah** by **Rabbi Yissachar Ber HaKohen**. (Poland, 16th century).

Me'Am Loez: An anthology of commentaries on the **Tanach** initiated by **Rabbi Yaakov Culi** (Turkey, 1689-1732) and completed after his death by other scholars.

Mechilta: **Midrashic** commentary on Exodus written by **Rabbi Yishmael** (Land of Israel, 2nd century C.E.) and his disciples.

Melecheth Shlomo: Commentary on the **Mishnah** by **Rabbi Shlomo Adeni** of Yemen and the Land of Israel (1567-1625).

Menachem Azariah of Fano, Rabbi: Italian master of the **Kabbalah** who lived from 1548 to 1620.

Mesilath Yesharim: An ethical treatise based upon a **Braitha** in the **Talmud** which traces the ideal path of spiritual development. This work was produced by **Rabbi Moshe Chaim Luzzatto** who was born in Italy in 1707 and died in the Land of Israel in 1746.

Metzudoth David: Commentary on the **Tanach** by **Rabbi David Altschuler** (Poland, 18th century), parts of which were completed by his son, **Rabbi Yechiel Hillel Altschuler.**

Mezuzah: Parchment scroll containing the first two verse of the **Shema** which Jews attach to the doorways of their homes. (Plural = **Mezuzoth**)

Michtav MiEliyahu: Ethical treatise written by **Rabbi Eliyahu Dessler** (Russia and Great Britain, 1891-1954).

Midrash: Homiletic interpretations of the **Tanach**. **Midrashic** works are often classified into **Halachic Midrash** which explains how religious law is derived from the text of the **Tanach** and **Aggadic Midrash** which discusses the philosophical, theological and ethical aspects of the text.

Midrash Othioth Rabbi Akiva HaShalem: **Midrash** contained in **Batei Midrashoth**, an anthology of **Midrashic** material originally compiled by **Rabbi Shlomo Aharon Wertheimer** (Land of Israel, 1866-1935) and reprinted with additions and correction during the 1950's by his grandson, **Rabbi Yosef Avraham Wertheimer.**

Midrash Rabbah: "The Great **Midrash**" is the most extensive collection of **Midrashic** interpretation.

Almost all of the **Midrash Rabbah** is Aggadic in nature. The **Midrash Rabbah** follows the text of the **Tanach** and so is identified as, for example, **Breishith Rabbah**, Midrashim on the text of **Breishith** (Genesis).

Midrash Tehillim: A **Midrashic** work on the Book of Psalms, also known as **Midrash Shocher Tov** because it opens with the words "שחר טוב".

Mishnah: The Oral Law. A compilation of traditions passed down from generation to generation by word of mouth until committed to writing in the third century C.E.

Mizrachi, Rabbi Eliyahu: Author of a widely read commentary on **Rashi**. (Turkey, 1450-1526).

Moreh Nevuchim: A wide-ranging philosophical treatise written by the **Rambam** (**Rabbi Moses Maimonides**).

Mussaf HeAruch: The **Aruch** was a seminal work on Hebrew lexicography written by Rabbi Nathan ben Yechiel (Rome, 1035-1110). The **Ma'arecheth HeAruch** published in the Romm Vilna edition of the Jerusalem **Talmud** contains excerpts from the **Aruch** which help explain words or phrases in the text. The editors also added material from the **Mussaf HeAruch**, a supplement written by **Rabbi Benjamin Mussafia**.

Nachman of Breslau, Rabbi: Famous **Chassidic** leader who was a great grandson of the **Baal Shem Tov**. (1772-1811).

Ne'ilah: Special additional prayer recited at the conclusion fast days such as **Yom Kippur**.

Nethivoth Olam: A set of philosophical treatises written by **Rabbi Yehudah Loewy**, the **Maharal** of Prague. (1526-1609).

No'am Elimelech: **Chassidic Torah** commentary by **Rabbi Elimelech** of Lizensk (Poland, 1717-1787).

Ohr HaChaim: Major commentary on the **Torah** written by **Rabbi Chaim ben Attar** (Morocco, Italy and the Land of Israel, 1696-1743).

Oppenheim, Rabbi David: Commentator on the Jerusalem **Talmud**. (Nicholsburg, Moravia, 1664-1736).

Orach Chaim: Section of the **Shulchan Aruch** written by **Rabbi Yosef Karo** who lived from 1488-1575 and died in the Land of Israel containing laws concerning everyday ritual practice.

Otzar HaMidrashim: A two volume collection of **Midrashim** compiled by **Yehudah David Eisenstein**, a businessman and scholar. (United States, 1854-1956).

Pesach: Passover.

Pesikta D'Rav Kahana: A collection of **Midrashim** attributed to **Rav Kahana** (2nd century, Babylon and the Land of Israel).

Pesikta Rabbathai: A collection of **Midrashim** from the early Medieval period (probably 8th century C.E.).

Pirkei D'Rabbi Nathan: See **Avoth D'Rabbi Nathan**.

Pithchei Chochmah VeDa'ath: Treatise written by **Rabbi Moshe Chaim Luzzatto** who was born in Italy in 1707 and died in the Land of Israel in 1746.

Pithchei Teshuvah: Commentary on the **Shulchan Aruch** by **Rabbi Avraham Tzvi Eisenstadt** (Lithuania, 1812-1868).

P'nei Moshe: Commentary by **Rabbi Moshe Margolies** of Lithuania (died 1781) on the Jerusalem **Talmud** which provides a basic understanding of the text. **Rabbi Margolies** also wrote **Marei HaPanim** which delves into more complex issues raised by the text of the Jerusalem **Talmud**.

P'nei Yehoshua: **Talmudic** commentary by **Rabbi Yaakov Yehoshua Falk** (Germany, 1681-1756).

Rabbeinu Nissim: Early Talmudic commentator and author of numerous sermons and responsa. (1290-1375).

Rabbeinu Tam: **Rabbi Yaakov ben Meir** who lived in France from 1100 to 1171 was a grandson of **Rashi**.

Radbaz: Acronym for **Rabbi David Ben Zimra**, chief rabbi of Egypt who lived from 1480 to 1573.

Rama: Acronym for **Rabbi Moshe Isserles** who flourished in Poland from 1530-1572. he is most famous for his glosses on the **Shulchan Aruch**.

Rambam: An acrostic for "Rabbi Moshe Ben Maimon," known in English as **Rabbi Moses Maimonides**. He was born in Spain in 1135 and died in Egypt in 1204.

Ramban: An acrostic for "Rabbi Moshe Ben Nachman," known in English as **Rabbi Moses Nachmanides**. He lived in Spain from 1194 to 1270.

Rashi: An acrostic for the name of **Rabbi Shlomo Yitzchaki** who lived in France from 1040-1105. **Rashi's** commentaries on the **Tanach** and Babylonian **Talmud** are considered the most basic and essential for every student to learn.

Romm Vilna Talmud: Romm publishing house was founded in 1789 by **Baruch ben Yosef Romm** and changed hands several times. The editions of the Babylonian and Jerusalem **Talmud** as well as numerous other classic texts published by this house have become the standard editions most widely used by Jewish scholars. **Shmuel Shraga Feigensohn** served as editor in the late nineteenth and early twentieth centuries. He hired scholars to annotate the texts Romm published, noting variant readings. These scholars also compiled commentaries on the texts.

Rosh HaShannah: The Jewish New Year.

Sanhedrin: An academy of seventy-one **Torah** sages which served as the supreme arbiter of Jewish law in ancient times.

Scherman, Rabbi Nosson: Contemporary author and editor.

Sefer Chareidim: Treatise on the **mitzvoth** by **Rabbi Elazar Azkari** of Turkey and the Land of Israel, 1533-1600.

Sefer HaBahir: A **Kabbalistic** text attributed to **Rabbi Nechuniah ben Hakana** (Land of Israel, 1st century C.E.).

Sefer HaGilgulim: A volume of the **Kithvei HaAri** by **Rabbi Chaim Vital** (Land of Israel, 1542-1620).

Sefer HaIkarim: A work which discusses the fundamental tenets of the Jewish faith authored by **Rabbi Yitzchak Albo**. (Spain, late 1300's to early 1400's).

Sefer Likutei HaShas (Likutim MiEtz Chaim): Selections from **Etz Chaim**, a **Kabbalistic** work written by **Rabbi Chaim Vital** as part of his monumental compendium of teachings of the **Arizal**.

Sefer Mashbiach: Commentary on the Jerusalem **Talmud** by **Rabbi Moshe Shimon Sivitz** of Pittsburgh, published in 1918. The commentary has an approbation from the renowned **Rabbi Yisrael Meir Kagan**, popularly known as the "**Chafetz Chaim**."

Sefer Ta'amei Hamitzvoth: A Kabbalistic work written by **Rabbi Chaim Vital** as part of his monumental compendium of teachings of the **Arizal**.

Sefer Yuchasin: Chronicle of Jewish history by **Rabbi Avraham Zacut** (Spain and Syria, c. 1440-1515).

Sha'ar HaGemul: Treatise on the afterlife, resurrection, Heaven and Hell by **Rabbi Moshe ben Nachman** (Spain, 1194-1270).

Shavuoth: The festival which occurs fifty days after Passover when God gave the **Torah** to the Jewish people. This holiday is called "Pentecost" in English.

Shayarei HaKorban: Commentary on the Jerusalem **Talmud** by **Rabbi David Fraenkel** (Germany, 1707-1762), author of the **Korban HaEidah**.

Shema: A prayer consisting of three paragraphs from the **Chumash** (Pentateuch) which Jews recite every morning and evening.

Shemoth: The Book of Exodus. **Shemoth Rabbah** is the portion of the **Midrash Rabbah** on the Book of Exodus.

Shir HaShirim: The Book of Songs. **Shir HaShirim Rabbah** is the portion of the **Midrash Rabbah** on the Book of Songs.

Shneur Zalman of Liadi, Rabbi: Author of numerous works including **Likutei Amarim Tanya,** a Chassidic work which discusses a wide range of theological issues. **Rabbi Shneur Zalman** founded the **Lubavitch Chassidic** dynasty. He lived in Russia from 1745 to 1812.

Shofar: Ram's horn which Jews blow on the holiday of **Rosh HaShannah**.

Shulchan Aruch: A codification of Jewish law written by **Rabbi Yosef Karo** who lived from 1488-1575 and died in the Land of Israel. The **Shulchan Aruch** is divided into four sections: **Orach Chaim** concerning everyday ritual practice; **Even HaEzer** concerning marital law; **Choshen Mishpat** concerning business and financial matters; **Yoreh Deah** concerning several topics which do not fit conveniently into the other categories such as dietary laws and agricultural laws which apply to the Land of Israel.

Siach Yitzchak: Collection of homiletic discourses by **Rabbi Yitzchak Isaac Chaver**, a disciple of **Rabbi Chaim of Volozhin**. (Lithuania, early nineteenth century).

Sifthei Kohen: Commentary on the **Yoreh Deah** section of **Shulchan Aruch** by **Rabbi Shabbethai ben Meir HaKohen,** popularly known as the **Shach**. (Lithuania and Moravia, 1622-1663).

Sirilio, Rabbi Shlomo: Author of a commentary on the **Jerusalem Talmud**. (Spain and Jerusalem, 1485-1558).

Sukkah: A hut Jews live in during the Festival of Tabernacles (**Sukkoth** in Hebrew) which falls in autumn.

Sukkoth: A festival which occurs in autumn after **Yom Kippur** (the Day of Atonement). Jews live in huts during this holiday reminiscent of the huts or clouds of glory in which they lived when traveling through the desert after departing Egypt. (This holiday is called the Festival of Tabernacles or Booths in English).

Tamid offerings: Two lambs which the *Torah* commands Jews to sacrifice daily, one in the morning and one in the afternoon. (Exodus 29:38).

Tanach: An acrostic for the Jewish Bible consisting the *T̲orah* (Pentateuch), *N̲eviim* (Prophets) and *K̲ethuvim* (Hagiographa).

Tanchuma: **Midrashic** commentary on the **Torah** written by **Rabbi Tanchuma bar Abba** (Land of Israel, 4th century C.E.) and his disciples.

Tanna: Sage who lived during the time of the **Mishnah**. (Plural = **Tannaim**).

Tannaim: Sages who lived during the time of the **Mishnah**.

Tanna D'Bei Eliyahu: A set of **Midrashim** which the Prophet Elijah taught to **Rabbi Anan** (Babylonia, 3rd century C.E.). The longer portion (**Tanna D'Bei Eliyahu Rabbah**) was taught to **Rabbi Anan** before he fell out of favor with Elijah. The shorter portion (**Tanna D'Bei Eliyahu Zuta**) was taught to Rabbi Anan after that. (B.T. *Kethuboth* 106A).

Targum Yonathan ben Uziel: An Aramaic translation and commentary of the **Tanach** written by **Rabbi Yonathan ben Uziel** (Land of Israel, 1st century C.E.).

Tefillin: Leather boxes containing upon which are written sections of the **Torah** worn by adult Jewish males during weekday morning services.

Tifereth Yisrael: A commentary on the **Mishnah** by **Rabbi Yisrael Lipschitz** (Germany, 1782-1860).

Tikunei Zohar: **Kabbalistic** work attributed to **Rabbi Shimon bar Yochai** (Land of Israel, 2nd century C.E.) and his disciples.

Torah Temimah: A commentary on the **Torah** which quotes classical sources such as **Talmud** and **Midrash** on each verse and explains them. Written by **Rabbi Baruch HaLevi Epstein** of Poland in the 19th century.

Torathan Shel Rishonim: An anthology of comments on the Jerusalem **Talmud** gleaned from the work of **Rabbi Ber Ratner** by **Shalom Shraga Feigensohn** editor of the Romm Vilna edition.

Tosafoth: A group of approximately two hundred **Talmudic** scholars who flourished in Europe during the twelfth and thirteenth centuries. These scholars wrote and disseminated several versions of their commentaries on the **Talmud**.

Tosafoth HaRosh: Commentary on the **Talmud** by **Rabbeinu Asher ben Yechiel**, known by the acronym **HaRosh**, who was born in Germany and later settled in Spain. (circa 1250-1327).

Tosafoth Yom Tov: Commentary on the **Mishnah** by **Rabbi Yom Tov Lipman Heller** 1579-1654.

Tosefta: A collection of traditional teachings organized by **Rabbi Nechemiah** (Land of Israel, 2nd century C.E.) and his disciples, paralleling the material of the **Mishnah**. (B.T. *Sanhedrin* 86A)

Tur Shulchan Aruch: Code of Jewish law written by **Rabbi Jacob ben Asher** (Germany and Spain, 1270-1340) which served as a model for the **Shulchan Aruch** written about two hundred years later by **Rabbi Yosef Karo**.

Turei Zahav: Commentary on the **Yoreh Deah** section of **Shulchan Aruch** written by **Rabbi David ben Shmuel HaLevy** (1586-1667).

Tzaddikim: Righteous men. (Singular = **Tzaddik**).

Tzedakah: Charity.

Tzitz Eliezer: Collection of responsa by contemporary **Halachic** scholar, **Rabbi Eliezer Waldenburg**. (Jerusalem, born 1917).

Tzitzioth: Ritual fringes which the **Torah** commands Jews to wear on four-cornered garments.

VaYikra: The Book of Leviticus. **VaYikra Rabbah** is the portion of the **Midrash Rabbah** on the Book of Leviticus.

Vilna Gaon: **Rabbi Eliyahu Kramer** (Lithuania, 1720-1797). The word "**gaon**" means "genius." The **Vilna Gaon** was a child prodigy who wrote extensively on just about every aspect of the **Torah**.

Vital, Rabbi Chaim: Chief disciple of the **Kabbalistic** master known as the **Arizal**. **Rabbi Vital** authored the **Kithvei HaAri**, a compendium of his master's teachings. (Land of Israel, 1542-1620).

Waldenburg, Rabbi Eliezer Yehudah: Author of the major work of responsa known as **Tzitz Eliezer**. (Jerusalem, born 1917).

Yaakov Ibn Chaviv, Rabbi: Author of the "**Ein Yaakov**" collection of **Aggadoth** who lived in Spain and Turkey from 1445-1516.

Ya'aroth D'vash: Homiletic work by **Rabbi Yonathan Eibeschutz**, an outstanding scholar of **Talmud** and **Kabbalah**. (Poland, Moravia, Prague, 1690(?)-1764).

Yad HaChazakah: A comprehensive codification of Jewish law written by the **Rambam** (**Rabbi Moses Maimonides**).

Yalkut Reuveni: Anthology of **Midrashim** and other classical Jewish literature edited by **Rabbi Avraham Reuven Sopher Katz** (Prague, died 1673).

Yalkut Shimoni: Anthology of **Midrashim** on the **Tanach** edited by **Rabbi Shimon HaDarshan** (Frankfort, 13th century C.E.).

Y'dei Moshe: Commentary on the **Midrash Rabbah** written by **Rabbi Yaakov Moshe Hellin Ashkenazi**, a grandson the the renowned **Talmudist, Rabbi Shlomo Luria**. (Early 17th century).

Yechaveh Da'ath: A book of responsa by **Rabbi Ovadiah Yosef**, formerly the Chief Rabbi of Israel and major contemporary scholar.

Yeshiva: Academy.

Y'feh Mareh: Commentary of the **Aggadoth** of the Jerusalem **Talmud** written by **Rabbi Shmuel Yafeh Ashkenazi**. (Turkey, 1525-1595).

Yismach Moshe: **Chassidic** commentary on the **Torah** by **Rabbi Moshe Teitelbaum** (Hungary 1759-1841).

Yismach Yisrael: **Rabbi Yerachmiel Yisrael Yitzchak Danziger**, a **Chassidic** master who lived in Poland from 1853 to 1910. He was known by the name **Yismach Yisrael** after the popular work he wrote of that name.

Yoreh Deah: Section of the **Shulchan Aruch** written by **Rabbi Yosef Karo** who lived from 1488-1575 and died in the Land of Israel containing laws on various subjects.

Yosef, Rabbi Ovadiah: Chief Rabbi Emeritus of Israel and major contemporary scholar. **Rabbi Ovadiah's** numerous works include an extensive collection of responsa. (Born in Iraq in 1920.)

Yosef Tehilloth: Commentary on the Book of Psalms by **Rabbi Chaim Yosef David Azulai,** popularly known by the acronym **"Chida."** (1724-1806).

Zohar: **Kabbalistic** commentary on the **Torah** attributed to **Rabbi Shimon bar Yochai** (Land of Israel, 2nd century C.E.) and his disciples.

INDEX

Aaron, 384
Aaron, and evil gossip, 75
Abishag, 92-93
Abishai, 105
Abner, 98, 103-106
Abraham (see also Patriarchs)
Abraham, and peace with Sarah, 90
Abraham, God rose before, 400-401
Abraham, righteousness and generosity of, 410-412
Abraham, rose early to sacrifice Isaac, 187
Abraham, those who bless will be blessed, 120-121 (note 276)
Abraham, told of Egyptian slavery by God, 356
Absalom, 98, 107
Acco, 265
Achish, King, 334
Adam, and evil gossip, 77-79
Adam, before sin, 274
Adam, body of, 251
Adam, gave names to animals, 201
Adam, seduced by snake, 295 (note 646), 311-312
Adam, sin of, 141, 205-209, 244, 246-247, 311-312, 319
Adar, 353-354
Adonijah, 92-93
Adultery, 86, 166, 307-308
Africa, 291-292
Aftergrowth of Sabbatical year, 161-162, 295-296
Aged, see Elderly
Aggadoth, study of, 4-5, 61, 230, 336-340
Ahab, King, 99, 101, 245, 254-257
Ahasuerus, King, 127
Ahijah, 255-256
Ahimelech, 103

Ahitophel, 98
Akiva, Rabbi, daughter saved from snake, 14-15
Akiva, Rabbi, had twelve thousand pairs of students, 231
Alphabet, Hillel taught potential convert, 289
Altar, see Temple, altar of
Amalek, 110, 316, 317
Amen, 277, 279, 282
Ancestors, deeds of influence later generations, 238 (note 501)
Ancestors, merit of, 226, 281, 408, 410-412
Ancestry, choosing leaders with good, 223, 224-226
Angel, in likeness of Rabbi Pinchas ben Yair, 200
Angel Michael sacrifices souls of righteous, 169 (note 369)
Angel of death, 255-256
Angel of Esau, 314 (note 695)
Angel, spoke to Zachariah, 374
Angel, teaches baby entire *Torah*, 281
Angels, appear in likeness of person whose merit caused salvation, 200 (note 419), 229 (note 485)
Angels, challenged God's show of favoritism, 285
Angels, defined as spiritual forces, 207
Angels, have free will, 207
Angels, Jews are like on *Yom Kippur*, 95
Angels, Jews greater than, 279
Angels, objected to giving of *Torah* to people, 64-65
Angels, objected to saving Jews at Reed Sea, 202
Angels, predecessors likened to, 195
Angels, prevented heathens from stealing from Jews, 153
Angels, visited Abraham, 400
Anger, of God, 174, 183, 337, 386
Animal, prohibition against eating limb of living, 81-82
Animal fodder, 160, 196
Animals, dangerous, 199 (note 417), 204
Animals, kosher, 165
Animals, life force of, 390

Animals, named by Adam, 201
Animals, slaughter of, 308
Animals, which represent Gentile empires, 165
Animals, will find relief at time of redemption, 269-270
Antbila, 176
Antigeras, demon which inhabits bathhouses, 331-332
Antoninus, 210
Apparel, see Garment or Garments
Arab, 326
Arabs, 145 (note 330)
Aramaic, 1
Argonaut, 331 (note 742)
Aristobolus, 24, 168
Aristotle, 68, 207
Ark, see Holy Ark
Arnan the Jebusite, 176
Arrow, implies contention, 145 (note 332)
Arrows, evil gossip likened to, 98-99, 106
Artebon, 66-68
Ashkelon, 30, 153
Assyrians, 249, 292
Baal Shem Tov, had special spiritual sensitivity, 266
Baby, see also Children
Baby, King Saul resembled one year old, 404
Babylon or Babylonia, 165, 223, 250, 259, 277, 370, see also Babylonian and Babylonians
Babylonian, Rabbi Chiya was, 235
Babylonian Aramaic, 1-2
Babylonian exile, 283-284, 286, 378
Babylonian sages, 3
Babylonian *Talmud*, compared to Jerusalem *Talmud*, 2-4
Babylonians, 250, 370
Balsam, 364
Bar Mitzvah, 150

Barzillai, 387
Basemath, 404
Batheira Family, 223-224
Bathroom, going to, 351
Bathroom, students observed teachers in, 315
Baths, heated for seven days and seven nights, 332
Baths, Rabbi Chiya in, 229-230
Baths, Rabbi Shimon bar Yochai visited, 297, 300, 302
Baths, Rabbi Yochanan and Resh Lakish visited, 182, 187, 190
Baths, Rabbi Yudan Nessiah and Rabbi Shmuel bar Nachman
visited, 331-332
Bathsheba, 92
Beautifying *Mitzvoth*, 7-8
Bedframe, 351
Bedroom, students observed teachers in, 315
Beggar, and Nachum Ish Gamzu, 185, 190-192
Beggar, and Rabbi Akiva's daughter, 14
Beggar, died due to change in diet, 184
Beggar, disqualified from accepting tithes, 175-176
Beggar, Hillel treated well, 177
Beggar, provided with poultry, 177-178
Beggar, of wealthy background, 177-178, 181-182
Beggar, shaming, 188-189
Beggar, warned husband against eating poisoned food, 307-308
Beggars, and Rabbi Pinchas ben Yair, 196
Beggars, delaying contribution to, 181-182, 187-192
Beggars, soothing, 41
Beggars, dishonest, 181-190
Benjamin, 30, 31 (note 67), 108 (note 245), 223, 248
Bezalel, 9
Bias, against Jews, 17 (note 45)
Bilaam, 201 (note 421)
Bilhah, 83
Bird, cannot be trapped contrary to will of Heaven, 297

Bird, shooing away mother, 46-49, 51
Blessings, merited by giving *Tzedakah*, 41
Blind, placing hazard before, 365-366
Blind man, honored by rabbis, 185-186
Blindness, spiritual, 50
Bloodshed, see Murder
Body, comes from the Earth, 208-209, 251-252
Body, receives life force from soul, 390
Body, soul will be revealed in after resurrection, 301
Body chemistry, 354
Bone, *luz*, 303
Bone, Rabbi Yochanan carried with him, 327
Bones, pile of, 299, 303-304
Bribery, 285, 322 (note 724), 334, 360-361, 409
Bride and groom, 21, 53-54
Brothers, of Joseph, 75 (note 159), 81-84, 91, 108 (note 245), 238
Bulimia, 191
Burial, see also Funeral
Burial, in Land of Israel, 250-251, 260-264
Burial, of babies, 278-279
Burning, of Land of Israel, 249-253
Business, angels do not engage in, 64
Business, carried on by Joseph's brothers, 83
Business, dreams related to, 348-349
Business, Jews regarded as successful at, 16-18
Business, obligation to teach one's son a trade, 22
Businessman, 270 (note 591)
Butcher, who sold non-Kosher meat, 308-309
Buy low, sell high, 17-18
Cabbage, 164, 295
Cain, 73
Caleb, 317-318
Camel, 160-161, 164-165, 169-170, 196

Canaanite women, 404-405
Canaanites, 291-293
Candles, 369
Capricious behavior, 314-320
Carob tree, and Rabbi Shimon bar Yochai, 296, 301
Carob tree, of unusually large dimensions, 160
Cave, David approached Saul in, 104-105, 334 (note 750)
Cave, Obadiah hid prophets in, 99-100
Cave, of Pameas, 260 (note 552), 330-332
Cave, Rabbi Chiya and his sons buried in, 235-237
Cave, Rabbi Shimon bar Yochai hid in, 296-297, 300-302
Cave, thieves took Rabbi Pinchas ben Yair's donkey to, 195
Census, 386 (note 867)
Chaim of Volozhin, Rabbi, upset over financial loss, 328
Chametz, 26-27
Chaninah ben Tradyon, Rabbi, murdered by Romans, 83
Charity, see *Tzedakah*
Chavah, and snake, 77-78, 311-312, 315, 318
Chavah, sin of, see Adam, sin of
Chicken house, 153
Children, angel teaches *Torah* to prior to birth, 281
Children, at what point merit entrance to World to Come, 276-282
Children, captured by Gentiles, 391
Children, death of Rabbi Yochanan's, 327
Children, *Torah* study of, 231-233, 369
Chiya, Rabbi, and his sons as great as the Patriarchs, 237
Chiya, Rabbi, had spiritual traits similar to Joseph's, 237-239
Chiya, Rabbi, greatness of, 230-234
Chiya, Rabbi, tomb of, 235-239
Cinnamon, 160
Circumcision, 12 (note 28), 129 (note 294), 135, 277-279, 282
Citron, 208 (note 440)
Cloak, see Garment or Garments

Clothing, see Garment or Garments
Coffin, of Rabbi Huna the Exilarch, 223
Coffin, of Rabbi Meir to be placed on seashore, 260, 261 (note 553)
Coffin, of Rabbi Shmuel bar Rabbi Yitzchak, 54
Coffins, coming from outside Land of Israel, 262
Coffins, of Rabbi Chiya and his sons, 236 (note 494)
Coffins, placing clod of earth on, 262
Colleague, rising before, 398
Commerce, see Business
Community, doing something beneficial for when miracle occurs, 298-302
Community, surrendering one of its members to marauders, 321-323
Community, leaders of, see Leaders
Community, may not turn over one of its members to be harmed, 321-323
Community, merit of exceeds that of individual, 226, 408-409
Community, reward for serving, 173-174
Community, those who aid protected from harm, 27
Contractions, employed by Jerusalem *Talmud*, 1-2
Convert, rejected by Shammai but accepted by Hillel, 289
Convert, sins of are forgiven, 403-405
Converts, 12 (note 28), 67-68, 176-177, 210 (note 443)
Corpse, handling on Sabbath, 308
Corpse, hidden by Samaritan, 298-299
Corpses, of wicked burned, 248-249, 252-253
Corpses, raised by Rabbi Shimon bar Yochai, 298-303
Corpses, will be clothed with flesh at time of resurrection, 210 (note 442)
Court, Heavenly, see Heavenly Court
Covenant, 86, 146-147, 249
Covenant, of circumcision, 129, 135, 282
Covenant, of *Torah*, 282

Coveting one's neighbors belongings, 154-156
Cow, broke loose and was chased to Babylon, 370
Cubit, modern equivalent, 288 (note 636)
Curse, against those who curse Abraham, 120 (note 276)
Curse, converted to blessing by *Mitzvah* performance, 373-377
Curse, Earth cursed at time Adam and Chavah sinned, 205-207
Curse, had snake not been cursed it would have served people, 319
Curse, Nachum of Gamzu cursed himself, 185
Curse, tongue caused primordial snake to be cursed, 106
Curse, which will befall Jews if they disobey *Torah*, 269
Cursed be the man who teaches his son Greek philosophy, 24
Dama ben Nathina, 30-33, 39, 79
Dancing, before bride and groom, 53-56
Dancing, of King David, 55, 110-111
Daniel, 118-119, 121
Darkness, changing to light, 329
Darius, King, ministers jealous of Daniel, 118
Darius, King, tried to save Daniel, 119, 121
David, King, 141, 176, 177 (note 383), 224, 333 (note 743), 334, 387
David, King, contrasted to King Saul, 109-113
David, King, danced before Holy Ark, 55, 110-111
David, King, deposed by Absalom, 107
David, King, may have believed evil gossip, 107-113
David, King, victim of evil gossip, 80, 97-99, 103-105
David, King, settled conflicting claims to throne, 92-93
Death, angel of, See angel of death
Death, atones for sin, 257-258
Death, before a certain age, 383-391
Death, by choking, 15 (note 41)
Death, by kiss, 15 (note 41)
Death, caused by sin in general, 245 (note 511)
Death, caused by sin of Adam and Chavah, 244, 246

Death, caused by stinginess, 52
Death, elixir of, 314 (note 695)
Death, life after, see World to Come
Death, location of predetermined, 254-258
Death, *Mitzvah* performance after, 262, 273-275
Death, of Abner, 103-105
Death, of beggar, 182, 185, 191-192
Death, of children, 278-280
Death, of Jacob, 91
Death, of King David, 92
Death, of Levites, 384
Death, of Nabal, 388-389
Death, of Samuel, 383, 385
Death, of righteous, 277
Death, of sinners, 383-391
Death, of Ulla, 259, 264
Death, outside Land of Israel, 251, 262
Death, predicted in dream, 353-354
Death, premature, 383-391
Death, repentance before, 103, 220 (note 465)
Death, scholar whose garments have grease stain worthy of, 55
Death, student who rules before his master deserves, 287-288
Death, *Torah* study after, 273-275
Death, *Tzedakah* saves from, 14-16
Death penalty, 76, 322 (note 723)
Deception, by evil inclination, 311-312, 319
Deception, by Gibeonites, 292-293
Deception, related to evil gossip, 74-75, 77-78, 101
Democracy, 225-226
Demon, who haunts bathhouses (Antigeras), 331-332
Demons, God will protect from, 10
Demons, no longer prevalent today, 314, 359-360
Demons, repelled by *Mitzvah* of *Tzedakah*, 183
Desert, and Mount Yeshimon, 261

Desert, Generation of, 80, 386-387
Desert, King David fled to, 107
Desert, Sinai, 288
Design of universe, proof of God's existence, 207-208
Dinar, 31, 175-176, 182
Diocletian, 261, 330-333
Disciple, see Student(s)
Disobedience, of Adam and Chavah, 209
Disobedience, of King Saul, 109-113
Disobedience, to God, 145, 271, 274-275
Disobedience, to God causes famine, 162
Disobedience, to parents, 37
Disobedience, to the Torah publicly, 136
Divine Presence, goes into exile with Jews, 380-381
Divine Presence, King David asked God to remove it, 99
Divine Presence, no longer manifest among Israel, 390
Divine Presence, rose for Abraham, 400
Doctor, difference between good and bad, 327
Doeg, 80, 98, 103
Dog, protected its masters from eating contaminated food, 310
Dog, protected its masters from kidnaping, 310
Dog, son called father a, 40, 43
Dogs, lapped up blood of butcher, 308-309
Dogs, lapped up blood of King Ahab, 255
Dogs, lapped up blood of Naboth, 255
Dogs, symbolize evil inclination, 316
Dogs, symbolize rash behavior, 316-320
Dogs, vicious, 203-204
Donkey, 154, 190, 191, 406, 407
Donkey, of Rabbi Pinchas ben Yair, 195-196, 200-201
Donkey drivers, 159, 160
Doorframe, dream about, 351-352
Dove, prefers bitter food from God to sweet food from humans, 188-189

Dream, rabbi appeared in and named successor, 342-343
Dream, that coins hidden in certain place, 341-342, 347
Dream, weaver saw Rabbi Yossi support sky in, 230
Dream interpreters of Jerusalem, 356
Dreams, cannot be relied on for *Halachic* decisions, 342-343
Dreams, influenced by thoughts during day, 342
Dreams, interpretation of, 347-362
Drunk, 353
Dust, of Evil gossip, see Evil gossip
Dust, of the Land of Israel, 265-268
Dyers' Tower, 369
Earth, amassing wealth upon, 13
Earth, disobeyed God, 205-209
Earth, of the Land of Israel heavier than elsewhere, 265-268
Earth, punished because people sin, 205-209, 251
Earth, The refers to Land of Israel, 241
Earth, *Torah* is on Earth, not in Heaven, 65
Edom, 119, 165
Education, of children, 231-234, 238
Egypt, 64, 73, 134, 221, 222 (note 468), 238, 241, 356, 386
Egyptian army, 374
Elazar ben Arach, Rabbi, greatness of, 149-150
Elazar ben Azariah, appointed head of Sanhedrin, 224-225, 232 (note 489)
Elazar ben Shamua, Rabbi, aided Roman, 333
Elazar, Rabbi, bemoaned his fate, 411-412
Elder, unlearned, 399
Elder, who violates *Torah*, 388
Elderliness, death of, 383, 387
Elders, accepted *Tzedakah* only between *Rosh HaShannah* and *Yom Kippur*, 184
Elders, and Joshua, 292
Elders, of Batheira, 223
Elders, respect for, 47, 54, 386 (note 867), 394-403, 411

Eliezer ben Hyrcanus, Rabbi, retained his learning perfectly, 149
Elihoreph, 255-256
Elijah, decreed that no rain fall, 100
Elijah, predicted Ahab's death, 255-257
Elijah, received report from Obadiah, 99-100
Elijah, sole remaining prophet, 100
Elijah, visited Rabbi Yehoshua ben Levi, 321-322
Elijah, visited Rebbi, 228-229
Elisha ben Abuya, Rabbi, could not enter *Gehinnom*, 251
Embarrassment, see Shame
Enemies, make peace with one who pleases God, 309-310
Engagement, see Marriage
Esau, guardian angel of, 314 (note 695)
Esau, married daughter of Ishmael, 404-405
Esau, plotted against Jacob, 119, 121-122, 298
Ethrog, see Citron
Eve, see Chavah
Evil eye, 51-52
Evil gossip, accepted by King David, 107-113
Evil gossip, atoned for on *Yom Kippur*, 95-96
Evil gossip, caused destruction of Temple, 77
Evil gossip, compared to murder, 103, 106-107
Evil gossip, entails denying God's existence, 85-87
Evil gossip, leads to other sins, 79-80
Evil gossip, permitted against those who foment conflict, 89-91
Evil gossip, references to in *Torah*, 89-90
Evil gossip, sneaky form of, 93-94
Evil gossip, spoken against David, 97-99
Evil gossip, spoken by Joseph, 75 (note 159), 81-84
Evil gossip, spreading of, 115
Evil gossip, taint of, 90-91, 94-95, 109, 203
Evil gossip, worse than any other sin, 72, 74-80, 97-101, 133
Evil inclination, causes people to feel rebellious, 285-286
Evil inclination, converting to good, 375

Evil inclination, dog as symbol of, 316-317
Evil inclination, extent of, 313
Evil inclination, identical to primordial snake, 311-312
Evil inclination, King David destroyed his, 112-113
Evil inclination, starts in subtle ways, 78
Evil inclination, crooked ג symbol of, 319
Evil inclination, will be highly attenuated in future, 274
Evil thought, 115-116, 118-119, 120 (note 276), 125
Evildoers, see Wicked
Excision, 383-385, 388-391
Exile, atones for sin, 256
Exile, Babylonian, 251, 283-284, 286
Exile, caused by hypocritical flattery, 169 (note 368)
Exile, caused by sin, 245
Exile, Divine Presence goes into with Jews, 380-381
Exile, Egyptian, 238
Exile, for purposes of studying *Torah*, 231, 233, 238
Exile, Land of Israel burned during, 251
Exile, Land of Israel shrank due to, 371
Exile, means "revealed" or "uncovered," 313
Exile, of the Jewish people in general, 3, 280
Eyes, 185, 236, 384, 411, see also Eyesight
Eyes, of Rabbi Yossi became weak after observing Rabbi Chiya, 230
Eyes, visualized in dreams, 348
Eyesight, 47-48, 50-51, 150
Family, leaving for the sake of *Torah* study, 233
Fasting, to avert consequences of evil dream, 360
Father and mother, honoring, 30-43
Favoritism, God does not show, 285
Favoritism, Joseph showed to Benjamin, 108 (note 245)
Fear of Heaven, 139 (note 318), 225
Fences, breaching, 295
Fences, snakes frequent, 107, 295

Festivals, ascending to Jerusalem on, 152-155, 170, 248, 391
Fever, 309
Figs, 161-163, 188-189, 269, 369
Finger, mentioned in dream, 350-351
Finger, of God, 147
Fire, accompanied coffin of Rabbi Shmuel bar Rabbi Yitzchak, 54
Fire, descended to protect Rabbi Pinchas ben Yair, 199
Fire, one-sixtieth of *Gehinnom*, 251
Fire, preceded Rabbi Yehudah bar Chiya, 399 (note 894)
Fire, purifies body, 251-253
Fire, represents *Gehinnom*, 251-253
Fire, *Torah* compared to, 199 (note 418)
Fire, which breaks out on Sabbath, 340
Fire, words of God like, 147, 267
First, Israel is called, 203
First Cause, 68
First fruits, 394-395
Firstborn cattle and sheep, 284
Flattery, 169 (note 368)
Flax, 93, 232, 378-379
Flood, of the generation of Noah, 188, 251, 253, 364-366
Flood, swept away pious man's daughter, 200, 412
Forgotten teachings restored by rabbis, 8-11
Four species, used during *Sukkoth*, 233-234
Fox, 162
Free will, 139, 207
Friends, of groom, 270
Friends, reciting formula before to improve dream, 358
Friendship, caused Jews to overlook crowded conditions, 170
Friendship, of Antoninus and Rebbi, 212 (443)
Fruit, of the Tree of Knowledge, 77-78
Fruit trees, 206-209

Fruits, brought by sharecropper to Rabbi Yishmael ben Rabbi Yossi, 360-361

Fruits, fourth year, 363-365, 368-369

Fruits, immature, 363-365

Fruits, of Sabbatical year, 363-364

Fruits, of the Land of Israel, 159-165, 171

Fruits, of the Messianic era, 269-271, 279

Funeral, attending is an act of kindness, 19-20

Funeral, of Rabbi Huna the Exilarch, 235-237

Funeral, of Rebbi, 219-220

Funeral, rising before procession, 395

Funeral, setting aside *Torah* study to attend, 54

Garlic, 310, 311 (note 682)

Garment, David cut corner of Saul's, 105-106, 334 (note 750)

Garment, in dream, 349 (note 770)

Garment, in Hebrew means betrayal, 124

Garment, stories are for truths of *Torah*, 5

Garments, for burial, 7 (note 13), 210-217

Garments, Joseph gave his brothers, 108 (note 243)

Garments, *Mitzvoth* are for the soul, 62

Garments, of Mipibosheth, 108

Garments, of Rabbi Shimon bar Yochai, 296

Garments, Rabbi Elazar ben Shamua provided Roman, 333

Garments, Rabbi Zera did not remove when crossing Jordan, 265

Garments, torn for mourning, 218, 219

Garments, used by Gibeonites to fool Jews, 292

Garments, will be restored at time of resurrection, 210-217

Garments, worn by rabbis and judges, 55, 407 (note 911)

Garments, worn in bathhouse, 229 (note 486)

Gath, 334

Gehinnom, 16 (note 44), 40, 42, 138, 214, 251-252, 264, 337 (note 754), 389

Gematriah, see Numerical value

Generosity, 52, 412, 414

Gentile neighbors, 153
Gentiles, brought into Land of Israel by Assyrians, 249
Gentiles, child raised among, 391
Gentiles, contaminated because did not receive the *Torah*, 318
Gentiles, conversion of, 67-68, 289
Gentiles, good deeds of, 118-122
Gentiles, have used *Torah* to invent their own religions, 144-146
Gentiles, judging favorably, 120
Gentiles, placed restrictions on Jews, 16-18
Gentiles, recognize importance of certain *Mitzvoth*, 79
Gentiles, righteous, 120 (note 276), 281 (note 622), 400 (note 896)
Gentiles, studying works of, 26
Gentiles, threats against Jews, 321-323
Gentiles, who attempted to rob Jewish neighbors, 153-155
Gentiles, wicked, 120-121
Gibeonites, 292-293
Ginai River, split for Rabbi Pinchas ben Yair, 198, 202
Girgashites, 291-292
Goat, 82, 160, 161
God, honored Abraham, 400-401
God, imitating ways of, 7-8, 333 (note 743), 381
God, proof of existence, 207-208
God's existence, denial of, 85-87
God's Name, desecration of, 76, 136
God's Name, spitting when mentioning, 134-135 (note 304)
God's Name, resemblance to, 317
Gog and Magog, 270-271
Golden calf, 138
Good thought, 115-116, 118, 120
Goslings, 46, 48, 51
Gossip, see Evil Gossip
Grace after meals, 188, 285-286
Grace of God, 139-140, 189, 379

Grape cluster, unusually large
Grapevine, 269, 352
Grass, 205-207, 216 (note 460), 269, 390 (note 879)
Grasshoppers, 38
Greed, see stinginess
Greek, philosophy and language, 22-28
Greek and Roman mythology, 68
Groom, 270, see also Bride and Groom
Groom, sins forgiven when married, 403-404
Gueber, 197 note (414), 332
Hadrian, 67
Haifa, 288, 397
Halachah, deciding in front of teacher forbidden, 287-290
Halachah, follows majority opinion, 295
Haman, 127
Hammer, 267
Hasmonean kings, 12 (note 28), 24, 168
Hatred, 51, 77 (note 162), 167-169
Heart, all limbs dependent upon, 326, 329
Heart, dependent upon purse, 326, 329
Heart, Israel camped at Mount Sinai with one, 202
Heart, Holy One, Blessed be He, desires, 41
Heathens, see Gentiles
Heaven, see also World to Come
Heaven, 169 (note 369), 174, 358, 390 (note 879)
Heaven, acting for sake of, 226, 232, 234, 316 (note 702), 408-409
Heaven, all gates of closed except those of mistreatment, 188
Heaven, amassing wealth in, 13
Heaven, and evil gossip, 85, 107
Heaven, bestows mercy upon those who are merciful, 405
Heaven, charity seen from, 13
Heaven, commands snakes to bite, 107
Heaven, death at hands of, 389-390

Heaven, directing one's heart to, 41
Heaven, fear of, 139 (note 318), 225
Heaven, fire from, 199
Heaven, *Hashem* looks from, 373
Heaven, Moses ascended to, 64-65
Heaven, not proper place for *Torah* to remain, 65
Heaven, statement made in concerning Rabbi Huna the Exilarch, 237
Heaven, *Torah* given from, 135
Heaven, whatever exists on Earth has parallel in, 258
Heaven, will of, 297
Heavens, God is exalted above, 99
Heavenly academy, 231
Heavenly Court, 191
Heavenly Court, does not punish before age twenty, 384
Heavenly voice, 54, 219-220, 236 (note 494), 297
Helen, Queen, 12 (note 28)
Hell, see *Gehinnom*
Heretic, 125, 134, 251, 389
Heretical books, 134
High Priest, 374-376, 397
High Priest's breastplate, 30
Hillel the Elder, accepted non-Jew who wished to convert, 289
Hillel the Elder, treated beggar well, 177
Holocaust, 121
Holiness, of *Torah*, 4-5
Holiness, one increases but does not decrease, 401
Holiness, spirit of, 299
Holy Ark, King David danced before, 55, 110-111
Holy Ark, took up no space, 371
Holy of Holies, 384
Homily or Homilies, see *Aggadoth*
Honey, 162, 163-164, 189, 373
Honoring father and mother, 30-43

Horse, Hillel the Elder brought for beggar, 177

Horseradish, 350

Huldah, 357

Humiliation, see Shame

Humility, 140

Humility, of Joshua, 317-318

Humility, of King Saul, 317-318

Humility, of Rabbi Yochanan, 212-213

Humility, of Rebbi, 222-223

Humility, required for *Torah* study, 313

Hypocrisy, 165-170

Hypocrisy, Rabbi Yoshayah sought to avoid, 212-213

Hypocrites, Pharisees symbol of, 176

Hyrcanus, 24, 168

Idol, 30, 407

Idolatry, 72-73, 76-77, 80, 115, 132, 166, 293

Idolatry, contrasted to Judaism, 66-68

Idolatry, introduced by Jeroboam, 249

Idolatry, not as bad as slander, 99-101

Idolatry, thoughts of, 125

Imma Shalom, 288

Immature fruits, 363, 365

Impurity, ritual, 299-300

Impurity, spiritual, 314

Interpreter, 407-408

Isaac, 121 (see also Patriarchs)

Isaac, birth of, 357

Isaac, disapproved of Esau's wives, 404-405

Isaac, sacrifice of, 187

Isabel, 99

Ishmael, 201

Ishmaelites, 145 (note 330)

Israel, all responsible for one another, 117 (note 268)

Israel, Land of, acquired through hardship, 263-264

Israel, Land of, air of makes one smart, 263
Israel, Land of, burial in, 235, 241-247, 249-253, 259-264
Israel, Land of, burned, 249-253
Israel, Land of, certain *Mitzvoth* only performed in, 64, 283-284, 286, 295, 368
Israel, Land of, conquest of, 291-293
Israel, Land of, dimensions of, 370-372
Israel, Land of, division of when Jews arrived, 70, 258
Israel, Land of, produce of, 159-171
Israel, Land of, rabbis' affection for, 265-268
Israel, Land of, resurrection and, 241-247, 264
Israel, Land of, Shimon bar Vava traveled to, 411
Israel, Land of, special qualities withdrawn when Jews exiled from, 370-372
Israel, Land of, spies slandered, 80, 317, 386
Israel, Land of, stones and earth weigh more than elsewhere, 265-268
Israel, Land of, surrounded by seven seas, 260-261, 264
Israel, Land of, *Torah* study and, 263-264, 267-268
Israel, Land of, vulnerable when Jews ascend to Jerusalem, 152-155
Israel, Land of, wealthy people of, 362 (note 810)
Israel, Land of, women protected by Rebbi's merit, 222, 229
Jacob, 91, 350 (see also Patriarchs)
Jacob, and Esau, 119, 121, 298
Jacob, established markets in Shechem, 298
Jacob, heard evil reports from Joseph, 84
Jacob, honesty of, 168
Jacob, lived in Egypt seventeen years, 221
Jacob, retrieved earthenware vessels, 327 (note 734)
Jacob, wished to be buried in Land of Israel, 241-242, 244, 246-247
Jehoiakim, 135-136
Jeremiah, 357

Jeroboam, King, 245, 248-249, 252-253
Jerusalem, ascending to for festivals, 152-155, 170, 248, 391
Jerusalem, bringing fruits to, 341, 363 (note 811), 368-369, 394
Jerusalem, bringing Holy Ark to, 55, 110
Jerusalem, celestial, 258, 264
Jerusalem, converts living in, 176-177
Jerusalem, distance to border of Land of Israel, 372
Jerusalem, distance to Sepphoris, 369 (note 824)
Jerusalem, dream interpreters in, 356
Jerusalem, miracles in, 170
Jerusalem, spiritual, 258, 264
Jerusalem, will be decorated with huge jewels, 280
Jerusalem, word of the Lord shall go forth from, 263
Jewel, lost by Saracen king, 197-198
Jewel, sent by Artebon to Rebbi, 66-70
Jewel, swallowed by mouse, 197-198
Jewels, *Torah* study more valuable than, 60
Jewels, will decorate Jerusalem in future, 280
Joab, 98 (note 217), 104
Jordan River, 69-70, 260 (note 551), 265, 293, 330
Joseph, buried with Rabbi Chiya, 236-238
Joseph, interpreted dreams, 352, 355, 356, 359
Joseph, Potiphar's wife attempted to seduce, 73
Joseph, showed favoritism towards Benjamin, 108 (note 245)
Joseph, spoke evil gossip about his brothers, 75 (note 159), 81-84
Joseph, swore to bury Jacob in the Land of Israel, 240-241
Joseph, was implored to excuse his brothers, 91
Joshua, as disciple of Moses, 9
Joshua, exceedingly humble, 317
Joshua, led Jews into Land of Israel, 283, 291-293
Josiah, King, 136, 357
Jubilee, 258
Kappadokia, 347

Killing, see Murder
Kindness, compared to *Tzedakah*, 19-21
Kindness, God created world as object for His, 189
King, God as, 67, 161
King, must act strictly according to the *Torah*, 112
King, must maintain dignity of his office, 111
King, of Persia/Medea note allowed to nullify decrees, 121
King, of Saracen, 197-198
King, Rav Shesheth predicted arrival of his entourage, 50
King, rebel against, 93
Kings, three who will not be resurrected, 245-246
Klipah, 167
Kohanim, 10, 283, 394
Kohanim, blessings of, 285, 358, 361-362
Kohanim, gifts for, 284, 296 (note 649)
Kohanim, hats of, 198 (note 415)
Kohanim, must not relinquish right to be called up first to *Torah*, 225 (note 482)
Kohanim, of Nob killed by King Saul, 98, 103, 106
Kohanim, purifying Tiberias for, 298-300
Kohathi, 384
Kohen Gadol, see High Priest
Kosher animals, 165
Kosher food, 36, 38
Laban, 298
Lambs, 24, 161, 164, 168-170 and see also Sheep
Land of Israel, See Israel, Land of
Lashon Hara, see Evil Gossip
Laughter, of angel of death, 255
Laughter, of Sarah, 90-91
Laundryman, 219-220
Leaders, see also Rabbis
Leaders, appointment of, 172, 222-226

Leaders, community must be consulted about selection of, 225-226

Leaders, difficulties of, 173-174

Leaders, disobedience to *Torah* extremely detrimental, 136

Leaders, may need to study non-Jewish philosophies, 25-27

Leaders, of each generation must be obeyed, 11

Leaders, should be devoted to the people, 380-381, 408-409

Leaders, who purchase their positions, 406-409

Ledger, 349

Leg, seen in dream, 353

Legs, ensure that person will die where destined, 254-258

Levites, 10, 283, 284, 394

Levites, lifespan of, 384-385

Levites, tithes of, 176-177, 341, 376

Lifespan, 16, 383-388

Lineage, see Ancestry

Lion, 106

Lions, 98-99, 121, 153

Lizard, 244-245 (note 511)

Locusts, 163-164

Loophole, 142

Love, for fellow Jews, 170

Love, for God, 116, 126

Love, for Jerusalem, 170

Love, for Mitzvoth, 286, 306

Love, for Rebbi, 218

Love, for *Torah*, 148

Love, repentance out of, 126, 201 (note 421)

Luck, 410-412

Lupines, 298, 302-303

Mahalul, 369

Mahalath, 404

Mar Zutra, prayers answered for others but not for himself, 379

Marriage, causes atonement, 404-405

Marriage, feast, 270
Marriage, of Rabbi Akiva's daughter, 14
Marriage, selling *Torah* scroll to finance, 413
Mazal, 410-412
Menasseh, 245
Merit, has principal and has proceeds, 114
Merits, relative to sins, 129
Messenger, announced coming of those bearing first fruits, 394
Messenger, of Diocletian, 331
Messengers, Abner sent to King David, 104
Messengers, Rebbi sent to appease Rabbi Pinchas ben Yair, 199
Messiah, arrival of not miraculous event, 245
Messiah, era of, 241
Messiah, generation preceding advent of, 316-317
Messiah, miracles and, 271-272
Messiah, nations of world will attack Jews after arrival of, 271
Messiah, numerical equivalent of snake, 319 (note 719)
Messiah, will be a descendent of Nahshon, 319
Messiah, would come if Rabbi Chiya and his sons prayed together, 231
Messianic era, evil will change to good, 319
Messianic era, fruits of 270
Messianic era, miracles during, 272
Messianic era, not proper topic of speculation, 212, 278
Messianic era, Romans will make false claims during, 166
Messianic era, will entail suffering, 247
Metatron, 282 (note 625)
Mezuzah, 66-67, 266, 398
Mice, 197, 222
Michal (daughter of King Saul), 55, 80, 110-111
Milk, death resembling drawing hair from, 15 (note 41)
Milk, leaving uncovered, 306-320
Milk and honey, 161, 373
Mill, binding one's father to, 40-41

Minors, see Children
Mipibosheth, 107-108, 112
Miracle, cannot be performed out of nothing, 302
Miracle, causes person's merits to diminish, 299, 354, 379
Miracle, deserving, 202-203
Miracle, flax and wine did not spoil, 379
Miracle, God will reconstitute clothing at time of resurrection, 211
Miracle, Holy Ark took up no space, 371
Miracle, no one ever complained of lack of space in Jerusalem, 170
Miracle, performed by Antigeras, 332
Miracle, performed by Rabbi Shimon bar Yochai, 302-303
Miracle, pregnant women did not miscarry, 222
Miracle, resurrection not a, 244, 245 (note 512)
Miracle, return to Land of Israel not a, 245
Miracles, at time of Rebbi's funeral, 219
Miracles, during Messianic era, 271-272
Miracles, forbidden to rely upon, 309, 316
Miracles, Nachum Ish Gamzu accustomed to, 191
Miriam, and evil gossip, 75
Miriam, well of, 261
Mishnah, of the pious, 322
Mitzvah, converted to sin, 42-43
Mitzvah, observing just one saves from *Gehinnom,* 214
Mitzvoth, after death, 262, 273-275
Mitzvoth, beautifying, 7-8
Mitzvoth, between person and God, 376-377
Mitzvoth, between person and his or her fellows, 376-377
Mitzvoth, compared to *Torah* study, 59-65
Mitzvoth, delaying, 187
Mitzvoth, diligent go early to do, 187
Mitzvoth, easiest and most difficult, 44-50
Mitzvoth, greatness of those who perform, 373-377

Mitzvoth, means for "earning" reward, 189
Mitzvoth, motives for performing, 408-409
Mitzvoth, number of provides Jews excuse for lapses in observance, 141-142
Mitzvoth, performed for the sake of Heaven, 233-234
Mitzvoth, reward for commensurate with effort, 49-50
Mitzvoth, reward for not known, 44-50
Mitzvoth, scholar excused from, 45 (note 93)
Mitzvoth, voluntary observance of, 82-84, 281-284
Money, appointment of leaders on account of, 406-409
Mount Sinai, 8, 9, 147, 148, 151, 202, 290, 318, 399
Moses, ascended to Heaven, 64-65
Moses, as teacher of Joshua, 9
Moses, God angry with, 174
Moses, Nadab and Abihu ruled in his presence, 287
Moses, people rose for, 397
Moses, pleads on behalf of Israel, 73, 138
Moses, prayed for Joshua, 317
Moses, served as High Priest, 397
Moses, spies incited rebellion against, 318
Moses, subject of gossip, 75, 397, 402
Moses, took leave of the Jewish people, 70-71
Mules, of Rebbi, 198-199, 204
Munbaz, King, 12-14, 17-18
Murder, as cardinal sin, 72-74, 76-77, 115, 133, 166
Murder, by Nazis, 121
Murder, David suspected of plotting by King Saul, 105-106, 111-112
Murder, of inhabitants of, 112
Murder, of Jew, 350
Murder, of Naboth, 257
Murder, of prophets by Ahab and Isabel, 99-100
Murder, of Rabbi Chanina ben Tradyon, 83
Murder, planning of, 119, 121

Murder, related to evil gossip, 80, 103, 107
Murder, related to sexual immorality, 308
Murder, revealed by dream, 350
Murder, shaming one's fellow comparable to, 188
Murder, suicide a form of, 220
Murder, threat against the Terror of the Kingdom, 326
Mustard, 162-163
Mythology, Greek and Roman, 68
Nabal, 388-389
Naboth, 254-257
Nachum of Gamzu, 185, 190-192
Nadab and Abihu, 287
Nahshon ben Aminadab, 315, 319
Nazi war criminals, 121
Nebuchadnezzar, King, 165
Nechemiah, Rabbi, and death of beggar, 184-185
Nikkai, 369
Nineveh, 357
Nissan, 353-354
Noah, 188, 253
Noahide commandments, 292
Nob, priests of, 98, 103, 106, 112
Non-Jews, see Gentiles
Numerical value, 269, 271 (note 593), 301, 312 (note 688), 319 (note 719), 387
Obadiah, hid prophets, 99-100
Obadiah, prophesied destruction of Edom, 119
Obedience, to God, 51, 109-113, 145, 312
Obedience, to God by the Earth, 205-209
Obedience, to parents, 37
Obedience, to the law, 121
Obedience, to the rabbis, 10-11, 286
Obedience, to the *Torah*, 32-33, 136, 318-319, 375-376
Olive, seen in dream, 348

Olive branch, in beak of dove, 189
Olive branches, seen in dream, 347-348
Olive oil, seen in dream, 348
Olive oil, used to anoint King and High Priest, 375
Olive size, 285
Olive trees, 269, 374
Omen, ill, 191-192
Onkelos, 67
Oral *Torah*, consists of two parts, 148
Oral *Torah*, contrasted to Written *Torah*, 144-151, 289
Oral *Torah*, prohibition against writing down, 339-340
Orphans, 176, 177, 232
Outlaw, see Theft
Ovens, 348
Ox, 154, 161
Pameas, cave which is source for Jordan River, 260 (note 552), 330-332
Paradise, see World to Come
Pashchor, 250
Passover, see *Pesach*
Patriarchs, see also Ancestors
Patriarchs, God swore that Land of Israel would belong to, 245
Patriarchs, observed *Torah* voluntarily, 82-83
Patriarchs, Rabbi Chiya and his sons as great as, 237
Pauper, see Beggar
Peace, creating, 53, 57-58, 69-70, 79, 90-91
Peace, offered by Joshua to Canaanites, 291-293
Peace, with one's natural enemies, 309-310
Peach, 159
Peddler, 90
Penitents, greater than the completely righteous, 127-128
Penitents, nothing stands in way of, 132
Persian government, 118, 121
Persian miles, 168, 372

Pesach, 26, 106, 152, 373
Pharaoh's butler, 352
Pharisees, 167, 176
Philosophy, non-Jewish, 22-28
Phinehas, 167, 316 (note 702)
Piety, false, 94, 167, 176, 312, 313-314, 322
Pig, 24, 165, 168
Pigkeeper, 330, 332, 335
Pinchas ben Yair, Rabbi, and mice, 197-198
Pinchas ben Yair, Rabbi, donkey of, 195-196, 200-201
Pinchas ben Yair, Rabbi, split Ginai River, 198, 202-204
Piety, defined, 313-314
Pious, see also Righteous
Pious person, Rabbi Yossi HaKohen was, 149
Pious person, who dug pits for wayfarers, 199-200
Pious person, who ridiculed danger of exposed wine, 309, 313-314
Poor people, see Beggars
Potiphar's wife, 73
Prayer, and Rabbi Shimon bar Yochai, 296
Prayer, anticipating results of, 109
Prayer, before entering bathhouse, 297 (note 651)
Prayer, during priestly blessings, 358, 361
Prayer, for others cause supplicant's prayers to be answered first, 405
Prayer, for Rabbi Elazar, 173
Prayer, for sick, 134
Prayer, interruption of, 398
Prayer, of blind man, 186
Prayer, of Daniel, 118-119, 121
Prayer, of Hannah, 385
Prayer, of hypocritical people, 166
Prayer, of Jewish farmers, 373
Prayer, of Moses, 138, 317

Prayer, of Rabbi Chiya and his sons, 231
Prayer, of Rabbi Yochanan for bandits, 325
Prayer, of Rabbi Zera to forget his learning, 3 (note 4)
Prayer, of thief, 366
Prayer, Rabbi Tarfon's mother requested of rabbis, 35
Prayer, that one not fall prey to speaking evil gossip, 95
Prayers, of Jews at Reed Sea, 202
Prayers, of righteous, 273, 379-381
Predestination, 254-258, 410-412
President, of the Jewish people, 400, 403-404, 407
President, of the *Sanhedrin*, 25, 223-224, 232 (note 489)
Priests, Jewish, see *Kohanim*
Priests, Zoroastrian, 197 (note 414), 332 (note 744)
Principal, of good deeds, 53, 69-71, 114, 115 (note 263)
Principal, of sin, 72, 114, 129-130
Prophecy, 50, 242, 250, 270, 299
Prophecy, related to dreams, 355-360
Prophecy, no longer exists, 314
Prophecy, of Elijah, 256
Prophecy, of Moses, 75
Prophet, Rabbi Eliezer denied being, 288
Prophetic vision, called "sight" in *Tanach*, 50
Prophetic vision, of Jews at Mount Sinai, 358
Prophetic vision, of Zachariah, 374
Prophets, false sent to King Ahab, 255
Prophets, female are more merciful, 357
Prophets, ignored by Israel, 144
Prophets, murdered by King Ahab and Isabel, 99-100
Prophets, removal of a ring greater than, 127
Pruning shears, 338
Punishment, according to severity of sin, 76
Punishment, by untimely death, 383-391
Punishment, converted to reward, 377
Punishment, fear of, 126

Punishment, for failing to object to wrongdoing, 174
Punishment, for idolatrous thoughts, 125
Punishment, held off if repentance possible, 166
Punishment, in World to Come, 42, 73, 125-126, 130-131, 132, 136, 337, 389
Punishment, measure for measure, 48, 82, 257
Punishment, of Miriam, 75
Punishment, of pious man who mocked prohibition against consuming exposed wine, 309, 316
Punishment, of those who mocked Rabbi Shimon bar Yochai, 298-299, 303-304
Pupil, see Student(s)
Rabashakeh, 292
Rabbi, buying position as, 406-409
Rabbi, selecting successor for, 343
Rabbinical decrees, 286
Rabbinical student, see Student(s)
Rabbis, see also Leaders
Rabbis, see also *Torah* scholars
Rabbis, could tell they were in Land of Israel by weight of stones, 265-268
Rabbis, denigration of, 134 (note 302), 332 (note 744)
Rabbis, dignity of, 53-56
Rabbis, excused from *Mitzvah* performance, 45 (note 93)
Rabbis, have ability to reconstruct forgotten teachings, 8-11
Rabbis, must be relied on to transmit tradition, 289-290
Rabbis, of each generation must be obeyed, 11
Rabbis, reciting their teachings causes their lips to move in grave, 274 (note 601)
Rabbis, should build fence around the *Torah*, 285-286, 296
Radishes, harvested just after Sabbatical year, 161
Rafter, 347
Rain, Elijah decreed stopping of, 100
Rav, flax ruined by worm infestation, 378-379

Rav, nephew of Rabbi Chiya, 224, 378 (note 843)
Rebbi, death of, 218-219
Rebbi, exceedingly humble, 222-223
Rebbi, offended by Rabbi Chiya, 223-244, 228-229
Rebbi, pained by teeth, 222, 228
Rebbi, punished for insensitivity to calf, 222
Red heifer, 31-33
Reed Sea, 202, 315
Rehoboam, 248
Reincarnation, 49, (note 105), 131, 246-247
Reincarnation of Ishmael, 201
Repentance, averts punishment, 337
Repentance, by wicked converts their sins to good, 124, 126-128
Repentance, causes redemption, 381
Repentance, difficult for hypocrites, 101, 166-167
Repentance, difficult for idolaters, 115
Repentance, difficult for those who speak evil gossip, 101, 79
Repentance, erases sin, 76, 142
Repentance, Nabal failed to repent, 389
Repentance, not necessary for *Yom Kippur* to cause atonement, 132 (note 300)
Repentance, not possible for suicide, 220 (note 465)
Repentance, nothing stands in way of, 132
Repentance, of Esau, 405
Repentance, of Ishmael, 201 (note 421)
Repentance, of Jews saves their leaders, 381
Repentance, of King Saul, 103
Repentance, of Rabbi Shimon ben Lakish, 329
Repentance, out of fear, 201 (note 421)
Repentance, possibility of averts punishment, 166-167
Repentance, Ten Days of, 388-389
Resh Lakish, risked life to save Rabbi Immi, 325
Resh Lakish, risked life to save Rabbi Yochanan's money, 326, 328-329

Resurrection, clothing of dead will be restored at time of, 210-215

Resurrection, denial of, 125, 134, 303

Resurrection, faith in, 212

Resurrection, fundamental doctrine of Judaism, 303

Resurrection, Land of Israel and, 241-246, 249, 264

Resurrection, not a miracle, 244-245

Resurrection, not directly mentioned in *Torah*, 243

Resurrection, of babies, 276-282

Resurrection, Rabbi Shimon bar Yochai had experience similar to, 301-303

Resurrection, reincarnation and, 246

Resurrection, sun will shine brighter at time of, 302

Resurrection, *Torah* scholars will continue studies after, 273-274

Resurrection, wicked merit after punishment, 249, 252

Reward, see also World to Come and Resurrection

Reward, commensurate with effort, 20, 128

Reward, for acts of kindness, 20-21, 53

Reward, for giving charity, 21, 338

Reward, for honoring parents, 31-33

Reward, for learning *Torah* in hostile environment, 233

Reward, for *Mitzvah* does not exist in this world, 130, 271

Reward, for *Mitzvoth* not known, 48-49, 45-50

Reward, for preparation to do *Mitzvah*, 115 (note 263)

Reward, for public service, 173-174

Reward, granted even if *Mitzvah* planned but not performed, 115-117

Reward, greater for those commanded, 286

Reward, measure for measure, 20, 82, 281, 375

Reward, of communal leaders, 173-174

Reward, of Dama ben Nathina, 31-33

Reward, of Girgashites, 292

Reward, of *Mitzvah* contrasted to punishment for sin, 315

Reward, of Rabbi Shimon bar Yochai kept intact, 300
Reward, of wicked, 129-131
Reward, reduced when miracle performed, 299-300
Reward, Vilna Gaon did not wish to receive for performing *Mitzvoth*, 233-234
Rich, *Mitzvah* to act kindly towards, 19, 21
Rich, of the Land of Israel, 362 (note 810)
Rich, one who is happy with what he has is, 170 (note 372)
Rich, person of rich background forced to accept charity, 177-178, 184
Rich, who buy rabbinical positions should not be recognized, 406-409
Righteous ancestors of the Jewish people, 281
Righteous brothers and sisters who have never sinned, 280
Righteous non-Jews, 121 (note 276), 281 (note 622), 400 (note 896)
Righteous, and miracles, 302
Righteous, cannot stand in place of penitent, 127-128
Righteous, death of, 277, 388
Righteous, do not need God's grace to prosper, 378-379
Righteous, have free will, 139-140
Righteous, held to higher standard than others, 84, 192-193
Righteous, may be punished in this world rather than the next, 132
Righteous, offspring of are good deeds, 199 (note 418)
Righteous, prayers answered for others but not for themselves, 379-381
Righteous, recognize God's goodness, 337
Righteous, reward of, 251, 271-272, 280, 389 (note 877)
Righteous, souls of sacrificed, 169 (note 369)
Righteous, use material things to serve *Hashem*, 327
Righteous, who are buried inside the Land of Israel, 250 (note 528)
Righteous, who are buried outside Land of Israel, 242, 244

Righteous, will feel pleasure when evil is defeated, 271
Righteous, will pray and study *Torah* after resurrection, 273-275
Righteous, will rise from the dead dressed in white, 211, 215
Righteous person, who turns to evil, 123-126
Ritual fringes, 211 (note 446), 213-216
Robbery, see Theft
Rock, see also Stone
Rock, where well of Miriam located, 261
Rolling underground at time of resurrection, 242-247
Roman, aided by Rabbi Elazar ben Shamua, 333
Roman, one should not humiliate, 332
Roman mythology, 68
Romans, see also Rome
Romans, murdered Rabbi Chanina ben Tradyon, 83
Romans, persecuted Rabbi Shimon bar Yochai, 296
Rome, 67, 107, 370
Rome, hypocrisy of, 165-166
Rome, symbolized by pig, 165, 168-169
Rosh HaShannah, 161, 162, 184, 389
Rules, for calculating numerical values, 312 (note 688)
Rules, for interpreting *Torah*, 144, 148
Ruth, 224
Sabbath, ascending to the Temple prior to, 369
Sabbath, ascending to the Temple to spend, 369
Sabbath, desecration of, 388, 390
Sabbath, Diocletian ordered rabbis to appear immediately after, 330-332
Sabbath, drinking wine on eve of, 308
Sabbath, fasting on, 360
Sabbath, fire breaking out on, 340
Sabbath, Michael sacrifices souls of righteous on eve of, 169 (note 369)
Sabbath, observance meaningless to angels, 64
Sabbath, observance takes priority over honoring parents, 37

Sabbath, "Observe" and "Remember" uttered simultaneously, 358

Sabbath, protecting corpse on, 309 (note 677)

Sabbath, Rabbi Yannai awaited son-in-law on eve of, 399

Sabbath, Rebbi buried on eve of, 219

Sabbath, utensils may not be repaired on, 35

Sabbatical cycle, 175, 341, 363, 373

Sabbatical year, 161-162, 295-296, 363

Sacrifice, of Isaac, 187

Sacrifice, of red heifer, 31 (note 68), 32

Sacrifices, King Saul saved Amalekite flocks for, 110

Sacrifices, must be offered on earthen altar, 252

Sacrifices, of hypocrites, 166

Sacrifices, two daily *Tamid*, 160-161, 164

Saddle, 406-407

Sages, see Rabbis

Samaritan, played trick on Rabbi Shimon bar Yochai, 298-299, 304

Samaritan, played trick on Rabbi Yishmael ben Rabbi Yossi, 351

Samaritans, during time when Land of Israel was burning, 249-250

Samuel, 104

Samuel, declared that King Saul would not establish dynasty, 111, 317-318

Samuel, died at age fifty-two, 383, 385

Samuel, died just before Nabal, 388

Samuel, King Saul disobeyed him, 109-110

Sanhedrin, 8, 25, 221 (note 468), 223-224, 232 (note 489)

Saracen, king of, 197

Sarah, 90-91

Satan, 312 (note 688), 319-320, 399 (note 895)

Saul, King, 55, 80, 98-99, 103-105, 107, 109-113, 317, 334, 404

Scale, for "weighing" sages, 149

Scales of justice, 81-82, 139-141
Scholars, see Rabbis
Scribe, mocked Rabbi Shimon bar Yochai, 299, 304
Scribes, of King Solomon, 255-256
Scribes, who made copies of *Talmud*, 1
Sea, ritual fringes remind wearer of, 216
Seas, surround Land of Israel, 260-261, 264
Secret matters, 241-243
Secretary, 255 (note 540)
Serpent, see Snake
Sexual immorality, as cardinal sin, 72-73, 76-77, 115, 132
Sexual immorality, prevalence of, 109
Sexual immorality, related to evil gossip, 80
Shame, at time of resurrection, 211-212
Shame, prevents people from learning, 315
Shaming beggars, 183, 188-190
Shaming people publicly, 188
Shammai, rejected non-Jew who wished to convert, 289
Sharecropper, 159, 360
Sharing, 171-172
Shavuoth, 152
Shechem, 298
Sheep, see also Lambs
Sheep, among seventy wolves, 169
Sheep, firstborn, 284
Sheep, of Amalekites, 110
Shema, 61, 187, 396, 398
Shesheth, Rav, predicted arrival of king's entourage, 50
Shimon bar Yochai, Rabbi, hid in cave, 296-297, 300-302
Shimon bar Yochai, Rabbi, purified Tiberias, 297-300, 302-303
Shimon ben Lakish, Rabbi, see Resh Lakish
Shimon bar Vava, Rabbi, 410-412
Ship, sank and stranded Roman, 333
Shmuel, fled from his father, 181

Shroud, 325
Sight, see Eyesight
Sign, Kosher, 165
Sign, of blessing, 413
Sign, of Divine displeasure, 191-192
Sin, principal of, 72, 114, 129-130
Sinai, Mount, see Mount Sinai
Sinai desert, 288
Sins, accidental, 314, 363, 390-391
Sins, atoned by burning of Land of Israel, 249-253
Sins, caused by spirit of folly, 314-315
Sins, less or more than merits, 129
Sins, minor, 132
Sisra, 311
Slander, see Evil gossip
Slave, Hillel provided beggar with, 177
Slave, Joseph was to Potiphar, 73, 82, 91
Slave, Ziba to Mipibosheth, 107
Slaves, Jacob's sons called their brothers, 81-82
Slaves, Jews in Egypt were, 64, 356-357
Snake, and evil gossip, 77-79, 107
Snake, and Rabbi Akiva's daughter, 14
Snake, bites those who violate rulings of sages, 295
Snake, bites to punish those who speak evil gossip, 107
Snake, prevented injury, 310
Snake, thwarted intruders, 153
Snake, tongue of, 106
Snake, which seduced Adam and Chavah, 77-79, 207, 295 (note 646), 311-312, 318-319
Snakes, liable to drink from uncovered liquids, 306-320
Snakes, symbolize rash behavior, 315-316
Snakes, will eventually be helpful, 320-321
Sodom and Gomorrah, 357, 374
Soldiers, of Abner and Joab, 104

Soldiers, of Hyrcanus and Aristobolus, 24, 168
Soldiers, of King Saul, 105, 317
Soldiers, sent to capture Onkelos, 67
Solomon, King, and angel of death, 255-256
Solomon, King, quoted, 333, 353
Solomon, King, rulership challenged, 92-93
Solomon, King's son, 248
Sons, receive part of soul from father, 237 (note 496)
Sons, should inherit leadership positions from fathers, 225
Sons, who are *Torah* scholars, 338
Sorcerer, 197
Sorcerers' books, 336, 340
Soul, ascends to upper spiritual realms during sleep, 354
Soul, damaged by sin, 390
Soul, father transmits to son, 237 (note 496)
Soul, giving up in unclean land, 260
Soul, *Mitzvoth* are garments for, 62
Soul, purified by reincarnation, 49 (note 103)
Soul, purified in *Gehinnom*, 251, 389
Soul, source is in Heaven, 208-209, 251-252
Soul, *Torah* study is "food" for, 62
Soul, will be fully revealed in body in future, 301
Souls, of righteous sacrificed, 169 (note 369)
Spies, sent by Moses to see Land of Israel, 80, 317-318, 386
Spiritual level, of humanity has declined, 314
Spring, Rabbi Elazar ben Arach compared to, 149
Spring, stopped supplying water due to failure to tithe, 198
Spring water, used for ritual purification, 31 (note 68), 32
Star, dream about swallowing, 349-350
Stealing, see Theft
Stillborns, 278, 280
Stinginess, 50-52
Stone, see also Rock
Stone, those who buy leadership positions compared to, 407

Stone, *Torah* compared to, 267
Stone, upon which Dama ben Nathina's father sat, 30
Stone fences, snakes found among, 107
Stones, of the Land of Israel, 265-268
Stones, *Torah* scholars compared to, 267-268
Student, of Rebbi who collected tithe of poor, 175-176
Student, rises before master, 397-398
Student, who is humiliated will not seek revenge, 332 (note 744)
Student, who rules in presence of master deserves death, 287-290
Students, assigned by Rebbi to escort Rabbi Chiya, 230
Students, must greet their teachers, 396
Students, observed their teachers in bathroom and bedroom, 315
Students, of Rabban Yochanan ben Zakkai, 149-150
Students, of Rabbi Eliezer "killed" a man, 352, 355
Students, of Rabbi Pinchas ben Yair asked to cross Ginai River, 198
Students, of Rabbi Akiva, 173, 231, 353
Students, of Rebbi threatened by angel of death, 256
Students, Rabbi Chiya selected boys as, 231-233
Students, teased Diocletian, 330
Students, who recite master's teachings after his death, 274
Subterranean passages, 370-372
Suicide, 219-220
Sukkoth, 106, 152, 233
Sulphur, 249, 252
Sun, will glow seven times brighter in future, 302
Sunset, 119, 331
Synagogue, answering *Amen* in, 277, 282
Synagogue, of Serongin, 261-262
Synagogues, building of, 186-187
Synagogues, of the future, 273
Syria, 107
Syrian border, 325 (note 729)

Tablets, of the covenant, 147
Taint of Evil gossip, see Evil gossip
Talmudic mile, 288 (note 636)
Tamid offerings, 160-161, 164
Tarfon, Rabbi, honored his mother, 34-36, 39
Tartiroy, 369
Teachers, every community must supply, 233
Teeth, angel of death gnashed, 255, 256
Teeth, letters formed using, 253 (note 535)
Teeth, of Rebbi, 222, 228-229
Tefillin, 7, 215 (note 457), 266, 398
Tooth, displayed by Rabbi Yochanan,
Temple, altar of, 169 (note 369), 176, 177 (note 383), 252
Temple, destruction of, 3-4, 77, 161, 162, 166-171, 188,
371-372, 390
Temple service, 24-25, 161, 164, 168, 169 (note 369), 376, 391
Ten Commandments, 32, 154
Ten Tribes, 248
Terror of the Kingdom, 325-326
Tetragrammaton, 83, 135
Theft, 86
Theft, attempted by heathens during Sabbatical year, 153-155
Theft, different forms compared, 167 (note 363)
Theft, failing to tithe considered, 201
Theft, from farmers, 363-367
Theft, from righteous person, 326-329
Theft, most people engage in, 109
Theft, of donkey of Rabbi Pinchas ben Yair, 195-196, 200-201
Theft, shows lack of faith in God, 42
Theft, sin of Ishmael, 201
Thief, feeding non-kosher food to, 363-367
Thief, prays for success, 365-366
Themis, 297 (note 651)
Thornbush, 105-106

Thorns, 349
Three-ply cord, 140
Throne of Glory, 216
Tiberias, baths of, 182, 297, 331
Tiberias, dust of, 265
Tiberias, home of Rabbi Yehudah Nessiah, 330
Tiberias, home of Rabbi Yochanan, 325 (note 729)
Tiberias, home of Rebbi, 221 (note 468)
Tiberias, purification of by Rabbi Shimon bar Yochai, 298-303
Tiberias, Sea of, 260, 261
Tithe, 42
Tithe, Biblical versus rabbinical, 283-284
Tithe, doubtful, 196
Tithe, failure to remove, 197-198, 201
Tithe, merit of protected wealthy people of Land of Israel, 362 (note 810)
Tithe, power of to transform evil decrees, 375-377
Tithe, qualifications for, 175-176
Tithe, second, 341-342\
Torah, compared to water, 264, 312
Torah, denial of Divine origin of, 135
Torah, does not rise for her son, 397-398
Torah, holiness of, 4-5
Torah, Jews willingly accepted, 318
Torah, proof of Divine origin of, 155
Torah, shall go forth from Zion, 263
Torah, twisting meaning of, 129 (note 295), 135, 317
Torah knowledge, acquired through hardship, 263-264
Torah scholar, see also Rabbi(s) and Student(s)
Torah scholar, must not twist meaning of *Torah*, 313
Torah scholar, son who is, 150-151
Torah scholars, see also Rabbis
Torah scholars, and the Land of Israel, 267-268
Torah scholars, called builders, 267 (note 585)

Torah scholars, compared to stones, 267-268
Torah scholars, *Mitzvah* of visiting, 94 (note 206)
Torah scholars, poor, 187
Torah scholars, prominence atones for sins of, 403, 405
Torah scholars, setting aside studies to perform *Mitzvoth*, 61
Torah scholars, those who give *Tzedakah* will have sons who are, 338
Torah scroll, 74, 172 (note 374), 398, 413-414
Torah study, antidote to evil inclination, 79-80
Torah study, compared to *Mitzvah* performance, 59-65
Torah study, entering exile for, 231-233
Torah study, for purpose of ridiculing others, 43
Torah study, great because it brings to action, 62, 79-80
Torah study, humility required for, 313
Torah study, interrupting, 45 (note 93), 54, 61, 398
Torah study, more valuable than any other *Mitzvah*, 53, 69
Torah study, of children, 231-233, 369
Torah study, prerequisite to resurrection, 281-282
Torah study, requires effort, 8
Torah study, reveals subtleties of *Mitzvoth*, 79-80
Torah study, selling *Torah* scroll to finance, 413
Torah study, value of commensurate with effort, 41
Torah study, with impure motives, 42-43
Torah study, worth more than all the world, 59-60
Trade, see Business
Tree of Knowledge, 77-78, 208 (note 440), 312, 315
T'rumah, 296 (note 649)
Tunnels, 370-372
Turquoise, 211, 213-217
Twain, Mark, 17 (note 45)
Twisted, shall be made straight, 320
Tzaddik, see Righteous Person
Tzedakah, and dishonest beggars, 181-183, 187-190

Tzedakah, does not necessarily require giving anything away, 414

Tzedakah, contrasted to acts of kindness, 19-21

Tzedakah, contributing in order to gain prestige, 130, 409

Tzedakah, delaying contribution of, 182, 185, 187-192

Tzedakah, giving can avert consequences of bad dreams, 362

Tzedakah, giving saves from other financial loss, 10

Tzedakah, giving secretly, 183, 188 (note 401)

Tzedakah, includes commiserating with beggar, 178

Tzedakah, limited to one-fifth of one's wealth, 8

Tzedakah, not a favor to poor, 13 (note 29)

Tzedakah, one who gives will have sons who are *Torah* scholars, 338

Tzedakah, Rabbi Shimon bar Vava did not want to accept, 411 (note 924)

Tzedakah, referred to as "the *Mitzvah*," 183 (note 390)

Tzedakah, saves from death, 14-16

Tzedakah, shrewd way of giving, 184

Tzedakah, the best investment, 12-18

Uriah the Hittite, 98 (note 217)

Vilna Gaon, delighted to perform *Mitzvoth* for their own sake, 233-234

Vineyard, adjacent to King Ahab's palace, 255

Vineyard, and Rabbi Shimon ben Lakish, 159

Vineyard, four year old, 363 (note 811)

Vineyard, in dream, 350

Vineyard, of Rabbi Prida, 161

Vineyard, rabbis compared to rows in, 231

Vision, see Eyesight

Voluntary observance of *Mitzvoth*, 283-286

Water, alludes to kindness, 203

Water, bodies of border Land of Israel, 261

Water, caused wheat to rot, 350-351

Water, covering to prevent contamination by snakes, 306-320

Water, hot, 297 (note 651)
Water, *Torah* compared to, 264
Water, served by Obadiah to prophets, 100
Water, used for ritual purification, 31 (note 68), 32
Water, used to wash Rabbi Yishmael's feet, 35-39
Water flask, 105-106
Wealthy, see Rich
Wedding, see Marriage
Well of Miriam, 261
Wheat, development of compared to resurrection, 214-215
Wheat, finished product after grinding depends on owner's luck, 36
Wheat, in dream, 350-351
Wheat, of the Land of Israel, 160
Wheat, stealing, 42
Wicked, acknowledge wrongdoing when punished in next world, 337
Wicked, always suspected of acting improperly, 120-122
Wicked, and repentance, 124, 126-128
Wicked, and resurrection, 211, 213, 246, 249, 252, 277
Wicked, cause others to be cursed, 206
Wicked, enter Paradise after purification in *Gehinnom*, 251
Wicked, good deeds of rejected by *Hashem*, 86
Wicked, have free will, 139-140
Wicked, influence of, 317
Wicked, must undergo reincarnations to be purified, 131
Wicked, never attain spiritual reward of the righteous, 389 (note 877)
Wicked, no need to be solicitous of welfare of, 363-367
Wicked, outlook of, 130-131
Wicked, punished measure for measure, 114
Wicked, rewarded for good deeds in this world, 129-131
Wicked, shall not attain half their days, 385
Wicked, strengthening hands of, 37

Wicked Gentiles, 118-122
Widow, 176, 177
Wife, coveting neighbor's, 154
Wife, dog protected, 310
Wife, David's, 55, 80, 110-111
Wife, Esau's, 404
Wife, not prohibited though secluded with beggar, 307-308
Wife, Moses separated from, 75, 397 (note 891)
Wife, of rabbi, showing respect for, 401
Wife, Potiphar's, 73, 82
Wife, Rabbi Akiva consulted, 172
Wife, Rabbi Eliezer commented to, 287-288
Wine, beggars drinking, 183
Wine, in dreams, 350, 352-353
Wine, left exposed, 306-314, 316
Wine, never soured for righteous, 378-379
Wine, overly sweet, 350
Wine, *Torah* compared to, 312-313
Wine barrels or jugs, 162, 349
Witnesses, false, 255
Witnesses, who sign documents, 71
Wolf, 106
Wolves, 169
Woman, rising for elderly, 401
Work, interrupting, 394-395, 398
World to come, 14-15, 16 (note 44), 36, 40-41, 52, 53, 57, 69, 72, 103, 125-127, 129-131, 134-136, 138, 188, 199, 219-220, 245-246, 251, 263-264, 271-272, 273, 280-281, 299, 337, 339, 389
Written *Torah*, contrasted to Oral *Torah*, 144-151, 289
Wrongdoers, see Wicked
Yael, 311
Yannai, King, 167

Yannai, Rabbi, rose our of respect for Rabbi Yehudah bar Chiya, 399, 401

Yavneh, 231

Yehudah bar Chiya, Rabbi, 236-237, 399, 401

Yeshimon, Mount, 261

Yetzer HaRa, see Evil Inclination

Yishmael, Rabbi, honored his mother, 35-39

Yochanan ben Zakkai, Rabbi, chief disciples of, 149

Yochanan, Rabbi, displayed bone of son, 327

Yochanan, Rabbi, robbed by bandits, 326-329

Yochanan, Rabbi, saved others but not himself, 381

Yom Kippur, and evil gossip, 95

Yom Kippur, and wine left exposed, 309, 316

Yom Kippur, atones for sin even without repentance, 132 (note 300)

Yom Kippur, atones for violations of negative commandments, 76

Yom Kippur, ten days between *Rosh HaShannah* and, 161, 184, 389

Zachariah, 374

Ziba, 107-109

Zilpah, 83

Zimri, 167, 316 (note 702)

Ziphites, denounced David, 99, 105

Zuz, see *Dinar*